ROUTLEDGE LIBRARY EDITIONS: POLITICS OF THE MIDDLE EAST

Volume 6

BEYOND COERCION

BEYOND COERCION
The Durability of the Arab State

Edited by
ADEED DAWISHA AND I. WILLIAM ZARTMAN

LONDON AND NEW YORK

First published in 1988 by Croom Helm Ltd

This edition first published in 2016
by Routledge
2 Park Square, Milton Park, Abingdon, Oxon OX14 4RN

and by Routledge
711 Third Avenue, New York, NY 10017

Routledge is an imprint of the Taylor & Francis Group, an informa business

© 1988 Istituto Affari Internazionali

All rights reserved. No part of this book may be reprinted or reproduced or utilised in any form or by any electronic, mechanical, or other means, now known or hereafter invented, including photocopying and recording, or in any information storage or retrieval system, without permission in writing from the publishers.

Trademark notice: Product or corporate names may be trademarks or registered trademarks, and are used only for identification and explanation without intent to infringe.

British Library Cataloguing in Publication Data
A catalogue record for this book is available from the British Library

ISBN: 978-1-138-83939-7 (Set)
ISBN: 978-1-315-68049-1 (Set) (ebk)
ISBN: 978-1-138-92379-9 (Volume 6) (hbk)
ISBN: 978-1-315-68481-9 (Volume 6) (ebk)

Publisher's Note
The publisher has gone to great lengths to ensure the quality of this reprint but points out that some imperfections in the original copies may be apparent.

Disclaimer
The publisher has made every effort to trace copyright holders and would welcome correspondence from those they have been unable to trace.

Volume III:

Beyond Coercion

The Durability of the Arab State

Edited by
Adeed Dawisha
and I. William Zartman

CROOM HELM
London • New York • Sydney

© 1988 Istituto Affari Internazionali

Croom Helm Publishers Ltd, Provident House,
Burrell Row, Beckenham, Kent, BR3 1AT

Croom Helm Australia, 44–50 Waterloo Road,
North Ryde, 2113, New South Wales

Published in the USA by
Croom Helm
in association with Methuen, Inc.
29 West 35th Street
New York, NY 10001

British Library Cataloguing in Publication Data

Beyond coercion. The Durability of the Arab state. — (Nation,
    state and integration in the Arab world ; v.3)
    1. Arab countries — Social conditions
    2. Arab countries — Politics and
    government
    I. Dawisha, Adeed I.   II. Zartman, I.
    William III. Series
    306′.0917′4927   HN766.A8

    ISBN 0–7099–4149–8

Library of Congress Cataloging-in-Publication Data

Beyond coercion. The Durability of the Arab state.

    (Nation, state, and integration in the Arab world ;
    v. 3)
    1. Arab countries — Politics and government — 1945-
    I. Dawisha, A.I. II. Zartman, I. William. III. Series.
    DS39.N34 vol. 3 [DS63.1]   956 s [909′.0974927]   87-22157
    ISBN 0-7099-4149-8

Photosetting by Mayhew Typesetting, Bristol, England
Printed and bound in Great Britain by Mackays of Chatham Ltd, Kent

Contents

List of Tables	viii
Foreword	ix

Introduction	1
I. William Zartman	
Contemporary Arab regimes	2
Definitions of the concept of state	6
Characteristics	9
Static and dynamic theories of stability	11

1. Arab Bureaucracies: Expanding Size, Changing Roles	14
Nazih Ayubi	
Expanding size	15
Expansion described	15
Why the expansion?	20
Role in development	24

2. Political Parties in the Arab State: Libya, Syria, Egypt	35
Raymond A. Hinnebusch	
Libya: charismatic mobilisation from above	36
Syria: single party in a divided society	43
Egypt: party adaptation to a pluralising society	50
Arab party systems: differences and similarities	57

3. Opposition as Support of the State	61
I. William Zartman	
Manipulated pluralism: Morocco	64
Controlled pluralism: Egypt	73
Emerging pluralism: Tunisia	81
Conclusion	84

4. Professional Associations and National Integration in the Arab World, with Special Reference to Lawyers Associations	88
Mustapha K. El Sayed	
Framework for the study of interest groups and Arab integration	90
Method of study	93
Law associations	94

v

CONTENTS

Membership of bar associations	95
Purpose and policies	100
Public policies towards bar associations	111
Arab Lawyers Union	112
Conclusion	114

5. Arab Military in Politics: from Revolutionary Plot to
Authoritarian State   116
Elizabeth Picard

Towards the stabilisation of Arab military regimes	120
Armed forces and the state	122
The military and society	129
Military regimes and economic development	136

6. Role of Religious Institutions in Support of the State   147
Sadok Belaid

General context	147
Partnership: the Arabian Peninsula — Saudi Arabia	149
Split: the Maghreb states	154
Confrontation: Egypt and Sudan	159

7. Social Structure and Political Stability: Comparative
Evidence from the Algerian, Syrian, and Iraqi Cases   164
Jean Leca

Political stability and social structure: a static model	164
Social challenges to political stability: the split in the middle class and the dilemmas of redistribution	166
Algeria: 1962–85	170
The 'corrective' movement in Syria: 1970–85	183
Iraq: 1963–85	192
Conclusion: class society, class politics and social upheavals	196

8. Social Transformation and Political Power in the
Radical Arab States   203
Rashid Khalidi

Changing ruling elites	206
New and prosperous class	209
Distance between ruler and ruled	214

9. Limits of Ruling Elites: Autonomy in Comparative
Perspective   220
Hamid Ansari

10. Class and the State in Rural Arab Communities 239
   Nicholas Hopkins
      Testour (Tunisia) 241
      Musha (Egypt) 246
      Al-Murrah Bedouin (Saudi Arabia) 251
      Conclusion 257

11. Arab Regimes: Legitimacy and Foreign Policy 260
   Adeed Dawisha

12. Conclusion: Reasons for Resilience 276
   Adeed Dawisha

   Bibliography 284

   Index 305

List of Tables

4.1	Registered lawyers in Arab countries (1978–81)	96
5.1	Arab armed forces (1966–84)	119
5.2	Arab states and military service	131
5.3	Gross Domestic Product and military budgets (1982)	136
7.1	Algeria: share of agriculture and industry in labour force, GDP and planned public investment (1965–84)	172
7.2	Working male population of Algeria, by professional status (1966 an 1977)	173
7.3	Growth in employment in selected sectors (1967 and 1982)	174
7.4	Growth in non-agricultural employment (1980–2 and 1982–4)	177
7.5	Non-agricultural employment in the private sector (at 31 December 1984)	178
7.6	Incomes (1979 and 1984)	179
7.7	Expenditure — production balance (1980–3)	184
7.8	Land ownership and distribution (1913 and 1945)	186
7.9	Class structure of Syrian society (1960 and 1970)	187
7.10	Evolution of GDP (1970–83)	188
7.11	Labour force in agriculture and industry (1960–80)	193
7.12	Public sector and private sector in certain economic sectors of the GDP (%)	194

Foreword

Nation, State and Integration in the Arab World is a series of four volumes exploring the origins, foundations, impact and stability of Arab states. This volume, which is the third in the series, analyses the process of stabilisation amongst the Arab states, a process that has contradicted all predictions of impending disintegration and political collapse. Although there are some cases of disintegration, there are quite evidently mechanisms at work that have helped to consolidate a majority of the Arab states and the Arab state system. Stability may not be a virtue *per se*, and some of the stabilising factors may not be equated with progress but we feel that it is nevertheless important to overcome the stereotype of extreme political volatility that is commonly associated with the Arab states, and to realise that, while change is possible and indeed likely, it is neither without limits nor without rules. Revolutions, as in Iran or the Sudan, or political collapse and disintegration, as in Lebanon, are highly visible but nevertheless exceptions.

The series is the result of collective research organised by the Istituto Affari Internazionali over a period of three years, under the general title *Nation, State and Integration in the Arab World*. The undertaking was made possible by a generous main grant from the Ford Foundation, and an equally generous additional grant from the International Development Research Centre (IDRC) of Canada, which supports the work of Arab scholars writing on economic issues. Further financial support was received from the Italian Ministry of Foreign Affairs, and from the Commission for Cultural Exchanges between Italy and the United States.

The Istituto Affari Internazionali worked in cooperation with the Panteios School of Political Science in Athens, which organised the two international gatherings that brought together the authors of this series to discuss their ideas in depth. As a result, while these are collective volumes, we believe that they have reached a degree of homogeneity which is not normally found in such undertakings. The Panteios School also supported one of the meetings with its own funds, decisively contributing to the success of the project.

Help was received also from The Gustav E. von Grünebaum Centre for Near Eastern Studies at the University of California, Los Angeles, which hosted me in February and March 1984 and again in the autumn of 1986.

FOREWORD

The project was directed by an international steering committee in which the following participated: Roberto Aliboni, Director, Istituto Affari Internazionali; Hazem Beblawi, Chairman, Egyptian Export Development Bank; Ursula Braun, Consultant, Stiftung Wissenschaft und Politik; Marwan Buheiry, Director, Centre for Lebanese Studies; Alexander Cudsi, Professor, Panteios School of Political Science; Adeed Dawisha, Professor, George Mason University; Omaymah Dahhan, Professor, University of Jordan; Georges Sabagh, Director, The Gustav E. von Grünebaum Centre for Near Eastern Studies, University of California, Los Angeles; Ghassan Salamé, Professor, American University of Beirut; and I. William Zartman, Director, Africa Programme, SAIS, Johns Hopkins University.

The steering committee played a major role to which I, as director of the project, am very substantially indebted for its advice in planning the research and selecting the contributors. Some of the members, by acting as editors of a volume, have taken on closer responsibility for the material included. This third volume was edited by Adeed Dawisha and I. William Zartman.

I also received substantial help and advice from other friends. Ali Hillal Dessouki was expected to be on the committee, but a variety of circumstances prevented him from taking part in its deliberations. I did, nevertheless, greatly benefit from his generous advice and detailed comments, during numerous interviews in Cairo, and my debt to him is substantial. I also benefited from the friendly advice I received from Judy Barsalou of the Ford Foundation in Cairo, Ann Lesch of the American Field Staff in Cairo, Andrew Watson of IDRC in Cairo, and Gary Sick of the Ford Foundation in New York.

My personal thanks also to the staff of the Istituto Affari Internazionali, who contributed with sympathy and dedication to the complex organisation of this undertaking.

The shape of this project was deeply influenced by the advice of two friends who unfortunately did not live to see its completion. The steering committee decided to dedicate the four volumes to their memory.

When I met Malcolm Kerr in Los Angeles when the project was still at the planning stage, he gave me valuable advice. I asked him to be a member of the committee, but he was then expecting to be appointed President of the American University of Beirut. He insisted, however, that he wanted to be associated with the project, so much so that the first meeting of the steering committee was hosted by him at Marquand House in June 1983. He took part in our deliberations then and contributed to the formation of the basic decisions which shaped the project. His assassination was a tragedy for us personally and professionally, and has marked a disastrous turning point in West Beirut's struggle to remain one of the intellectual centres of the world.

The same circumstances finally drove Marwan Beheiry out of Beirut. Marwan was, personally and intellectually, a living example of West Beirut's intellectual curiosity and non-sectarian spirit. He played an intense part in the work of the steering committee and in the meetings connected with this project, until death struck him unexpectedly in exile.

It has been an honour, and an education, for me to serve as director of this project, and I wish to thank all contributors for the very many things I learned. I hope that the reader will find these volumes equally instructive. Any shortcoming should be ascribed to my responsibility only.

Giacomo Luciani
Director of Studies
Istituto Affari Internazionali

This series is dedicated to the memory of
Malcolm Kerr and Marwan Buheiry

Introduction

I. William Zartman

This collection focuses on a problem: explaining the stability and persistence of the state in the Arab world. Coming from various angles to the problem it tries to answer the question: is the Arab state a solid creation? And why? The question is not new, but the answers today are quite different from a previous round of answers. Thirty years ago the same question was raised in many writings, when analysts concluded that the state was a weak creation, an artificial part of a naturally evolving social entity called the Arab nation (Halpern, 1963; Sharabi, 1966; even Hudson, 1977). Writers judged that the state existed as a dependent artifice at the whim and tolerance of socio-political interactions across its borders, and they often completely neglected it when they turned to development sociology and away from politics. The 'artificial Arab states' was a frequent theme and a frequent answer to questions about the nature and stability of politics and society in the Middle East.

Now it is obvious that those answers no longer apply. Today, states have at least the appearance of stability in the Arab world, and have persisted into the 1980s without fusion, secession, reconstitution, or dissolution into a larger pan-Arab entity. Despite earlier analysis to the contrary, the resilience of the post-colonial or post-imperial state should not be surprising; after all, it occurred in Latin America a century before the Arab states, in the Balkans a war before the Arab experience, and is now proving true in Africa a decade or two later. Taking 1970 as an average year, for over a decade and a half, Arab regimes have remained solidly in power and have created a stable organisational structure around them. This runs quite contrary to what happened in the 1950s and into the 1960s. The Arab defeat of 1967 seems to have been a turning point and partly responsible for the change (Ajami, 1981). But in a broader sense the

INTRODUCTION

cause is not obvious. Indeed, even the fact itself is not obvious. Many would contest the impression of stability and would claim that the state is a house of cards or a Potemkin village, its stability more apparent than real. Others would say that the Arab nation continues to be the dominant reality — although such a case is hard to make these days. These answers have a difficult time explaining away the evident fact of stability even if that stability may only prove to be transient.

Our answer is 'yes, but problematically'. That is to say, this volume finds that the state — defined as the authoritative political institution that is sovereign over a recognised territory — has been stable in the last decade and a half, and that durability is not simply an artificial vision. The answer, however, does imply that there are problems inherent in that stability, problems which both limit its present extent and have implications for its future. The chapters in this book start from the judgement that the decades of the 1970s and 1980s saw the creation of state structures that have frequently been unchallenged, and which when challenges did appear, overcame them without being severely wounded or weakened.

There are, of course, other answers than those put forward in this book. Our judgement is not negative, in that we do not believe that the apparent stability of the Arab state to be an illusion. But neither is it unqualifiedly positive, believing that there are no limitations to that stability. Nor do we suggest that the state is falsely stable; that is, that its stability is real but essentially irrelevant to the more important politics that are going on around it — a judgement held by some of the students and practitioners of Muslim fundamentalism. Thus, this collective study starts with a judgement which it then seeks to explain. It does not seek simply to describe the aspects of politics and society which it examines. Instead it attempts to bring to bear evidence from various points of view into a focused explanation of the enduring nature of the Arab state.

CONTEMPORARY ARAB REGIMES

It would be well to begin with a review of this durability on a country by country basis, since one of the implications of the answer is that there is no Arab world but rather a collection of Arab states. It is important to do this not simply for historical reasons, in order to establish a general factual basis for the succeeding analyses, but above all because a brief review of the histories of these states will

2

throw light on the meaning of stability as used in this book. Events or periods which indicate stability in some judgements may not do so in others. In this way the debate can be sharpened by a clear characterisation of different national histories.

Morocco, it may be claimed, has been stable since its independence, since the state has continued essentially unchallenged since 1956. Even the single transfer of power from Mohammed V to his son Hassan II in 1961 was accompanied neither by major structural change nor by violence. It was a purely constitutional event. However, the monarchical succession did provide a major change in leadership and there have been a number of institutional — and even constitutional — changes since independence. A narrower definition of stability might identify the early 1970s as the beginning of the most recent period of stable state operation (Waterbury, 1970; Zartman, 1987). It required the political negotiations of 1974–76 to put Morocco's 1972 constitution back into force. A new team was brought in under Hassan II, and a new political unity was forged under the banner of national integrity — the Saharan campaign. To be sure this stability has been interrupted on a number of occasions since the early 1970s. In 1981 and 1984 there were serious outbursts of violence. But once the smoke had cleared, it was apparent that in both cases the violence was demonstrative rather than instrumental: the state structures were neither challenged nor shaken.

Algeria has experienced remarkable stability since 1965 — remarkable if only because of the revolutionary origins of the government. The period immediately after independence, from 1962 to 1965, was a one of institutional and political instability in which even the hasty structures established after independence were repeatedly shaken by violence (Leca and Vatin, 1975; Entelis, 1985). However after the coup of Colonel Boumedienne in 1965, a non-constitutional regime was established that — apart from the abortive coup of 1967 — remained basically unshaken. After the constitution of 1976, this informal political instability was formalised and the succession of Chadli Benjedid in 1979 brought in a new team without shaking the structures of the state. The Benjedid succession took the whole first term and perhaps the second to consolidate its power but this consolidation was carried out within stable state structures with changes only in personnel.

Tunisia too can be said to have known state stability since independence in 1956, under the unchallenged regime of President Habib Bourguiba and his Destourian Party (see relevant chapters in

INTRODUCTION

Anderson, 1983; Zartman, 1982; Hermassi, 1972). A narrower definition of stability would suggest it began in 1969, when a gradual move towards a more authoritarian left was blocked and the state returned to its liberal policies and somewhat rigid party structures. The changes of prime minister and presidential successor in 1980 and 1986 brought in somewhat different teams but did not change the basic stability or policies of the state. As in the case of Morocco, Tunisia's stability was punctuated by serious outbursts of violence in 1978, 1980 and 1984. Yet these brought no changes to the nature or structure of the state. The succession to Bourguiba is expected to be no more disruptive than the succession to Mohammed V in Morocco or Boumedienne in Algeria.

Libya's very different state structure may stretch the term stability (see Anderson, 1986; Zartman, 1982; Wright, 1982). Nonetheless, the regime of Colonel Qadhafi has been in power since 1969 and has been in control of innumerable structural changes under the umbrella of its leadership. In the mid-1970s military coups and a new set of state institutions brought a shift in the structure of the state and since then a number of abortive coups have been attempted which have shaken the notion of stability. Yet they have all been overcome, without a change in the political and administrative apparatus presided over by Qadhafi's junta, so it is not inappropriate to speak of state stability in Libya since 1969 or at least since 1973–5.

The beginning of the 1970s also saw the Egyptian state take its current form (Waterbury, 1983; Hinnebusch, 1985). Although some of the policies of the Sadat regime began after the Arab defeat of 1967, the new directions were not firmly in place until Sadat actually came to power in 1970, and particularly not until after the Corrective Revolution of 1971. Perhaps the most remarkable aspect of Egyptian state stability was the lack of basic change in the nature of the state after the assassination of Sadat. The assassination of 1981 was a personal accident rather than a state revolution; although the chief of state was removed with violence, the structures and indeed even the nature of the policies of the state did not change.

Syria's stability dates from the takeover by Hafez Assad in 1970 (Van Dam, 1979). The structures of the state have changed little since then, nor has the leadership. As in the case of some of the other countries, there have been serious enough events and instances of violence to raise questions about that stability but in each case, and notably in the destruction of Hama by the regime in 1982, the state ran roughshod over its challengers and continued without undergoing major change. Like the other countries, Syria's example shows that extra-constitutional challenges to the state should not be confused with instability; instability only occurs, in this meaning of the term, when such challenges result in the destruction of the state.

Jordan's stability goes back to before the 1960s, when King Hussein came to power. The significant date is 1967, when the new additions to the kingdom were removed by Israeli occupation and when the Nasserite challenges to the regime were overcome (Day, 1986; Gubser, 1983). After the major threat to the state was removed by the events of Black September in 1970, the kingdom, reduced to its trans-Jordanian dimensions, has been unchanged in its structures and leadership.

In Iraq, where events with a curious irony frequently parallel those of its arch-rival Syria, stability has prevailed since 1968 (Helms, 1984; Niblock, 1982). The regime of Saddam Hussein has remained in power without notable changes in the structure of its state. Although that stability has been won at the cost of an endless and potentially destabilising war with Iran going on a decade, structural and personal continuity still characterise internal affairs.

The house of Saud has shown remarkable durability in its Arabia since the end of World War One. The contemporary era began in 1964 with the elevation of Feisal II to the throne, giving the system the stability it has enjoyed ever since (Quandt, 1983; Safran, 1984). The enlargement of the cabinet to include members outside the royal family in 1975, and the succession of King Khalid upon Feisal's assassination in the same year, only strengthened the state's structures and policies. The seizure of the Great Mosque and the Gulf Coast demonstrations of 1979 were weathered without significant impact, and King Fahd succeeded to the throne in 1982.

The exception is Sudan (Wai, 1981). Not only does the *coup d'état* which removed President Numeiry in 1985 qualify as an unstable event but it would be very hard to claim that Numeiry's state itself was a good case of stability. The fluidity of Sudanese politics was obvious on several occasions during the Numeiry regime, between his advent to power in 1969 and his removal 16 years later. Sudan must stand as a test case against which generalisations can be made.

Lebanon is the other exception (Dubar and Nasr, 1976). Indeed, Lebanon has frequently been an exception to the rule: it had a competitive democracy at times when such practices were rare, and showed dynamic stability in its own affairs during earlier periods when instability prevailed elsewhere. But since 1975, Lebanon has been undergoing such a high degree of instability that it must be

INTRODUCTION

counted as a case of the collapse of the state.

For the most part, the nearly two decades between 1970 and the present were a time of stability, often a continuation of characteristics that began several years before. This often relates to the position of a single strongman at the head of an institutionalised state. There could be real challenges to the stability of the institutions in Morocco, Tunisia, Libya, Syria, Jordan, Iraq and Saudi Arabia when the strong leaders pass away, even by natural causes. On the other hand, it has been seen that in Morocco, Algeria, Saudi Arabia and Egypt, a strong leader has died or been removed by an assassin's bullet, and nonetheless stability has prevailed.

State stability refers to the fact that the sovereign, geographic entities of the Arab Middle East and their internal structures have persisted over the period without undergoing sudden, violent change. Not only union and secession, but also revolution, revolt and even military coups have been strikingly absent in a region which previously seemed to mass produce them. Change is not absent, nor can it be, but it is gradual and evolutionary. New figures of power have entered and left the political structures but the chief of state has been able to stay in office. Historically, the period under consideration is often stage two of independence — the period of stability which follows several decades of instability, contested regimes and structural upheaval. The first period might be interpreted as a one of struggle over the form of government, after the struggle for independence itself has been won. Once the structure of government was decided by the emergence of a dominant sociopolitical force, it was possible to govern within the established state structures. No judgement of 'governing well' is implied, nor is stability equated with legitimacy. A regime could be considered illegitimate by some of its people and still be stable if they are unwilling or unable to shake it, indeed this is the condition of most Arab and many other states. Legitimacy here is not considered to be the prime — and tautological — indicator of stability but only a resource among others to be used to produce it. Beyond these definitions and assumptions, the search for explanations for the constancy of the Arab state proceeds.

DEFINITIONS OF THE CONCEPT OF STATE

The explanation for this stability must begin with an analysis of the nature of the Arab state. State is defined as the authoritative political institution that is sovereign over a recognised territory. There are many other definitions of state, and much of the confusion over its nature can be resolved by choosing one definition and separating empirical from definitional elements (Laski, 1935; MacIver, 1926; Weber, 1947; Nettl, 1968; Tilly, 1975; Evans *et al.*, 1985; Schatzenberg, 1987; Kaplan and Lasswell, 1950; Bodie and Birnbaum, 1983; Cohen and Service, 1978; Gordon, 1986; Callaghy, 1984).

This definition focuses on three elements: it considers the state to be authoritative and sovereign and hence an accepted focus of identity and arena of politics; it regards the state as an institution and therefore an organisation differentiated from other, informal practices of politics; and it sees the state as associated with a particular territory. The third element is probably the least controversial but the other two introduce some complexity.

The state as institution is both tangible organisation and intangible symbol; and such duality is in the nature of institutions. A family, for example, is the people who compose it but also an identity which they represent. A state is not merely a large family, since state-as-organisation is not equivalent to the population of the country but only to state functionaries and politicians, it is ultimately distinguished from 'private' personnel and organisations. Yet state-as-symbol is larger than the sum of its parts (like family and other institutions). What is 'private' operates under it or within it, even if separate from it. Try as one might, it does not capture the essential nature of the state to separate the organisational from the symbolic component and attempt to consider the state as only one or the other.

The implications of this definition are, first, that it suggests that some politics are outside the state. Although ultimately carried out with the aim of controlling (or abolishing) the state, some political action lies beyond officially authorised or permitted rules, and even beyond the state's recognised territoriality. Most politics, however, is carried out within the state arena, according to rules or routines established within the state.

Second, the definition of state as receptacle of legitimacy stems from the use of the word authority — usually defined as legitimate or rightful power. Although this is a standard assumption, it carries certain operational problems. Operationally the state can undergo an apparent loss of legitimacy. This occurred most recently in Sudan, and some writers have suggested that the Arab state in general has a very contested legitimacy, in the eyes of many intellectuals at least (Hudson, 1977; Adam, 1985). But whatever the operational problems of the loss of legitimacy, definitionally legitimacy must be attached to state power — that is, rule carried out in the name of the state. The state must be considered the receptacle of political legitimacy, since even opposition groups seek to take it over in order to benefit from its legitimate power. What happens in the exceptional cases when this definitional assumption is challenged must be considered as they arise. Of course, the legitimacy of state power is not the same thing as the legitimacy of a particular ruling group, which has to face the test of its right to rule or actually to exercise state power.

Third, in official party regimes such as those in Algeria or Russia, the party is part of the state because it is part of the authoritative political organisation. In other countries, such as the United States, France or Morocco, parties are not considered part of the state. This implication is important, because it draws a sharp distinction between different kinds of party not usually considered when they are discussed. There may be other implications that will become apparent as the discussion continues.

There is also a distinction to be made between regime and state. Governments and regimes are the groups of people who run the state at a given time. It is clear, for example, that there is a difference between the Egyptian state and the regimes of Nasser, Sadat and Mubarak. The state continues, although one may extend this in order to talk about 'the state under Sadat' or 'the state under Nasser', or even the 'Nasserite state' (it is little harder to make an adjective out of Sadat or Mubarak). Regimes, administrations or leaders may rise and fall, but only when the nature of the organisation and its structures change, can one say a state has been altered.

Clearly, state, stability, and legitimacy are core concepts whose essential or ideal nature is usually qualified in reality by empirical impurities and surrounded by large gray areas (Watkins, 1934). How much constitutional change or amendment is required to change the basic nature of the state; how many constitutional amendments and how fast, or how many new institutions (as for example in Libya) are required before one can say that the state is unstable, are all matters that are hard to set up as a quantitative test beforehand. Similarly, where is the threshold marking the degree of challenge that becomes an indicator of state instability? What degree of recovery confirms state stability? And in either case how long after the event must one wait to draw the conclusion? The change from Ben Bella to Boumedienne/Benjedid in 1965, or from Idris to Qadhafi in 1969, or from King Farouk to Nasser/Sadat/Mubarak in

1952–3 are seen as changes in the state, whereas other changes already indicated, as in Lebanon after 1975, Mauritania and Chad after 1978, Egypt in 1952, or North Yemen during the civil war are indications of chronic state instability or state collapse (Chazan, 1983).

Some personalised polities, such as those in the Arabian peninsula, are only slowly developing into states, and often still have a way to go. Despite the effort to make sharp definitions, the subject is mainly painted in grays; there are no easy indicators. Many judgements suggest reasoning that is more enlightening than the final label.

CHARACTERISTICS

Moving beyond definitions, the characteristics of a specific type of state — the Arab state of the Middle East — can be identified.[1] Many of these characteristics are political, both because the state is seen as a political institution and because they refer to structures and functions which imply an exercise of power or a means of accomplishing goals. Other characteristics may be intimately tied to other aspects of society, but the political dominates.

The most important characteristic of the stable Arab state of the 1970s and 1980s is the position of a central strongman, leader and orchestrator. The Graet Patron or Manipulator may adopt many different styles of leadership and may have a position that runs through many shades of centralisation and control but in all cases of state stability, that stability is associated with one or successive single leaders. Although the Great Patron is surrounded by followers, he clearly emerges as the single manipulating and deciding leader even if he had to rise from the pack in the early years of his tenure.

Second, the political organisation of the contemporary state is associated with periodic personnel changes, when the leader from time to time introduces sweeping changes to the group around him, associated with new programmes and directions. The periodicity of the changes is neither fixed nor regular. They can be compared to the changes in elected governments imposed by electoral realignments in critical elections. Such shifts can also be related to changes in the social composition of the population and their political demands. For example, Sadat's and Benjedid's liberalised policy responded to the demands of groups which obtained new importance

INTRODUCTION

as a result of the policies of Nasser and Boumedienne and the soften-
ing of Sadat's liberalisation under Mubarak responded to popular
reaction against the Open Door Policy. An aspect of state structure
is periodic revision of political organisation and its direction.

A third characteristic of the Arab state is the practice of politics
of limited association. The term is distinct from politics of mobilisation, in which there is a direct link between mass organisations and
political leadership, with the public pressing the leader and the
leader playing on demands of the public. The term is also used in
distinction to politics of control, in which there is no participation
and in which politics is wrung out of the body politic by stifling
political activity. The Arab states of the 1970s and 1980s are
characterised by the intermediate stage, in which there is enough
democracy to point to, but not enough to have to bow to. Therefore
there is an outlet for those interested in political activity, and
continual manoeuvering along a spectrum that runs from opposition
to loyal support, but which never reaches in any significant way to
the mobilised masses. The years of economic growth of the 1970s
gave the Arab state the resources to meet demands of its people —
satisficing rather than satisfying — but at least responding to the
politics of association.

Fourth, the group that runs the state is based on a broad urban
middle class. The class may either have been only recently urbanised
or it may have been urban of longer standing, but the urban population, including both bourgeoisie and proletariat, represents a specific
base for the government. This characteristic differs from a number
of claims which are often made about the Arab state. It is not run
by a ruling class, for example, which would be drawn from a much
narrower social base, and one in which the rulers would hand on
power to members of their own family or at least people who
resembled them socially. Nor is an urban middle class base the same
as a capitalist class, since the capitalist bourgeoisie is only a part of
the class base and often a very small part at that. Nor, very clearly,
is the Arab state a workers state. Urban workers may be part of the
social basis of power, but they are only one among many and their
role, as indicated, is one of limited association rather than of
mobilisation. Nor, especially, is the Arab state a peasant state.
Peasants are generally the neglected part of the society and are
nowhere near the social basis of power. Locating the base of power
in the urban middle class does not mean that the state is the organ
of the middle class. It acts in relation to it, as a separate entity with
which spokesmen for the urban middle class or parts of it interact.

10

The representatives of the urban middle class or its components may have a very specific understanding of their interests and try to operationalise that understanding in policies. Those who run the state, however, look to their own interests even where their strongest power base is drawn from the urban middle class.

Fifth, in all the Arab countries the state does contain a large administrative organisation. This organisation is important because it gives the state a means of operation and also because it constitutes a section of the population part of whose interests are associated with the state itself. This complex relationship is rarely studied. A group of civil servants may see their interests associated with particular practices of the state on some occasions but on others may think politically as members of the urban middle class and consumers. As 'producers' of state outputs and consumers, their interests may vary widely. Nonetheless, one component of their interests is associated with the maintenance of the state, reflecting a certain professionalism, although that term must often be used extremely narrowly.

Sixth, the Arab state operates as an organisation of control or regulation. That is its role in the economy and society. Again, the distinctions here are important. The state is rarely an organisation of economic production, though it spends much of its energy controlling those which are. Even when a large part of the economy is under the control of the state, the element of control is more important than the element of productivity. This is one of the problems of para-statal and other official organisations. The state is an organisation of political control through instruments of violence. Army, police and regulations which control the political freedom of the citizens are all important aspects of the Arab state, often to the point where the custodians actually take over, or at least play as important a role as, one of the leadership groups.

STATIC AND DYNAMIC THEORIES OF STABILITY

A theory of stability is needed to convert these six characteristics into an explanation of the persistence of the Arab state over the past decade and more. Of the dichotomies that divide the universe, the distinction between static and dynamic types provides a useful starting point.

Static theory of stability examines the matter from the point of view of challenge and response. It seeks to explain state stability by

INTRODUCTION

ascribing to the state sufficient responsiveness to handle oppposing challenges. Such a theory tells nothing about the levels of challenge and response, nor about their nature, but it focuses the analyst in the direction to probe into these questions. Thus a state may be stable because its challengers are weak; therefore, only a weak response is needed. Or, a state may be stable because it is able to muster tremendous energies to overcome tremendous challenges. Both effects produce the stability although the nature of that stability is likely to differ. The challenges may come from very different types of sources — internal and external, upper class and lower class, diversified and concentrated and so on. In the challenge and response theory, stability is static, like the stability of a pyramid, and it is achieved by keeping up with the pressures exerted on the state.

Dynamic theory of stability deals with the stability of motion, like the stability of a bicycle. It sees stability as arising from the inherent operations of the state, which converts change into energies that maintain the state structure. Dynamic stability comes from keeping ahead of pressures and is the result of structures, myths and functions which interact to provide internal coherence.

The previous discussion on the characteristics of the contemporary Arab state suggests that its stability should be explained by a dual theory, taking into account both static and dynamic aspects. To begin with, the state has been able to maintain itself over the past decade and half because it has effectively exercised instruments of control to lower the possibility and the expectation of violent attack. The internal security apparatuses in the Arab state control potential opposition and combat it if it becomes more blatant. Through them, the state lowers the expectations of potential opponents, who learn that if they are to have any effect on the state they should seek to operate on it rather than against it, to bring limited pressures to bear in specific policy directions rather than to seek to change its basic nature. Potential oppositions tend to forget this as their members grow old and are replaced by younger, rasher upstarts. They then have to be taught again and state instruments of internal security emerge from the shadows to drive the lesson home. Once the lesson is learned, it remains until a new generation arises to challenge the leaders. Events from each of the Arab countries illustrate this. Whether it is students or the military in Morocco, politicians or other military members in Algeria, fundamentalists or politicians in Egypt, or Sunnis in Syria, opposition and its control are a cycle of social engineering and constraint.

12

There is also a dynamic aspect to stability which makes it something other than a temporary freezing of politics. Stability, as the characteristics of the Arab state have shown, is the result of a dynamic exercise in which rulers regroup periodically around issues and adopt new policy directions. Such changes are achieved either by co-opting representatives of new groups and/or by the adopting of new policies to meet the challenges. The state therefore not only controls the demands put on it but meets some of them by drawing on — if not actually representing — the key element of society through its relations with the urban middle class. There are specific instances in the history of the Arab states over the past decade and a half that illustrate such shifts of policy. The policy change towards consumerism in Algeria, the move towards liberalisation in Egypt later followed by partial control, and even the opening up of opportunities to a new class in Libya that was followed by austerity, are all examples of new shifts and new teams around the Great Patron and Orchestrator.

The following chapters illustrate aspects of this dual nature of stability. They point to particular roles played in society and by the state, and to the relationships between them which produce persistence and responsive change. It may be objected that there is no state in this volume, only reasons for its durability, but that would be to miss the concept of the state that informs this work, a concept that has its place in current state-society literature. The state is seen here as the whole that is larger than the sum of its parts, a combination of bureaucracy, parties, military, classes and ideology (religion); it is itself a part of society, the economy and the polity and also a member of the world society of states.

The state is where bureaucracy, parties, military and others meet, and it is the product of that meeting. It is impossible to think of it as separate from the society in which it operates. Thus, this is a book about the state. Like a cathedral, its supports are part of it, rather than separate, like the supports of a roof.

NOTE

1. I am grateful to Ghassan Salamé for discussions on the Arab state, and to Michael Schatzenberg for discussions on the concept of nature of the state.

1

Arab Bureaucracies: Expanding Size, Changing Roles

Nazih Ayubi

Few can fail to notice the process of bureaucratisation that has swept the Arab world since the 1950s. 'Bureaucratisation' means two things: (a) bureaucratic growth, i.e. expansion in public bodies of the sort that can be measured by increases in the numbers of administrative units and personnel as well as the rise in public expenditure, including in particular, wages and salaries; and (b) an orientation whereby the administrative and technical dominate over the social. Generally it is a tendency that goes very much in the direction of centralisation, hierarchy and control.

Both aspects of bureaucratisation have grown substantially in the Arab world in the last 30 years. The remarkable thing is that this has happened in all states. For the purposes of this study, the Arab states are classified along three scales: 'old' vs 'new', large vs small, rich vs poor. A fourth scale — 'radical' vs 'conservative' — should not be forgotten, although it is of less significance at present to the issue at hand.

It is possible to argue that the expansion and role of the public bureaucracy are affected by the position of any particular Arab state along these three scales. Given that we could not cover all Arab states in detail, the study has concentrated (without excluding others) on Egypt on the one hand, and three Gulf states (Saudi Arabia, Kuwait and the United Arab Emirates)[1] on the other. These were chosen to represent 'extreme types' on the three scales: Egypt is old, large and poor, while the Gulf states are on the whole new, small and rich. The choice is also useful in that in the 1960s Egypt was usually characterised as 'radical' and Saudi Arabia as 'conservative'. Two 'intermediate' cases — those of Jordan and Syria — are also touched upon briefly in order to provide the chapter with more of a comparative nature.

EXPANDING SIZE

It is remarkable how extensively and rapidly the bureaucracy has expanded in practically all Arab countries, even though the relative weight of the various causes of this expansion has differed from one type of country to another. Four criteria are used to measure bureaucratic growth: increase in the number of administrative units, increase in the number of public employees, increase in current government expenditure and, within that, increase in the wages and salaries of the employees. In considering the extent of bureaucratic growth, these four criteria should be taken together in the sense that a relatively limited or slow increase in one category at any particular stage should not distract the analyst from observing the phenomenon of bureaucratic growth in its totality; i.e. as represented by a combination of all four factors together.

EXPANSION DESCRIBED

The dynamics of bureaucratic growth in a number of Arab countries will be described before we investigate possible reasons for expansion.

Bureaucratic growth in Egypt

The disproportionate group of Egypt's public 'establishment' is not a new phenomenon. However, with the 1952 revolution, the public bureaucracy grew more rapidly and extensively under the impact of the regime's policies to expand industrial activities, welfare services and free education (Ayubi 1980, Chapter 3). This growth was particularly striking after the 'socialist measures' of the early 1960s, which involved widescale nationalisation of industry, trade and finance, worker participation in management and profits, and an extensive programme for social services and insurance. Thus from 1962–3 to 1970, Egypt's national income increased by 68 per cent, resting on an increase in the labour force of no more than 20 per cent. Yet at the same time, posts in the public bureaucracy increased by 70 per cent and salaries by 123 per cent (Ayubi 1980, pp. 218–32). Thus far, the rate of bureaucratic growth had substantially exceeded the rate of growth in population, employment and production.

The main irony, however, is that in the 1970s, and indeed following the adoption of the economic open door policy in 1974, the impetus of institutional growth continued under its own momentum even though the role of the government and the scope of the public sector were starting to diminish in importance. For example, the 1975 budget indicated that current expenditure accounted for 66.2 per cent of the total financial outlay of the budget, while wages and salaries accounted for 10.5 per cent (Ministry of Finance, *The State Budget*, 1975). Indeed, considering governmental outlays in the period from 1973 to 1978 as a whole, one finds that salaries more than doubled while current expenditure trebled during this time.

In terms of manpower, in 1978 the public bureaucracy — *i.e.* the civil service and the public sector excluding enterprise workers — employed over 1,900,000 persons. If state companies are added, the public 'establishment' at the beginning of 1978 was employing about 3,200,000 officials and workers (CAOA and Ministry of Finance, 1978 and 1979). At the beginning of the 1980s, the still-expanding Egyptian bureaucracy looked even bigger. It employed 2,876,000 individuals in central and local government as well as in the public sector.

One of the main problems about bureaucratic inflation that has occurred since the adoption of *infitah* is that it has happened at a time when the public economy as a whole and state industry in particular are not — given the reorientation of policy and the changing role of the government — expanding fast enough to make these increases in personnel and expenditure a rewarding exercise. It is therefore probable that bureaucratic inflation will increasingly represent a strain on national resources. One of the unhealthy aspects that accompanied this inflation in public expenditure was the decline in the percentage of such expenditure on economic activities from 35 per cent in 1962 to only 22 per cent of the total outlay in 1976. Other problems to emanate from bureaucratic growth include excessively slow action, very low remuneration and as a result, extremely poor performance.

Bureaucratic growth in the Gulf

Compared to Egypt, the origin of whose bureaucracy goes back thousands of years and whose formation in modern form dates back over a century, the bureaucracies of the Gulf have been created from scratch. Their main expansion has been an outcome of oil wealth, which moved the states towards large-scale social welfare programmes and ambitious economic development plans.

Saudi Arabia

The Saudi bureaucracy was initiated in the 1950s and its growth has been remarkable in the three decades it has existed so far. The number of ministries has grown from four to 20, and over 40 public authorities and corporations have been established since 1950.

Civil service employees, who numbered no more than a few hundred in 1950, increased to about 37,000 in 1962–3, to 85,000 in 1970–1 and to over 245,000 in 1979–80. The ratio of public employees to the total population in the early 1980s was approximately 3.5 to 4 per cent, which is admittedly not excessive, but government civil servants represented 10 per cent of the total labour force and 13 per cent if one counts non-career personnel.

The oil boom manifested itself in a massive increase in revenues which jumped from $2.7 billion in 1972 to $22.6 billion in 1974. This was immediately followed by large increases in expenditure. Between 1973 and 1982, salaries and benefits, as well as current expenditure, grew thirteen-fold (*The Statistical Yearbook*, 1981–2). Without doubt, the expansion in public expenditure in Saudi Arabia has been most impressive.

Kuwait

The handful of administrations and directorates that existed in the early 1950s developed into ten departments in 1959. These were turned into ministries in 1962, when three more were added, making a total of 13 ministries. By 1976, the number of operating ministries had reached 16 in addition to two ministers of state (Marouf, 1982, pp. 32–9). Furthermore, a number of higher councils have been created (for Petroleum Affairs, for Housing Affairs etc.) and over 25 public authorities and corporations.

The numbers of government employees grew rapidly: from 22,073 in 1966, to 113,274 in 1976, to 145,451 in 1980. According to official figures, government employees represented 12.5 per cent of the population and about 34 per cent of the total labour force of Kuwait in 1975.[2] In 1979 the Amir of Kuwait expressed the view that some 65,000 civil servants in Kuwait were unnecessary and a World Bank report on Kuwaiti public administration suggested a total freeze on all new appointments.

Government expenditure also soared. Between 1973 and 1979, domestic expenditure increased by 388 per cent and salaries and wages by 242 per cent (Central Bank of Kuwait, *Economic Report*, 1978). It is estimated that nearly 39 per cent of government expenditure can be classified as organisational: this includes the substantial incomes provided to the head of state and the Amiri Diwan as well as more standard expenses such as the Employees Bureau and supplementary allocations.

United Arab Emirates (UAE)

The first federal government was formed immediately after the Union was declared in 1971, with Abu Dhabi as the main sponsor. In 1968 Abu Dhabi had some 20 government directorates, which increased to 25 by 1970. The first council of ministers of Abu Dhabi, which was formed in 1971, included 15 ministers, but this was abolished in 1973, and replaced by a federal cabinet with 28 ministers. Abu Dhabi also established an executive council to run its own affairs. Public authorities and corporations were set up, including the Abu Dhabi Steel Works, the General Industry Corporation and the Abu Dhabi Investment Authority.

In 1968 the Abu Dhabi administration employed 2,000 officials. By 1970, their number had doubled and by 1974 it reached 5,352, of which 37 per cent were UAE citizens, 42 per cent were other Arabs and 21 per cent were foreign nationals (Rashid, 1975). Eight years later, the number of public employees in Abu Dhabi had jumped to 24,078 (AIPK, 1983, p. 358).

Public employment on the federal level quadrupled between 1972 and 1982, from 10,500 to over 40,000 (Arabian Government, 1983, p. 213). The explosion in numbers of public employees is the most dramatic among the three Gulf countries studied, given the country's minute population base, its recent independence and the fact that the oil boom more or less immediately followed its formation. The UAE is representative, but in an extreme way, of what happened in other desert states where the local human base could not support the required expansion, leading therefore to heavy reliance upon expatriate labour. In the Abu Dhabi bureaucracy (which is the largest and most established within the UAE), a ludicrous 83.6 per cent of all officials are foreign nationals.

There are several indications that the state bureaucracy may have stretched itself beyond its capabilities. In 1983, this country, which ranks among the highest in the world in terms of *per capita* income, ran up a budgetary deficit which forced it to defer payment of salaries to public employees for a number of months. As the budgetary deficit was expected to increase in 1984, the Ministry of

Finance and Industry forbad the creation of new public posts for non-citizens in the following financial year (*al-Watan*, 7 May 1984).

There has been a vast expansion in public finances in the UAE since the oil boom. The federal budget, which is mainly financed by Abu Dhabi, quadrupled between 1971 and 1974.[3] Between 1973 and 1974, for example, Abu Dhabi's budget more than doubled. Payment for national and federal ministries accounted for nearly 40 per cent of the total (Aziz, 1979, pp. 55–70). In the Abu Dhabi budget for 1976, expenditure on both Emirate and the federation continued to grow; expenditure in 1977 was 74.8 per cent of the total, rising to 84.3 in 1982.

Bureaucratic growth outside the Gulf

Bureaucratic inflation followed the same pattern outside the Gulf. Where there were fewer than ten ministries at the time of independence, there were more than 20 by the 1980s (22 in Jordan, 24 in Syria). Public sector organisations proliferated: in Syria in the early 1980s there were 60 public organisations (*mu'assasat*) and 25 public corporations; in Jordan, there were about 38 public organisations of various descriptions.

In 1982, Syria had 440,000 public officials in the civil service and public sector (excluding the armed forces, police and security). Compared to a total population for the same year of 10,788,000, the ratio is one in 25, or 4 per cent (Syria Minister of State, 1984). Related to a total labour force of 2,174,000 in 1979, this means that civilian public employment represented 20 per cent of total employment (Syria, Central Statistical Office, 1981).

Jordan's 1979 census records a population of 2,152,000, of which the labour force constituted 18 per cent. In 1982, 59,000 people worked for the government (excluding casual workers) (Public Statistics Department, 1982; *al-Khidma al-Madaniyya*, June 1983). Thus government officials represented 2.75 per cent of the population and 14.9 per cent of the labour force.

Current expenditure came to over half of the total outlay in Jordan's 1981 budget; of that, 21 per cent went on salaries and wages (State Budget Department, 1981). In Syria, current expenditure amounted to 57 per cent of total outgoings. Of that, about 18 per cent went on salaries and wages (*Statistical Yearbook*, 1984).

WHY THE EXPANSION?

Reasons for bureaucratic expansion are multiple. Some is due purely to demographic growth and to the need to supply services for increasing populations. But as the percentage of public officials within the population in general and the labour force in particular tends to be higher than in many other societies, one has to examine other causes. The following seem to be of particular importance: traditional prestige of public office (for long associated with powerful foreign rulers); strong belief in the developmental role of the bureaucracy; the relationship of public office to creating the contacts vital for private business; and possibly the impact of the Egyptian model, both as an example and through the role of the large number of Egyptian officials working in many other Arab countries.[4]

Some of the reasons for bureaucratic growth are entrenched in the social and political conditions of the society. Most important is the expansion in formal higher education that is in no way related to the economic needs and manpower requirements of the society. Under pressure from people aspiring to higher social prestige, and the belief that qualifications lead to economic development, the Middle East has witnessed a strong case of what one expert has called 'diploma disease'.

This tendency, which reached alarming proportions in Egypt, has caught up with even the small city states of the Gulf, where everybody is racing to build yet another new university, regardless not only of whether the market needs graduates but even of the availability of students. In Egypt, where there are three times the number of engineers that are required by the country's industrial base, and where only 20 per cent of agronomists work in agriculture, where can the remaining graduates go but into the public bureaucracy, where they do very little but drain the public purse. The share of wages and salaries in Egypt's total expenditure has risen steadily over the past 20 years.

Proportionately, too much attention has been given to formal higher education in comparison with technical education and vocational training in all Arab countries. In most countries of the world, educational expansion has in fact followed, not preceded, industrial development (the only possible exception is Japan, where the two went more or less hand in hand). Muhammad Ali's experiment in nineteenth century Egypt to expand higher education without a similar expansion in on-the-job training resulted in virtually no real industrial development and the country had to start almost from scratch in the inter-war period. All Middle Eastern countries are currently making the same mistake, with high ratios of university graduates and relatively low levels of industrial development. One important outcome is to inflate public bureaucracy, with too many controllers, inspectors and supervisors but few functioning personnel to control, inspect or supervise.

Another major reason behind the expansion in the size (and role) of the government bureaucracy in some Arab countries is associated with the growing *rentier* nature of the state in these countries, mainly as a consequence of the oil boom. The description is meant to indicate that a dominant or significant proportion of the national income is derived from rents rather than from the productive (mainly commodity) sectors of the economy; these revenues mostly go to the state, which takes charge of their allocation and distribution. Palmer, Alghofaily and Alnimir (1984) maintain that:

> 'Rentierism' is not only an economic phenomenon. Rentier criteria . . . also possess concomitant cultural-behavioural characteristics that make it difficult for the rentier state to increase its productive capacity and to maximise the economic and political advantages at its disposal.

The rentier nature of the oil-rich states like Saudi Arabia, Kuwait and the UAE is obvious enough. The percentage of oil exports to total exports in these countries ranges between 90 and 99 per cent; the percentage of oil revenues to total government revenues ranges between 85 and 99 per cent; oil's contribution to GDP in turn is to a large extent related to government expenditure, which is almost totally dependent on oil revenues. It one excludes the direct and indirect impact of oil, it is clear how weak the economic base of the society is (Abd al-Rahman, 1982, pp. 67–8).

The fact that oil revenues accrue to the state before they are distributed has made the economic role of the state in the oil-rich countries extremely powerful, in spite of the anti-socialist rhetoric of the governing elites. Saudi development plans may extol the virtues of free enterprise, and the advisers to the Saudis may assure us that the rapidly growing role of the Saudi government in the Saudi economy is viewed as only a 'temporary evil', but the fact cannot be concealed that the government sector was responsible for over 62 per cent, or nearly two-thirds, of GDP (as expenditure) during the third plan (KSA, *Third Development Plan*, p.29). In 1976 the share of government in total consumption was 59.8 per cent, the share of government purchases in GDP was 33.3 per cent and the share of government in Gross Fixed Capital Formation was 69.6 per cent (Mallakh, 1982, p. 276). As Usama Abd al-Rahman (1982, p. 40) observes, 'The government's hegemony over the economy is large — possibly exceeding government hegemony in most developing countries, and not differing very much from the hegemony of government in countries following a socialist path'. Another writer has tried to reconcile the two contradictory aspects by concluding that the government has in effect 'become the senior partner in a system of Islamic state capitalism' (Long, 1976, p. 56).

For the rulers of the oil-rich states, the bureaucracy serves as a respectable and modern-looking method of distributing part of the revenues. Unlike traditional, straightforward handouts, bureaucracy provides a more dignified way of disbursing largesse, camouflaged in the language of meritocracy and national objectives. And sure enough, the Gulf bureaucracy is, in spite of all its paternalism, a redistributive instrument that provides people of lesser status and income with opportunities for social promotion through state education and bureaucratic careers.

The creation of jobs in the 'oil state' becomes almost an objective in its own right, with little regard for what these recruits should (or can) do. This explains, among other things, the high numbers of illiterate and other poorly educated nationals who tend to be employed by the bureaucracies of the oil-rich states. It may also partly explain why many officials are not in their offices for much of the time. According to studies made by the Saudi Institute of Public Administration, 75 per cent of officials arrive at work late, 69 per cent often leave the office for private business, and 51 per cent are frequently absent without leave; when the employee is actually at his desk, only 48 per cent of his time is spent on his official job (*al-Yamama*, 9 to 15 March 1982, pp. 4–7).

Foreign and local advisers who recommend things like job descriptions and reductions in the number of jobs, are often mistaken: the inefficiency may be at least partly intentional. Even before the oil bonanza, one analyst observed:

Some of the inefficiency is deliberate, because civil service appointments are viewed as a vehicle for distributing oil wealth among the citizenry and as a means of giving idle Kuwaitis a job. Consequently, most offices are grossly overstaffed; five people are commonly employed to do work that one could perform (al-Marayati, 1972, p. 290).

22

Public employment is also perceived to be a political safety valve; and this does not apply only to oil-rich states. The government in Egypt, as much in Saudi Arabia, cannot fail to see, for example, that most members of the militant Islamic groups are either university students in their final years or newly graduated. Public employment may be regarded as one way of reducing their anger, and if not of co-opting them, at least controlling them through attendance requirements and official tasks. Little wonder that the most extreme among these militant groups (such as *Takfir* in Egypt and *Ikhwan* in Arabia) dissuade their followers from working for the government (Ayubi, 1982–3).

Even the growing number of foreigners in the bureaucracy of the oil states, which is often regarded as a potential political risk, is not without its rewards. It gives locals the opportunity to command and supervise a respectable number of subordinates (who are, further-more, frequently better qualified and more experienced than their superiors). This is bound to represent an element of satisfaction for the native officials and to lessen possible antagonism between them and their rulers, by emphasising instead the citizen-expatriate dichotomy. The assignment of technical tasks to outsiders in the oil states fits the established tradition and represents an element of continuity. Nomadic societies have traditionally assigned technical jobs to slaves, minorities and outcasts, keeping for the insiders — in addition to the pastoral activities — the honour of carrying arms (Gellner, 1981). Given that only Kuwait has military conscription and that various foreign military advisers now work for the Gulf states, one wonders whether the oil boom is moving the Arab away from even this time-honoured function?

The oil bonanza, superimposed upon a bedouin society, has produced a rentier economy, with a dominant state sector and a sizeable commercial sector.

The oil boom's effects on Egypt have tended in the opposite direction. The erosion of Nasser's populist regime and the reverberations of the oil boom led to the emergence of an inverted-rentier economy characterised by the state's shrinking economic role and fast expansion in the commercial sector. The country has depended increasingly in the last decade on revenues that are not production-based and in particular on the remittances of workers in the oil-rich states. Muhammad Duwaidar (1983, p. 160) writes:

At the expense of the productive sector (in agriculture and industry) Egypt is becoming more dependent on income: income from oil, income from their overseas labour force, income derived from the Suez Canal and from tourism, and income from interest payments, as investors look for high returns on capital instead of turning to entrepreneurial activity.

Jordan and Syria have also become increasingly dependent on these sources of income, especially worker remittances, and Syria is adopting its own mini open-door policy. Although the Egyptian government has earned considerable revenue since 1973 from oil and the Suez Canal, income from tourism has benefited primarily the private sector, while remittances from people working in the oil-rich states have helped the private sector — in the absence of taxation — almost exclusively. Put differently, the state is richer in the Gulf, and society is richer in Egypt.

Because wealth does not translate immediately and automatically into power, the state in Egypt remains much stronger than the society. This was made clear during the seventies: the bureaucracy that had been expanded and strengthened mainly for development purposes under Nasser, was used for control under Sadat. By the same token, the state in the Gulf is not becoming stronger as fast as it is becoming richer. Institution-building is much more recent in the Gulf and is being implanted in a society in which primordial loyalties (familial, tribal, regional and sectarian) are stronger than they are in Egypt.

This, however, is to anticipate an aspect that will be examined more closely elsewhere in this study.

ROLE IN DEVELOPMENT

Marx explained that bureaucracy survives by projecting an image of serving the general interest. In the Middle East the bureaucracy does the same, but it also projects the image of being the main vehicle for development.

Middle Eastern leaders called upon the bureaucracy not only to fulfill the conventional law and order functions, but also to be involved in industry, trade, education, culture and so forth. The literature of the fifties and sixties was full of praise for the potential for progress of the public bureaucracy — for many people it represented an orderly alternative to the agonies of a social or cultural revolution. The direction of development administration was clear: expand and consolidate departmental-type administration, involve the bureaucracy in national comprehensive planning, in extensive industrialisation programmes, in urban construction and in a fast-expanding system of conventional higher education.

Discovering — usually half way along — that bureaucracy is probably ill-equipped to deal with this heavy load, the authorities declared that in order to have successful development administration there must first be effective administrative development. Since administration is regarded as a science that has reached its maturity in the West, administrative development was to a large extent regarded as an exercise in the transfer of technology, and the modernisation of administration was regarded as the solution to most of its problems (Wickwar, 1963). The fifties and sixties were also the heyday of technical assistance (both national and international), concentrating first — in the Middle East — on Turkey, Egypt and Iran, and then proceeding to the rest of the Middle East.[5] A combination of the ideas of such people as Fayol, Taylor and Weber, with their underlying concepts of economy, efficiency and rationalisation, were presented — sometimes in the simplified form of POSDCORB — as the *passe partout* 'science of administration'.

It is unnecessary to go out of one's way to illustrate the hold that the ideas of such authors, particularly those of Max Weber, had and still have on experts on administration in the Arab world. All one has to do is to pick up any piece of writing by any reputable Arab expert on administration, and there it is. Of course, there is nothing wrong with referring to these writers: the problem is that the exercise often not only begins with them but ends with them, and makes no reference to the relevance of their ideas to an Arab society.

Guided by this 'science of administration', improvements were introduced in the functions of personnel, budgeting, planning, organisation and training, changes that were usually confined to the central secretariats and the capital city. The line agencies, functional departments, sectoral units and operating levels of organisations — the real carriers of development — did not benefit as much (Islam and Henault, 1979, p. 259).

The cost, inefficiency and authoritarianism of an omnipotent bureaucracy afflicts most Middle Eastern countries. As in many other countries of the Third World, dependence on a central bureaucracy as a vehicle for economic development has given rise to the irony that it is the societies which lack good administration which are the ones to establish the most comprehensive and complex array of administrative controls over every aspect of investment, production and trade (Weinstein, 1981, p. 120). Egypt under the open door policy — as I have illustrated elsewhere — is a very good case in point, for even while trying (or claiming) to liberalise the economy, the bureaucracy continues to play a domineering and obstructive role (Ayubi, 1982b). Even the bureaucracy of a presumably shining example of a welfare state, such as Kuwait, does not always rise to the level of expectations. In a study on government services in Kuwait, 65 per cent of all respondents thought that the performance of the administrative machinery was poor, 30 per cent thought it was moderate and no more than 5 per cent thought it was good (al-Salim, 1982, p. 51).

Middle Eastern bureaucracies have not, on the whole, succeeded in solving the development problems they have been called upon to solve. Poverty persists, although it has often been modernised. Technology-intensive industrialisation has failed to create a sufficient number of jobs to absorb a rapidly expanding labour force, and the so-called trickle-down effect from the modern industrial sector to the poor in general and to the countryside in particular remains negligible. In short, the quality of life for the majority of the population has remained abysmally low with many of the basic needs for food, water, shelter, health and education still unsatisfied. Nor has the administration managed to reform itself and improve its own performance as an instrument of service.

Practitioners and experts alike are not prepared to accept much of the blame for the poor performance of the administration. It is always somebody else's fault: the politicians for interfering too much (but sometimes for not interfering enough, through a 'lack of political will'); the financial or technical resources (*imkaniyyat* in Egyptian terminology) for being meagre; or the whole population for not possessing a rational culture.

ORGANS OF CONTROL

Part of the reason why central, monocratic types of administration are favoured in the Arab World is the useful control functions that this type of bureaucracy can serve. This is why other types of organisation are not tried, and why, when they are adopted within programmes of administrative reform, they are used only as techniques void of power-sharing devices.

Rulers become impatient with the Weberian-style 'machine bureaucracy'[6] because its narrow minded, routine-bound instrumentalism seems incapable of confronting developments needed for innovations and mobilisation (Mintzberg, 1979, pp. 314–47). But its elaborate hierarchy and strict chain of command is also an invaluable instrument of control. They feel bound to criticise the dysfunctions of the monocratic-type bureaucracy that they inherited from the colonial period,[7] but they know that its control qualities should never be eroded. Most leaders in Arab countries now want (or say they want) development; but many want power too, and in most cases power is the more immediate and pressing of the two objectives. According to Fathaly and Chackerian (1983, pp. 202–7):

> Part of the superficial attractiveness of machine bureaucracies is that they cope quite well with hostile political environments. Power is centralised in the administrative apex and this arrangement provides clear responsibility for administrative action and quick response to *political* threats.

Rulers continue to lament the inefficiency of machine bureaucracy, but they overlook the fact that it is their obsession with control that lies behind its survival and strength.[8] Arab rulers appear to prefer a system of administrative authority in which all power emanates from a single political leader and where the influence of others is derivative in rough proportion to their perceived access to him or their share in his largesse. They often subject their bureaucracies to frequent and unpredictable transfers of administrators. Shifting people around is a continuous reminder of how those in superior positions can intervene on whim and at will. Ministries fight for funds with other units of government, not as a means to pursue particular programmes but as an on-going test of their standing in the bureaucratic pecking order. The often-criticised overlapping of jurisdictions may also be politically functional from the ruler's point of view. To ensure competition among a leader's subordinates, they are endowed with roughly equal power and given overlapping areas of authority. Absence of defined responsibility fits the system's informal modes and enhances the leader's flexibility to choose among personnel and policies (Weinbaum, 1979, pp. 3–7). An element of tolerated corruption goes a reasonable way towards ensuring the official's loyalty. Not only does he benefit but he is always under the threat that the authorities may decide to put a stop to that tolerance and apply the law.

Should it come as a surprise, given the Arab rulers' obsession with the control functions of bureaucracy, that security organisations tend to be the most 'efficient' public organisation in most Middle East countries.

The top and middle administrators themselves — given their cultural and social background — are likely to be just as power conscious. A study of 52 executives from six Arab countries (Egypt, Jordan, Kuwait, Lebanon, Saudi Arabia and the UAE) showed that out of a range of seven decisions, 22 per cent are likely to be the executive's own decision, 55 per cent a consultative decision (discussion with a small selected group followed by his own decision), 13 per cent a joint decision and only 10 per cent a decision based on delegation. There is even less power-sharing, more autocratic behaviour in organisational decision-making (Muna, 1980, pp. 47–60).

If subordinates oppose the Arab executive's decision, he is most likely to pull rank and go ahead in spite of the opposition. In situations where the executive opposes a decision that the subordinate favours, the power tactic most often used is inaction — freeze it or give it time to die. The Arab executive is so frightened of losing power if discussion is allowed and managerial conflict is tolerated, that he usually seeks security in what appears to be complete subordinate compliance. As one Egyptian executive said, 'If a leader, whether on the national or organisational level, does not suppress opposition, people (including my employees) think he is weak and he loses respect'[9] (Muna, 1980, pp. 63–8).

It is hard to imagine that anything but a monocratic, hierarchical bureaucracy could suit the inclinations of such a power-conscious executive. It is no wonder administrative reform based on power-sharing, participation and delegation, tends to die a speedy death almost as soon as it is tried in the Arab world.

Even when rulers and executives are prepared, under popular pressure or expert advice, to consider some measure of reform that involves delegation and decentralisation, they will tend to apply it in such a way that it is robbed of its participatory ethos. In Egypt, the introduction of a system for management by objects (MBO) in the mid-seventies was unsuccessful since, among other things, the executives though of it more as a means of increasing their managerial power than as a way of achieving a high level of consensus among the employees over the policies and programmes of the organisation (Ayubi, 1982a).

Bureaucracy vs Bedoucracy

The dynamics of bureaucratisation are quite easy to comprehend in a hydraulic society with old state traditions like Egypt. They are more difficult to understand in bedouin societies, that are known for autonomy and individualism. 'Bedoucracy' and bureaucracy seem to be completely at odds with each other. As Ernest Gellner (1981, p. 77) explains, bureaucracy is the antithesis of kinship. They have been developed to deal with completely different sets of problems. Arid-zone tribalism is a technique of maintaining order which dispenses with the specialised enforcement agencies that are associated with the state (and, in a way, *are* the state) (Gellner, 1983, pp. 439–40). Yet the opposites are partly reconciled by *petrocracy*.[10]

Through the creation of a bureaucracy, the rulers of the oil states are paying the citizen — by way of lucrative government employment — in return for a cessation of the old tribal wars, for tacit acceptance of the political supremacy of one tribe or fraction of a tribe (the royal or princely family) over the others. What the central administration does for the modern urban sector, the system of local subsidies achieves for the rural and nomadic areas. This can be likened to a system of indirect administration that recognises the traditional authority networks of the bedouin and incorporates them in the state structure.

The taxation function is thus reversed in the oil state: instead of the usual situation, where the state taxes the citizen in return for services, here the citizen taxes the state — by acquiring a government payment — in return for staying quiet, for not invoking tribal rivalries and for not challenging the ruling family's position.

The relationship that is being established between the official and the state is quite complex. On the one hand he knows that the state (or more specifically the ruling family) needs his acquiescence; on the other he knows that he needs a public post not only for the financial benefits it offers him but also for the contacts it provides (which are indispensable for the conduct of private business). In the short run, the official is tempted to feel that he is in the stronger position, that the state needs him more than he needs the state and that he can bargain with the state over the price of acquiescence.

Given this feeling and given the abundant oil reserves accruing to the state, the official is bound to think that he receives a meagre price for his service to the state. An empirical study conducted on 614 Saudi officials indicates that 79 per cent of the respondents were dissatisfied or neutral as far as their pay was concerned: the petrodollar flood has obviously created very high pay expectations (Chackerian and Shadukhi, 1983, p. 321).

In the long run the individual is likely to be caught up in the web of organisational relations and eventually submit to the grasping hand of the state. For he has nothing to offer the state, in return for his salary and benefits, other than power over himself.

There is much evidence to suggest that most Arabs either have no alternative but to rely on the state bureaucracy or feel they cannot do without the wages, benefits and subsidies with which it supplies them. Such unilateral services offered by the state bureaucracy to meet the important needs of the populace provide those in control of the state apparatus with what Peter Blau calls the penultimate source of power — its ultimate source, of course, being physical coercion (Blau, 1964). This partly explains why governments of the oil-rich states, although hardly liberal and democratic, have on the whole managed to rule with less physical coercion than many governments of the oil-poor Arab states.

Hierarchy in organisation has two aspects. The first is as a channel for occupational mobility, with related status and economic rewards; the second is as an instrument of control (Chackerian, 1983, p. 94). When an Arab takes a government job because it has prospects, he cannot escape, at least in part, the control that it will have on him. Available empirical evidence tends to support this: the Arab *is* learning to obey. In Saudi Arabia, for example:

> While government workers are not highly motivated, they do seem to be responsive to demands from superiors. Hierarchical information flows are quite effective, but decisions are made at the top of the hierarchies regardless of competence (Chackerian and Shadukhi, 1983, p. 321).

Learning to obey indicates that the control functions of bureaucracy work successfully. But to respect hierarchy is not the same as becoming an 'organisation man'. The bedoucracy, with its emphasis on family and kin relationships, has survived into the petrocracy with its superficially large, complex and 'modern' (i.e. formal-rational) arrangements, and this has given rise to a new variety of state organisation that we may call a petro-bedoucracy.

Al-Awaji (1971, p. 187) explains the resulting conflicts within the bureaucrat most eloquently:

. . . Because he wants to maintain his position both with his kin, friends and neighbours, and with his superior or superiors, he either evades the issue to avoid possible conflict, or exploits it to his advantage. While his loyalty to his particular group is largely an emotional one, his loyalty to his superior and his organisational mandate is for expediency. Where there is no conflict between personal goals and those of his organisation or superior, his opportunism remains unrevealed. This may occur when a bureaucrat is able to satisfy the demands of one interest without violently offending the other. In such a case, he is an exploitationist. He can be boldly corrupt when the formal rules are flexible, or legalistic when this best serves his interests.

Nevertheless, in most cases, he is escapist. When the conflict is so sharp that it endangers his position at the office and/or at home or before his friends, he is most likely to evade it. The typical situation is when the interests involved are vital to both his particular group and to his supervisor or the formal regulations of his agency.

The existence of conflict should not be taken to mean that bureaucratic organisations will not develop: bureaucracy may co-exist with kinship, and bureaucratic organisations can be held together through patronage. The case of Jordan illustrates that the two apparent opposites can be blended rather well. Concerning the Gulf region, Amir al-Kubaisi has coined the term *sheikhocracy* to describe the behavioural outcome of the juxtaposition of the attitudes of the sheikhs who act the bureaucrats' role, and the bureaucrats who act the sheikhs' role (al-Kubaisi, 1982, pp. 152–4). Another use to which the rulers may also wish to put the bureaucracy is to maintain the *status quo* by co-opting the intelligentsia and other aspiring groups while blurring the class issue, under the guise of the bureaucracy's universality. Under the banner of 'meritocracy' people from a wider pool are recruited into the bureaucracy, which establishes the impression that social mobility is possible without the need for conflict. This takes the heat off potential class conflicts and allows the state to control the situation. In populist regimes (for example, those applying a strategy of 'developmental nationalism', such as Egypt under Nasser), a kind of 'Bonapartism' may emerge as the rulers declare that 'we are all workers', while trying to use the bureaucracy as a means for 'creating their own class' (Ayubi, 1980, Ch. 5 and 6). In the petro-bedoucracy, the bureaucracy seems to represent a vehicle by means of which the privileges of the royal entourage can become entrenched and class confrontation avoided altogether, sometimes in the name of the egalitarian ethos of the nomadic society and sometimes in the name of the brotherhood of Islam.

And sure enough, Arab officials have proved to be politically docile. They have not on the whole formed special trade unions. Those who join a professional (technically specialised) syndicate have usually been more of an asset to the government than to fellow members without government jobs — this is particularly the case with the professional syndicates in Egypt.

In situations like these, 'bureaucratic politics' are likely to assume a relatively important role. A job in the bureaucracy for an individual or one of his relatives represents access to sources of allocative and distributive power. Influence over decision-making related to important national or local projects represents one of the few available channels for 'participation' in the public affairs of the society.

In conclusion, one can say that the deficiencies of Arab bureaucracies in offering services and promoting development are not due simply to the lack of knowledge on the part of Arab officials. The rigidity, formality and arbitrariness of the bureaucracy is in no small measure the outcome of its use as an instrument of power: most Arab rulers find in the machine bureaucracy a useful control device, and most executives find it a means of acquiring authority and exercising influence. Most Arab rulers and executives want to see their bureaucracies play a part in developing their countries, but in their real order of priorities, power often comes before development.

NOTES

1. Three countries are chosen to represent the new, small and rich category of state so that, given the paucity of data, they can complement each other. It goes without saying that, although they share salient characteristics, there exist several differences among them.

2. Three per cent of the population and 17 to 20 per cent of the labour force is considered usual in many countries.

3. Bahrain dinars were later replaced by the United Arab Emirates dirham. One Bahrain dinar = 10 UAE dirham.

4. In the early 1980s, a million to a million and a half Egyptians worked in other Arab countries (Auybi, 1983, 'The Egyptian brain drain', *Journal of Middle East Studies, 15*). Many were in administrative and technical jobs, of which a significant proportion were employed in government.

5. The level of American technical assistance in Iran was by far the

largest and the relationship the closest. One of the earlier projects lasted from 1956 to 1961, cost over $2.3 billion, and involved about 26 advisers to each of the Iranian ministries except foreign affairs and war. The majority of such advisers, who remained in the country until 1978, had little knowledge of the local environment or culture. They spent most of their energy trying to change local practices without understanding why they existed. It is hardly surprising that, with the exception of the police, these advisers were not on the whole successful in transferring their techniques across cultural boundaries (Seitz, 1980, 'The failure of US technical assistance in public administration: the Iranian case', *Public Administration Review, vol. 10, No. 5*).

6. The 'machine bureaucracy' is a term used by Henry Mintzberg to connote the type of bureaucracy first described by Max Weber. The operating work of such a bureaucracy is routine, often simple and repetitive and hence easily standardised. If the tasks of the organisation, however, require a high degree of innovation and call for a flexible response to frequently occurring and not easily predictable changes (as is the case in developing countries), standardisation is not as easy, and other types of organisation would be needed to face the challenge.

7. Both the Ottomans and the European colonial powers had been more concerned with control than with development, and relied on authoritarian administrations to achieve their goals. As Arab countries gained their independence they retained the ex-colonial administrations more or less intact, and whenever they introduced changes, they drew their inspiration from the French or the Egyptian models, which are both strongly control-oriented (Alderfer, 1967, *Public administration in newer nations*, Praeger, New York, pp. 5–62).

8. In the literature on organisation there are two orientations in studying control: one that views it mainly as a technical managerial device for enduring efficiency in fulfilling organisational goals, another that views control mainly as the ability to use power *vis-à-vis* others within the organisation. Although the two senses are not mutually exclusive, we are more interested in the second, as it is more relevant to the subject of the state (compare Dunsire, 1978, *Control in a bureaucracy*, Martin Robertson & Co, Oxford, pp. 21–72).

9. It is interesting to note that this statement came from an Egyptian. Muna's study (1980, *The Arab executive*, Macmillan, London, pp. 56–7) found that executives from Egypt shared less of their decision-making power with their subordinates than executives from the other five countries. Among these executives from Saudi Arabia showed more power-sharing in departmental decisions than the others. Could this be a reflection of the hierarchical traditions of the hydraulic society in the case of Egypt, and the egalitarian traditions of a bedouin society in the case of Saudi Arabia?

10. The term 'bedoucracy' is adapted from Muhammad al-Rumaihi. It is meant to imply that in spite of modern technology and equipment, the Arabian administrator is still predominantly a traditional nomad in his way of thinking and patterns of behaviour (al-Rumaihi, 1977, *Muawwiqat al-tanmiya*, Kazima, Kuwait, p.137). The term 'petrocracy' is our own coinage, but inspired by the title of Usama Abd al-Rahman's book *The petroleum bureaucracy and the development dilemma* (Abu Shikha, Nadir,

33

ARAB BUREAUCRACIES

1983. *Al-Tanzim al-idari* [administrative organisation in thirteen Arab states], Amman: Arab Organisation for Administrative Sciences.) It is meant to indicate a system whose politics as well as economics are dominated by the 'oil factor'.

2

Political Parties in the Arab State: Libya, Syria, Egypt

Raymond A. Hinnebusch

Few authoritarian states fail to develop some sort of single or dominant party system in this age of mass politics. What about the place of political parties in the Arab world? Under what conditions do they develop? What functions do they perform and how? This study will examine these questions through an analysis of the role of parties in Egypt, Syria and Libya, three important but variant cases of the dominant political formation in the area, the authoritarian-modernising state.

The Arab world seems to provide special, even hostile conditions for the development of party systems. No truly competitive party systems survive today, much less perform the functions they do in Western 'democracies', although their rudiments existed in the early independence period. Moreover, parties do not appear to be 'system requisites' in parts of the Arab world: this area contains a disproportionate number of no-party states, notably the traditional monarchies which dominate the Arabian Peninsula. In the more pervasive authoritarian-modernising regimes, party systems usually do exist, but even there they typically play less central roles than in competitive and totalitarian politics, often being subordinated to personalistic executives, the military or the bureaucracy. They are exclusively either single or dominant-party systems with low tolerance for opposition. Nevertheless, roughly two-thirds of today's Arab states do have a party system of sorts and although their role is hardly identical to that of parties in competitive or totalitarian systems, similar institutions are unlikely to be totally dissimilar in function. In fact, these party systems do perform functions more or less useful and sometimes central to the stability and effectiveness of Arab political systems.

In the Arab world, as elsewhere, party systems develop where regimes exist in societies which require some institutionalisation of elite-mass linkage. Where the ruler seeks social transformation or where he embarks on a national struggle against an 'imperialist' foe, he is likely to want the mobilisation of popular support and hence to have need of a party, although he is unlikely to tolerate opposition parties. In more modernised Arab societies, where traditional legitimacy and elite-mass ties rooted in religion and kinship are being eroded and social mobilisation is generating new participatory propensities, a party system may be needed to generate new bases of legitimacy and to absorb participatory pressures. But where great oil wealth allows massive co-optation by the state, this may neutralise participatory pressures and substitute for a party system. Generally, a party system is more likely to exist and more likely to perform central political functions in more advanced societies in which leaders seek radical change. The subordinate role of party systems in most Arab states by comparison to that in Western democracies and totalitarian regimes may, by the same logic, result from a lesser level of modernisation than in the former and a lesser level of commitment to radical change than in the latter. Competitive party systems are virtually non-existent in the Arab world, reflecting the rulers' preoccupation with concentration of power and a still limited level of social and political mobilisation, at which pressures for its diffusion can still be absorbed by a single, or failing that, a dominant party system. The following analysis will try to show how these variables help account for the similarities and contrasts in the party systems of the three case countries.

LIBYA: CHARISMATIC MOBILISATION FROM ABOVE

Libya under Qadhafi is a classic example of charismatic leadership in which a leader enjoying unbounded personal power makes his vision the source of all major innovation, his personal drive the principle dynamism in the political system. Qadhafi's power rests chiefly on charismatic legitimacy, an army controlled by personal followers, a compliant bureaucracy and the dependence of the people on an oil-rich state. But Qadhafi has wanted, not just to stay in power, but to carry out a revolution in Libya, to turn a people attached to traditional parochialism or infected by Westernisation into a virtuous participant citizenry loyal to Arabism and Islam, and to fashion an egalitarian social order and a productive new economy. This has demanded the mobilisation of mass participation and, if the new order was to endure, its 'routinisation' in new political institutions; in fact, in a party-like structure. The conditions of post-1969 Libya gave Qadhafi special opportunities to construct a new political order. Power had long been dominated by a small traditional elite, while most Libyans were politically passive. The old regime had lost much of its traditional legitimacy, and Qadhafi's overthrow of this discredited regime and his nationalist assertiveness quickly won him a mass following. Thus he acquired the fund of political capital needed to dominate, expand and reshape a small and pliant political arena.

Determined to enact the revolution from above, Qadhafi rejected the liberal model which, to him, divided the nation between competing private interests. Nor did he want the Leninist system, typical of the modern revolutionary state, viewing it as the domination of one class over others. His institution-building effort therefore took a Nasserite form which, though altered over time, has persisted. A single all-embracing mass political organisation, initially called the Arab Socialist Union (ASU) was erected through which the leader hoped to expand and organise his largely lower-middle and lower class following. All participation had to be channelled through the ASU on an individual basis; no autonomous political group activity, whether based on segmental, class or 'alien' ideological differences (liberalism, Marxism), was permitted; the press and secondary associations were brought under regime control and the rudiments of pluralistic party politics were repressed.

Qadhafi was soon dissatisfied with his initial party-like experiment. He met growing resistance from a multitude of interests and opponents: traditional elites, angry at their displacement or opposed to the effort to capture their tribal mass bases; the middle class, alienated by the repression of political freedoms; the bureaucracy, resistant to reform; military colleagues, unhappy with his unilateral initiatives. At a growing disadvantage in the small elite political arena, Qadhafi needed to mobilise mass support on his side, but the ASU, infiltrated by unsympathetic tribal or opposition elements and largely lacking political cadres was unavailable for this task. Qadhafi needed to generate a new activist mass political culture amenable to his revolutionary vision, but the masses remained largely passive, often still beholden to traditional political symbols.

Hence, Qadhafi launched his Popular Revolution in which he aimed to go over the heads of his elite opponents and mobilise the masses in direct action against them. This effort resulted in the emergence of pro-Qadhafi 'popular committees' across the country manned by a new group of activists drawn from the lower social strata which Qadhafi saw as his constituency. The move strengthened Qadhafi's hand but the power struggle went on. It was only after the 1975 fall of his military rivals that Qadhafi could begin his effort to transform Libya according to the ideological blueprint contained in his *Green Book*. In his effort to replace Libya's mixed economy with a socialist worker-controlled one, he challenged the vital interests of the bourgeoisie large and small. In his insistence that the *Green Book* was the authentic expression of Islam, he challenged the religious establishment. In his foreign policy, Qadhafi challenged Western imperialism and its local clients. To contain the opposition these challenges were bound to provoke, and to consolidate popular support, the mass activism he had tried to mobilise in the Popular Revolution had to be broadened and incorporated into an effective political organisation. By 1979, Qadhafi's efforts to do this had culminated in a new party-like structure called 'people's power'.

In principle, 'people's power' embodies a direct democracy which puts both executive and legislative power in the hands of the whole people. In practice, it is an altered and apparently more effective form of Nasserite mass organisation. Authority theoretically flows upward from the sovereign people through a four-tiered set of assemblies and committees. At the bottom, are popular committees acting as neighbourhood authorities or management committees in economic enterprises. Next, in the sub-districts, are 187 Basic People's Congresses composed of the people assembled; they are, in principle, the focus of all sovereignty, the building blocks of direct democracy. They elect their own political leadership bodies, called secretariats and also sub-district popular committees with administrative powers. At the district level, there are 45 Popular Congresses elected from the basic congresses, also with political secretariats. They are paralleled by administrative popular committees, regional cabinets composed of specialists corresponding to national administrative departments. At the national level is the General People's Congress of about 1,000 delegates, drawn mostly from the secretariats of the basic congresses, and approximating to a national legislature. Responsible to it is a cabinet-like General Popular Committee, composed of technical elements picked by the general people's congress from lower level popular committees.

The general congress also elects a supreme political leadership, the General Secretariat. This body was filled by Qadhafi and his close military colleagues until 1979, when he turned formal political

POLITICAL PARTIES IN THE ARAB STATE

leadership over to civilian followers. Parallel to this geographically-based structure, is a series of occupational syndicates for farmers, students, professionals, workers and others, which are also represented in the general congress. Finally, in 1979 a distinct line of informal political authority was created, composed of so-called revolutionary committees: it was made up of Qadhafi zealots charged with exercising ideological leadership of the masses *inside* the popular democracy structure, and acting as 'watchdogs of the revolution'. The revolutionary committees represent a recognition by Qadhafi of the need for an ideological vanguard of true believers to lead his revolution at the base as well as at the top. But these followers have not been formally organised as a vanguard party, being self-selected enthusiasts rather than carefully chosen and indoctrinated militants, linked to Qadhafi in a more personal and sporadic, than disciplined or organised, fashion. Despite the claim that this system embodies a direct popular democracy, which dissolves barriers between the people and the exercise of power, an examination of several actual political processes — recruitment and policymaking — makes it clear that democracy from below is channelled and controlled from above.

Leadership recruitment in the new Libya formally takes place by election from below. In practice, Qadhafi and his close colleagues remain the top political elite, ruling on the basis of charismatic legitimacy and coercive power. Top administrators, formally elected by the general people's congress, are nominated or approved by Qadhafi and his inner circle. One moves up in the system less through support from below than proven loyalty to those above. Political activism within people's power is probably a major channel through which aspirant elites become eligible for co-optation from above, but personal links to the top elite or professional career achievement counts for as much or more. Even elections at lower levels have increasingly come to be 'guided' from above. Earlier uncontrolled elections tended to reflect tribal solidarities, allowing larger kin-units to dominate smaller ones or resulting in election of local influentials uncongenial to the regime, or in the dominance of popular committees by persons lacking administrative qualifications. In response, the regime charged the revolutionary committees with screening candidates for political loyalty and technical competence.

The current system of guided nomination and open voting by hands is likely to preclude opposition candidates and to favour those enjoying regime approval or traditional local support, although it

39

does not exclude some debate over qualifications and some choice. As for the revolutionary committees, they seem to be virtually self-appointed in response to Qadhafi's call for their establishment. However, he subsequently took care to weed out unsuitable elements. In short, political recruitment in Libya is based on a combination of advancement from below and co-optation from above; the closer to the political apex, the greater the intervention from above. For those, often of modest social status, who are loyal to the leader's ideology, the system provides a relatively open channel of political advancement and apprenticeship. But it is closed to those who wish to contest Qadhafism. This results in the exclusion of those segments of the intelligentsia unwilling to accept the command of the sole leader. The irony is that it is these people who tend to have either the motivation and political vision needed to carry out the radical change Qadhafi wants or the technical qualifications on which his modernisation drive depends. The system provides no institutionalised means for leadership circulation at the very top, access to which, given the youth of the core elite, is effectively blocked. But the system may well be capable of reinvigorating elite ranks below this level.

The effect of mass participation in the policymaking process is also circumscribed by leadership priorities and controls. Foreign and defence policy is reserved to the leader; a major decision like the Uganda intervention was not even discussed in the popular congresses. In domestic matters there is a consultative process which typically begins with the despatch of leadership proposals for discussion in the basic people's congresses. A consensus is reached, no doubt under the influence of Qadhafi zealots, and delegates bound by it sent to the periodic general congresses. This imperative mandate is held to make the system a direct, rather than a representative, democracy. Many of the proposals so discussed have been reforms blueprinted in the *Green Book*. Measures such as nationalisation and conscription were both voted down at least once, but Qadhafi insisted and has ultimately prevailed on any matter he considered vital to his revolution.

On lesser who-gets-what issues, such as taxation, prices and the distribution of state expenditure, the system is more open to competitive articulation of interests and has become a vehicle for local demands on the national budget. But even this demand process has been constrained from above. The weight of the instructions of basic congresses to their delegates is diluted by aggregating their conflicting demands through a joint committee of the general congress and the cabinet in which demands are tailored to the priorities of a Five Year Plan drawn up in the national bureaucracy. Qadhafi has typically thrown his weight on the side of the cabinet against budget-busting raids from below, arguing that investments have to be made on a scientific cost-benefit basis.

Qadhafi has clearly been disappointed with opposition to his most cherished initiatives and the economically irrational and consumerist particularism expressed in the basic congresses. He has complained that the delegates often express the interests of small groups or individuals rather than the authentic will of the people. He expected that this would be overcome as the expertise and consciousness of the basic congresses was raised, and it was to undertake this that the revolutionary committees were created. Since these were not ideologically selected or disciplined, they, too, have often fallen below the leader's expectation of political virtue, but they give him a lever, however imperfect, to make sure his national priorities are favourably considered at the local base. Qadhafi has genuinely attempted to engage popular participation in policymaking, but when the outcome of this process departs from an authentic expression of the general will as he sees it, he has intervened to set it right.

People's power was also intended to engage mass participation in policy implementation, that is, to mobilise the masses in the construction of the new society, subordinate state officials to supervision by the supposedly Qadhafiite masses, and generally to create an active new citizenry in place of traditional passivity. In the most immediate sense, people's power aimed to distribute administrative power among appointed officials and popular elements. Policy implementation begins in the cabinet, which translates the consensus reached in the consultative process into concrete laws and programmes, but in 1969, responsibility for implementation was decentralised to the 45 regional popular committees, supposedly closer to the people. Thereafter, it proceeds downward to lower level popular committees, in sub-districts, neighbourhood and enterprises.

These popular committees at first combined political activists and career officials but this led to conflicts and the frequent presence of technically unqualified persons in administrative roles, compelling the regime to ensure that technocrats were selected for the committees. But popular committees remained accountable to local people's congresses as well as administrative superiors. In principle, this could keep officials responsive to both local popular and national technical needs, but it has often worked poorly: administrators can be paralysed or diverted into particularistic application of policies by excessive political intervention, or people's congresses may be too passive to exercise effective political oversight.

Many of the popular political activists have been as incompetent and negligent as the bureaucrats they are supposed to control. Many proved to be opportunists instead of true believers. Absenteeism in the basic people's congresses, reaching between 30 and 50 per cent, indicates the apathy or hostility of major parts of the population. In short, the system does not seem to have incorporated mass participation into the policy implementation process effectively enough to produce the kind of citizen responsibility and control over officials Qadhafi wants. Yet, it would be a mistake to see this system as inconsequential: it provides Qadhafi with a nucleus of organised followers at the base of society, giving him a remarkably ubiquitous presence in Libya's towns and villages without which the changes initiated at the centre would not be received locally. Pro-Qadhafi activism at the base plays a role in enforcing consensus, silencing those who will not be persuaded and pre-empting the potential for counter-revolutionary mobilisation. While coercion and economic co-optation also help to explain the relative lack of overt opposition to Qadhafi, it is unlikely he could have survived repeated challenges by so many powerful interests without the organised base created by people's power.

Despite its flaws, Qadhafi's political infrastructure does play a significant, if subordinate, role in the political system. It recruits sub-elites and prepares them for further political mobility. It plays a modest role in interest articulation, keeping the leader in touch with his base in a way perhaps not too different from traditional desert democracy, in which the leader consults with the people but takes the final decisions and brooks no opposition. If so, it may be compatible with the expectations of many Libyans. Even this very limited participation has consequences for individual careers and group interests, and to Qadhafi militants, it is of ideological significance. It has probably broadened and toughened the base of the state. Yet, lacking the ideological discipline and organisation to penetrate traditional values thoroughly and energise the people, it has shown limited ability to transform Libyans into virtuous new citizens. As long as the people fail to live up to his standards of virtue, Qadhafi must constantly intervene in the political process to set things right; but as long as he does so, the institutionalisation of participation remains fragile and Qadhafi risks that people's power will be bureaucratised and bypassed by clientelist means of approach to decision-makers, shrinking mass access to the centre. This is an in-built tension between charismatic leadership and institution-building. Without a more institutionalised incorporation of mass activism into the regime, the ideological orientation Qadhafi has given Libya is unlikely to outlast him (Hinnebusch, 1984a; Fathaly and Palmer, 1980).

SYRIA: SINGLE PARTY IN A DIVIDED SOCIETY

Syria's Baath regime rose out of a society fragmented by intense communal, class and urban-rural conflicts, locked in a nationalist struggle with powerful external forces, and ruled by a traditional, narrowly-based oligarchy of little legitimacy. The Baath Party, one of the most important of the ideological parties precipitated by the societal crisis, proposed to resolve the crisis through a mixture of pan-Arabism, the creation of a strong popular-based state, and radical social reform. Around this programme the party developed a significant middle class-peasant base, but never achieved the broad mass support necessary to win power through votes or popular revolution; so that when it took power in 1963 it was by military coup.

The Baath set out to establish a Baathist state and impose a revolution from above. This was immediately challenged by an array of rivals — the traditional oligarchy, the Muslim Brotherhood, liberals, Nasserites — all of whom had their own social bases. The Baath consolidated its rule only by virtue of the tightening grip Baathist officers established over the army. From the outset, the party was inevitably dominated by officer-politicians who had brought it to power and kept it there. But the Baathists knew that a stable state could not be based on military rule alone. Hence, they set out to forge a Leninist party-state: the party's collegial organs would become the centre of revolutionary authority, subordinating both military and bureaucracy. The party organisation represented a network of ideologically disciplined militants which stretched throughout society, displacing rival elites and mobilising mass support for revolution. In fact, a complex party apparatus was indeed forged and through it and its mass auxiliaries, a significant social base was incorporated into the regime.

At the same time, a 'socialist transformation', including nationalisations and land reform, weakened the traditional elite and brought the strategic points of the economy under Baathist control.

But ultimately the army could not be made subservient to party authority, and when the continued recalcitrance of social opposition, combined with military defeat, brought the army elite to advocate subordination of revolution to national unity, the party was powerless to stop it. Hafez al-Assad, the senior Baathist general, seized power in a 1970 coup and transformed the apex of the Baathist state, personalising and concentrating power in an authoritarian presidency, enjoying broad powers of appointment and decree. His power came to rest on a network of personal Alawite clients dominating the security apparatus, and loyal subordinates in the military high command. The party was reduced to becoming one of several pillars of a presidential-dominant regime. Under Assad, Baath ideology was gradually eroded as a determinant of policy by a realist foreign policy which tempered nationalist militancy, and by an economic liberalisation which diluted the Baath's statism and populism. The party elite itself was, through corruption and 'business on the side', transformed into a state bourgeoisie chiefly concerned with the defence of the *status quo*. This course provoked rising opposition from left and right which has only been contained by authoritarian controls and repression. Equally important to regime survival, however, has been the role of the party's political apparatus in defending the regime's social base.

In the Assad regime, high policymaking is chiefly the prerogative of the president, shared or delegated at his discretion with the party apparatus, military command and cabinet. By virtue of his unrivalled personal stature, leadership of the ruling coalition and command of the levers of institutional power, Assad is virtually unchallengeable and in no formal way accountable. Yet, he is as likely to act and speak in the name of an elite consensus or to broker conflicts within a divided elite, as to impose a personal view, and high policy is usually made in an inner circle of varying scope which typically includes military chieftains and top party politicians and ministers. Officially, the collegial leadership of the Baath Party is the most important centre of power below the presidency, yet the army high command carries greater weight in some spheres. Assad's clients in the security apparatus and key army commands have unrivalled positions as power brokers and the bureaucracy probably exercises more influence over the day-to-day running of the country. The party's collegial bodies in some ways remain pre-eminent: embracing top army and government elites who are normally senior party members, with formal authority over broad policy domains, they remain arenas of policy consultation and representation. The party apparatus penetrates the bureaucracy and through its military branches, it is symbiotically linked with the coercive base of the regime, reaching down into every corner of society. With a long history as an authentic political force, it is no mere creation of the president, but an important vehicle through which he protects his power and legitimacy. As such, the party cannot be taken lightly, but its role has been circumscribed by the presidential regime into which it has been incorporated.

The Baath Party organisation is a four-layered pyramid formally erected on democratic-centrist lines. Basic level organisations in villages, factories, neighbourhoods and public institutions are grouped into sub-branches in districts and towns, and these are combined into branches at the province or city level. In the armed forces, cells in smaller army units are grouped into sub-branches and branches at brigade and division levels. These two pyramids are joined in the countrywide (*qutri*) organisation. Each level of the pyramid has its own assembly and executive command, headed by a secretary. At the country level there is a Regional Congress and a Central Committee. The Regional Command issues from the Central Committee, representing the supreme party authority in Syria. The Syrian party, in addition to non-Syrian Baathists, comes together in a National Congress and a National Command which are technically superior to, but in fact are chiefly an appendage of, the Syrian organisation.

In theory, this party hierarchy emerges from elections from the bases: since 1971 the Central Committee and Regional Command have been elected from within its ranks by the Regional Congress, and the Congress itself has been elected from general assemblies at the sub-district level. Executive committees and secretaries at lower levels are appointed by the next higher level commands. A line of authority runs from the functional offices attached to the command to their lower level offshoots. The functional offices are responsible for internal party affairs and for supervision of popular organisations and state agencies in their functional domains. Clustered around the party are its auxiliaries, for workers, peasants, youth, students, women and various professions; most are headed by party members but also embrace segments of the non-party population that the regime seeks to incorporate into its base.

A major indicator of the importance of the party in an authoritarian regime is its weight in political recruitment; in Syria the Baath clearly plays a much greater role than in Libya or Egypt. It is true that decisive power struggles for succession at the very top have always been decided by military elites through coercion or threat rather than by party vote or seniority. The current top national elite was initially constituted from the party faction Assad brought to power in the 1970 coup. Since 1963, only Baathist officers were qualified contenders in this struggle. Moreover, the party has played the central role in the subsequent turnover and replenishment of this elite. Advancement into the national elite takes place through several channels. In addition to the party apparatus, the army, the ministerial bureaucracy, and to a lesser degree, the Baath's small allied parties, academic and professional careers also serve as channels of upward mobility. Assad has put personal loyalty as measured by kinship and sectarian status first in appointments to top intelligence and military posts critical to the regime's survival. In order to acquire access to strategic posts and the inner circle of power, even those who move up along non-party ladders, must normally have also party credentials and a demonstrated ability to advance within the party.

Advancement in the party chiefly takes place through co-option from above although elections from below have played a subsidiary, but decreasingly important role. The effect of elections has always been sharply circumscribed by the ability of incumbent elites to purge lower level activists and as such, an anti-leadership electoral challenge from below cannot be mounted unless leaders are divided. Lower level candidates for leadership have long considered it important to cultivate support for election to higher level assemblies which could bring them to the attention of national elites. Moreover incumbents who have been defeated in elections have normally suffered demotion in their political careers. In recent years, however, nominations from above have allowed less scope for real electoral contests below, and to reach the very top a pull from above has always been essential.

The president is the final arbiter of elite circulation. Those he wishes to protect are immune to defeat and there is no evidence that elite status can be attained from independent bases whether inside the party or outside it against his wishes. But Assad has often refrained from intervening in elections and allowed divided party elites to fight it out themselves. In fact, in two out of three major electoral rounds since 1970, there have been major turnovers at the top. The president has the legal powers to appoint whoever he pleases to government, and can, if he wishes, bypass the party or even arrange for rapid mobility of only nominal members inside the party. With certain important exceptions, however, he has not done so, and most persons who exercise power in Baathist Syria are senior partisans. This is even more the case further down the pyramid of power: party activism is the dominant route to sub-elite positions in Syria. Local party commands are the dominant political authority in the provinces and villages and appointment to administrative positions there depends on party credentials. To the extent that office in Syria brings with it spoils, big and small, the party in its recruitment function has been transformed into a font of patronage.

As a vanguard party, the Baath was never designed to aggregate societal interests into the policy process. But its rules did provide for 'intra-party' democracy, whereby local partisans were to be able to pass resolutions and elect delegates to the party congresses which set party strategy. This process was always controlled by the leadership's power to purge but it did go on and, until 1970, party congresses set high policy and helped decide conflicts between policy factions. This system remains today the only institutionalised channel of representation which carries any weight in the political system. Under Assad, its importance had indisputably declined as policymaking has gravitated to the presidency. The major policy initiatives under Assad — the economic opening, the search for diplomatic settlement with Israel, the Lebanese intervention — were all presidential *faits accomplis*, late ratified but not previously authorised by party congresses.

Nevertheless, the process retains a residual life. Discussion at lower levels keeps party elites in touch with the bases and they may, at their discretion, incorporate ideas and sentiments from below into their recommendations to the congresses. In the congresses themselves, so long as his major priorities are not challenged, Assad has not tried to impose a uniform policy on all matters, and as such, congresses remain arenas of debate and conflict over lesser, but still consequential matters. Factions of the top elite have battled at each congress, although the rivals have often been personal or sectarian coalitions, and the stakes more often power and patronage than basic policy issues. The struggles of rival factions to win support in the bases suggest that outcomes are not totally disconnected from opinion below. Congresses have also been occasions of vociferous criticism, even revolt, by the bases against elements of the top elite, the president always excepted.

The thrashing out of congress resolutions constitutes a kind of aggregative process through which the interests of various elements of the regime's constituency get heard and, to an extent, appeased and reconciled. These resolutions have often had a clear policy bias which has not always been on the same tangent as the dominant thrust from above. Thus, the resolutions of the 1975 Sixth Regional Congress incorporated a clear statist thrust which, while not overtly challenging the emerging economic liberalisation, subsequently translated into policies potentially at odds with it. The electoral defeat of some close Assad colleagues closely identified with liberalisation and corruption at this congress also acted as a kind of brake on economic liberalisation. That party congresses continue to carry some weight in the political system is not surprising; since many of those who sit in them are, after all, the regime middle elite and persons of consequence: party *apparatchicki*, heads of military party branches with senior command positions, chiefs of major administrative agencies and leaders of syndicates. Nevertheless, these 'public' consultative processes have, to a growing extent, been short-circuited by multiplying webs of clientelist and primordial forms of access to elites by which largely privileged interests sidetrack and reshape the policy thrusts issuing from the more broad-based and institutionalised intra-party aggregative process.

Finally, the party in Syria is supposed to play a major role, as in Leninist regimes, in supervising the implementation of regime policy by the state apparatus and in mobilising mass support for it. The party does have a structure specifically designed to do this, namely the specialised party offices through which parallel government ministries and popular organisations are supposed to coordinate and supervise their activities. Thus, the Peasant Bureau of the Regional Command and its derivatives at province and district levels, supervise both ministerial officials responsible for agriculture and peasant syndicate leaders in pursuance of their mission of ensuring the implementation of party agrarian policy. Similar offices operate analogously in labour and industry, education, economy, trade, youth and other fields. Their actual effectiveness in translating congress decisions into concrete policy is evidently very uneven. Some have vetoed ministerial initiatives outside party policy. Some have been active and effective in the formation and control of the party's array of popular organisations. But many seem preoccupied with patronage concerns, such as placing clients in public sector employment, or with corrupt practices, such as taking a cut on public contracts.

It is through its local cells, supposedly made up of ideological militants, and its popular organisations, that the party most directly tries to mobilise mass support and participation in policy implementation. This political apparatus penetrates towns, villages, factories, army units and government offices, representing a pervasive network of political control. The party itself has about 150,000 members and its auxiliaries may have organised between a quarter and a third of the population. Moreover, a recruitment policy deliberately aimed at mobilisation of a mass base and exclusion of hostile, largely higher class, elements has given a distinctly popular colouring to this base, compatible with official ideology. Though higher status elements are present at the party apex, the bulk of the party is petit bourgeois, worker and peasant in social composition. Moreover, until recently, radical nationalist and egalitarian ideological appeals played an important role in the recruitment of the party base. But careerist and personalist, localist and primordial connections have also always played an equally powerful role, increasingly so in recent years, and true militants have, as ideology declines, fallen by the way.

The party, moreover, has always been plagued by 'sick' tribalistic and sectarian factionalism; as ideological discipline has increasingly eroded, it has fallen victim to corruption, inefficiency and negligence. It is not, in short, a dynamic leadership capable of the true mass mobilisation needed for a radical transformation of society. But in hundreds of villages party cells represent a new local leadership, typically made up of educated youth and small and middle-income peasants, and these have helped bring a modest level of social reform and economic change to rural society. Through its various youth auxiliaries, the party has incorporated and indoctrinated thousands of school children. The party and its auxiliaries disproportionately incorporate and serve the interests of minorities, ex-rurals and the military, but they are not simply instruments. In their inclusion of thousands of Sunnis, city folk and civilians, they represent a web of shared interests and beliefs cutting across Syria's deep sectarian, urban-rural and institutional divides. The party thus incorporates the social base essential to a stable regime, excludes opposition access to major population segments, and helps to integrate a fragmented society.

It is clear that the party provides neither an effective mechanism for holding elites accountable nor for aggregating mass preferences into policy. But as a major channel of elite recruitment and patronage and an arena through which the interests of the regime's constituency may, so long as they do not conflict with the elite's priorities, be articulated and to an extent incorporated into policy, it remains a vital enough part of the political process to make participation worthwhile for its thousands of activists. By incorporating and organising a constituency with a stake in the regime, the party has given the regime a sturdiness and a modicum of legitimacy that contrasts sharply with the ephemeral narrowly-based pre-Baath regimes. It is also clear that the party has turned out to be a very pale copy of the Leninist prototype, incapable not only of social transformation, but even of firmly establishing and institutionalising a legitimate new political order. In carrying out its revolution from above, the regime has imposed structural change on society, but in doing so has alienated a multitude of interests that the party has been unable to submerge in the total mass mobilisation of true revolutionary regimes. Hence the regime has constantly had to alternate between repression of the opposition and concession to its demands. The opposition, on the other hand, has little hope of bringing down the regime. The outcome has been the supercession of the fragmented narrow political arena of the *ancien regime* by one much enlarged but sharply bifurcated between a powerful regime and a persisting intense opposition (Dawisha, 1978; Hinnebusch, 1982 and 1984b).

EGYPT: PARTY ADAPTATION TO A PLURALISING SOCIETY

The contemporary Egyptian party system is the product of the pressures of a pluralising society on the authoritarian state built by Nasser. Through a mixture of nationalist charisma and military force, Nasser concentrated power in an authoritarian presidency ruling through a massive bureaucracy. He repressed all opposition parties, mobilised broad cross-class support, imposed a nationalist-populist ideological consensus and organised an all-embracing official single party, the Arab Socialist Union (ASU). Possessed of unchallenged personal legitimacy and a reliable coercive and administrative apparatus, Nasser had little incentive to breathe life into this party; it remained subordinate to the government and never developed much autonomy, power or real function. Yet, while Nasser suppressed pluralistic political participation, his modernisation policies — industrialisation, mass communications and education, bureaucratic expansion — accelerated social mobilisation and class formation, thereby widening the social base of potential political participation.

Under his successor, Sadat, this widened political arena began to re-pluralise. Sadat inherited the levers of Nasser's authoritarian-bureaucratic state but lacked Nasser's mass popular stature. He thus sought to root his rule in one segment of Nasser's coalition, the bourgeoisie. As he steered Egypt right, abandoning Nasser's policies, the ideological consensus imposed under Nasser was shattered; left wing elements of the Nasserite coalition broke with Sadat while, to balance them, he allowed formerly repressed forces on the right — Islamic fundamentalists and the secular liberal bourgeoisie — to re-emerge politically. In the absence of unchallenged leadership legitimacy, the monolithic structures of the authoritarian state could not easily contain this deepening pluralisation of the political arena without resort to the kind of coercion that Sadat was reluctant to undertake. Moreover, a major part of Sadat's own constituency wanted political relaxation, even liberal political freedoms, if only for themselves. Thus, Sadat decided on a carefully controlled political liberalisation from above. The powers of the presidency to set basic policy remained undiminished, but state control over the political arena was relaxed. The single official party system was dismantled and three new protoparties emerged from it, one on the liberal right, soon to become the Ahrar Party, one on the left, the National Progressive Unionist Party (NPUP), and between them a pro-government centre, soon named the National Democratic Party (NDP). New parties could be formed with government approval so long as they were not based on the major fault lines of society, class, religion and region, and as long as they accepted the basic principles of the regime and refrained from threatening social peace. In 1977, the pre-1952 Wafd Party was resurrected and admitted to the party system.

The opposition parties were allowed to contest parliamentary elections and to propose constructive alternatives within the lines of presidential policy as long as they refrained from challenging this policy or mobilising mass support against the regime. Sadat hoped this experiment would please the liberal bourgeoisie he was courting, impress his new American patrons, provide the dose of political liberalisation needed to encourage the private sector and provide safety valves for or even co-opt opposition political activism. When the government party won the partially free elections of 1976, it appeared the regime could have both limited liberalisation and yet maintain control of the political arena. But when some of the opposition parties failed to play by the rules Sadat had laid down, he tightened controls, forced the Wafd to disband, and tried to replace the NPUP with a more loyal left of centre party, the Socialist Labour Party (SLP). In 1981, he suspended the whole experiment but after Sadat's death Mubarak restored it, an acknowledgement of the high risk and cost of attempting to reverse the pluralisation of the political arena. A dominant-party system seemed on its way to institutionalisation, made up of a large government party straddling the centre and an array of small opposition parties on its left and right.

The government party

The National Democratic Party (NDP) is a direct descendent of the ASU and, in fact, took over much of its organisation. At the top of the structure is a cabinet headed by a president and one or more secretary generals. The parliamentary caucus, an addition from Nasser's day made necessary by the appearance of parliamentary opposition, incorporates the party's deputies into the structure. At the province and district levels are party committees headed by secretaries. The NDP has inherited much of the structural and functional weaknesses of the ASU but, since the pluralisation of the party system, it has assumed a marginally enhanced functional role in the state.

The party leadership, free of the middle class left-wing officers and intellectuals who dominated the ASU, is a much more socially homogeneous coalition of ministerial technocrats, professional military and police officials and 'notables' with professional credentials and land or business interests, all chiefly of bourgeois background. It remains largely an extension of the state. The most powerful party leaders have either built their careers first as ministers or hold both government and party posts, with their real power base in the former. Leaders are supposed to be elected from below, but elections have been infrequent and presidential nominations and dismissals have played the dominant role in leadership formation. Upward movement in the party depends thus far more on co-option from above than support in the party bases; indeed some leaders have been imposed from outside the party. The party has yet to become a major channel for elite recruitment in the regime, a majority of ministerial elites still being co-opted from the civil and military establishments and from the universities. Thus it remains true, as under the ASU, that the executive provides the party with its leadership rather than vice versa.

Nonetheless, the party does play a limited and possibly widening recruitment role today. Party service has become more important for

POLITICAL PARTIES IN THE ARAB STATE

movement into the elite from bureaucratic and academic channels. One sign of this is the appointment of two recent prime ministers, Mustafa Khalil and Fuad Muhi al-Din, after extended party leadership. The practice has developed on a limited scale of co-opting to ministerial roles party or parliamentary notables with careers and interests chiefly in the private sector, a sign that the party may be developing into a recruitment channel distinct from the bureaucracy. Party recruitment to its local branches and to parliamentary seats plays a major role in the formation of the regime's middle and sub-elites.

The end of military and left-wing dominance of the party after Nasser should have made it easier to develop the party into a channel of interest aggregation for the regime's constituency, but this has happened to only a limited extent. The party's programme apparently emerged from interparty consultations in which the regime has tried to satisfy dominant interests in its constituency. Thus, the programme steers a middle course between individualistic capitalism and communism, and as such is compatible with both foreign investment and private sector revival as well as with the persisting large public sector. In this way, the regime appeases both the state and private sectors of its support base. But the party programme is too vague to determine high policy in any practical way and the government has never felt bound by it, its actual policy long being on a tangent considerably right of the official programme. Nor have party bodies been consulted shaping high policy: crucial decisions, like the 1977 cutting of food subsidies and the trip to Jerusalem, were taken without consultation and the government pursued the peace treaty and normalisation of relations with Israel in spite of opposition from its own party caucus.

On lesser matters, however, the government has accorded a growing role in policy making to the party's parliamentary caucus, making it the main arena in which the interests of its bourgeois constituency are articulated and conflicts, especially between its state and private wings, reconciled. Parliament has become a breeding ground for an endless stream of initiatives or responses to government meant to advance or protect these interests, which are often incorporated into policy. The caucus has also performed a modest government oversight function, allowing for the redressing of grievances among the regime's constituency. Sub-elites lower down in the party find party activity enhances their access to officials and helps to cultivate strategic personal connections further up, enforcing their status in the local community. Of course, the mass bases of the party are not formally incorporated into this process, although individuals may occasionally achieve access through clientelist ties.

The party is, in fact, expected to function as an elite-mass linkage incorporating a mass base into the regime. Formally, it does link a wide array of social forces to the regime, but this linkage is brittle. The party embraces large numbers of government employees, but many are nominal members who pay their dues to protect their jobs. The NDP youth organisation has had a hard time holding its own against Islamic youth groups. The party has successfully run pro-regime candidates in many professional syndicates, thus keeping large segments of the professional upper middle class in the fold, but it has failed to keep journalists and lawyers in line and its control has weakened since the sixties. It has had limited success in protecting the regime's bourgeois constituency from the New Wafd. The party co-opts top leaders of the trade union movement but has not been able to neutralise the special appeal of the left opposition to workers.

In the villages, the local notability often belongs to the party and to the extent that it represents the natural leadership of the village, helps link the peasant masses to the regime. In contrast to Nasser's ASU, however, the NDP lacks organisation at the village level, evidently content to rely on clientelism to do the job. In general, the party has been handicapped in its effort to mobilise a mass base by a lack of ideological discipline, a ramshackle organisation and a scarcity of voluntary activists. Even by comparison to Nasser's limited mobilisation efforts, the NDP seems uninterested in mass mobilisation, and its main linkage function is probably to prevent mobilisation by opposition forces. Still, as an organisational bond between the regime and the sub-elites which represent its core support and its informal linkage to wider social forces, it has proven its utility both in limiting opposition access to the masses and in getting out the pro-government vote. At its base, in fact, the party has taken on some of the features of a traditional patronage party.

Opposition parties in a dominant-party system

The formerly monolithic Egyptian political arena has given birth to a rich array of opposition parties which have become vehicles of political expression for significant parts of the population whose interests and values could not be served by the dominant party. Far from being personalistic factions lacking social roots, most are viable organisations which, despite government misgivings, have managed to root themselves in the basic fault lines of Egyptian society: classes, corporate groups, institutions. The party system reflects an authentic, if partial, ideological and social differentiation of the political arena.

On the right is the New Wafd, an advocate of economic and political liberalisation and a vehicle of the old *Bashawat* (the traditional notables) and the private bourgeoisie. The Ahrar Party, also on the liberal right, differs not in goals or composition but in its strategy of quiet advocacy rather than confrontation. Just to the left of the centre-right NDP, is the SLP, led by men similar in social background to the leaders of the centre and right parties, but with a distinctive radical nationalist political history: members of Misr al-Fatat, middle-class reformists who rose under Nasser and broke with Sadat over *infitah* and the separate peace with Israel. Islamic forces have not been permitted to form a party *per se*, but have been allowed to emerge as a real political movement with roots further down in the social system than the secular bourgeois parties. Led by *ulema*, merchants and students, its activists are drawn from the lower middle and middle class and command a popular following in the *baladi* quarters. Its affirmation of the Islamic way against Western penetration, its acceptance of small property holdings and advocacy of populist policies expresses the world view of this hard-pressed semi-traditionalist segment of society. Finally, on the left is the NPUP, a mix of middle class Nasserites and Marxists and working class trade unionists espousing a radical and nationalist-socialist ideology.

If one considers only the leadership and activists of the parties, there is the rough correspondence between conservative ideology and higher class composition and leftist or populist ideology and lower class composition which seems to indicate that Egyptian party politics may have moved beyond mere competition of patrons and clans without social roots. The limits of this movement are, however, also apparent. While the NPUP and the Islamic movement are spearheading the spread of ideological pluralisation downward, the great majority of the masses remains politically passive or, when active, is so in either a clientelist or 'anomic' fashion. This is clear from the fact that elections, despite the pluralisation of the party system, continue chiefly to be clientelist contests between competing notables with personal resources such as good access to the government needed to deliver local benefits or extensive personal and kinship connections associated with powerful families. Issue politics, given the limited economic security and literacy of the mass public, and the widespread suspicion that major policymaking power remains concentrated in a presidency immune to electoral outcomes, still counts only among a limited attentive public. This system greatly favours the government party since the bulk of notability is aligned with it. When added to the various persisting forms of government intervention in the elections, this has been enough to guarantee the regime an overwhelming majority in every post-liberalisation election. In short, the pluralisation of the political arena has advanced far enough to force a transformation from a single to a dominant-party system, but not far enough to force a thorough liberalisation which would make the executive accountable through the party system or allow the public a real choice between alternative programmes and leaders.

Legitimate opposition parties nevertheless make an important difference: they are evolving into 'parties of pressure' within the dominant-party system. Such parties cannot expect to take power. Their role is to articulate the interests and values of sectors of the population ignored by the dominant party. At worst, they help to frame the terms of public debate by raising issues and alternatives which would otherwise remain off the public agenda. But they may even sway the ruling party, because if they threaten to capture sufficient public support to jeopardise its position, it may alter its policies to take the wind out of the opposition's sails. Pressure parties essentially act as interest groups bringing pressure to bear for particular interests or promoting the fortunes of aspirant politicians hoping for co-option.

Under Sadat, a ruler intent on pursuing a mission at odds with most opposition sentiment, the ideological cleavage between government and opposition was too wide to allow the institutionalisation of this system. Loyal opposition constantly turned into anti-system activity, which Sadat periodically repressed. Yet it was partially operative. The Ahrar's low-key articulation of bourgeois interests helped widen economic liberalisation. Islamic militants forced some Islamising concessions from the regime and the NPUP and SLP probably helped to slow down or even reverse the regime's anti-statist and anti-populist policies.

Under Mubarak, these tendencies have developed further since, having no personal mission comparable to Sadat's, he arouses less opposition, and hence can be more tolerant of it. His reversal of some of the foreign policy excesses and corruption of the Sadat

56

regime, his adoption of Nasserite symbolism and the restoration of limited liberalisation were all efforts to placate the opposition and undercut its mass appeal. At present a tacit understanding exists between government and opposition: the latter knows that if it goes too far in challenging the regime, it invites repression, while the former knows that if it is too unresponsive it may invite mobilisation against the system.

The primary consequence of Egypt's dominant-party system, in the short run, is to legitimise the ruling establishment. The ruling party incorporates a significant constituency — major segments of the high bureaucracy and the military, professionals, businessmen and the rural notability, in short the most strategic social forces in Egypt. Through syndical and client ties, it also links a portion of the public to the regime. The legitimisation of opposition parties has channelled much political activity which might otherwise take a covert, even violent anti-regime direction into tamer, more manageable forms. In spite of their slim prospects of winning power and their limited ability in shaping policy, opposition elites have been remarkably willing to play the game and hence to incorporate their own mass bases into the regime.

Even if the regime is the winner, this system has resulted in a limited institutionalisation of participation which is meaningful for the participants and to a lesser extent provides the mass public with a modicum of leverage over elites. For many, membership in the ruling party is worthwhile: it is a channel of recruitment to the sub-elite and increasingly to higher elite roles. Its parliamentary caucus may not draft high policy but it is allowed to fill in many of the details which have serious consequences for strategic interests in Egypt. For activists in the opposition parties, the rewards are chiefly ideological: the chance to espouse ideas, reshape public opinion, occasionally even influence policymakers. As these parties continue to expand and pluralise the political arena they could, in the long run, become instrumental in imposing greater power-sharing on the ruling elite (Hinnebusch, 1985).

ARAB PARTY SYSTEMS: DIFFERENCES AND SIMILARITIES

Arab party systems, far from being uniform, vary, as the cases show, according to the purpose for which leaders build them and the nature of the environment in which they must operate. This variation is evidence, in itself, that parties are real, organic parts of their political systems, not mere paper structures. In Libya, the party is almost a personal emanation of a charismatic leader, an instrument through which he seeks to organise his mass following for revolution from above. Charisma and the malleability of the political arena have allowed him to impose his new order with relative ease; but in allowing him to avoid creation of an ideologically disciplined party, they have left Libya's revolution with a flimsy organisational weapon, lacking the muscle to transform traditional political culture and of dubious durability. Syrian Baath leaders also wanted to impose a revolution from above, but facing a more mobilised divided and intractable political arena, they had a strong incentive to build a Leninist-type party. The resultant ruling party is stronger than its counterparts in Libya or Egypt and it has imposed major changes on Syria and mobilised a constituency behind the regime, but it has proved too weak to obliterate the opposition which remains intense, stalemating creation of a legitimate new order. Ideological imperatives have gradually been subordinated, in varying degrees, to the interests of the president, the army and the dominant class and sectarian forces.

In Egypt, the post-populist elite seeks not change but stabilisation and can thus tolerate limited opposition. The dominant-party system is an appropriate adaptation which channels and absorbs the participatory pressures of Egypt's political arena. Given its increasing size and pluralisation, the only alternative, in the absence of Nasser's overwhelming legitimacy, was massive, inevitably costly, coercion. The greater level of political consensus, as compared to Syria, and the sturdy bureaucratic base of the state, made adaptation far less risky.[1]

Despite their differences, Arab party system share basic features imposed by similarities in origins, environments and leadership purpose which distinguish them from their counterparts in the Western and Communist worlds. In their origins, few Arab political parties have come to power through either mass votes or revolution; indeed many are creations or vehicles of military officers who seized power by coup, and were constructed or at least reshaped from above. Hence they are more instruments of state elites than vehicles through which social forces seize and make the state their instrument. As a consequence, they usually lack the ideological and organisational muscle and mass base which can only be forged in a protracted struggle for power from below. They also operate in a special environment which shapes the purposes to which leaders put them: unlike Western states, where muted social conflict and consensus on the rules of the political game ensure that elite circulation and the aggregation of demands through competitive parties can be allowed without threatening the established order, Arab states suffer from sharp social conflicts, and lack secure national identity and political consensus. Hence leaders build single, or dominant-party systems through which they aim to mobilise a mass consensus from above from the creation of a new socio-political order or to contain pressures from below threatening a precariously established one.

These forces shape the distinct structural, behavioural and functional features of Arab party systems. Arab parties have many of the features of authentic parties but their predominant character as instruments of state elites forged or manipulated from above, rather than mass parties mobilised from below, makes them very vulnerable to bureaucratisation and traditionalisation. Structurally, they differ from bureaucracies in that they have formal procedures for interest articulation and aggregation, and assemblies for the debate if not the deciding of major public issues, so they are not exclusively hierarchies for the passing down of orders. They differ from clientelist networks in the existence of modern organisations, rules and roles, to an extent independent of the persons who fill them. Behaviourally, they differ in that some of their members are activists, whether in the pursuit of private interests or the advocacy of public issues, rather than mere paid employees or deferential dependents of a patron. But the frequent subordination of the party to the executive, the consequent constraints on political expression and activity inside it, the careerism of many adherents, the overlap of party *apparatchiki* and state officials, tend to deaden intra-party political life, threatening to turn the party into a mere compliant political bureaucracy. In so far as this narrows access and excludes interests from expression, it, in turn, encourages the resort to personalistic connections of a clientelist nature which may either transform the party from within or bypass and render it irrelevant. Moreover, the modest penetrative and organisational capacity of some parties, and their consequent co-option of local notables, makes some of them little different from a client network at the base. The institutionalisation of distinctive party roles and rules for channelling participation is thus retarded by bureaucratic manipulation from above and traditional subversion from below.

Functionally, Arab party systems are of more limited significance than in Western or Communist polities. Elites are frequently self-recruited through the military or co-opted from the bureaucracy, and a largely immune from accountability to parties. But parties do seem to play some role in recruitment and turnover of elites and incumbent elites often need some party support to stay in power. The wishes of leaders often count for more in policymaking than the aggregation of social interests from below and even when aggregation takes place, the military or bureaucracy may be more crucial. Yet Arab parties play a limited role in channelling social demands and an even greater one in filtering and controlling them. No Arab party has achieved the capacity of totalitarian parties to mobilise the masses for social transformation; but they do play roles in incorporating a constituency into the regime and excluding opposition forces from access to the masses. In short, Arab parties have achieved only a very limited institutionalisation of participation — in principle, the major function of a party system. Parts of the public are typically excluded from participation, certain issues from the political agenda and the rules of participation are often manipulated by elites who remain immune from accountability. Nevertheless, a certain measure of real activism is channelled through Arab party systems and it can make a difference for political outcomes: it can influence and even constrain decision makers; for the ambitious, it can be a route to power and for the ideologues, a way of helping to shape public opinion. From the point of view of the state, this partial institutionalisation is not enough to solve the crisis of participation or eliminate praetorianism, but it is often sufficient to manage and control them. Certainly this is a major factor in the apparent stabilisation of the state in the Arab world.

NOTES

1. These three party systems seem to be representative of party systems in the Arab world. The Libyan case is similar to the Nasserite type of mass organisation created by personalised and reformist military regimes not only in Egypt, but in Shishakli's Syria, Numeiry's Sudan, Iraq under Aref, etc. The Syrian Baath is typical of the stronger type of party which shares power with the military, as in Baathist Iraq and Algeria. The Egyptian case is representative of more conservative states where a dominant or controlled multi-party system is tolerated, as in Tunisia or Morocco.

3

Opposition as Support of the State

I. William Zartman

In seeking to explain the reasons for the survival of the Arab state, one must come to terms with the problem of opposition. Since some opposition can be assumed to be a natural condition for any political system, the absence of opposition in Arab politics would provide both an explanation of state survival and a condition to be investigated. Overwhelming or persistent opposition, at the other extreme, would indicate a weak state. All political life goes on between these to extremes. Totalitarian regimes seek to eliminate all opposition, but are never successful for long. Overwhelming opposition is its own undoing, since if successful it becomes the government and weaker opinions are relegated to the new oppositional minority. Pure harmony and pure anarchy do not exist in anything but the short run, and are consequences rather than conditions (i.e. dependent rather than independent variables). This chapter faces the paradoxical challenge of using opposition as the independent variable to explain the durability of the Arab state in the 1970s and 1980s.

The picture drawn thus far carries implicit assumptions which may be less intuitively acceptable than those initial notions. It would appear that any government would seek to move from the extreme of oppositional majority to approach as closely as possible the opposite pole of total support. The conceptual ways of doing so are clear: it can physically eliminate the opposition, it can remove its causes and grievances, or it can co-opt its members. Yet not only is the goal impossible to reach in its totality, as has been seen; it is also impossible to attain even partially. Downs (1957) and Arrow (1951) have shown the impossibility of satisfying a constant majority in theoretical terms on a 'flat' surface — when there are merely many differences of interest and opinion. It is even more striking in

61

a developmental context where the nature of socio-political change introduces another dimension that makes the construction of consensus out of the traditional and modernised sectors impracticable. There will always be significant opposition anywhere, and even more in developing countries than elsewhere. Even if the government tries physical elimination, opposition, like the soldiers of Hercules, will continue to appear in new forms and places.

The other implicit assumption is the Western notion of democratic alternance between incumbents and opposition (Dahl, 1966, 1973; McLennan, 1973; Ionescu and de Madariaga, 1968). A democratic political system is held together by the restrained efforts of the ins to stay in and the outs to get in, with everyone following the rules because each has an interest in being guaranteed a chance to get back in from an out position. But democratic alternance is not a characteristic of Arab politics. Instead in the period under focus — the decade and a half of the 1970s and 1980s — the predominant characteristic of government is the presence of one socio-political group and no chance of alternance. Opposition is neither undercut, co-opted nor eliminated. It is used, and it tends to acquiesce to this use, for some reason other than the expectation of finding itself in power on the next occasion, electoral or otherwise.

One conclusion might be that opposition in such cases is merely the dupe or puppet of power, but this argument is not convincing. Such an interpretation gives more credit to the incumbents and less to the opposition than is warranted; there are too many valid politicians in the opposition to be dupes, and too little monopoly of wisdom for government to practise consistently successful puppetry.

Instead, the argument proposed here is that an understanding of opposition is to be found in the notion of role complementarity. Both government and opposition have interests to pursue within the political system, and this complementarity of pursuit reinforces the state. Neither uses the other, but each serves the other's interests in performing its own role. Thus, stability in the contemporary Arab state can be explained not only by the government's handling of opposition but also by the opposition's handling of itself and of government. This theme will be explored in this chapter, using a number of different states — Morocco, Egypt, Tunisia — as case studies.[1]

Whether authorised or unauthorised, opposition need not be restricted to political parties. Additional forms need to be considered: corporatism and functionalism. In addition to political parties and often more effectively, corporate and functional groups express opposition in the Arab world. When opposition parties are not authorised or when the political system is opened up to pluralistic forms, corporate groups are often the surrogate for or transition to formal opposition parties. Thus another assumption about opposition, drawn from another world's experience — the assumption of an identifiable partisan form — needs to be dropped to be realistic in the Arab world. Instead, opposition exists through a spectrum of formality, from some internal and informal fractions through organised surrogates to formal parties and informal movements inside and outside the authorised political system. Some of these forms are outside the present inquiry, since factions within a ruling group do not pose the same paradox nor do they have the same role. Furthermore, opposition does not take on the same significance and activity in an unorganised or informal form. The following discussion will take into account the oppositional status and activities of corporate groups as well as parties, but it will require some degree of organisational formality for the angle of role complementarity to be pursued.

The focus on formal organisation should not obscure the equally important matter of social base. Organisations are important only to the extent that they represent something. However, social basis is only a measure of reality in this analysis, not a term of the analysis itself. There is no indication — at least initially — that role complementarity demands any particular social sources of opposition or that social sources come into play at all in any way other than simply as a grounding for the power and existence of incumbent and oppositional organisations. Some incumbents and oppositions will be socially specific, representing identifiable social groups or activities or even classes, whereas others will be general and broadly representative. Indeed, some will compete for the same social clientele on the basis of things such as ideological, regional or personal appeals. Unlike some other structural analyses, this discussion focuses on the political, and assumes that in the Arab world of the 1970s and 1980s social structure is not the prime explanatory variable.

Like any structural explanation, this study assumes that stability — the condition to be explained — is found in some sort of balance, here seen as complementarity. It is important to emphasise that stability is not assumed: instability is as much to be accounted for as stability. The cases that follow will test, and hopefully show, the usefulness of this approach.

MANIPULATED PLURALISM: MOROCCO

Morocco is a centralised political system, with much power held by the king. The central figure is imbued with both traditional and modern legitimacy (to use Weber's concepts) and also with a charisma that is closer to its original religious meaning that to a merely personal transitional attribute. The king manipulates his support through a mystical bond which he cultivates with his people and through his control over the political elite. However, both of these activities are complicated by the fact that the nationalist movement also shared political legitimacy at the time of independence in 1956 and left its legacy to its successors, the political parties and national organisations, notably labour and student unions. Although parties and organisations have left their nationalist sources of legitimacy behind them as a quarter century has passed since independence, they have been given new life over the past decade by the fact that the king has found them to be useful to the functioning of the system. Thus parties and organisations have established a role in providing members of the political elite and in helping to mediate ties between the king and his people. This role is not to the king's liking, no doubt, but it is tolerated because the events of the preceding decade (1963–72) showed that without such organisations of support, the system was vulnerable to direct challenges from within and without.

However the king has also established limits to the power of mediating organisations of support (and demand). They are expressed in his graphic phrase, 'I will never be put into equation'; that is, king and party should not be equal centres of power but rather, parties must be subordinate to king and pluralistically competing and self-limiting. At the same time, other elements of support must be directly under royal control. A segment of the political elite must be directly dependent on the king, without independent sources of power such as party organisation, and a segment of the population — primarily rural society — must be directly supportive of the monarch, their representatives being spokesmen of support rather than spokesmen for demands (Marais and Waterbury, in Debbasch, *et al.*, 1970).

After 1973, the king began to recreate the polity, using the same elements of support which had been weakened and disorganised during the previous period — parties, army and networks of his own authority. Parties were brought back into activity in a painstakingly negotiated structure of roles which Abderrahim Bouabid has labelled 'limited democracy' (Rousset in Leca *et al.*, 1979). But, having learned from the previous period the lessons about the destabilising challenges that political parties with autonomous sources of power can bring, Hassan worked to tame the mass parties of the nationalist movement and confront them with patron parties under his sponsorship. Pluralism is in the Moroccan pre-constitutional political norms and is written into the Moroccan constitution to counterbalance the centralising effects of the monarchy. The king has always worked in various ways to replace the unity of the nationalist movement with an array of political organisations from amongst which he could pick his instruments of government.

Therefore, except at times of a government of national unity (i.e. national coalition, not single party), some parties would always be left in opposition. Some of them consider opposition status to be simply a time of reserve duty 'at the disposition of the king' but other see themselves in permanent opposition (until the millenial day when the nature of the system changes). Indeed, some can be recovered from the opposition personally with an appropriate government job, like Justice and then Prime Minister Maati Bouabid, formerly of the UNFP, but at the cost of being disowned by the opposition party. Still others constitute the disloyal opposition, rejecting the entire polity and suffering its rejection as well. Morocco therefore has a broad polity, widely (even if not universally) considered to be legitimate, and a wide spectrum of oppositions, most of them out of power for a very long time. It is thus an appropriate place to begin inquiry about the opposition's role in stability.

The most important of the parties is the Istiqlal, the venerable descendent of the nationalist movement, for a long time Morocco's largest as well as oldest party, with a coherent articulated structure and philosophy. Although the Istiqulal was on the oppositing side in 1959–60 and then again after 1963, it began a new era a decade later when its president and spiritual leader Allal al-Fasi died. The Ninth Party Congress of 1974 set out a programme based on national integrity, public liberty and economic reform that was in many details close to the existing Five Year Plan (1973–7), soon to be cancelled because of the Saharan campaign. When the regime's policy of liberalisation brought an invitation to the Istiqlal to return to power, the response in 1976 was more of a justification of cooperation than a declaration of demands that the party would bring to the new coalition (Rousset in Leca, 1979, p. 204f). The party's position is generally known to cover concerns of territorial recovery, economic nationalism, guarantees for organised participation in politics and parliamentary responsibility in government, Arabisation in culture and education, and welfare economics. With the death of al-Fasi, and the king's decision to share some power and responsibility in government, the two major obstacles to Istiqlal participation in government were removed. Neither of them concerned specific substantive demands. In a system in which legitimacy is attached to cooperation between monarchy and nationalist movement, association in government increases the attractiveness of the party to its constituents (and vice versa, as demonstrated popularity increases the party's claim on association in government).

Yet mobilisation and participation are part of the Istiqlal's day-to-day activities with its constituent activities with its constituents. This activity resembles party life reported in an earlier period (Ashford, 1961) and previous electoral campaigns (Leveau, 1976; or Santucci and Benhlal, in Leca, *et al.*, 1979), although there are few studies of the current period (Sehimi, 1979, 1985 on elections; and El-Mossadeq, 1981 on party life). Demands and discontents are raised in party cell meetings and electoral campaigns, and to some extent are passed on upwards. While it is likely that such transmission is not very important for the general nature, shape and functioning of the political system, it is also likely that the fate of individual demands is important to individuals and constitutes the grains of sand that comprise the edifice. At the same time, demands do not constitute the entire edifice. Much, and perhaps nearly all of the business at party cell meetings, as well as at higher levels, involves purely supportive participation, including reiteration of points that are already part of party and government programmes, attacks on the opposition, patriotic and nationalistic declarations, or simply association with party rituals. After all, a person is a supporter of the Istiqlal in part because he feels that it best handles his particular concerns (demands) but also because of regional and family connections with the party and because it is good to be associated with a party that enjoys the Istiqlal's relation to government (support).

Istiqlal alternance between government (1960–3, 1976–83) and opposition has trade-offs and implications for party interests in terms of both support and demands. Internally, there is a trade-off between the two; demands are expressed only within the basic decision to support the regime, but support is accorded only as long as it is compatible with the basic positions (demands) of the party. This sequence is unexceptional, no doubt, until it is added that it does not result in a continually recycling decision but rather in long-term commitments. Once it is decided that association in government is compatible with basic positions, the decision to support becomes a limitation on the expression of day-to-day demands. But when the decision is to oppose, the party is freed to reaffirm its demands in their full integrity. Participation in power compromises, as Al-Fasi knew it would, and opposition permits integrity. Participation also restrains the other participants, and that is the second trade-off. In providing support for the monarchy, the Istiqlal ties the king to its basic demands, and in voicing opposition it constrains him by showing up his deviation. Paradoxically, either position effects the Istiqlal policy of making the national integrity Saharan issue the bottom-line criterion for membership in the polity, thereby limiting the king's room for manoeuvre in international negotiations.

The Istiqlal is a waning party in Morocco, one that has suffered as much from participation as from opposition. Both positions have worked to discredit the party. Participation has shown its programmatic ineffectiveness, and opposition has shown royal disfavour. Programmatic ineffectiveness was the cause of the Istiqlal split in 1958–9, when royal restraints on socio-economic programmes made the party's left wing restive and finally led it to break away to form the National Union of Popular Forces (UNFP). Royal disfavour probably accounted for the Istiqlal's loss of voters in 1976–7 (after 13 years in the wilderness), and in 1984 (after a shorter time — a year out of power), despite the intervening six years in the government coalition. In the Istiqlal case, opposition has served party interest in integrity at the price of party fortunes. At the same time, it served government (royal) interests as well.

Undecided on the borders of the polity are the National and Socialist Unions of Popular Forces (UNFP and then USFP), the opposition parties, and also the labour unions and students, whether in their organised form of the National Union of Moroccan Students (UNEM) or not. In general, the undecided have the greatest interest in unhindered demand articulation and mobilisation, although they have also special roles in defining the limits of the political system and special meanings attached to their mobilisation mechanisms. These points will be developed in the following discussion.

The newly formed UNFP was the primary partner in the government of 1958–60, after which it entered into permanent opposition. In July 1972, however, it split into two factions over the question of whether any collaboration with the regime was possible. Although the hardest line was taken by the Rabat section, under

Abderrahim Bouabid, it gradually came around under the pressure of police measures and then offers of collaboration by the king and in 1975 became the USFP with participation in the political system, leaving the Casablanca section under Abdullah Ibrahim with the original party name and no role to play. The USFP joined the 1974 government with a Ministry of State and participated in the diplomatic campaign for the recovery of the Sahara and in the pre-election negotiations, but it could not reach an agreement to participate in government after the elections and has remained more or less the loyal opposition. During 1980 it rejected basic decisions of the regime, notably the constitutional amendments on the regency and the duration of parliament, and withdrew from participation in the by-elections of 1981 and from parliament itself after the expiration of its original mandate in the middle of the same year. In 1981, its leaders were jailed for a year for criticising the king for weakness in the Saharan policy, but in 1984 the same leaders were offered participation in the government, which they rejected. They then joined a government of national unity to guarantee the 1984 elections and emerged the largest of the non-government parties in the ensuing vote. But they continue to opt for opposition, having already undergone a second split in 1983 over the issue of whether to join the national unity government. Its opposition has, therefore, been accentuated to the point of straining the notion of 'loyalism', reinforcing its role as a boundary marker for the system.

Like the Istiqlal, the USFP is a real party, with ongoing constituency relations and functioning cells in contact with the party hierarchy and with their elected representatives. Its programme is socialist, and its local cells have their own ideas about their demands as well as about the degree of support the party should give to the regime and about the meaning of socialism (Benhlal, in Leca *et al.*, 1979). The USFP is wracked by continual debate on its relation to the system; 'support' is much less certain and more fragile than 'demand', and the party is made up of many factions and sections which take different positions on the question of the relation between the two. Thus, in a sort of Moroccan Watergate, with Moroccanly different consequences, the USFP was defeated in a major electoral battle in the Souss in 1977 by unnecessarily foul means piled on top of fair. The USFP congress of the following year had to keep a rebellious rank and file in line behind its policy of loyal opposition by means of a firm organisational hand. When the monarchy then extended the life of the national assembly whose initial election the USFP had challenged, the party could only hold itself together by

68

taking a further step out of loyalism into opposition and withdrawing from the assembly.

Nor did it hold together in 1983 when a minority withdrew in protest against association with government. Although its participation in guaranteeing the elections won the USFP a sizeable increase in votes, pressure from the members led to the party to decide 'to remain in opposition for two or three years rather than join in an incoherent government coalition'. Yet, to the extent that it supports the system, the USFP puts the monarchy into a dilemma, either of whose outcomes gives the party some satisfaction. If the king wins on the Saharan issue, the party benefits along with the rest of the country. But if the king is tied to an unshakeable goal with insufficient means to attain it and ends up weakened and vulnerable, the USFP — unlike the parties of the government — is not unhappy. The king has long played the USFP beyond all patience and credibility, never offering full association in government, always harrassing the party with police controls, and continually dangling the lure of participation in power before the leaders' eyes until the party cracks as a result (Barrada, 1980). Events that weaken the monarch and make the USFP more useful to it — such as the events of the constitutional breakdown (1963–72) and some conceivable outcomes of the Saharan affair — could work to the party's benefit. Yet as the decade of emergency showed, the cost of such an evolution in the political system is tremendous for the party in personal terms, for the monarchy does not allow itself to be weakened without weakening the other participants in the ring at the same time. The USFP has lived under repression and has been able to mobilise its membership under adverse conditions.

If the USFP's support role therefore results in a trade-off different to those available to sometime government parties, its demand role also involves a paradoxical exchange. The USFP is remarkably successful in achieving its demands, which it does only at the price of authorship, by 'ghostwriting' royal programmes. For example, while repressing the party for the plot of March 1973 and restricting civil liberties, the king undertook a programme of Moroccanisation of foreign-owned land and of the service sector, introduced a limited programme of labour participation in capital ownership of certain industries, and other measures, all part of the (then) UNFP platform. Again, in 1980, the king announced a reduction in poor people's rents by a third, while the USFP was calling for the simple freezing of rents. When the party and related unions heavily criticised ministerial decision on higher education, the king

69

(after a number of intervening steps) cancelled them. None of these measures, or others like them, have produced the procedural move which the party would prefer: a frank invitation to share power, to carry out programmes and to meet demands in the name and to the credit of the party. Instead, the king takes the credit for the measures. But the origins of the demands must certainly not be lost on UNFP members. Morocco is a political system in which initiatives come from the opposition but are enacted by the government in order to undercut the opposition's appeal.

Opposition on the outer fringes is organised under the name of the Front. The Front was the alliance between the Movement of 23 March growing out of the protest riots of 1965 in Casablanca and the 'Onward' (ila al amam) Movement which broke away from the Party of Progress and Socialism (PPS) — the authorised incarnation of the Communist Party (PCM) — in protest against its compromise with the government. The Frontists grew out of the republican element of the nationalist movement, as represented by Mahdi Ben Barka, who was assassinated in Paris by Moroccan Interior Ministry figures in 1965. They were typically members of the student movement, the National Union of Moroccan Students (UNEM), in contact with Communist organisations. Frontists were arrested in the early 1970s, sometimes tortured or liquidated, and then for the most part amnestied in 1980. By 1982 some were back in prison again. In subsequent trials, ties were alleged between Frontists and the protest riots of July 1981 and January 1984. Frontists were therefore the organised tip of an iceberg of unknown and varying size (Degenhardt, 1983). The key position of the Frontists, which put them beyond the political pale, was their rejection of the struggle for national integrity in the Sahara. Without that issue, they might have merely been subject to harrassment, albeit serious at times. However, they also opposed the regime on many other issues, so broad in nature that the Frontists basically rejected the form of the political system instead of simply imposing specific demands on it. They never sought collaboration within the system, on whatever terms.

Yet even Frontists were useful to the system, for they provided volunteers through whom the regime could show the limits of participation and the fate of total opponents, and once it had made its point it could also use them, through amnesty, to show both control and magnanimity. Thus even outside the system, the Frontists had a role to play, and they played it well.

Another element of opposition are the labour unions,[2] though each in a slightly different position with regard to the political system, since each is related (in a different way) to a political party — the General Union of Moroccan Workers (UGTM) to the Istiqlal, the Moroccan Labour Union (UMT) to the now-defunct UNFP, and the Democratic Labour Confederation (CDT) to the USFP (Eqbal, 1966; Forst, 1976). The Istiqlal dominates its union, the UMT dominated its party, and the CDT and USFP look on each other as equals with 'relations of . . . constant, privileged, . . . independent, militant . . . solidarity' (*Liberation*, 14 December 1978). Unions are active in Morocco and enjoy a good measure of freedom. They are an effective means for mobilisation of participants and the articulation of demands, and the government responds to their protests and pressures — never adequately by labour's standards, of course — as part of a bargaining process. Much of the recurring labour agitation concerns labour's demands for a sliding pay scale indexed to the inflation rate. In general, the government responds with a one-time pay rise and measures (including an Economic and Social Council in 1980) to maintain constructive contacts between government and labour. Labour demands are of two types — primary demands over wages and conditions of employment, and secondary demands for the revoking of punitive measures taken by the government against over-intense pressures for primary demands, such as arrest of strikers. These two levels allow for flexibility and face-saving in mobilisation and response.

In general, however, Moroccan labour unions operate within the polity, for they are aware of their vulnerability to the unemployed taking over their jobs. Both government and opposition are also aware that the real challenge comes from an event such as the 1965 Casablanca riots, when organised political forces were outflanked by anomic movements. Even the 1981 riots, which were union (CDT) instigated but got out of hand, point up the threat of anomic protest. The anomic threat is another of those paradoxical trade-offs which characterise Morocco. It brings government and unions together against a common danger but it is also brandished by each against the other in bargaining over labour demands. After the 1981 and 1984 riots, the king required all candidates to the September 1984 elections to be members of a party. Henceforth, opposition was to be organised and organisations were to be responsible, thereby enlisting them in the government job of control. With a common interest in avoiding anomie, government and unions bargain over demands, in support of the polity.

Yet the line between supporters and opponents of the polity is not sharp, as USFP behaviour indicates. Moreover, a link between organised and anomic demands exists among students, where the meanings of mobilisation, participation and demand are most complex of all. There are a number of ties between students, student unions, teachers unions and the main labour unions. Students are regarded by labour as natural allies, a vanguard which cannot be allowed to get too far ahead of the mass. The National Teachers Union (SNE) is a branch of the CDT and is one of the most radical of the unions, the instigator of the 1981 protest. UNEM is an established political organisation; banned in 1973, it was readmitted to legality in 1978 and is the most radical of the legal organisations in Morocco, wavering on the outside fringes of the polity. Mobilisation for demands not only exists within groups and organisations, but spreads from one to another because of overlapping membership in the education sector. Furthermore, the mobilisation cycle is an annual event. It begins soon after the opening of the calendar year (in the middle of the school year), and continues throughout the semester, mixing various types of demands and mobilisation groups — teachers, students, parents — both in secondary and in higher education. Vacations in the spring and summer provide cooling-off periods where life can return to normal without the protesters losing face. Demands here are on three levels: primary and secondary levels covering education and low-and-order grievances, and then residual demands against the political system in general, concerning its nature and existence (a point Hodges, 1981 confuses).

Strikes — the normal expression of demands — in this sector are thus different from strikes in the regular labour sector, and are met by a different response. On one hand, strikes are a frivolous 'panty-raid' type activity clothed in the form of serious political statements. On the other hand, strikes in the educational sector are a continual boundary-drawing device in which both sides of the line of legitimacy test their strength. It must not be overlooked that this aspect is not just a one-off test — the year's redrawing of the boundary that will hold until the sides have regrouped to meet again in a new tenporal context; it is also a crucial socialisation process for new elites and counterelites — new participants in the confrontation of *siba* and *makhzen*. Students are versed in distrust of authority and political cynicism, but they are also trained in observing encounters with the political system (whether they find its nature to their liking or not). Student leaders grow more and more radical in their job, as increasingly stiff government opposition to their demands drives

72

them to increasing opposition to the political system (opposition to primary and then secondary demands confirms their residual demands). In the end, radical leaders are purged from the political system, moderate students are co-opted into the system, and the lessons of the fruitlessness of fighting the system are conveyed to succeeding age levels or generations of students until a new generation which has not observed the cycle appears. In this cycle, the fortunes of the parents, their attitudes towards the system, and their rapport with their children also has a role to play. Morocco in the early 1980s appeared to be entering into a new cycle: the reappearance of the UNEM began a series of spring semester protests in 1979, 1980 and 1981, each slightly more intense and each mixing political and educational demands.

In the process, demands and discontents are not always well handled. As long as they can be subordinated to ongoing discussion about support, demand activity can be routinised or can be mobilised behind the continual manoeuvring over new role definitions. The Moroccan polity has a remarkable ability to keep its participants' hopes high, their demands dulled and their support cynical or at least self-interested. Each group, by playing its role, supports the polity in its way.

CONTROLLED PLURALISM: EGYPT

Egypt, too, is a centralised polity, governed by a royal household or palace elite as much as Morocco is governed by its *makhzen*. Within this republican palace, power is highly centralised in the hands of the president, who combines a high degree of institutional legitimacy and political skill — both in using his institutional power and in making the right policy decisions that keep the loyalty of his lieutenants and followers. There is pluralism at the level of the lieutenants, who have their own sources of power and bring their followers along with them, but who are totally at the mercy of the president for their positions. Conceivably a group of lieutenants could coalesce and react to their removal with enough weight to overthrow the president, but that has not happened since the uncertain days of 1954. There is considerable institutional pluralism under the centralised palace, including not only a highly articulated and entrenched bureaucracy but also a functioning parliament, many corporate groups (labour and professional syndicates), one or more armies, and, in the current period, political parties.

After an interregnum of factional pluralism in 1970 to 1971, the current period began with the 'corrective revolution' of 1971 which eliminated the internal opposition faction. Since the party (the Arab Socialist Union — ASU) was the organisational basis of that faction, it was natural that it be reorganised, opened up and then broken up under the controlled pluralism of President Anwar Sadat. Elections took place in 1972 with an enlarged party, in 1976 with three official 'tribunes' (*manabar*), in 1979 with competing parties, and in 1984 with competing parties under the new leadership of Hosni Mubarak. Throughout this evolution, one party remained dominant, the structural heir of the ASU, known as the Socialist Democractic Party of Egypt (1976–8) and then the National Democratic Party (NDP) thereafter. Scattered about this large central core was the opposition (Waterbury, 1983; Hinnebusch, 1985). During the time of the tribunes, the competitors of the Egypt Party were the Socialist Liberals on the right, the Progressive National Unity Party (PNUP) and the Nasserites on the left, and the unorganised independents, taking over the tribune of Nasserism. On the right, the old nationalist movement, the Wafd Party, appeared in new form in 1977 and then disappeared under official harrassment the following year, before it ever stood for elections. Subsequently the PNUP was nearly displaced by the Socialist Labour Party (SLP) on the left. The empty space on the right, at first co-opted by the NDP itself, was occupied under Mubarak by the New Wafd.

The decision to authorise an opposition came with Sadat's October paper in 1974 as an important part of the new regime's self-image of liberalisation. This thrust was crucial to the appearance that the regime was seeking to cultivate as a government of *laissez-faire* pluralism, but those appearances in turn were imperative to its public appeal in response to a popular thirst for relaxation of the Nasserist mobilisation and for time to absorb Nasser's social changes. Appearances were also important externally, where the government was seeking political forms that would help its appeals to Western sources of support and cared little about making itself attractive to the Communist countries. Finally, the government acted the way it did because it believed in its course, both negatively and positively. Sadat reacted against the perceived failure of the unitarist system of which he was earlier a part (political actions are frequently taken in rejection of a previous model rather than in sound analysis of a proposed one (Quandt, 1969; Zartman, 1980)). But there was a positive element as well: Sadat expected that opposition would be both constructive and manageable, a contribution but

OPPOSITION AS SUPPORT OF THE STATE

not a threat to successful and popular government. Moreover, pluralism at the government level was necessary to his view of father-like unity as the head of state. Paternally, the president would orchestrate his pluralism, and adjudicate his opposition. There were also more manipulative reasons for wanting an authorised opposition, the most important of which had to do with the delimitation of the polity. Although there is no *a priori* evidence, subsequent behaviour supports the common use of the opposition as a border marker for the authorised system. Opposition was subject to two sorts of control: 'unfair' competition with the massive official party (ASU — Egypt Party — NDP), and direct efforts to break or restrain the party over a specific oppositional action. Both can be viewed as efforts to use the opposition as an indicator of the limits of authorised action. Elections were less and less free and fair since the open elections of 1976; the opposition fluctuated and then declined (18 per cent in 1976, 21 per cent in 1979, 13 per cent in 1985). Rally breaking, ballot stuffing, newspaper seizures and harrassment, and eventually the legal requirement of 8 per cent of the total (not district vote) to qualify for elections (when the SLP received 7.1 per cent) all worked to define the polity as a consensus system and the opposition's role as an official devil's advocate (Dessouki, 1984).

Direct efforts to break the opposition parties also stake out the limits of the polity. The self-dissolution of the New Wafd in June 1978, official pressure for the SLP to do the same in 1981, and the harrassment of the informal opposition from the appearance of the National Coalition in the spring of 1980 to the police round up of September 1981 were all reactions to sweeping criticisms of government and its policies. They were designed to indicate that specific opposition in policy debates may be acceptable but opposition across the board, and particularly against the hallmark policies of the government such as the Peace Process, *infitah*, and communitarian cohabitation, was out. Although Sadat paid for his policies, the definition of the authorised political system has remained under Mubarak. Moreover, use of the opposition to delimit the polity had a threat value that was useful in diplomacy. Opposition was used to show Israel and the US the limits of Egypt's room to manoeuvre (Waterbury, 1983, p. 272). It was probably less useful against domestic third parties in bargaining, but was of some utility in counterbalancing the right and the left. Sadat used and indeed encouraged Muslim religious spokesmen both against the Coptic revival and against Muslim fundamentalists outside the authority system. All of these efforts to play parts of the opposition off against each other — both within and between parts of the political spectrum — failed in the end, but helped maintain dynamic stability for a while.

Lastly, opposition was useful in defining the position of the government on that spectrum. What is involved is a symbolic game that may not fool everyone, but since the basic mode of definition is by distinction or contrast, symbolism does have operational consequences. Initially, the official tribune was placed squarely in the middle of the road, but the 1976 elections gave it practically no official opposition to the left and only a timid Liberal Party to the right. However, instead of being a left-centre party defining itself against right-wing opposition, the Egypt Party found itself facing real and outspoken opposition from the unorganised left of the independents. The party reorganisation of 1978 and the elections of 1979 changed that, by providing an equally outspoken but organised (and therefore controllable) opposition from the SLP on the left, with the rightist opposition of the New Wafd stillborn. The government marked its new orientation by defending itself against the left, rather than by coming to terms with its vocal but formally impotent opposition. Ultimately this broad strategy, too, was unsuccessful, since Sadat was surrounded by informal opposition from all sides and was shot from the right.

The Mubarak regime shifted its position and its opposition. The 1984 elections eliminated the left and gave the government party an opposition from the right, forcing it either to defend itself against the right as a centre-left party or to come to terms with it as a centre-right party. The first has been the strategy of Mubarak, as it was of Sadat. Whether successful or not, it is an example of the ultimate use of the opposition to define the government (Ottoway, 1984).

In sum, opposition was useful to the government for many reasons, just as long as it was under control. But Sadat's government overestimated the leeway it had in exercising that control, and eventually succeeded only in channelling opposition into the terrorist group, a support group, and a climate of opinion (Waterbury, 1983, p. 387). To complete the analysis, a number of complementary questions need to be examined: under these conditions, what was the interest of the opposition in playing their particular roles? What kind of expectations did they hold? How complementary were the roles, and how did that complementarity break down? In dealing with these questions, distinctions can be made among four different opposition groups: tame opposition, vocal opposition, corporate opposition and unauthorised opposition, as well as a few groups that floated among

76

these forms. If the rest of the discussion proceeds in the manipulative terms of interest, roles and uses, it must be remembered that, basically, people entered different forms of opposition because of what they believed, and their actions fit the strength and direction of those beliefs. Opposition, whatever its form, was self-satisfying. Those who opposed only a little and were cowed in the process pretty much accepted the government position, whereas those who undertook unauthorised activity and ran its risks believed very strongly that the government was wrong. The first answer then to the question of motivations accepts action (or inaction) as the prima facie test of beliefs.

Tame opposition disagreed only a little with the government, criticised only a bit, and was easily co-opted. The Liberals, for example, were content with a chance to state their position and to contribute in the process to the diversity of power. Their expectations may have been greater individual visibility in opposition than in government, or a greater chance of being bought off than of being rewarded. The NPUP and some parts of the SLP were in the same position (Hinnebusch, 1984d). The role of Mahmud Abu Wafia, Sadat's brother-in-law, who organised both the debate on pluralism and the Egypt Party and then was one of the leaders of the SLP until it got too critical, is a symbol as well as an example of roles and their limits.

Others played their roles more wholeheartedly, both providing a home for opponents of the regime and expressing their own opposition across the board. The SLP and the New Wafd are the best examples of vocal opposition, although their expectations differ. SLP was an active 'pressure party' (Hinnebusch, 1985), seeking to affect government policy and limit some of the directions which it criticised. It understood and operated within government's procedural limitations, and in return sought to impose substantive limitations of government policy. There is no evidence that it was specifically effective on any policy measure, and that may have led it into broader criticism of the government in press and parliament after 1980. Nor is there any evidence that the party had any illusions about its ability to join in, let alone form, a government. It was not only a 'corrective opposition'; it was also a permanent opposition. It must have been satisfied with that role (had it been allowed to play it fully), since from the very outset it could not have expected anything else. Indeed, both the Wafd and the SLP were torn apart (in 1984 and 1980, respectively) over whether to accept appointed seats to parliament, lest they be compromised by that much dependence on the government.

The New Wafd just as clearly has wider aspirations. If it seems unlikely that they be fulfilled, one must remember that the 65-year history of the Wafd is not only one of unfulfilled expectations but, more deeply, of role imbalance, in which the three main actors of the system — crown, coloniser and party — pulled in different directions and eventually destroyed the polity by 1952 (Deeb, 1979; Colombe, 1951). The Wafd seeks to be the government party. Curiously, as long as it maintains that optimism, it implicitly redefines the political system as one of two potential governing parties and adds to its legitimacy. The fact that it makes its demands as an aspirant to power, not just a constructive and permanent opposition, is a support for the system. Other role complementarities are not evident as yet: the Wafd has neither served as a limitation nor a source of ideas, nor has it drawn off a dissident part of the government's social support group and left it with a more coherent social base (Hinnebusch, 1984c) — all roles it could potentially play as the future unfolds.

Is there some mechanism that can bring roles and role expectations into balance, so that the Wafd only does and aspires to do what serves the government's purposes at the same time as it serves its own, and the same for government? Conceivably so, and it would be accomplished by conditioning or on-the-job socialisation, as has happened to some degree with the USFP in Morocco and also to some degree with the old Wafd. Neither of these cases is an exact parallel, though, nor is the SLP, which became more vocal as it became learner. Present divergences of views on the proper role for the New Wafd suggest that unless one or the other or both sides adjust their roles and expectations to fit the other's (as seems unlikely), there is likely to be continued conflict that will point up the incapacities of the authorised system and drive people to play their politics on its unauthorised fringes.

Corporate opposition groups in Egypt are in a different position. Their primary interest is in representing their members' interests, not in opposing government, and their members' interests are relatively homogeneous. Egypt has a more active corporatist structure than many Arab countries. If its labour unions have been dominated by a long association with the ASU, its professional syndicates are vigorous defenders of their own interests and autonomy, and hence of a liberal pluralism that includes opposition. Besides the press, which operates in competition with one another rather than as a syndicalised corps, the most independent profession

78

is the lawyers. Another non-opposition professional group are engineers. Sadat in 1981 and Mubarak in 1983 tangled with the Lawyer's Syndicate, with a little help from parliament and then the constitutional court. In the end, the presidential measures of control of 1981 were declared illegal and the lawyers' leadership restored to office. Sadat's umbrage was originally roused by the syndicate's critical statements on Egyptian relations with Israel, statements which stopped after the leadership was changed. By the time the leadership was restored, it was the presidency which had changed, and a *modus vivendi* was reached by which the syndicate's oppositional activity would be reduced. Functional groups can function without being an opposition, if the government will let them do so. If they do take on an oppositional role, it is either because opposition has become widespread or because no one else can play the role effectively. In neither case is there any complementarity of roles for government.

The Egyptian case brings out the fact that roles are not necessarily complementary by definition, and that systems are not necessarily in equilibrium. Some people are not content with the limits government places on their activity and government does not feel served by the form their behaviour takes. The resulting conflict may occur within the polity (as in the case of the Wafd) but it may also serve to drive the opposition outside the polity and into unauthorised activity. Examples of this effect include borderline groups such as Dawa, the National Coalition, and eventually the victims of the September (1981) round up, but also out-and-out out groups such as *Takfir wa al-Hijra*. The latter justify their righteous opposition by entering into conflict with the government, since the source of the evils they perceive is blatant and close at hand. The government justifies their existence but the reverse is not true; they have been too far from the frontiers of authorised activity to be useful to government as a frontier marker or even as an example. As true believers, they find persecution of their comrades only an encouragement in their defence of high stakes and noble purposes, not a deterrent.

The most interesting cases are the undecided or borderline groups. Al-Dawa and its leader Omar Tilimsani were brought into the polity by Sadat, to strengthen his position on the religious right. That served the purpose of the Dawa group well enough but it also legitimised the general platform of the extremists and aroused, if not alienated, the Copts. Al-Dawa and the government served each other's purposes while serving their own, but in the process they helped strengthen the very opposition they sought to undermine. In the discussion thus far, a frequent conclusion has been that it is better to authorise opposition than to force it outside the policy; yet in the case of religious opposition, there are advantages to both courses.[3] The attempt to co-opt a part of the religious opposition was not effective in taming the rest, even in the presence of a complementarity of roles. At this point, it is not yet clear whether the case stands as an exception or a conclusion.

The remaining groups of undecided include the National Coalition, which issued a number of proclamations against Sadat's policy in the spring of 1980, and the large number of people (including some of the National Coalition's signatories) who were arrested in September 1981 and only gradually released by Mubarak in the following year, who are evidence of shrinking consensus. The opponents' action served two of their interests — that of conscience, and that of enlarging the area of debate. They ran into the government's intention to do just the opposite. It was no doubt the massive scale of the arrests that caused or confirmed the climate of opinion within which Sadat's assassins and their support group operated.

In general, the Egypt of Sadat and Mubarak supports the analytical notion of system stability through role complementarity. For the most part, government opposition has followed its own interests, accepting both the position of the other party in the state and its own, and using the other for its own purposes. To the extent that this complementarity worked, the stability of the system was maintained. But Sadat's message of liberalism fuelled greater expectations than he was ready to fulfill, particularly as time went on. Some opposition groups were content to play a limited official or tame role, as seen, but others were not, and their members increased along with the limitations on their activity. This misfit provided the setting that permitted, if not legitimised, the assassination. It should be noted that nothing in this imbalance or in any other analysis that is essentially structural will explain the assassination itself. Assassination is a haphazard, individual act, and its chances of success are random, not a barometer of the stability of the regime or the strength of the opposition.

After the assassination and succession, relations between government and opposition returned to stalemate until the 1984 elections. Even then, the opposition parties seemed to be as confirmed in their various roles as the government in its own. Expectations have not yet crystallised: the Wafd has to grow used to its new role and government to its new opposition, and above all the polity has to decide whether it considers a president who in five years has crossed no canals, corrected no revolutions, and created no openings to be a welcome relief or a bore. Only then can roles be assigned and complementarities assayed, although in the interim stability is maintained, *faute de pire.*

EMERGING PLURALISM: TUNISIA

Tunisia is a presidential monarchy, dominated for its three decades of independence by the father figure of the Supreme Combattant, Habib Bourguiba, and by his companions in arms, the Socialist Constitutional (or Destourian) Party (PSD). Power is centralised at the top but the base of the political pyramid is small, since the country has a small and homogenous population with concentrated distribution over a small territory. Nonetheless, Tunisia has had repeated experiences with pluralism. Immediately after independence, Bourguiba not only had to eradicate fundamental opposition within his own party as he consolidated his power but also had to undo the pretensions of the General Union of Tunisian Workers (UGTT) to organise a socialist opposition party from scratch. By the end of the 1950s, the dangers of opposition has been eliminated and an open party co-opting new elites as they arose was established under the benevolent aegis of the president. He placed and replaced his lieutenants at will, for though they might represent different currents of opinion, none had any independent source of power that escaped his control.

Although the 1960s might be termed the socialist decade of Ahmed ben Salah, the former UGTT leader and economic czar lost his position because he was busily building an independent source of power. The 1970s became the liberal decade of Hedi Nouira, the prime minister. A more important watershed in the latter period however was 1974, when young, liberal, pluralist elites were evicted from the party leadership. The PSD closed its ranks and became a bureaucracy, just at the moment when pluralism began to emerge in Tunisian society as a result of the successful economic management of Nouira's administration. Heretofore, opposition had been a matter of individuals, who could be sent into private life for a while to cool their heels before being recalled to service by the president. After the mid-1970s, opposition began to find a social base, and since it was no longer accommodated within the nation-party it began to look for organised expression of its own. The Nouira era had the liberal option, actually made pluralism and civil rights its platform and found supporters among the middle class and scattered disaffected regions. Ahmed ben Salah's Popular Unity Movement (MUP), representing the socialist option, had first to be separated from its exiled leader, but the MUP II was acceptable and also tapped middle-class dissatisfaction. The Tunisian Communist Party (PCT) should probably also be included in this list, since it was the first party to be authorised in the 1980s, and was a companion of the Destourian movement in the nationalist struggle, even if not a branch. Like the others, the PCT is a movement of professionals and intellectuals, a safety valve for dissatisfaction rather than a mass challenge to PSD. The government party looks on these movements with some scorn or with patronising camaraderie, since the leaders are former colleagues and the parties pose no real threat.

The Islamic Tendency movement is another matter, being neither a Destourian offshoot nor a negligible safety valve. Hence it is not authorised. Until 1983, there was not the slightest indication that the government found any value in the MTI. The only usefulness of the movement was to facilitate the identification of hostile opposition leaders, who were in fact tried and sentenced to jail in 1981. In 1985, during the Tunisian-American crisis over the Israeli bombing of Hammamet, Prime Minister Mzali received an MTI leader, as a move to signal his foreign policy dissatisfaction and his domestic policy to pass before the polity could react to these developments but in the pluralist 1980s of Mohammad Mzali, the new prime minister, a number of responses emerged. The first was a reinvigoration of the party itself, reopening the leadership of party auxiliaries to new voices and recalling liberals back to the party fold. The second was the opening of elections to multiple candidacies under the single party in 1980. And the third was the cautious tolerance and finally authorisation of opposition parties, first as movements and newspaper publishers, then as contenders in the 1981 parliamentary elections (which were then rigged to prevent the true size of the opposition being known), and finally as authorised parties.

Observers have long felt that the inevitable evolution of Destourian politics was towards a multi-party system. As socio-economic pluralism developed as a result of the impressive Tunisian growth, political pluralism pressed for recognition within the party. Acceptable at first, it became too broad in the mid-1970s, just at the same time as internal pressures within the leadership called for a narrowing of political positions. Thus, most of the opposition movements were spin-offs from the single party, and they were welcomed by the government to the extent that they removed the tendency to form factions from within the PSD and took it outside, where it would attract a minimum of followers. Opposition parties became the functional equivalent of the temporary political banishment of individuals of the 1960s. Ahmed Mestiri's Socialist Democratic Party (PDS) represented breadth, but the MTI was in general of little use to the government.

The most serious challenge to the government has been the UGTT. The nationalist trade union, both partner and member of the Destourian nationalist movement, has long had a dual nature, as single overarching labour union and as potential opposition party. It made its bid for party status in 1956 and was denied; eight years later it was back in an opposition role over economic (devaluation) and social (wage freeze) policies, and in the late 1970s — beginning in 1976 — it was in open conflict with the government. The next year the government repeated its tactic of 20 years earlier and broke labour unity by creating its own Destourian labour movement, the National Union of Tunisian Workers (UNTT), but the UGTT only pushed its own opposition further to the point of precipitating the bloody riots of January 1978. The government gave strength to this ticket and prestige to the UGTT claim of being a party when it ran a successful joint slate of PSD-UGTT candidates in 1981, but that did not prevent continuing conflict and finally arrest of the UGTT leadership. Certainly the conflict after 1968 was closely tied to the personality of the UGTT leader, Habib Achour, but he was broadly supported by the union membership. When Tunisia finally becomes a multi-party system, a socialist labour party based on the UGTT will be the PSD's main opposition.

It was the long-term hope of alternance that kept up the faith of the various opposition groups, coupled in varying measures with belief in the rightness of their cause. Thus, the Tunisian oppositions were closer in their reasoning to the Wafd than to the other Egyptian or Moroccan parties. Nothing in the government's behaviour confirmed the parties' long-term hopes, but all of them read the multi-party prospects of the political system and the pluralist evolution of the society and economy as foundations for their fortunes. Like the Wafd, they have not yet faced the test of their faith, but unlike the Egyptian situation, the slowly evolving nature of a Tunisian multi-party system can keep their hopes alive for a longer time without being satisfied than the already proclaimed doctrines of pluralism in Egypt. Thus the Tunisian opposition parties have also been inspired by a certain notion of patriotism, that justifies their role in bringing about political pluralism for the good of the country and in accordance with various waves of history (liberal, socialist, Islamic), even if the government does not recognise that such actions are in Tunisia's best interest. In sum, it is largely supported by the perceived evolution of the country towards a functioning multi-party system and eventually toward party alternance in government.

Similarly, role complementarity is limited on the government side. The official single party is both scared and scornful of the opposition. It is still operating under the mystique (*fassabiya*, as it is called) of nationalist-movement-cum-single-party unity, and is fearful of the threat to omnipotence, predominance and employment that new parties might bring. Above all, the PSD is fearful that new parties might call into question the gains and accomplishments of the Bourguiba era, to the point where legislation authorising opposition parties requires them to pledge not to challenge or undo the measures of independence to date. To many Tunisians, this wariness and suspicion of opposition to the point of falsifying electoral returns that were only a small challenge to the PSD monopoly and none to its predominance, is unwise and unnecessary, but in Tunisia such decisions are made at the highest level by one or two persons (in this case, Bourguiba, Mzali and Interior Minister Driss Guiga in 1981).

On the positive side, the government can see two values in opposition. It can be a safety valve or lightening rod, which gives vent to criticism and indeed is happy to do so, but without being strong enough to challenge the PSD. It can also be a tamer and more easily controlled alternative to restive opposition imprisoned within the government party itself. Internal opposition would be more dangerous to single party unity, even if not successful, and would be more threatening to current directions of the party if it ever were actually to succeed in winning control of the PSD.

CONCLUSION

The argument of this analysis has been that the stability of contemporary Arab regimes can be partly explained by a complementarity of roles, expectations and activities between government and oppositions which provides support for the polity. The different types of polity in the countries studied support the analysis. But the analysis has left some important questions unanswered. Under what conditions (since the cases show that the answer must be conditional, not absolute) is stability served by bringing the opposition into the polity or by forcing upon it unauthorised status? What determines the opponents' decision to adopt one sort of role or another, or to work within the polity or outside it? The analysis has dealt with the perplexing question of explaining the opposition's acceptance of its seemingly hopeless position, by pointing out satisfactions in limited or even broader activity, but it has only noted these satisfactions, not explained them.

Attempts at a broader explanation can only be partial. Going back to the social basis of government and opposition, one might assert that if social (or class) demands are not met, dissatisfaction grows and opposition becomes too large for the polity to absorb, forcing it to move outside. When opposition is small or specific, it is better to keep it in the polity under control; when it becomes too large, it is a danger to government, whether in the polity or outside. But not all opposition is socially- or class-based, and not all dissatisfaction becomes opposition.

Another explanation can be traced back to conscience, asserting that there are objective levels or thresholds of discontent which correspond to and therefore explain various roles and expectations within the opposition. But conscience is subjective, not objective, and does not provide an independent measure of opposition (Moore, 1966, Appendix). Even if these thresholds are not fixed, however, conscience does offer an important ingredient in explaining satisfaction in opposition roles. Individuals can remain active, concerned participants in the polity but enjoy freedom from the constraints of a government party by joining an opposition party, preferring ineffectiveness with freedom to ineffectiveness without it. Government interest in this unusual mixture of 'exit, voice and loyalty' is more obvious.[7]

In the last analysis, the argument of role complementarity is a historical argument. It has served to explain stability in particular places at particular times, but its effectiveness depends finally on its acceptance. At a particular time, governments see opposition that is kept within bounds as useful and acceptable; and at a particular time, oppositions too are willing to fill a limited role, where their sense of purpose can be met without conflicting with the government's sense of purpose. This complementarity can even cover extended times of unfulfilled hopes of alternance — a revision of the initial hypothesis — as well as times when neither side has any prospect of alternance in mind. In such cases something must happen at some point to those unrequited aspirations: either they are finally realised, or they become mythicised and millenial, or they are dropped, or stability disappears. In the Middle East, the first occurred in Israel with Likud, the second has been the fate of most Communist parties, the third is the story of the parties of the Moroccan nationalist movement, and the fourth is the history of Egypt in its first 30 years of independence.

That historical period also has longer term implications. The choice among the four eventualities is part of the larger process of establishing myths of government, a large and elusive selection of interpretations. Some systems will never regard government and opposition as complementary in any form. At the end of the twentieth century, Algeria, Libya, Iraq and possibly Syria are in that category, and thus are not covered in this chapter since the explanation given does not cover their cases. Others accept a permanently subordinate opposition, where opponents 'know their place' and are satisfied to be there, content to provide policy suggestions and small but autonomous political organisations without hope of achieving power. Still others will only be satisfied with alternance, and role complementarity can only be an explanation over a transitional period. Thus, the explanation, while accurate, calls for a further explanation on a higher level where it cannot rationally be provided. Ultimately, there is no answer (as yet) to the question whether one or another type of political myth will obtain. Part of the explanation lies somewhere in the conditions of transition and the stability under which role-complementarity is effected. Contemporary Arab polities are still developing political systems, which means that political myths are still being set up. Once in place they undergo challenges and changes, to be sure, but that is a different period of evolution to the time of their actual creation. Creation means not only invention but also testing under use and over time. Role complementarity found in the supportive position of the opposition is, then, a temporary explanation of stability, but the extent to which it contributes to stability in the longer run — the next 15 years of the century — depends on the success with which it either becomes part of the political culture or serves to hold things still while institutions of democractic alternance are being prepared.

NOTES

1. It has been suggested that the PLO would also make a useful case study. On the other hand, it is worth noting that the oil windfall states of the Gulf and the Mediterranean would not.

2. A similarly 'symbiotic', but more positive, relation exists between king and *ulema*, and is examined by Donna Lee Bowen, (1985) 'The paradoxical linkage of the ulema and monarchy in Morocco', *Maghreb Review, vol. 1 no. 3*, p. 8.

3. Vatin (1982) suggests a more complex and convincing explanation: that religious language and locations are used to express opposition because other ways are blocked or restricted. The implication would be that secular oppositions should be allowed to perform, so as not to force disaffected elements to take refuge in the mosques, where they are harder to combat.

4. 'But there are many other cases where competition does not restrain monopoly as it is supposed to, but *comforts and bolsers* it by unburdening it of its more troublesome customers . . . Those who hold power in the lazy monopoly may actually have an interest in *creating* some limited opportunities for exit on the part of those whose voice might be uncomfortable,' Hirschman, 1970, *Exit, voice and loyalty*, Harvard University Press, Cambridge, (Massachusetts) p. 59, also 115f.

4

Professional Associations and National Integration in the Arab World, with Special Reference to Lawyers Associations

Mustapha K. El Sayed

Professional associations have been treated by political scientists as one type of interest group particularly relevant as a channel for political participation. Together with other interest groups, they have been a major concern for Western social scientists for a long time (Bianchi, 1984, pp. 5–27). De Tocqueville (1954, ch. 2, pp. 114–18) and Durkheim (1964, pp. 1–32) both noted how the rise of a multitude of associations enhanced political stability and checked the power of any omnipotent government. Contemporary Anglo-Saxon political scientists have focused on the relationship between interest groups and political participation in the Third World as well as in industrial capitalist countries and their views on the subject have widely diverged.

Although national integration was not the explicit focus in these studies, national cohesion and political stability were assumed to be features of developed societies. Schmitter (1971, pp. 2–11) for one, made such a relationship explicit. A primary hypothesis suggested that development — defined as a contrapuntal interaction between role differentiation and integration — would lead to an increase in the 'significance' of interest groups in the political development process. The number, influence and means of action available to such groups would increase throughout this process. New organisations would emerge to cover newly rising interests and their geographic scope would expand. The new groups would also become more functionally specific or more specialised compared to more general forms of interest representation that existed in the past. The work of these organisations would be more intensive as they became embedded in a dense network of interaction with other organisations throughout society. Finally, it is likely that the pluralism of such groups would be amplified, as the same interest could be represented by several competing organisations.

Schmitter dwelt also on the other side of the relationship, that of the influence of interest groups on political development. However, he offered few generalisations because much depended on a large number of intervening variables. Three were of particular importance: the policy adopted towards groups, the pattern of interaction between interest groups and authoritative decision makers, the prevailing political culture.

The major thrust of works on interest groups was concerned with their impact on political participation, but some propositions about integration can be formulated from the literature. The disruptive effect of political participation caused by the activities of interest groups can be equated with the weakening of national integration and *vice versa*.

Three trends were discerned. One trend attributed to the actions of interest groups in the early phases of political change a disruptive effect on political stability and hence on national integration. Huntington (1968, pp. 1–92) thought that the emergent interest groups in 'Praetorian societies' would not be capable of moderating the demands of their members in an age of rapid social mobilisation caused by the 'revolution of rising expectations'. This would not help successful political institutionalisation. Likewise, Almond was apprehensive of political instability which would ensue if interest groups did not manage to reduce the political demands of their members and thus help maintain the boundaries between the polity and other social systems (Almond and Coleman, 1960, pp. 3–64; Almond and Powell, 1966, chs. 5 and 7).

A second trend was expressed by social scientists who accepted the famous proposition of both de Tocqueville and Durkheim concerning the impact of the 'art of association' or 'organic solidarity' on the one hand and tranquil political order on the other. Eisenstadt (1966), Simmel (1955) and Coser (1956), each in his own way, seemed to concur in their belief that when citizens distribute their loyalties among a multitude of organisations, each defending only a peripheral aspect of their members' social existence this takes the pressure off impulses towards all-encompassing social conflict and replaces them with partial demands not requiring transformation of the social structure. Social conflict along these lines can contribute to orderly adaptation of the political system to citizens' diverse demands. Citizens' attachment to the political system and identification with it would tend to increase.

A third trend tends to qualify the positive impact of interest groups in terms of both political participation and national integration. Its advocates agree that interest groups offer channels for political participation. However, the possibility of using such channels would depend on legal access to them, which might not be granted to all citizens. Even when the right to participate is universal, the capacity to use such a right varies from one group to another, with some groups showing a large measure of political apathy (Rokkan and Stein, 1966, pp. 101–31). The organisation of interest groups reflects therefore the political privileges of a small elite and becomes itself the basis of new political inequalities (Bendix, 1964, pp. 33–144). Finally some American political scientists argue that the limited scope of participation via interest groups is the deliberate outcome of a focus on partial issues not of much concern to large numbers of people, and of such groups' representation at the centre of the political system (Schattschneider, 1960; Lowi, 1969). This trend suggests a selective and mixed effect. Interest groups tend to strengthen the integration of an elite within the political system at the expense of apathy and widening alienation of the masses of the people.

FRAMEWORK FOR THE STUDY OF INTEREST GROUPS AND ARAB INTEGRATION

Although the abundant literature on interest groups and political development has been the object of detailed critique elsewhere (Bianchi, 1984), some observations should be borne in mind.

The liberal bias of much of these writings is quite obvious. However, what is at stake is not the search for a so-called value-free social science nor an argument that a radical bias is better than a liberal one. But to equate development or, even more narrowly, political development with the rise of interest groups, is to overlook the fact that certain countries have found the path to modernisation without encountering the type of interest group depicted in the literature. On the contrary, these have limited the presence of such groups and regulated whatever manifestations remained of specific interest within a broader political framework, be it a single party or a single mass organisation. To deny that development can take place without the rise of a multitude of powerful competing interest groups is to claim that the Soviet Union, for example, is not a modern state.

Besides, none of the three trends amounts to a meaningful theory explaining why interest groups succeed in certain countries in enhancing orderly political change while they fail in others. The 'art of association' is a peculiar talent possessed by the American people according to de Tocqueville. Durkheim, on the other hand, suggests that 'organic solidarity' springs up almost automatically with increasing division of labour in modern societies. Schmitter is aware of this difficulty of generalising about the impact of interest groups on political development, as he recognises the number of intervening variables that can shape the final outcome and is content to suggest only the most prominent among those variables.

Moreover, little understanding of the nature of the political processes in Third World countries is gained if interest groups are defined as necessarily having formal organisations. Certain studies have shown that formal structures in such countries do not always carry much weight in the political process and that effective power is exercised by people linked through informal ties (Springborg, 1978, pp. 83–107; El Sayed, 1983).

The propositions outlined in the foregoing pages require extensive data to test them, although there are few detailed studies on interest groups in countries of the type necessary to verify these propositions. A theoretical framework of a narrower range would therefore be more adequate for an exploratory phase of research, which could later yield the data necessary to create more ambitious frameworks for empirical testing. The remainder of this section will present a more modest undertaking in the form of relevant questions to be asked about the relationship between professional associations and national integration in the Arab world. The same framework could be applied to other types of interest group.

Professional associations are understood to be the formal organisations set up by people who carry out non-manual activities in order to promote common interests that unite them by virtue of their work requiring similar or even identical skills. Such skills were acquired usually during an educational process very often at the university level, mostly in a modern institution, but those who acquired such training in traditional institutions, i.e. church education establishments in the West and old universities in the Orient, would also come under this definition, although their participation in the labour market has been on the decline for centuries.

Such professional associations can play an important role in enhancing or restraining national integration. Whether they become agents of national cohesion or, on the contrary, of national disunity depends on how open they allow their membership to be, on their state-wide organisational structure, the particular functions they perform in the national political system and the orientation of public policy towards them.

Membership

If the only criterion for membership is the possession of a specific type of training or the exercise of a particular job, without regard for factors such as the applicant's racial or ethnic origin, the professional association can provide a channel that enhances the sense of citizenship; otherwise it may tend to reflect and even aggravate racial, ethnic or other cleavages in the social structures.

State-wide organisation

American political scientists used to consider the capacity of the state to make its presence felt in all parts of its territory and in all sectors of social life an important sign of its upgrading to the status of a developed country. They considered the effort to acquire such a capacity a principal crisis of political development, calling it the crisis of penetration (La Palombara, in Leonard Binder *et al.*, 1971, pp. 205–32). Without subscribing to this line of thinking, it can still be accepted that such capacity 'kindly exercised' is an important foundation for a true sense of national identity. Professional associations can intensify such feeling by extending their organisation on a voluntary basis to cover the whole of the national territory, provided that their state-wide structure does not remain idle or shows its efficiency, and particularly its security apparatus, only to the government, without offering any 'real' service to its members.

Actions undertaken by professional associations

These are important in giving a concrete meaning to the expansion of their membership and organisation during two periods:

a) During the colonial period, given their position with respect to the independence struggle and extent of participation in it.

b) In the independent period, when professional associations can engage in four important functions, all of which call for intensive contacts with the authorities of the newly independent state. These are: promoting professional interests; providing a channel for political participation by voicing views on issues of broad national significance; mobilising efforts of nation-building; and serving as a force of political change.

In performing these functions, members of professional associations focus their attention on their new state, its authorities and its destiny. The attitude adopted by those authorities towards them determines whether such activities contribute to a heightened sense of citizenship or, on the contrary, give rise to a feeling of political apathy and hence weaken the legitimacy of that state.

Public policies towards professional associations

State authorities choose one of three options, or a combination of them, towards professional associations. They either content themselves with the mere sanctioning of the free play of professional associations (the pluralist option), a rare occurrence in Third World countries. They can mobilise energies of professional associations behind ideological goals of the regime (the corporatist option) (Lehmbruch and Schmitter, 1982, pp. 1–28, 259–80). Finally, they can manipulate professional associations in a power game behind a pluralist facade (the cynical option), somewhere in the middle ground between the first two.

Professional associations engage also in external relations with their counterparts in other countries. If such countries are tied by a common culture and feelings of solidarity, membership and organisation, the actions of professional associations at this level can be instrumental in enhancing suprastate integration or in weakening it. A positive impact in this respect is influenced by the intensity of their participation in three types of activities. These are: coordinating similar approaches to their tasks in their respective countries; engaging in common actions at a regional and sub-regional level; and upholding and pursuing common goals at the national, regional or international level.

How have Arab professional associations fared with respect to such tasks?

METHOD OF STUDY

It would have been useful to include several types of professional association in the Arab world in this study. However, the study of professional associations in the Arab world still has much ground to cover. Scholars of this topic have preferred either to examine all professional associations or interest groups in one country or to focus on one. Thus, substantial literature on professional associations in Egypt already exists (Reid, 1981; Springborg, 1978; El Sayed, 1983; Abdel-Moneim, 1984; Ziadeh, 1968; and *Lawyers and politics in Arab countries*, Reid, 1981). Apart from that, the subject remains *terra incognita*.

It would seem inevitable therefore to focus on one type of professional association and to find out how it has helped to enhance or weaken national solidarity in several Arab countries. Otherwise, to generalise about professional associations in Arab countries without the help of such case studies would definitely be impossible.

This study should be considered as only one step in the direction of a more general and comprehensive study of those associations in the Arab world.

LAW ASSOCIATIONS

Lawyers took the lead in setting up professional associations in the Arab world. The first bar association was established in Egypt in 1912, followed by Syria and Lebanon in 1921; a short-lived bar association was established in Aleppo in 1912 but did not continue after a few meetings. Iraq and the Maghreb countries knew the first stirrings of professional associations among lawyers when their first bar organisations were set up at the beginning of the 1930s (Reid, 1981, p. 381; Bu Roways, 1982, vols 1, 2 and 3).

Medical doctors, journalists and engineers followed the steps of the lawyers, the doctors one decade later but as much as three decades later in the case of the other two groups. Reid (1981, pp. 380–7) dwelt on the conditions which enabled the lawyers to take such a lead. With commercial expansion of Western capital into Arab lands and the adoption of Western and notably French civil codes, a strong need arose for lawyers with knowledge of Western law. The vanguard of the modern educated elite in the Arab world consisted mostly of lawyers, accounting for between half to almost all of the first generation of university students in Egypt, Syria and Iraq (62 to 73 per cent; 28 to 53 per cent and 94 to 100 per cent respectively) (Reid, 1981, p. 385). Under colonial rule, the bar association soon became a focal point in local politics. In Egypt,

94

Syria and Morocco, bar associations became either a launching ground for future ministers and party leaders or the stronghold of opposition when autocratic rulers dismissed a popular party from the government. The political fortunes of the bar associations were drastically eclipsed under the military regimes that ruled over the destinies of many countries in the Arab world in the 1950s and 1960s. However, new conditions in some of these countries favoured a sort of comeback in the 1970s of the bar association, as a mirror of the true political forces in their countries or even as an agent of political change.

Bar associations have therefore become an important landmark in the national politics in Egypt, Lebanon, Syria, Iraq, Jordan, Kuwait, Bahrain, South Yemen, Sudan, Libya, Tunisia, Algeria, Morocco, Mauritania and Palestine. There is a society for jurists in the United Arab Emirates (consisting of 150 members) and the Arab Lawyers Union has recommended constituting a special branch of UAE lawyers with the promise to assist the establishment of a bar association. Saudi Arabia, Qatar, and Oman do not have any formal lawyers organisation (Arab Lawyers Union, 1984, p. 117). The continued claim by ruling families that they are guided only by principles of Islamic *shariah* has definitely hindered not only the establishment of a bar association but the growth of such a secular profession of law as well. All types of professional association or trade union are virtually banned in the three countries.

MEMBERSHIP OF BAR ASSOCIATIONS

According to *Mawsouat al Muhami Al Arabi* (Encyclopaedia of Arab lawyer) (Bu Roways, 1982) the number of registered lawyers in the 14 Arab countries which had formal professional associations for lawyers was about 25,000 during the period 1978–81. This number would increase by almost 20,000 if lawyer trainees are included.

Bar associations vary considerably in terms of numerical strength and political importance. More than half the registered lawyers come only from one country, Egypt. The first four countries in the Arab world to establish bar associations — Egypt, Lebanon, Syria and Iraq — account for over three-quarters of the total; and when two other countries — Jordan and Morocco — are included, the share of these six countries amounts to over 90 per cent of the total. Obviously, such extreme concentration of lawyers in only six of 15 countries cannot be attributed merely to population. In the six

PROFESSIONAL ASSOCIATIONS AND NATIONAL INTEGRATION

Table 4.1: Registered lawyers in Arab countries (1978–81)

Country	No. of registered lawyers	% of total	No. of lawyers per 100,000 people
Egypt	13,972	53.3	35
Lebanon	1,920	7.3	71
Syria	1,884	7.2	22
Iraq	2,693	10.8	21
Jordan	1,158	4.4	37
Kuwait	104	0.4	8
Bahrain	48	0.2	
South Yemen	28	0.1	1
Sudan	663	2.5	4
Libya	225	0.9	8
Tunisia	547	2.1	9
Algeria	654	2.5	4
Morocco	1,037	8.4	11
Total	24,933	100	

Note: The figure for Egypt is a conservative estimate. The same source also gives another figure (37,563), but adds that it might not be very accurate as it probably includes not only the trainees but those whose names should have been dropped, and the deceased (Bu Roways, 1982, vol. 3, p. 14). Egyptian Bar Association authorities currently quote the figure of 30,000 for the total number of Egyptian lawyers.

countries, the ratio exceeds 10 lawyers for every 100,000 people.

The three bar association on which this chapter focuses are those of Egypt, Syria and Morocco, which together include two-thirds of all lawyers in the Arab world.

The number of lawyers has increased at a rapid rate in some of these countries. The number of registered lawyers in Egypt in 1960 was only 3,921 and jumped to 13,972 two decades later (Bu Roways, 1982, vol. 3, p. 14). During that period the number of lawyers in Egypt more than doubled in each decade. A study presented to the Eighteenth Congress of the Society of Bar Associations in Morocco observed a similar trend, arguing that the total number of lawyers — registered and trainees — in the country was 3,246 in 1985, and would rise to above 10,000 by the end of the century. Thus the lawyer/population ratio would rise to five for every 100,000 citizens. The study proceeded to suggest ways of limiting entry into the lawyer profession.

Apart from the Egyptian Bar Association with its massive membership, the bar association in most other Arab countries really represents an elite in terms of number and education, and most probably also in terms of social standing and prestige. Conditions of

96

membership in the bar associations of Egypt, Syria and Maghreb show certain common features (Bu Roways, 1982: vol. 1, pp. 273–382; vol. 2, pp. 221–60; vol. 3, pp. 17–99). According to internal regulations, no one in any of the three countries should exercise the profession of advocacy unless his name figures on the lawyers' lists approved by the bar association of his country or his place of residence. Requirements related to nationality, residence in the country, possession of a law degree and period of training. In the case of Syria, employment by the Ministry of Defence or membership in another professional association is a bar to entry. Such conditions can cause friction, as when the Syrian Bar Association insisted that former army officers go through a period of training before being qualified as practising lawyers (*al-Muhamoun*, 1979, pp. 17–18). Egyptian legislation was unique in requiring active membership in the Arab Socialist Union for candidates for office in the bar association. This provision was replaced in 1975 by the requirement of formal approval of all candidates by the so-called socialist public prosecutor appointed by the National Assembly, which is dominated by the ruling party and led by the head of state.

In none of the three countries was there any provision concerning sex, ethnic origin or religion of members of the bar association and its leading organs. In fact, lawyers of minority groups in the three countries played a prominent role in the establishment of their bar associations (Reid, 1981, pp. 48–9, pp. 190–1). A Copt, Murqus Fahmi, and a protestant, Fares el-Khoury, were associated with the establishment of the bar association of Egypt in 1912 and of Damascus in 1921, and several Copts led the Egyptian Bar Association during the first half of the twentieth century. Fares el-Khoury and his cousin Fayez el-Khoury headed the Damascus Bar Association for seven years in the 1920s and 1930s, and several times, the Aleppo Bar Association was headed by Christians during at least eight of the 32 terms of its elected council between 1918 and 1980. As for Morocco, several European and Jewish names were on the lists of registered lawyers. It seems therefore almost certain that bar associations in the three countries did not practise discrimination on the basis of religion in the admission of new members and probably also in the election of their officers. It could even be argued that people of minority groups were over-represented among lawyers. The prominent role played by lawyers during the first half of the twentieth century in nationalist movements with a secular outlook suggests that the bar associations took the lead in emphasising the secular orientation of the new institutions in their countries and in enhancing national unity in the face of European colonial powers who were suspected of being too willing to exploit possible ethnic cleavages in colonised societies.

However, it is noteworthy that although lawyers of minority groups continued to figure among members of the elected councils of bar associations in the three countries — ten per cent of the council of the Egyptian Bar Association during the period 1978–85, for example, were Copts — it became increasingly rare for a lawyer from a minority group to head any of these organisations. Perhaps, the eclipse of nationalist parties that led to struggle for independence in Egypt and Syria took away with it the secular nationalism, and ethnic particularisms came to the fore under new ruling elites despite the radical slogans they expounded.

Organisation

Bar associations in the Arab world do not adhere to a single organisational scheme, although variations in the past were greater than they are at present. Three types of internal structure prevail.

1. The professional organisation of the lawyers is called the Lawyers Society in some countries, notably Kuwait and Bahrain, whereas in others it is called the Lawyers Syndicate (*Niquabat al-Muhameen*). The difference is not merely the label, for a look at the law regulating the profession in Kuwait for example (Bu Roways, vol.1) reveals that unlike in other Arab countries, the lawyers Society does not have the power to determine who is a lawyer and who is not. The official list of registered lawyers is established in the Court of Appeal under the supervision of a committee including three judges, the attorney general, the undersecretary of the Ministry of Justice and two layers chosen by the Lawyers Society from its own members. Other provisions of the same law (42, 1964) reveal that the Lawyers Society, unlike the Lawyers Syndicate, does not have much control over the organisation of the profession.

2. A second pattern is that of the multiplicity of associations representing lawyers in the same country. A pluralist organisation prevailed among three syndicates in Syria from 1921 to 1972 and still prevails among the two syndicates in Lebanon and nine in Morocco. Although such pluralism was in fact a reflection of the administrative divisions and local traditions of particular countries, the letter of the law did not preclude the presence of two independent syndicates in the same region or town. The only condition attached

was that their membership should be no fewer than 30 registered lawyers. Local branches of the single national bar associations are called affiliated syndicates (*Niqabat Farqeyya*), but they lack the autonomy of the pluralist syndicates, since they are subordinate to the central council of the bar association, and bound by law to submit reports to it and to carry out its policies. While syndicates of the pluralist type coordinate their activities, engage in common action and even observe certain uniform rules in their organisation, each is free to determine its own internal regulations.

The rise and demise of the pluralist organisation of the lawyers' profession in Syria began with plans of the colonial power (France) to divide it into several states. Its continuation under a multi-party system in independent Syria fits national politics. However, what is really striking is that it survived under the military regimes which ruled Syria until 1972. In the end, as the political system itself tended gradually to be less pluralistic — to say the least — it found the single bar association easier to control and manipulate. Thus Syria had three active independent syndicates in Damascus (1921), Aleppo (1921) and Latakia from 1929 until 1972. They used to meet in a conference of Syrian bar associations and cooperated in the publication of a review, *al-Muhamoun*, which had been published earlier by the Damascus Bar Association. After 1972, local syndicates lost their autonomy and became branches of the central bar association in Damascus. At present, besides Damascus, there are eight other branches in Aleppo, Latakia, Homs, Hama, Tartous, Dir El Zour, Al Haska and Adelp. However, Syrian lawyers are concentrated in the first two cities; Damascus has nearly half (48 per cent) and Aleppo almost a quarter (23 per cent). Latakia and Homs each have 7 per cent of the total and the five other branches share 15 per cent (Bu Roways, 1982, vol. 1, pp. 360–410).

Morocco and Lebanon remain the only two countries that still practise pluralism in the organisation of their bar associations. Moroccan lawyers at present belong to 15 syndicates scattered throughout the country. The 15 organisations meet periodically in a conference of the Society of Bar Associations of the Maghreb. Eighteen such conferences have been held so far. Pluralism in this particular case is reinforced by size. The largest bar association in Rabat has only one-third of all registered lawyers. Casablanca, Fes and Marakesh come next with almost one-third (31 per cent) of the membership (13 per cent, 10 per cent and 8 per cent respectively). Slightly more than one-third (36 per cent) are affiliated to eleven other syndicates in Tangiers (5 per cent), Meknes (6 per cent),

Agadir, Beni Melal, Nadour, Quneitra, Oujda, Tetuan, Asfi, Jedida and Satat. Nothing suggests that this pattern of pluralist organisation will be abandoned in the near future.

3. The third type of structure is that of the single bar association prevailing in most other Arab countries including Egypt. The only pluralism is based on categories of law, i.e. lawyers registered with Mixed Courts, or Shariah lawyers in the case of Egypt. Single bar associations seem to have been easily established without any challenge or questioning. Such associations can be divided into branches. The branches can either be attributed broad functions concerning services rendered to members, as in Syria since 1972; or they can be called affiliated syndicates, as in Egypt. However, they are subordinate to their central organ from which they receive guidance and are under the formal obligation to carry out its decisions within their own spheres. The Egyptian Bar Association has 21 such affiliated syndicates.

Over and above such varieties of organisation, all bar associations in the Arab world, and more particularly in the three countries under discussion, have a similar internal structure. The highest authority is the general conference or the general assembly. The Egyptian Bar Association is open to all registered lawyers, but in Syria and Morocco, it is open only to delegates of the branches, who are usually elected.

The second level in the structure of authority is probably the most important. It is the council of the bar association, which ranges from ten members in the case of Syria to 24 in the case of Egypt. In Morocco, it depends on the size of the bar association. The council is really the central leadership of the bar association. Headed by a president usually called *Naqib al-Muhameen*, the council is delegated the power of the general conference during the intervals between its very short sessions (a few days but in most cases only one day). It is the council, and more particularly the *Naqib*, who speaks on behalf of the lawyers and takes initiatives, expecting the lawyer members to follow suit. The councils are elected for a period of three years in the case of Morocco and Syria and four years in the case of Egypt.

PURPOSE AND POLICIES

The three bar associations under study, and indeed most other bar associations in Arab countries, strove to pursue two lines of action simultaneously. First they acted as the organisations of a group of people exercising the same profession, who consequently have certain concerns to look after and particular interests to promote. Secondly, as enlightened citizens, they cared about the destiny of their countries, particularly their national independence and the fundamental human rights of their countrymen, since their education and skills equipped them more than any other segment of the educated elite to know about these questions and to serve these two goals.

This section argues that the bar associations in the three countries tried with the means available to them, to carry out the first task. As for the second, it was performed with such enthusiasm that it put the lawyers at the forefront of political forces in their countries, a role for which they had often to pay the price in terms of the autonomy of their organisation if not the safety of their leaders.

The prominence of the bar associations in the national politics of the three countries reached its apex in the case of Egypt, particularly during the 1920s and the 1930s and again in the 1980s. To a much lesser degree, that was also the case in Syria, especially in the period between independence and the Baath Party's accession to power in 1963. The Syrian Bar Association was at the forefront of opposition forces in the 1970s. Finally, although lawyers' organisations in Morocco were also active political forces, their importance in national politics probably did not match that of their Mashreq counterparts.

This section is not concerned so much with the role of lawyers in national politics as it is with their professional organisations. As the largest segment of the modern educated elite, lawyers manned ministerial posts, sometimes even whole cabinets, established political parties, constituted a sizeable minority in the parliaments of the three countries and stood at the top of the administrative ladder in many ministries, particularly in the first half of this century in Egypt and till the 1960s in Syria. However, they did not do this in a concerted manner as members of a specific organisation. The next pages will trace the lines of action pursued by their professional associations.

Promotion of professional interests

The bar associations in Egypt, Syria and Morocco engaged in a variety of activities for their members. They published journals not only to express views on matters affecting them as citizens but to

PROFESSIONAL ASSOCIATIONS AND NATIONAL INTEGRATION

provide them with the information necessary for the exercise of their professional duties — such as texts of laws and decrees, judicial decisions and comments on the organisation of justice. Thus the Egyptian Bar Association published *ah-Muhamat* (1920), and the Damascus Bar Association published *Niquabat al-Muhameen* (1935), later called *al-Muhamoun*, since 1964 the organ of all lawyers organisations in Syria (Bu Roways 1982). The Society of Bar Associations of Morocco published *al-Muhamat* (Bu Roways, 1982, vol. 3, pp. 215–20), in addition to journals of its affiliated associations (*al-Meeiar* in Fez, *Mejallat Al Mahakem Al Maghrebeyya* in Casablanca and in Marakesh).

The associations established pension funds and disciplinary committees, and defended lawyers in dispute with the state. The Syrian association provided services such as consumer cooperatives and the Egyptian bar sold cars at reduced prices and organised pilgrimages to the holy places in Saudi Arabia. A sign of continued interest in such matters was the special committee set up at the last congress of the Moroccan bar associations to look into the affairs of the profession.

Governments of the three countries would prefer bar associations to concern themselves solely with professional services. The Egyptian government accused the elected council of its bar association of neglecting members' interests by engaging too much in politics (*al-Ahram*, 24 July, 1981). The first congress of bar associations in Syria, held after the dissolution of elected councils and the appointment of new ones in 1980, had only two items on the agenda: a declaration of total support for the policies of President Hafez al Assad in all fields, and the social services provided to its members — (*al-Muhamoun*, March 1981).

Political participation

Almost from their inception, bar associations have been active participants in the political process in Egypt, Syria and Morocco. They issued statements, contacted top government leaders, held conferences, organised lectures and debates and even asked their members to strike in defence of national causes.

The capacity to engage in such actions varied from one country to the other, and within the same country from one period to another. When the three countries were under foreign occupation, the Egyptian Bar Association enjoyed a larger measure of autonomy

102

because the administration of the internal affairs of the country was in national hands, particularly after 1922. During the period of the single-party, mass-organisation system in both Egypt and Syria, the political activities of bar associations were limited to those authorised by the leadership of the dominant party or organisation. However, lawyers organisations in the two countries still managed to take positions unfavourable to the ruling party. The range of action available to them greatly increased and became more varied during periods of multi-party experiments. This review will focus on issues of confrontation during recent decades, in line with the thrust.

Egypt

The last strike action threatened by the Egyptian Bar Association was in March 1954 when its General Assembly demanded parliamentary elections, freeing of political prisoners and an immediate end to the military regime. The bar's council was still dominated by a Wafdist majority. Thereafter, the association was run by an appointed council including former council members who were either independent or belonged to minority parties. The situation was normalised in 1958 after a new advocacy law was issued and new elections were organised. During the following 18 years, the bar did little to displease the Nasser or Sadat governments and confined its participation in public affairs to channels open for any organised interest during that period, i.e. through its single mass organisation and its own journal. However, even during this period, the bar did not turn into an enthusiastic supporter of the ruling group, for whenever an occasion for free expression of opinion presented itself, members of the elected councils seized it to voice their liberal view. In 1962, the late Mustapha El Baradei, the bar's president, called for the establishment of an opposition party in the Congress of the Forces of the Working People. He expressed the same views at a conference of the association on 15 May 1972, and in 1976 in debates within the Committee on Political Action which was charged with proposing changes in Egyptian political structures (El Sayed, 1983, pp. 139–40).

Similarly, the lawyers organisation took the risk of echoing demands put forward by other social groups which resorted to strikes, demonstrations and public marches in order to oppose aspects of government policy. The council issued statements in January 1972 supporting students' demands for a more active policy to wipe out Israeli occupation of Arab territories, and in January

1977 endorsing demands of the workers and other poor people for a change in the government's economic policy. Criticism backed by the bar association became more frequent in the 1970s but, until 1976, the critical positions were taken within the broader framework of the Arab Socialist Union, since all members of the bar's council were necessarily also members of the single mass organisation.

The situation became qualitatively different after November 1976. Not only was the association no longer bound to confine its dissent within the limits defined by the ideology of the mass organis-ation, which ceased practically to exist after a return to a form of multi-party structure in that month, but the association, with more freedom of action, increasingly expressed its opposition to the very orientation of Sadat's government in both domestic and foreign policy.

Thus through various channels — well-attended public meetings in its headquarters in the very crowded centre of Cairo, statements to the press, interviews in opposition newspapers, its own journal and publications, Arab lines of influence and contacts with officials — the bar's council, particularly after the re-election of Ahmed el-Khawaga as President in 1979, voiced its objections to laws affecting citizens' fundamental rights, the independence of judicial organs and autonomy of the Journalists Syndicate. It also mobilised opposition to a project for the commercial exploitation of the plateau on which many of the ancient Egyptian pyramids were built. However, what particularly outraged Sadat was the bar's opposition to his treaty with Israel and its declared resistance to normalisation of relations with the Jewish state. Thus, for nearly two and a half years, from January 1979 to July 1981, hostility mounted between the ruling National Democratic Party and the bar association. The climax was reached in July 1981, when despite massive protests by the lawyers, President Sadat signed a law dissolving the elected council and appointed a new one. On 5 September of the same year, at least five members of the elected council were detained together with Abdel Aziz el-Shourbagui, the ageing former president of the bar association.

The elected council refused to recognise the measures and waged a legal battle with the government. It finally won in July 1983, when the Supreme Constitutional Court decided that such measures violated the constitution. The elected council was formally reinstated. Later it helped draft new laws for the profession in 1984. New elections were organised in May 1985. Former members of the council who opposed Sadat's policies with Ahmed el-Khawaga as leader had a landslide victory. The *al-Wafd* newspaper claimed that out of 24 members in the new council, 14 at least were Wafdists. Others belonged to the Nasserite, Marxist and Muslim Fundamentalist trends (El Sayed, 1983, pp. 156–68; *al-Muhamat*, special issue, *vol. 63, no. 5* and *6*, May–June 1983; *vol. 65, no. 5* and *6*, May–June 1985, pp. 162–5).

However, the situation faced by the re-elected council is different to the problems faced by the country in the last years of Sadat's regime. Political parties now have greater freedom of action. For the time being, public expression of dissent does not involve much risk. Although the Egyptian Bar Association continues to concern itself with issues of national politics, it no longer stands at the head of the opposition, a place now occupied by political parties.

Syria

Syrian lawyers' political involvement in the independent period has a certain affinity with that of their Egyptian colleagues, although Syrian bar associations showed more concern for pan-Arab national politics. For example, after the arrest of several lawyers and others prominent at the bar, arrests which seemed to disregard their political leanings, Zakir al-Qasimi, the Damascus bar president, held a press conference in January 1954 at which he urged lawyers and journalists to work together against Shishakli's military regime. The Aleppo bar president was forced to resign. Lawyers followed suit, joining students and workers in massive protest movements which led finally to the fall of Adib Shishakli in February 1954. A month later, Egyptian lawyers were engaged in milder protest actions against the continuation of the military regime in Egypt.

As in Egypt, the period from the mid-fifties to the late seventies was a dormant one, as far as the political activities of the Syrian bar associations are concerned, although, unlike in Egypt, lawyers and their leaders remained prominent in national politics. Political parties were outlawed under the merger with Egypt in the United Arab Republic. The Baath Party came to power two years after Syria's secession from the UAR and imposed on Syria an effectively single party state, in which other 'nationalist' and 'progressive' parties had only a symbolic presence in the national front. Part of that period was spent in reorganising of the associations into one, in accordance with a law issued in 1972.

The bar association came again to the fore in the late 1970s, as it was suspected by General al-Assad's government of being a haven for its political opponents.

Copies of *al-Muhamoun* from 1979 to 1981 reflect the gulf that existed between the bar and the regime, and the way loyalist lawyers attempted to bridge it. An article in issue 2–3 (1979), for example, on the power of the president to ratify decisions made by the state security tribunals attributed absolute powers to the president. Another article suggested that when a detention order was issued *in absentia*, it should remain in force for no more than a limited period. The news section included an item on the bar association's opposition to the attempt to exempt internal security officers from the conditions of training when they applied for registration as lawyers.

Other issues (6, 7 and 8) published proceedings of a symposium on fundamental human rights and freedoms in the Arab world held in Baghdad in August 1979, including contributions by Syrian participants. Mahmoud el-Geyoushi, vice-president of the Association for the Defence of Human Rights in Syria surveyed the restrictions on fundamental human rights and freedom resulting from emergency laws in the Arab world. Dr Mowaffaq al-Kozbari, president of the Prisoners and Prisoners' Families Care Society, lamented the wider implications of the suppression of liberties in the Arab world.

Following the publication of four further issues, *al-Muhamoun* ceased to appear for ten months in 1980. When publication was resumed, the new editor expressed his sorrow for the interruption and promised regular publication. The issue listed the names of the lawyers appointed to run the affairs of the central council of the association in Damascus and councils of the branches in other Syrian cities. It included a statement that disapproved of the refusal of the Arab Lawyers Union to admit members of the new council to represent Syria at its permanent office and at the Fourteenth Congress of Arab Lawyers held in Rabat in June 1980, arguing that the dissolution of the councils and appointment of new councils was a purely internal Syrian affair.

The original councils were accused of failing to condemn violent action by the Muslim Brotherhood in Syria and of encouraging protest strikes by traders.

The same issue, while publishing the proceedings of a congress of Syrian bar associations, failed to discuss changes in the councils or the arrest of the association's president. Instead, it covered the financial affairs of the various branches of the association, which had decided on an increase in several fringe benefits accruing to lawyers. It condemned the actions of the Muslim Brotherhood and declared its total support for the policies of President Assad. The

106

congress decided to confer on President Assad the title of 'Honorary President of the Syrian Bar Association and First Advocate of Right and Arabism' (*al-Muhamoun* 1 to 8, 1980). The congress approved changes in the advocacy law in 1972. The changes prohibited discussion in the congress of any matter not included on the agenda set in advance by the council, and disqualified any Syrian lawyer from seeking election to a post in all Arab or international associations without prior approval from the association's council (*al-Muhamoun*, 1 to 8, 1980, pp. 370–1).

Finally, a new law was promulgated. It did not affect the structure of the bar association, though the Arab Lawyers Union maintained that it violated the independence of the association. Elections were subsequently organised in all branches of the association and many members of the appointed councils retained their seats. Members of these councils also held seats in a newly elected national assembly. The president of the bar association is the the chairman of the legislative commission of the assembly. Leading members of the association present in the national assembly may propose amendments to the advocacy law, but none have so far done so.

Morocco

Available data suggest that conditions of political participation by bar associations in Morocco are quite different to those prevailing in Syria. Violations of human rights are reported in both countries. At its eighteenth congress held in Fez from 27 to 29 June 1985, the Society of the Bar Associations of the Maghreb was nevertheless able to debate questions of fundamental human rights, freedoms and national issues. The congress was divided into committees, one of which was concerned with public affairs. In its resolutions, the congress noted that guarantees of personal liberties and public freedom were no longer upheld, that laws which violated public freedom continued in force, that international documents of human rights had not been ratified and that the practice of political detention continued. It also noted the lack of guarantees for the exercise of the rights of defence and independence of the judiciary in political trials and observed that some newspapers were still illegally banned while others were object of harassment. The congress lamented violations of freedom of speech in the elections held for local councils and the national assembly during the last two years and noted that such violations made those elections void of any credibility in the eyes of the public. It remarked moreover that economic, social and cultural plans did not guarantee rights to work, education, housing and medical care for the majority of people, which was incompatible with obligations emanating from the ratified international convention on economic, social and cultural rights.

Finally, the eighteenth congress approved a special motion recommending the release of Ahmed Ben Amru, a former president of the Society of the Bar Associations of the Maghreb, together with that of other lawyers who have been detained for the last two years.

Agents of nation-building

The bar associations in Egypt, Syria and Morocco demonstrated their determination to take part in the shaping of new national policies, not only in the struggle for independence from colonial powers. An indirect means of influence was through studies of the different legal aspects of nation-building. Through their journals and conferences they commented publically on relations among the three classic powers, legal and judicial reform, organisation of the government, the legal status of state enterprises, rights of citizens and a host of other subjects.

Members of bar associations took a more direct part in nation-building through legislative assemblies, working within the political parties and taking on executive office as ministers and even prime ministers. Some of them, particularly in Egypt under the monarchy, occasionally combined their membership in both the government and the council of the bar associations.

Those who occupied the post of prime minister in Syria included three who were presidents of the Damascus Bar Association (Fares el-Khoury, Said el-Ghazzi, Maamoun el-Kozbari) and one who was its secretary general (Sabri el-Asali). In Morocco two leading ministers — Maati Bouabid and Muhammad Bucetta were former presidents of bar associations. In Egypt, despite the prominence of its bar association, none of the leading members assumed the premiership, although many were ministers and Makram Obeid was the secretary general of the Wafd Party (Bu Roways, 1982, vols 1, 2 and 3).

It is difficult to assess the impact of those lawyer politicians on the process of nation-building. For one thing, they did not all share the same ideologies or political positions. In Syria, for example, whereas Fares el-Khoury belonged to the People's Party or joined the National Bloc, Sabri el-Asali led the National Party. In Morocco, Maati Bouabid was once a member of the Socialist Union

108

of Popular Forces, the major leftist opposition party in the country, and Bucetta was a supporter of the king and president of the Istiqlal Party. It is even more difficult to find a common denominator amongst them in terms of a commitment towards broad orientations of the lawyers profession such as liberalism, secularism and nationalism.

The rule of such leading lawyers did not have a lasting impact on the process of nation-building in their countries, though none of them lasted in power very long. Their golden age in both Egypt and Syria came to an end with the overthrow of the parliamentary system in those countries and the advent of military regimes of a more radical nature (1952 and 1963 respectively). One does not need to wonder much about the impact of such rule by the lawyers, had it lasted longer or been more stable, because it was obviously losing support among the masses and radical sections of the intelligentsia before it was dealt the decisive blow by the military (Abdel Malek, 1968; Seale, 1965). It would be incorrect to attribute the failure of the parliamentary system in the two countries to those lawyer politicians who led it, for they were not the only force directing it. However, they were too closely linked to the big landowners and commercial bourgeoisie who were its principal beneficiaries. Despite the good intentions of some, they could not break with such classes and finally had to be condemned along with them.

A force of political change

Although the rule of lawyers did not leave an enduring impact, their bar associations nevertheless remained an important force for political change. On several occasions, the bar associations of Egypt and Syria joined hands with other opposition forces in resisting authoritarian regimes. In 1954 and again in 1980, they were involved in major confrontations, with openly military regimes in the first case or with authoritarian regimes led by former army officers in the second. Such confrontations came to a successful conclusion from the point of view of the bar associations in Syria in April 1954, when Shishakli's dictatorship collapsed; and in 1983 in Egypt, when the Supreme Constitutional Court ruled that Sadat's measures against the lawyers professional organisation were unconstitutional, two years after Sadat's death. The Society of Bar Associations of Morocco is one of the forces militating for a more profound liberalisation of King Hassan's regime.

The lawyers probably constitute an elite in some Arab countries, but they are not divorced from the population at large. Through their direct links with the masses and affiliation to political parties, their associations can engender sufficient resistance to topple an authoritarian regime. A recent example was given by the Sudanese Bar Association, which had been involved since 1980 in a confrontation with the military regime of General Gaafar Numeiry and which together with other professional associations, helped to canalise the protest actions of the masses, which culminated in the overthrow of his regime. They then constituted a national front to govern the country through a transitional period leading to elections in April 1985 (Arab Lawyers Union, 1985).

Besides this direct role, bar associations can influence the process of political change indirectly. The struggles of the associations in the three countries against authoritarian measures and regimes have given birth to a powerful liberal tradition among the intelligentsia of these countries which has to be reckoned with by their governments. The political liberalisation measures introduced in both Egypt and Morocco since the mid-seventies were in part an acknowledgement by the late President Sadat and King Hassan II of Morocco of the presence of this tradition and an attempt to gain legitimacy through the formal adoption of some of its demands (Dessouki, 1978, pp. 7–24; al-Qabbaj, 1984).

Finally, such confrontations helped define the rules of a new political game based on the government's respect for the autonomy of professional associations and their right to express dissenting views. Both the late President Sadat and King Hassan II expected opposition political parties and interest groups to reciprocate their consent to a larger measure of freedom of action by abstaining from any radical critique of their policies. When some of these parties and groups did not abide by such 'rules of good behaviour', the heads of government retorted by cutting the already limited scope of action left to them. The Egyptian Bar Association persisted in its struggle against this reversal of policy and the government of President Hosni Mubarak accepted a supreme constitutional court's ruling to respect the autonomy of the bar association. At present, although the bar's council is made up predominantly of opposition figures, the government does not interfere any more in the internal affairs of the bar, and even responds favourably to many of the association's demands. More importantly, the move towards a more pluralistic organisation of relations between the government and the lawyers' formal organisation has benefited other professional associations as well, notably those of the journalists and university professors, in which government supporters do not always have a decisive weight. In this manner too, it can be said that the Egyptian Bar Association has contributed to political change in the country.

PUBLIC POLICIES TOWARDS BAR ASSOCIATIONS

Because the governments of Egypt, Syria and Morocco would not allow the bar associations to look after their own affairs, their policies have varied depending on the nature of the political system, the alignment of political forces within the bar association and the degree of the governments' domination of the political system. Policies have ranged from direct control of the associations through appointment of all members of its council or board, to tolerance of the existence of a bar association dominated by lawyers who were either independent or belonged to opposition groups. Such policies can be summed up as follows:

1. Bar associations run by councils fully appointed by the government when the government, dissatisfied with an elected council, decided to dissolve it and appoint another to its liking. This method was employed in Egypt by Ismail Sidqi's government in 1934, by Nasser's in December 1954 (Reid, 1981, pp. 159, 166–7) and by Sadat in July 1981. General Hafez Assad in Syria did the same in 1980.

2. The right to appoint some of the members of the bar's council. The mandate government in Syria reserved the right to appoint three members of the council of the Damascus Bar Association (Reid, 1981, p. 198).

3. Approval by the Ministry of Justice or any other administrative organ necessary for candidacy or election to posts in the bar's leading organs. Such a right was also possessed by the mandate authorities in Syria (Reid, 1981, p. 197) and is possessed by the Public Socialist Prosecutor in Egypt at present, although he did not exercise it in the 1985 election of the Egyptian Bar Association.

4. Mandatory membership of the single party or mass organisation before putting forward a candidacy to posts of the leading organs of the association, as in Egypt in the period 1962 to 1975.

5. Suppression of an independent organisation for lawyers and integration into other professional groups, so as to constitute single organisation. Nasser suggested, in the mid-1960s, that there was no need for independent professional associations in a socialist country

PROFESSIONAL ASSOCIATIONS AND NATIONAL INTEGRATION

and that they should be integrated with the trade unions (El Sayed, 1983, p. 90). This is the situation prevailing at present in Libya, in which a complete reorganisation of the profession was introduced within a special branch of the People's Congresses.

6. Pressures on lawyers to elect persons known for their loyalty to the government, or manipulation of election procedures so as to favour government supporters. These methods were used in Egypt under the minority governments of Muhammad Mahmud and Ismail Sidqi (Reid, 1981, pp. 158–64) and were probably used by the Syrian government in 1982.

7. Arrest of leading members of bar associations, was used in the three countries under review during almost all the periods under discussion — notably in Syria in 1980 (arrest of Mesbah al-Rokabi, president of the bar association), Egypt (five leading members of the bar detained in September 1981) and Morocco (arrest in 1983 of a former president of the bar who led the radical faction of a major opposition party).

8. Restrictions on the independence of certain organs within the bar association. According to changes in the law governing Syrian lawyers organisations, the general conference lost the right to fix the agenda of its own meetings (al-Muhamoun, 1981, pp. 370–1).

9. Tolerance of autonomy irrespective of the particular alignment of political forces within an association. This happened in Egypt under both Wafd and minority parties before 1952, and in Syria, particularly in the immediate post-independence period (1945–8) and seems to be the case in Egypt and Morocco at present.

ARAB LAWYERS UNION

Arab bar associations have shown great interest in strengthening professional solidarity across national frontiers. The Damascus Bar Association took the initiative and convened the first conference of Arab Lawyers in 1944 which was attended by 268 lawyers, almost two-fifths of whom were Syrians and the others from Lebanon, Egypt, Iraq, Palestine and the Trans-Jordanian Kingdom. The conference called for the establishment of an Arab Lawyers Union, an event which took place in Cairo twelve years later. The membership now includes 22 bar associations from 15 different countries.

The Arab Lawyers Union aims to work for the good of the Arab world, to realise its national goals, to strengthen ties of friendship and solidarity among Arab lawyers, to guarantee lawyers' liberties

112

in performing their duties and ensure the independence of the judiciary, to enable Arab lawyers to work in any Arab country provided they have a licence from the local bar association, to promote judicial agreements among Arab countries, and introduce common standards for members of the legal professions in Arab countries.

The organisational structure of the union consists of its general conference, open to all registered Arab lawyers, a permanent bureau in which all affiliated associations are members and a general secretariat.

The conference has already met 15 times in eight Arab capitals. The four oldest associations of the Mashreq countries dominated its conferences till the mid-seventies, when the associations of the Maghreb countries started to participate more intensively. The last three conferences were held in Maghreb states. Out of the 35 sessions of the permanent bureau between 1960 and 1980, eight were held in Cairo where the union has its headquarters, seven in Damascus and four in Baghdad. The post of secretary general has been held by two Syrians (1958–61 and 1979–83), a Jordanian (1964–78) and the Sudanese Farouk Abu Issas, who has been in office since 1983,

The union has undertaken the diffusion of a national legal culture. Besides its journal, which began publishing in 1970 and has appeared on a more regular basis since 1983 , it has published more than 30 books including six on legal questions, three on occupied Arab territories, two on Arab unity, and two on petroleum affairs.

Arab lawyers conferences are important gatherings, usually addressed by the head of state of the host country and given much publicity in Arab media. The first conferences were devoted to issues of nation-building and liberation from colonialism and the last conferences to issues of human rights.

The union has intervened with the governments of several Arab countries in defence of persecuted citizens or in solidarity with lawyers or judges organisations which were the object of repressive measures. The conference recently established permanent committees for liberties and for women's affairs, and a centre for legal research and studies.

The last Conference of Arab Lawyers, which was held in Tunis in November 1984, endorsed a report submitted by the secretary general on ways of increasing the effectiveness of the union's work. It called for a a stronger role for the research centre, more union publications and intensified contacts with member associations. The conference focused on the defence of human rights in the Arab world and drew members' attention in this context to the union's international connections, particularly through participation in the activities of United Nations bodies in which the union is recognised as a non-government organisation.

CONCLUSION

Whether or not bar associations in Egypt, Syria and Morocco are considered elite organisations, which they definitely were during a certain period of their history, their members have maintained strong links with their countrymen that have allowed them to lead nationalist movements and become principal actors in national politics.

These bar associations have performed integrative functions at both the national and pan-Arab level. Membership is open to people of all creeds who fulfill the necessary professional conditions, and lawyers of minority groups continue to hold senior posts in numbers exceeding their ratio within the total population.

The organisational structure of the bar association covers almost all parts of their territories. The cohesion of the lawyers professional associations has been little affected by their structure so long as their members subscribed to the common objectives pursued by their general councils.

When bar associations confine their energies to a narrowly defined promotion of their members' professional interests, this is more than welcome by the authorities of their countries. However, being the vanguard of the educated elite, lawyers organisations cannot keep out of the liberation struggle nor the process of nation-building. This has given rise to clashes with governments, a dilemma common to labour unions as well.

Can such confrontations be interpreted as likely to lead to disintegration of the national polity? The answer seems to depend on the outcome of the confrontation. If it ends in the subjugation of the bar association to more restrictive regulations, this further alienates lawyers and their supporters (usually the middle classes) from the authority structures in their country and weakens the legitimacy of the government. This is perhaps the situation prevailing in Syria since the confrontation of 1980. If on the contrary, the conflict results in some sort of accommodation between the government and the bar association, this can increase respect and attachment by the lawyers to the authority structures in their countries and heighten their legitimacy. This may be the case in Egypt since 1983 and in Morocco in the future. In such a situation, conflict has a positive function as an integrative mechanism. However, the mid-1950s to the late 1970s was generally free of such conflict in the countries studied.

Although it might be difficult to pin-point any lasting impact left by lawyers who joined the ruling caucus, bar associations remained an important force for political change in the three countries, as they contributed to the rise of a powerful liberal tradition in their political culture and were principal antagonists in the decisive moments of their countries' history. However, the prominence of the bar association in the recent national politics of the countries under study seems to coincide with a return to more liberal economic policies accompanied by continued restrictions on the activities of organised opposition. Interest groups in general and professional associations in particular, in this situation turn into vehicles for the expression of demands that would otherwise find their way to political parties. It follows from this observation that the bar association tends to focus more on professional questions in a freely functioning multi-party system.

Finally, Arab bar associations are also interested in enhancing pan-Arab solidarity and cooperation. Lawyers organisations of Mashreq countries established the Arab Lawyers Union, the oldest pan-Arab professional association and one of the few which is still functioning. The Arab Lawyers Union has already acted as an integrating mechanism among Arab countries, although the evaluation of its role in this respect goes beyond the limits of this work.

5

Arab Military in Politics: from Revolutionary Plot to Authoritarian State

Elizabeth Picard

> Stoop, Romans, stoop
> And let us bathe our hands in Caesar's blood
> Up to the elbows, and besmear our swords;
> Then walk we forth, even to the market place,
> And, waving our red weapons o'er our heads,
> let's all cry, 'Peace, freedom, and liberty!'
> Julius Caesar, III

Twenty years ago, for someone who studied Arab politics either on the local, the regional, and even more on the national level, armed forces appeared to play a central part in the system and to stand at the core of analysis. A first reason for this importance was to be found in the dramatic tension on the international scene in the Middle East and North Africa at that time: the last episodes of a long struggle for national liberation were being acted out, such as the Suez triple aggression (1956), the Algerian struggle for independence (until 1962) and finally the departure of the British from the Gulf. Moreover, the rising warfare between Israel and its Arab neighbours and the catastrophic Arab defeat of June 1967 contributed to stress the special importance of armed forces in politics. When reading a periodical like *Dirasat Arabiyya* in the late 1960s, one would find in nearly every issue an article dealing with such topics as 'the revolutionary army' or 'the popular war for national liberation' (Allush, 1968; Abu Uras, 1969).

Arab armies appeared even more central for the study of Arab politics on account of their growing concern for civilian affairs and their various involvements in governmental processes. Since the first aborted attempts in Iraq, the Bakr Sudki coup in 1936, (Batatu, 1978, p. 337), Rashid Ali al-Kaylani's revolt in 1941 (Batatu, 1978,

116

pp. 451–61), there had been a long series after World War Two in Syria, soon followed by Egypt's Free Officers in 1952, and by many others.[1] As a result, military intervention in politics had become commonplace in many Arab states, actually with a much higher frequency than in most Third World countries during the 1950s and 1960s.[2]

Even when erratic and bloody, as was the Iraqi 1958 revolution against the Hashemite monarchy, military coups were looked upon rather positively at that time. They were explained by an urgent need for authority in countries where the state was still embryonic and the public services defective. They were praised because of the disciplined and hierarchical character commonly attributed to armed forces. Many observers stressed the assumed penchant of the officers for modern technology and consequently implied they might authoritatively convey their various qualities to their citizens as a whole. Armies were also deemed to operate mainly at a national-state level and consequently to have the capacity to reinforce their country's cohesion. To summarise, armed forces were seen by many a scholar, be he an Arab,[3] a Westerner[4] or even a Soviet,[5] as a strongly modernising instrument, a major agent for change and renouncement of tradition, especially because the new generation of officers who initiated most of these coups came from a more rural and less privileged origin than their elders.

This 'new middle class' with its main tool, the armed forces (Halpern, 1962, p. 278), was considered bound to set up a state-controlled economy and to give an impulse to the process of intensive industrialisation in order to substitute nationally-made products for imported products, a process then considered key to Third World development. The military would also be able to prescribe a new citizenship and to encourage such values as secularism and political participation, in the sense that Lerner praised in those years: Nasser's Egypt, Iraq after Qasim's revolution, Baathist Syria and, soon after, Boumedienne's Algeria were the paramount examples of the successful intervention of the military in Arab politics.

The reaction against such a positive view of the armed forces in the Arab world was not long to come. Both the rather negative performances of the new military regimes and the criticisms which arose regarding the so-called modernising capability of the officers when they became involved in politics decreased appreciation of the army.

The years 1967–70 represented a dramatic turn in Arab history: after the June *naksa*, leaders had to comply with a very new situation and adopt a lower path. They shifted from the nationalist, socialising and triumphant rhetoric which had prevailed for a decade or more, to pragmatism and a withdrawal towards more limited state interests. A new moderate style had to be found, and the model became Saudi Arabia. As for the flamboyant officers who had allegedly prepared the Syrian citadel for the 'decisive battle', and such a charismatic leader as Nasser, not only had they failed to repel the Israeli attack or to make the slightest gains for the Palestinians in whose name they had mobilised and disciplined the masses, but on the domestic scene, they had met serious setbacks in their policy of authoritarian nationalisation, of extensive agrarian reform, of industrialisation, and finally in their stiff control of state apparatus and bureaucracy. Their attempt at imposing social development had fallen short of the masses' expectations as well as scholars' predictions.

Thus, beyond each country's special character and peculiar events, beyond the unbearable burden of a state of continuous warfare against Israel, even beyond the strengthening ties of Arab state economies with the capitalist world system, stands the major issue of the role of the armed forces in the state-building and nation-development processes at work in the Arab world.

During the 1970s, various studies appeared in Western countries, which stressed the internal rivalries and continual feuds among Arab military elites, their communal and clan cleavages and alliances, resulting in a costly and endless series of plots and coups reflecting the mosaic social structure of Middle East Societies.[6] Once freed from the conservative monarchies as in Egypt and Iraq, or having got rid of colonial rule as in Algeria, or of patrician oligarchy as in Syria, the new authoritarian governments led by the military had no other destiny than to become the stage of rivalries between coteries of officers: the Free Officers in Cairo, Qasim's followers in Baghdad, then the Revolutionary Command Council and, in Damascus, the famous and secret Baathist Military Command. In each of these countries, officers would perpetuate their domination over the civilian masses in the very tradition of the Ottoman Empire when *askaris* were opposed to *reayas*, and they would primarily concentrate on internal adjustments and negotiations between factions.[7]

In the meantime, the debate on the nature of the military regimes in the Arab world had lost much of its importance in the Arab Middle East and the Maghreb. The main concerns had become the oil and post-oil era economy along with the cultural heritage, the

118

Table 5.1: Arab armed forces (1966–84)

	Population		Active military duty			Paramilitary			Reserves
	1974	1984	1966	1975	1984	1966	1975	1984	1984
Algeria	16.4	21.7	65,000	63,000	130,000	8,000	10,000	25,000	100,000
Egypt	36.6	47.2	180,000	298,000	460,000	90,000	100,000	140,000	300,000
Iraq	10.7	14.9	80,000	101,000	640,000	10,000	19,000	650,000	75,000
Jordan	2.0	2.6	35,000	37,000	68,000	8,500	22,000	20,000	35,000
Lebanon	3.1	2.7	10,800	15,200	20,300	2,500	5,000	7,500	—
Libya	2.2	3.5	5,000	25,000	73,000	—	23,000	10,000	40,000
Morocco	16.8	23.3	35,000	56,000	144,000	3,000	23,000	30,000	
Saudi Arabia	8.7	10.0	30,000	43,000	51,000	20,000	32,000	45,000	
Sudan	17.4	23.2	12,000	38,600	58,000	3,000	5,000	7,000	
Syria	7.1	10.4	60,000	137,000	362,000	8,000	9,500	38,500	
N. Yemen	6.3	7.5	—	20,900	36,500	—	—	25,000	
S. Yemen	1.6	2.2	10,000	9,500	27,000	—	—	45,000	
Tunisia	5.6	7.0	20,000	24,000	35,000	5,000	10,000	8,500	

Sources: M. Jancwitz, *Military institutions and coercion in the developing nation*, pp. 36–42; International Institute for Strategic Studies, *Military Balance 1984–5*.

turath, and national identity. As for the issue of military participation in politics, it gained a new dimension which requires the adoption of a new perspective when we want to discuss it in the mid-eighties.

TOWARDS THE STABILISATION OF ARAB MILITARY REGIMES

As far as Arab military are concerned, a first important change relates to size: armies have grown considerably beyond the numbers that they used to have when their officers initiated their coups. The Syrian army, for example, counted only a few thousand men at the time of the Palestinian war and of the first coup by Husni Zaim, and thirty to forty thousand when the Baathist revolution took place in 1963. It is ten times larger in the 1980s (see Table 5.1). This growth is not only significant in itself, it is also impressive when related to the country's population and, secondarily, to the part of the state budget allocated to defence expenditures, even without taking the 'special expenditures' into account.

Another change lies in the general professionalisation of the armed forces in the Arab world, and their renunciation of previous formulas such as guerrilla or revolutionary armies. Arab armies carry armaments which are among the most sophisticated in the world, like the Mirage 2000 in Egypt, the Mig-27 (which has not been deployed yet in the USSR's European allied countries) or the SAM-5 in Syria. They also undergo intensive training in order to maximise skills and knowledge and to meet the challenge of this new weaponry. In 1985, conscripts in the Egyptian army were 66 per cent high school graduates, 14 per cent university graduates and 20 per cent vocational school graduates (*New York Times*, 24 February 1986).

In Algeria, the decision to turn the revolutionary army into a professional one was taken by Colonel Boumedienne as early as 1962 (Quandt, 1969, p. 219). His accession to the state presidency in 1965 and his suppression of Zbiri's rebellion in 1967 were further steps in his move to break with the National Liberation tradition in order to rebuild a monolithic National People's Army that he might more closely control. Difficulties in confronting the Moroccan troops during the first Saharan war in October 1963 also played a part in Boumedienne's decision to reinforce the Algerian military capability and to provide it with more weaponry and funds.

120

Similarly the June 1967 defeat led the Baathist leaders of Syria to feel the need to entrust the country's defence to skilled officers rather than to highly politicised ones, and to stress better preparation of troops and equipment.[8] This new trend had no miraculous result but clearly improved performance, as could be noticed from the Algerian stand during the war of October 1973, from the length of the Egyptian–Israeli war of attrition in 1969–70, and from the substantial steps taken by the Syrian army on the Golan Heights during the first days of October 1973. As for Iraq, it seems that the Irani attacks on Fajr 4 (1982) and Fajr 5 (1984) induced its leader Saddam Hussein to reshuffle the military command in order to keep 'political' (Baathist) officers off the battlefield and let competent officers reorganise the army and especially the air force.[9]

This move towards a professionalisation, or a re-professionalisation of Arab armies should not be interpreted as a return of the military 'to the barracks'. After all, General Mustafa Tlas who has been in charge of Syrian defence for nearly 16 years, warned the world at the time of the neo-Baathist radical coup of February 1966 in which he had taken a minor part, 'We will never surrender power to civilians' (Picard, 1979a, p. 58). As far as Arab armies are concerned, there is no evidence of any link between an increase in professional skill and a de-politicisation, as argued by Huntington (1969). The precarious loyalty of the highly professional Jordanian armed forces to the Hashemite throne (Haddad, 1971, pp. 47 ff) seems to have been secured at the price of large exclusions. The Saudis perpetually seek to maintain a balance of power between their paramilitary units and the national military establishment. If they were compelled to enlarge these forces, to train them and to give their command more initiative in order to resist an Iranian threat in the Gulf, they might not only have to face a military lobby in their administration but possibly an eruption of the officer corps onto the political stage (indeed, rumours of various attempted coups have already been heard). In Morocco the army combines high professional standards with a persistent tendency to interfere in politics.

Rather than deal with these three traditional personal authoritarian regimes, however, this chapter deals with four Arab countries that have ranked high in military coups: Syria, Egypt, Iraq and Algeria. In the 1980s their armies play a decisive or even a central part in politics, and their strong involvement in civilian affairs clearly distinguishes them from the three traditional states or from the Tunisian presidential regime,[10] or even from the party

121

dictatorship in the PDRY. Libya might have fitted in this set, although it is rather a charismatic-leadership regime — curiously close to Tunisia — rather than a military one. As for Sudan, the country shows that no military dictatorship is settled for ever.

The counterexample offered by Sudan stresses the impressive longevity of the four regimes under discussion. Syrian Baathists came to power as early as 1963, and General Assad in November 1970. The authoritarian state established by Nasser in 1954 succeeded in institutionalising its succession process, from one *rais* to the next, as did the Algerian regime. Saddam Hussein, who has been a member of the Iraqi Baathist command since 1968, raised himself to supreme power in 1979. Of course, longevity does not necessarily mean stability. Numerous failed coups and rebellions are known to have taken place within the Syrian armed forces since 1970: at the beginning of 1972 and in July 1973, with Jadid supporters; in March 1976 when 30 senior officers tried to stand against their country's intervention in Lebanon; in December of the same year, during the festivities of Aid al-Adha; in January 1982, a large plot involving several Alawaite air force officers was discovered.[11] A similar record can be listed for Egypt in 1972, 1974, 1981 (in Mansurah, a few days before Sadat's assassination) and, to a lesser extent, for Algeria and Iraq. But on the whole, the endurance in power of more stable military groups clearly indicates a change of trend for the Arab military regimes and requires a reflection upon the causes and meaning of such longevity and apparent stabilisation. Among the issues at stake are the nature of the state dominated by armed forces; the role of the military towards the society of the country; and their growing participation in the domestic economy. All three issues raise the question of the role of armed forces in Arab politics, whether it is either conservative or modernising, and the extent of their commitment to the public good. Analysis is based on scarce information and dubious facts: where the military is concerned, even on the political stage, suspicion and secrecy become the rule.

ARMED FORCES AND THE STATE

It is altogether striking and enlightening to discover the variety and the looseness of the terminology used by academics to describe the regimes of the Arab states where the military have successfully engineered a coup and happen to share in the political power: it includes 'military dictatorship', 'army-party rule', 'military oligarchy' and 'civil-military coalition'. Such variety not only relates to situations changing according to place and time; it also reflects a controversial appraisal of the role of armed forces in politics as illustrated by the examples under discussion.

The longevity of the Syrian and Iraqi regimes cannot be ascribed to the peaceful operation of democratic processes. It is founded upon authoritarian, if not dictatorial, power. Competitive processes which characterise open societies are excluded in such a way that these regimes must be described as 'authoritarian personal' regimes supported by armed forces (Picard, 1979, p. 52). The first national authority in revolutionary Syria was a National Revolutionary Council Command which appointed itself in the days following the 1963 Baathist coup. Its 15 members were officers only until July, when Baathist civilians replaced the Nasserist military members who had been removed. Its chairman was of course military General Amin al-Hafez, and officers never accounted for less than 20 per cent of its total membership. As for the governments since 1963, the military steadily held 15 to 25 per cent of the ministerial portfolios (Van Dam, 1979).

Since the revolution, sensitive ministries like Defence and the Interior have been their constant prerogative, but they have often taken charge of the Ministry of Agriculture at times when rural structures were undergoing fundamental change, and sometimes even the prime ministry. It is more difficult to appraise the part they played within the Baath Party, which is nevertheless essential. During some periods, senior officers have accounted for a third of the members in the National (pan-Arab) Command and in the Regional (Syrian) Command. Even after the decision was made at the Kisweh military meeting of April 1965 to restrain the responsibilities of the esoteric and powerful Baathist Military Command and to limit the participation of the military in the RC to three of its eleven members, those three still managed to secure their hegemony through civilian alliances (Van Dam, 1979, pp. 31–51).

The influence of the military also spread down the party to its lower levels from the very first months of the revolution, with nine new military branches were authoritatively created by the BMC. The army's overwhelming influence is summarised by the multiple civilian functions of General Hafez al-Assad, its commander-in-chief, who is president of the State, and secretary-general of the Baath and of the National Progressive Front since 1971.

Through a formal reading of Iraqi institutions, the 'civilian' character of the political regime in Baghdad is frequently contrasted with the hegemony of the military in Damascus. However, such a contrast fades before the high state positions occupied by army officers and the importance given by Saddam Hussein to the apparatus of repression and coercion. Five officers, and no civilians, sat in the first Revolutionary Council Command, the first executive body after the 1968 Baathist coup. Until 1973, the military held all the key state positions: the presidency of the RCC, the prime ministry, the ministries of Defence and the Interior, the secretary-generalship of the Baath, and naturally the army command. After-wards, the growing influence of the civilian wing of the party around Saddam Hussein — who was appointed general in 1976 — cannot conceal the strong reliance of the regime on both the regular and the 'popular' army (*jaysh ash-shab*) (*al-Thawra*, 6 January 1976; *New York Times*, 11 January 1981), a tendency which has been accen-tuated since the war with Iran. As a whole, the move observed in Baghdad as well as in Damascus in the mid-seventies to transfer key positions in the Baath Party and the government from officers to civilian technocrats, in an attempt to set the conditions for a successful economic liberalisation (Picard, 1979b, p. 665; Spring-borg, 1986, p. 33) has been slowed down in both countries: in Iraq, because of its deepening involvement in the Gulf war, and in Syria after the intervention in Lebanon and the extension of an internal state of warfare. This stresses opportunely the fact that a major cause for Arab military intervention in politics and the main reason for the stay of the armed forces in power are to be found in an external threat to state security.

Has a similar secularisation of political power occurred in Egypt and Algeria? The five years of the Nasserist revolution and the period of Ben Bella's rule were marked by harsh competition between the military and other rival groups: revolutionaries, intellectuals and technocrats (Abdel Malek, 1962, pp. 178–9; Quandt, 1969, p. 110). The historical importance of armed struggle in Algeria's accession to independence had conferred a major political role on officers, either from the guerrilla or professional armies. At the time Boumedienne replaced Ben Bella with the support of a reshaped army, the Revolutionary Council, then the upper executive body in the country, counted as many as 22 officers from both armies out of 26 members. Another institution, the National Liberation Front, the only official party, barely had any formal existence, in spite of the resolutions of the Soummam Congress in 1956 and of the text of the National Charter (1963),

124

both guaranteeing its pre-eminence over the military. But the move had already begun and the homogeneous coalition of professional military men and technically competent administrators under Boumedienne (Zartman, 1970, p. 342) turned year after year into a more technocratic group, while the FLN's role expanded slowly. From the mid-seventies on, the military command has been mainly devoted to the custody of the state and of its legitimacy. During the FLN Congress of January 1979 following Boumedienne's death, it demonstrated its influence in the designation of Chadli Benjedid as his successor. The continuing importance of the National People's Army was well illustrated by the accession of the highest ranking officer to the state presidency, and then to the office of secretary-general of the FLN (Entelis, 1982, pp. 108–9). But this primarily conservative mission no longer implies that the military outnumber the civilians in key government positions nor that they have authority to initiate Algerian state social and economic policy.

As the power of decision lies mainly in the executive, and because the command of the executive is a necessary condition for military control of society, the proportion of the military inside the executive can give an indication of its role and importance in the state. The figures available for Egypt indicate that army officers occupied 20.6 per cent of the ministerial portfolios under Nasser, with a peak of 51 percent in 1961. This percentage fell to 7.5 under Sadat (Cooper, 1982, p. 209) and after 1971, the military had charge of only certain ministries: Transport and Communications, War, and War Production. The demilitarisation process took place in two stages. First, after the Yemen debacle in 1963 and the June 1967 disaster, Nasser lost confidence in his army and tried to rely more upon the progressive forces and the Arab Socialist Union, the party in which the military were not eligible for membership, unlike in the Syrian and Iraqui Baath. Later, the election of a new assembly in October 1971 and the publication of the October Working Paper in April 1974 clearly showed Sadat's intention to demilitarise the polity and institutionalise a civilian power, a decision strongly supported by most segments of the political class. At the same time, when the Egyptian army recovered its lost honour by nearly securing a victory on the Canal, it was eliminated from central points of political influence on the national as well as at the local levels, in an apparent agreement to send the military permanently back to the barracks (Waterbury, 1983, p. 376; Cooper, 1982, p. 223). However, the demilitarisation process should not be overemphasised; a clear indication of its limits was given by the nomination of Hosni

Mubarak, the commander-in-chief of the army, to the position of vice-president of the state, a sensitive position for communications between the government and the armed forces, and by his accession to the state presidency after Sadat's assassination. Another indication is the growing popularity of the Defence Minister, General Abu Ghazala, a potential rival for an executive power weakened by Egypt's hopeless predicament.

Such attempts at demilitarising the political system in Egypt and in other Arab states are meant to initiate stable civilian patterns of government and to codify the revolutionary process in order to balance the country's power centres successfully. In various public addresses as early as 1966, Nasser argued about the necessity of codifiction (*taqnin*). Actually he, and Sadat after him, developed an important legislative and institutional apparatus both at the local and the national levels, thus contributing to the renewal of political institutions such as the legislature, various political organisations and parties, and local government. The Algerian move on the same path was impressive after Colonel Boumedienne had strengthened his hold of the state: in 1976 he ordered referenda on the National Charter and the new Constitution, and in the following year, presidential and legislative elections. Afterwards, a party congress of the FLN was convened in January 1979, while the local and regional assemblies (*assemblées populaires communales* and *assemblées populaires de Wilaya*) were revived (Entelis, 1982, p. 108). As in the succession from Sadat to Mubarak in Egypt, the transmission of presidency from Boumedienne to Benjedid took place through an institutional process in an apparently cohesive and stable mood. This confirmed at first sight the thesis of the capability of a military regime to bring about a 'state of institutions', as Sadat's October document put it: it was up to the holders of power openly to determine its rules and procedures. There were to be clearly designated mechanisms for making decisions in such a way that the danger of arbitrary and coercive interference would be eliminated.

But once they have attained power and set themselves up as arbitrators, how qualified are the Arab military to work out such a project? The political processes at work in each of these four cases after new institutions have been prescribed lead to questions about the meaning of value of such institutionalisation. In Egypt, for example, the new government chosen by Anwar al-Sadat following the legislative elections of 1976 took so little account of electoral results that it was as if they had no meaning for the president.

126

Indeed, do elections, 'platforms' (*manabir*) and pluripartism really mean much for a population whose participation in the electoral process approximates 20 per cent and whose lives, for the most part are lived outside the political (and economic) system? Given such weakness and mediocre pervasiveness of the institutions, the likelihood of military intervention, or of the strengthening of military rule can never be dismissed, should the social situation or the regional balance further deteriorate. The mutiny by police conscripts in February 1986 was overcome through massive action by the regular army. Order was restored but no negotiation followed, nor any political debate on the real issues at stake: the extreme poverty and the crisis of identity of the Egyptian people.

In Algeria, structural and especially demographic problems are not as serious. The country did not undergo mob riots in January 1984 as its Tunisian and Moroccan neighbours did. It offers a rather successful image of transition to a civilian and liberal regime. However, the army remains strongly influential in the civilian decision-making bodies, in the government and even in the party. It has a tendency to react authoritatively to political or social contests and to rely on repression rather than on dialogue, as the events of 1985 proved, when a group of lawyers who had established an association for the defence of human rights were severely sentenced.

Another example of the limited effect of an imposed institutionalisation is the Iraqi National Assembly, elected in June 1980 after ten years of delayed promises by the regime. The method of selecting the candidates, described as a process of 'controlled democracy' (Baram, 1981), gave the new parliament a merely symbolic function. But the extreme example of contradiction between institutionalisation and reinforcement of coercion is Syria. The country has experienced tremendous institutional development since November 1970: not only was a new Constitution promulgated in 1973, but people's representation was set at the national level (*majlis ash-shab*) as well as the regional (*majlis al-muhafaza*) and local (*majlis an-nahiyya*) levels. Ever since, these assemblies have been duly renewed through elections, while throughout the 1970s and 1980s the Baath party and the Worker's Union (*Ittihad al-ummal*) have held regular congresses. Competition for nominations as delegates has become more intense, and the delegates of their congresses more often reviewed in the national press than under the previous secretive neo-Baath regime (1966–70). The government has been enlarged to about 30 ministers, nearly half of whom come from 'independent' back-grounds and have no official connection with the political leadership in the Progressive National Front. The judiciary and administration have been considerably expanded, thus increasing the number of institutions to which an individual might refer in order to escape arbitrary treatment. Judged purely by this record, the military regime of General Assad seems to have been successful in improving political communication and participation, and in promoting a stronger relationship between the citizens and the state.

What does such a 'return to democracy' initiated by the Syrian authorities really mean? The Syrians have gone to the polls nearly once a year, but the turnout in the elections has decreased as regularly as the government's success has grown (Picard, 1978). Notwithstanding the fact that many of these institutions have been created purely for international purposes,[12] they can only result in bureaucratic overdevelopment and ideological indoctrination as long as they are not accompanied by a reduction in state coercion. In Syria, emergency laws promulgated in 1963, at the beginning of the revolution, have never been lifted. Despite presidential promises, arbitrary arrests, kidnappings and imprisonments are frequent and have even increased since 1976, when personalities of the higher military command became the target of attacks by opponents. A limiting clause concerning the Progressive National Front restricts political activities in the army and the university to the Baath party only. Another clause in the 1973 Constitution assigns more than half of the 195 parliament seats to 'representatives of the workers and peasants', which means to appointed militants of the popular organisations affiliated with the Baath. Even more, political practices frequently diverge from the law, when they do not contradict it altogether: elections are engineered by state agents in order to eliminate disturbing candidates and secure favourable results. The press of the progressive parties allied to the Baath in the PNF is freely printed but not displayed in public newsrooms; as for the opposition press, it is totally forbidden. Even the semi-official Baathist periodicals are censored (*Le Monde*, 20 April 1979). Finally, in an ambitious attempt at destructuring the civilian society, the military regime dissolved the main professional unions, including those of the physicians, engineers and lawyers, for having criticised the repression of Islamic militants and the lack of democratic liberty, and replaced them authoritatively in early 1980.

Of special significance is the amazing growth of paramilitary forces in the Arab military regimes in their stabilising and institutionalising phase since 1970 (Janowitz 1977, ch. 5, p. 17). These

128

paramilitary units were created to reinforce and combat together with the regular forces. In Iraq, the *Jaysh ash-shab* is linked to the Baath party and recruits larger numbers than the army, around 600,000 men. It was long dedicated to internal security and 'peace-making' tasks, especially in the Kursish areas, until the war with Iran, when it was sent to the battlefront. In Egypt, the Ministry of the Interior heads some 300,000 members of security forces. Algerian gendarmes number 25,000. The strategy of multiplying and diversifying armed forces has even been adopted by other Arab authoritarian regimes such as Saudi Arabia whose White Guard numbers 45,000 men, nearly as many as the regular army.

In Syria, the regimes' militias underwent tremendous growth owing to the development of political sectarianism and to the seizure of power by Hafez al-Assad's fellow Alawite officers. His brother Rifat's militia, the Defence Companies *(saraya l-difa)* mobilised as many as 50,000 men until February 1984[13] and included armoured companies, a mechanised brigade equipped with T72s, missiles and paratroop units. It had serious rivals such as General Ali Hydar's 15,000-strong 'Special Forces' or Adnan Makhluf's Presidential Guard. Each established its own intelligence and acted independently. At times, militias would operate out of the country's boundaries, in Lebanon, but it is rather the regular army which intervenes on the domestic stage, along with the police and the militias, hence a long list of military operations in Syria's streets, from the shelling of the great mosque in Hama in January 1965 to the devastation of that town in February 1982.

Reflecting upon the longevity of some Arab military regimes, one should thus consider the huge technological progress of their armies and wonder whether the 'stability' which has been remarked on since 1970 does not owe much to an increasingly pervasive state machinery and especially state police: today, the seizure of the radio building and the broadcasting of a *communiqué no. 1* are no longer enough to ensure the success of a revolutionary coup. A bloody battle must be fought, whose outcome is far from certain, as shown in the fighting between rival militias in Damascus from February to May 1984, or the uprising of the Security Forces in Egypt in February 1986.

THE MILITARY AND SOCIETY

In view of such circumstances, the hypothesis that Arab armies are especially effective at carrying out the autonomisation of the state appears highly disputable. So, too, is the description of their intervention as 'praetorianism', under the pretext that the army has a central role that leaves it free to induce constitutional changes and to take governmental decisions (Perlmutter, 1974, p. 4) and that this is consistent with the Ottoman tradition and necessary for industrialisation and modernisation (Perlmutter, 1974, pp. 27, 52). If the military succeeds in controlling society and in exercising power over it, this power should not be mistaken for the true authority of the state (Haddad, 1971, p. 33). In the long run, military rulers will have to seek popular consent, they will need to secure their legitimacy and to enlarge their social basis, lest they be regarded not as state rulers but as a mere clique, a gang (*jamaa*) as Michaud (1983) once described the military regime of Syria. A full understanding of the political role of the military in the Arab world thus requires an examination of the attitude of the military towards society as a whole, and of the special linkages between the officers in power and certain parts of society.

In order to gain the legitimacy which will allow it to implement its authoritarian decisions and to feel free from the hegemony of any social group, the military aims at representing the nation as a whole, on the ideological as well as on the social stage. It does not rely so much on the so-called historical and highly controversial legitimacy of the kind granted by the *hadith* tradition: 'obey those who wield power'. It rather claims a revolutionary legitimacy, gained through political struggle or, in the case of Algeria, through armed struggle. In many circumstances, this legitimacy proves strong enough to resist the erosion caused by the regime's mediocre achievements on the regional as well as the domestic level, and to survive internal feuds between rival factions. It has even benefited from the involvement of the military in the defence of its country, as all four states have had to fight on their borders since the beginning of the revolutionary period: Egypt and Syria against Israel, Algeria with Morocco, and Iraq in the Gulf war. Another way of strengthening its legitimacy is by acting as an authentic instrument for organising socio-economic goals, such as implementing agrarian reform, participating in public works, educational campaigns or emergency rescue (Leca and Vatin, 1975, pp. 398f).

The legitimising process of the military regime and the conveyance of patriotic values to the nation as a whole, operated through military service (Devlin, 1982, p. 237). Universal conscription was set up in Iraq, in Syria and in Algeria shortly after the revolution, and both Iraq and Syria gradually renounced the *badal*, a system which allowed fortunate conscripts the option of paying in order to escape their military duty. In Algeria, the conscripts serve for six months only (Table 5.2). In Syria, because of the permanent tensions both on Israel's eastern front, and in Iraq, since the beginning of the war with Iran, they are kept in the army for several years. Military service in Egypt also lasts several years but conscription has been kept selective because of the rapid growth of the population and the low educational level among the rural masses. Both the army and a teaching career in the government schools offer a way out from impoverished origins. It is well known, that in Iraq as well as in Syria, many of the revolutionary officers were recruited among youngsters from modest origins, the 'village generation' (Van Dusen, 1971). In Algeria,

> The ANP has a popular base, drawing largely from the lower social strata: 'sons of *fellahin* and sons of workers'. But social origins are less important for the ANP than social change; the army is composed not of workers and *fellahin* but of their sons (Zartman, 1970, p. 246).

But beyond the ability of the army to provide individual educational opportunities and upwards mobility lies the issue of the extent to which it can mould individuals into a common process of political socialisation. In other words, does the country depend on mobilisation for conscripts to develop their identities as citizens and soliders? Does conscription offer a national tradition, common values, and a set of relations between the state and the citizen? In

Table 5.2: Arab states and military service

Country	Conscription	Length of service
Algeria	General	6 months
Egypt	Selective	3 years
Iraq	General	2 years
Jordan	Selective	2 years
Lebanon	General (never effective)	
Libya	Selective	
Morocco	General	18 months
Saudi Arabia	Selective	
Sudan	General	not implemented
Syria	General	30 months
N Yemen		
S Yemen		2 years
Tunisia	Selective	12 months

the states of the Arab world, such common national values are still very weak. National solidarity competes with and overlaps clan, communal and religious solidarities, thus obstructing army attempts at conveying a national ideology and a unified political culture. And, on the other hand, the persistence of authoritarianism and military regimes is in itself an impediment to the development of any kind of political culture (Khuri and Obermayer, 1974, p. 55).

Even Arab nationalist ideology, as put forward by the military, is burdened with flaws. While Baathist regimes have put themselves forward as propagators of pan-Arabism, especially through their stance on the liberation of Palestine, their ambitions emerge purely on the nation-state level, as mere Iraqi or Syrian ambitions (Hurewitz, 1969, p. 423). They dedicate themselves to the defence of their state and the recovery of its lost territories, and they mobilise the population within the state borders. Hence the limited objectives of the October 1973 war, the Syrian attempts at recovering the Golan, or the launching of a war against Iran by Saddam Hussein. An even more conclusive demonstration was offered by the deterioration of the relations between Damascus and Baghdad in 1974–5, and again after the brief episode of the failed merger of the two Baathist states from October 1978 to July 1979. Not only had both countries rival economic interests as far as oil and commercial transit or the division of the Euphrates' waters was concerned, the process of unifying the two branches of the Baath party and the armed forces in both regions (*aqtar*) of the Arab nation also presented a threat for the leadership in each country: members of the party national command in Damascus would have had to yield to Michel Aflaq's historical leadership in Baghdad, while the militias should have surrendered to a unified regular army authority. Such a process was very soon seen as a menace to the hegemony of the military in each country; it had to be avoided, and a plot was uncovered in Baghdad, which put an end to the negotiations (Picard, 1979c, p. 9).

Have Egypt and Algeria been more successful in using the army as the backbone of their national cohesion? Have they been able to escape the contradiction between their Arab identity and their nation-state identity, and find their way through the contradictions? The choices of Anwar Sadat when initiating the October war, or opening peace negotiations with Israel in 1977 appear to indicate the greater homogeneity of Egyptian society and cohesion in the country's army, that it is capable of representing all the nation's strata, both urban or rural on a national level (Vatikiotis, 1961, pp. 44–68).

However, the failed coup of October 1972, the attempt in April 1974 by Takfir wal Hijra involving cadets at the military academy, and Sadat's assassination in October 1981 at the very moment he was presiding over the annual military parade in celebration of the October war, challenge the indications of reinforced cohesion by disclosing the existence of an Islamic contest in the midst of the Egyptian armed forces.

In Algeria, Colonel Boumedienne's policy (Criscuolo, 1975, p. 206), resumed after his death by Colonel Benjedid, clearly aimed at reinforcing the army's cohesion and capability in order to turn it into a modern professional force, but also to use it as the central apparatus in the state-building process and the protection of the state. The integrity and homogeneity of the Algerian state are less endangered by border conflict with Morocco or by short-lived uprisings in Berber areas, than by the family and regional cleavages which split the political and economic leadership into rival groups, such as the Oujda group which dominated the state under Boumedienne. Of course, Algerian society should not be compared to the mosaic diversity of the Arab East, but its social cleavages threaten the country's stability whenever they permeate the armed forces, and they are carried by military officers into administration, party and government, or into private business. Civilian conflicts then turn into open armed interventions: although little is known about the abortive coup against Chadli Benjedid in June 1979, in which senior officers might have been involved along with top civil servants, it is an indication of the extension of the cleavages and rivalries within civilian society into the military command.

It is interesting to compare Algeria with Iraq as regards the position of armed forces towards national identity and the state-building process, as well as their links with the various segments of society. Although Iraqi armed forces became involved in civilian tasks and responsibilities, they still acted primarily as the defender of the land and state legitimacy. Confronted with an external threat such as the Iranian invasion of national territory during the Gulf war, the Iraqi army succeeded in maintaining cohesion, even if it lacked the mystical impetus of the Iranian *basijin* and *mujahidin*. Desertions and cases of insubordination did occur, especially among the Kurds, but on the whole, no major dissension appeared either among the conscripts or at the command level, between Sunni Arabs (20 per cent of the country's population) and the Shia (55 per cent). One might eventually conclude that where there is a threat to the national entity, and in spite of the artificial character of the 'colonial' borders, the army does play an efficient part as the catalyst of a superior common interest. Such a conclusion might even apply to the Syrian army, however surprising it may seem at first sight. In June 1982, confronted with the invasion of Lebanon by Israel, its Sunni as well as its Alawite brigades fought in the Shouf mountains and the Beqaa valley without restriction. While the battle was soon lost by the Syrian air force and on the diplomatic scene (Schiff, 1984), armoured and infantry units kept on resisting valiantly for what was unanimously regarded in Syria as a national (Syrian) issue.

However, such cohesion in the face of an external threat does not prevent the Iraqi armed forces from being caught in communal conflict and civilian ideological dissent. Recent Iraqi history offers a long record of struggle, eliminations and changes of leadership inside the country's military and political command: in 1970, General Hardan al-Takriti was mysteriously murdered after he opposed his country's intervention on the Palestinian side in Jordan. In 1973, the army was shaken by the Nadhim Kazar plot and rebellion (Batatu, 1978, pp. 1093, 1094). One year before Saddam Hussein ascended to power in July 1979, 39 officers were executed in Baghdad on the charge of having reorganised Communist cells in the army. On the whole, the tight control of the Baath, the army and the security services by a small group originating from the Sunni area of Takrit is evidence that the military dictatorship is permeated by civilian cleavages; power imbalance does not come so much from an uneven regional distribution of key positions as from the impact of clan and family ties on the economy of the state and eventually the nature of its society.

Of all examples of an hegemonic army being drawn into the process of civilianisation, the most obvious is the Syrian case. Before independence, troops and officers were mainly recruited along communal lines. The French mandate purposely kept Sunni Arabs out on account of their nationalistic tendencies, although they were more than three-quarters of the population, and chose to rely on ethnic and religious minorities. After independence, the army was opened to all, but the new generation of officers were attracted to the political parties that were competing at the time for the leadership of the young republic: the Baath, the Communists, the Muslim Brotherhood and the Syrian Social Nationalists.[15] The incorporation of civilian political conflicts within the army and the failure to organise it efficiently resulted in 1949 in the shift of controlling power in the state from the civilian leaders to the military. But once Baathist officers had triumphed over their rivals from other

134

progressive parties in July 1963, they were not a homogeneous and cohesive group, even though they unanimously called for socialism and Arab unity. Their cleavages and internal struggles reflected Syria's regional and communal diversity. Kurds and Christians were almost completely barred from military and political command after the United Arab Republic (1958–61). In 1964–5 came the turn of the Sunnis, then the Druse and the Ismailis in 1967. The confrontation and successive elimination process between military 'parties' reached down to clan and family divisions within the Alawite community itself, with the elimination of Jadid in 1970, Umran's assassination in 1973, and finally the battle among the brothers, cousins and relatives of Hafez al-Assad and all his lieutenants, in the Rawdha district of Damascus in February 1984 (Batatu, 1981, pp. 331 ff).

An army which devotes so much of its strength and activity to internal feuds is no more able than the armies of more homogeneous countries such as Egypt and Algeria, to fulfill its task of guarding the state and standing for national unity. Syrian officers had entered politics in the 1950s and 1960s through personal and conspiratorial networks, relying mainly on secrecy and selective coercive control. Once in power, they could not escape involvement in civilian linkages; they enlarged their networks into factions and were drawn into bargaining and negotiations in order to protect their access to state, material and symbolic benefits. They were compelled to rely heavily on paramilitary units in order to control those sectors of the civilian population that were not incorporated in their political bargaining (Janowitz, 1977, pp. 45–6). Thus, in spite of the institutionalisation mentioned earlier, every part of Syrian public life fell under direct control of the military who became the brokers (*wasta*) between the state and the people for any kind of public transaction, thus eradicating the civilian society they had wanted to shape.[16]

While in Egypt and Algeria the army stands to preserve the unity of the state and contributes to the construction of national identity through governmental and political institutions, as long as it is able to silence its internal divisions, in plural societies such as Syria, and Iraq to a lesser degree, the hegemony of armed forces over the polity is far from having a strengthening and unifying effect or promoting democratic institutions. It freezes political debate and turns it into a struggle between factions, which can be resolved only by coercive means. It has created an immobile and oppressive society.

MILITARY REGIMES AND ECONOMIC DEVELOPMENT

Among the central objectives of the Arab military regimes and among their primary justifications for using coercion over their people, was the need to accelerate economic development. In a move inspired by Atatürk's experience in Turkey, they intended to initiate an intensive industrialisation process through public enterprises in order to eliminate the old elites — especially the urban industrial bourgeoisie that had presided over the Egyptian economy for several decades, that had grown rapidly in Syria during the 1950s, and that was present even in Iraq. The state was to become the main and nearly exclusive agent of economic decisions, through a series of seizures and nationalisations which would give it the necessary legal and economic means.

As far as the military is concerned, such a project involves two corollaries. First, the capacity of armed forces to bring about national development through their internal modernisation process and through cooperation with civilian elites. Secondly, their ability, once they become an hegemonic group in power, to free themselves from their social origins and thereby to secure the autonomy of the state.

A dramatic statement must be made from the start: the military in the Arab world are budget devourers. Since the extension of the war with Iran, Iraqi military expenditures as a proportion of GDP are particularly high (Table 5.3), and Syria is close behind. The contrast made earlier between these two military regimes on one hand, and bureaucratic regimes controlled by the military on the other, shows up here again: Egypt devotes 'only' 8.56 per cent of GDP to national defence; Algeria has an even lower level. The

Table 5.3: Gross Domestic Product and military budgets (1982) ($m)

		GDP	Defence	%
1	Iraq	34,600	8,043	23.25
2	Syria	18,467	3,210	17.38
3	Saudi Arabia	153,099	21,952	14.33
4	Jordan	3,831	542	14.21
5	Morocco	14,697	1,328	9.03
6	Egypt	29,141	2,495	8.56
7	Libya	28,520	709	2.50
8	Algeria	43,584	847	1.94

Source: *Military Balance (1984–5)*, International Institute for Strategic Studies, London.

question is how massive expenditure on arms and equipment dedicated to destruction can have a constructive effect on these countries economies. Answering it requires consideration of alternative uses to which their financial resources might have been put. But Egypt since its 1979 peace treaty with Israel has not altered its public investment policy or its economic priorities. It is also often suggested that the army serves as a training ground for technical and administrative skills. Thousands of young men either belonging to the professional army or recruited as conscripts come into contact with modern technology and management: a basic skill such as driving is taught to hundreds of young Iraqis every year in the barracks. In Damascus, the army weekly *Jaysh ash-shab* offers a regular review of the different kinds of technical and professional education provided by the army for the conscripts.

The counter-argument is that much weaponry is relatively simple to import and to operate (Murad, 1966, p. 46), and that military training does not really offer the type of education relevant afterwards in industrial management or agricultural machinery. Furthermore, the rigid military ethics and authoritarian pattern of decision-making lessen the soldier's ability to adapt to his own society. In the field of civilian technology and management, choices that have to comply to complex social requirements benefit from a relaxation of the military's political influence and supervision (Owen, 1983, p. 144). The low level of military educational efficiency is also shown by the fact that so many young Egyptians and Algerians are unemployed after leaving the army, while young Syrians have to emigrate to the Gulf to be able to acquire useful knowledge and skills.

It must also be remembered that in these four states, as in most countries of the Arab world, the army is a different world with its security of employment, standardised patterns of work, housing and other economic advantages. In Syria, the military earns four to ten times more than its civilian counterparts. Officers' privileged positions do not predispose them to innovation nor to social, political or even technological change, but rather to caste consciousness and conservatism. Another handicap is the lasting domination of the 'political' officers over the 'professionals', since civilian divisions have permeated the armed forces. It led to disastrous consequences on the Iraqi army's performance during air battles in the Gulf war. It still burdens the Syrian military where any officer, especially the Sunnis or Christians, with serious technological and professional ability has to be supervised by another, closely related to the regime.

Could officers become part of a dynamic development process in their country's economy, while insisting on stability and hierarchy, and closely controlling their own corps? First, their number and influence in the civilian field should not be overestimated: although figures are not available for all four countries, it appears that officers have not filled many technical and administrative posts and constitute only a small part of those elites termed 'strategic' in the development process. In Egypt, for instance, the importance of the military in the managerial elite was never very great, and soon declined (Ayubi, 1980, p. 248; Owen, 1983). At the height of military influence in the Egyptian economy and polity, around 1967, officers accounted for 2 per cent of the 18,000 top-level civil servants. Syria's state and bureaucratic elites further clarify the role of the military: when they enter civilian positions, they taken charge of political rather than technical functions; they command, decide, organise, and even maintain order. Most gravitate to the Ministry of the Interior, where they can dedicate themselves to protecting the state and regime, with special emphasis on order and hierarchical transmission of 'revolutionary' values. The dichotomy suggested by the title of Entelis's study of the Algerian elite, *Technocratic rule, military power*, points to military who do not directly contribute to the good of the economy. Although officers enter the civil administration, government, national enterprises and private companies with their managerial skill and professionalism their influence generally results in the perpetuation of a meddlesome, complex and often inefficient bureaucracy.

Because of the growth of their armies and the diversification of their requirements, the military has recently turned to economic procurement, entering as a major partner in the industrial world, international and domestic services, and commercial networks. The growth and size of the Egyptian army's stake in the country's industrial and building enterprises has become a frequent subject of criticism in the national press. Officers coordinate government departments, run industries and public works enterprises and even administer land reform. No survey has been published so far on the Egyptian army's global economic participation, but the intensive development of its arms industries in vast plants at Saqr and Abou Zabal is an indication of the Egyptian military's increasingly diverse economic production.

The Algerian military does not appear on the frontlines of business, possibly because large state public enterprises like the Sonatrach and its offshoots are difficult to challenge, and the private sector is still small and insecure. However, the army's own industries and suppliers are extensive and productive, under military management. In Iraq and in Syria also, the armies have become first rank entrepreneurs. They started out by producing military supplies like equipment and uniforms, moved into manufacturing that required special skills and imported technology, and soon enlarged their range of activities to produce consumer goods such as construction equipment and aluminium window frames, and even bottled mineral water. From there, they have diversified into public works, road and house building, poultry farming, and even the cultivation of thousands of acres of newly irrigated state land along the Euphrates. Army officers control economic empires and employ tens of thousands of civilians, whose pay is better than in either the civil public sector, or the private sector. They share successfully in their country's economic growth, especially by running its most technologically advanced and economically productive units.

When the time comes to evaluate the impact of the military-managed sector, its effect on other enterprises appears questionable despite the economic success. Not only do military enterprises transgress the law by escaping the social and monetary constraints which burden other companies, they often fail to respect employment laws or observe either import restrictions or the financial rules of the currency market. The most famous example in Syria is the *Sharikat al-Iskan al-Askari* (Milihouse), a contracting firm headed by Major Bahloi (Jarry, 1984), which in five years has become the country's leading enterprise. In Iraq, the equivalent is the Saddam Military Establishment for Prefabricated Housing. But alongside the fact that Milihouse manufactures quality products, delivers them on time and earns large profits, the distorting effect of its methods on the social and financial balance of the country cannot be easily dismissed.

The revolutionary military which seized control of the state has tended to base its management on political rather than economic logic. The Egyptian 1962 National Charter and after it the Baathist 'Theoretical Perspectives'[17] of October 1963 proclaimed 'the abolition of the feudal system' to be the first revolutionary priority. The new leaders would do away with the old, exploitative bourgeoisie. Secondly, and only secondly, came the need to set up import-substitution industrialisation (ISI) under state control. An investigation into the decision-making process regarding important moves such as nationalisation of trading and industrial companies in Syria or Algeria often reveals that the decision was made as a reaction to regional or domestic events, like Nasser's challenge to the Syrian

Baath, or a feud between Algiers and Paris, or even internal competition within the group of military leaders. Although dealing with economic matters, the officers respond mainly to ideological necessities because this aim is to impose a new system. Besides this, they pursue personal, family and clan interests and often impose strategies likely to benefit themselves when dealing with public affairs.

Many state-owned industrial plants in Syria are less dependent on local or national requirements than on the amount of expenditure at stake, and above all, on the identity of the partners involved. Rather than developing the state sector, the role of the 'strategic elites' and especially of the officers who hold civilian functions, lies in allocating the benefits of government operations. Their purpose is to enlist politically devoted clients from the state bureaucracy, who benefit from the patronage process in which goods and services are traded for loyalty and obedience. The Syrian press[18] regularly denounces these petty or powerful clients as 'parasite' (*tufayliyya*) bourgeoisie.

Patronage was a feature in Syrian politics long before the revolution but it became more extensive under the military regime, especially under *infitah*, the economic liberalisation. Theft of public property, bribery of civil servants, graft and nepotism have become commonplace. These informal practices are today an integral part of a new political order, in which authority, or rather power, is the main means of acquiring material and symbolic goods. The supremacy of strength and coercion at state level, which is the prerogative of the military, has led to the embezzlement of the revolutionary Baathist programme: the party slogan *Wahda*, *Ishtirakiyya*, *Huriyya* (Unity, Socialism, Liberty) has been turned by popular derision into *Wahda*, *Ishtirakiyya*, *Haramiyya* (Unity, Socialism, Banditry).

Being in charge of the external security of the state, the Syrian army has extended its control to the country's foreign trade and imposed a tax on all imported goods and equipment. Not satisfied with regular commerce, the military heads a vast smuggling network across the Lebanese and Turkish borders,[19] which provides an extensive income and has become an essential part of the country's economy: to suppress it would hurt production and lead to a dangerous shortage of consumer goods. In July 1984, General Assad officially condemned these practices and ordered the restoration of regular control over trade at the Lebanese border and the arrest of a dozen junior officers, along with a general, accused of illicit trafficking in construction material. His purpose was not so much to forbid the trade as to check members of the military caste competing for hegemonic position. Finally, while a high-ranking officer, General Ibrahim Salameh, was arrested in Damascus (*Le Monde*, 14 August 1984), and an ex-minister of the Interior was indicted in Egypt in May 1983 during a similar anti-corruption campaign,[20] the economic basis of the military power remained untouched.

Illegal profit and scandalous abuses by the military (and technocratic) elites have not been as important in Algeria as they have been in Syria. Does this difference allow us to make a distinction between 'production states' and 'allocation states' when the influence of the military on their country's economy is at stake? Nothing is more questionable: Iraq, which turned into an archetypal *rentier* state in the middle of the seventies never underwent the distortions and prevarication known in the Syrian system although the costs of industrial production are generally 50 per cent higher than in the West (Stork, 1979, p. 145). A more convincing explanation lies in the balance between the technocratic and the military elites in the key state positions. In both Algeria and Egypt, the technocrats were successful in containing the officers and confining them to the role of guardians of the state, as well as in keeping control of the decision-making processes. A similar balance prevailed in Iraq until the Gulf war propelled the military to the fore. Syria's armed forces, however, have always kept a strong hold on civilian power.

General Assad's regime even succeeded in the uncommon strategy of turning its regional policy into a major source of income. Since the Arab summits following the October war, Syria has been granted an annual subsidy from the Gulf oil states. This allocation was decided on in order to underwrite the military effort of confronting Israel, and was raised to nearly 2 billion dollars a year at the Baghdad summit of 1979 following Egypt's defection. In some years, the amount received by the Syrian regime represented half the state budget, and it rapidly became indispensable to match the level of expenditure of the country. The subsidy's main object was to allow Syria to maintain a new strategic balance with Israel on the eastern front, but the country came to depend on its relationship with the other states in the Arab East: in 1976, the oil states' aid was drastically cut as a reprisal for Damascus' military intervention in Lebanon, and again in the 1983, because of the Syrian confrontation with the PLO in the Beqaa and around Tripoli. In the meantime, the Baathist military has become a master at playing on political and military tensions on their borders, with Iraq in 1979 and 1985, with Jordan in 1981, and even in Lebanon. Each crisis allows it to take advantage of its Arab financial protectors and to receive a new subsidy to reward its political compliance. Because the allocations come from abroad, because a part is given direct to high-ranking officers and often registered on 'special budgets', it further escapes official governmental supervision.

In all four countries, members of the ruling elite have reacted to the intervention of the military in their countries' economies and to their regimes' uneven achievements. They have stressed the necessity of reinstating populism by complying with socialist ideas of redistribution. These requests and criticism come mainly from civilians, members of the parties which inspired their revolutions: Baathists in Syria and Iraq, militants of the Algerian FLN, or of the ASU in Egypt. The extension and regulation of the allocation process, they claimed, would have helped civil servants, skilled workers and peasants alike, and enhanced a class formation process. The authoritarian military regimes instead chose to reinforce state capitalism by linking the state sector with the newly flourishing private sector. This choice was strongly influenced by the evolution of the international balance of power in the region after 1973; it was encouraged by the surplus capital provided by the oil booms of 1973 and 1979. On the domestic front, it meant the estrangement of the leaders from the classes from which they came and their alliance, instead, with bourgeois entrepreneurs.

The *infitah* period has allowed private contractors to increase their share in the national economy, in domestic and foreign trade, in housing, in the production of consumer goods and even in agriculture. Their cooperation with the military has facilitated the obtaining of permits, credit and raw materials; together with the officers, they have shared in ventures and eventually tightened their economic links through matrimonial strategies. In Algeria, criticism was raised of the new wealth of high-ranking officers as well as civil servants dealing with private business and foreign trade. In Egypt, the connection between Anwar Sadat and the famous contractor, A. Osman Ahmad, aroused much popular suspicion. In Iraq, the manager of Maktab Khalid, a major public building contractor in charge of the construction of Baghdad's new airport and several military bases along the front was known to be married to a close relative of the Iraqi Minister of Defence, Adnan Khairallah, himself the brother-in-law of Saddam Hussein (Springborg, 1986, p. 44).

In Syria, Alawite senior offices have extended their hold on trading and building companies. The best known of all, Rifat al-Assad, has been involved in trade with a Damascene businessman, Muhammad Ali, who had to leave for France suddenly when the Prime Minister General Khlaifawi set up a Committee for the Investigation of Illegal Profits in July 1977. Rifat also supervises imports into Syria of cement from the Shikkan plant in Lebanon, which belongs to his friends, the Frangiahs, and is involved in the hashish trade in the Beqaa valley. In order to secure his business, he has extended his matrimonial strategy towards other Alawite officers, the ruling Saudi family, and the Damascene bourgeoisie. As such, he is a paramount example of military patronage.

The categories involved with the military in power are less the 'new middle class' from which the officers themselves originate and recruit their new members, than a coalition of old and new landowners, merchants and contractors. Due to the personal, familial and communal nature of their ties with the military command, they are unable to coalesce into a social class — an *infitah* class — which might have made up the main basis of the state. On the contrary, the officers' strategy is to play their various segments against each other, and to oppose them to the mass of state clients, in order to hold into their own power. Still, the military regimes have succeeded in staying free from class hegemony. But in the long run, their strategy fosters the upper bourgeois interests while weakening the state-building process.

Few of the features of military intervention in Arab politics described here should be considered specific to the Arab world. 'Oriental' society is not uniquely fated to rule by armed despots estranged from the masses. These characteristics are common to many underdeveloped countries, bound in economic dependency and impeded by weak institutions. The intervention of armed forces results in temporary stability which can be considered as positive, although it hampers the establishment of regular institutions for discussions and decision. Because of military oppression, the alternatives appear to be primary solidarities and religious eschatology. In that respect, the kind of response Arab tribalism and Islamic fundamentalism offer to the suppression of society by the coercive state is not much different from the various African, South American and even Eastern European responses.

It is the history of the region itself which gives the intervention of armed forces in politics its specific features, and which help explain the transformation of a revolutionary plot into a lasting authoritarian military regime, the officers' abuse of coercive power in a society they had intended to transform, and their appropriation of their country's economy. Except for Egypt, which enjoys a better record of civilian institutions, most Arab states were founded only recently. Most have endured colonialism and still resent its violence through the perpetuation of the war with Israel — which is central in the analysis of the Syrian regime. The sudden and fragile changes in their economy resulting from oil wealth have conveyed to their leaders a feeling of overestimated strength — it led Iran to military adventurism and the interruption of its demilitarisation. And finally, they have to balance their moves towards modernisation and democracy with the preservation of their societies' culture and values — Algeria's slow steps towards institutionalisation illustrates the difficulties. However, the growing population and the continuing pressure for social change in the Arab world are issues which no military regime can resolve politically, unless it chooses to work towards its own dissolution.

NOTES

1. E. Beeri who in 1969 wrote on Syrian and Egyptian experiments, comes back to the subject in the disenchanted and critical article published in 1982 in *Middle Eastern Studies, vol. 18, no. 1*, 'The waning of the military coup in Arab politics'.

2. M. Janowitz (1977), *Military institutions and coercion in the developing nations*, University of Chicago Press, (Chicago), p. 88: of the twelve Arab countries with modern armies of a professional type, the military constitute the political ruling group or military oligarchy in four. They are actively involved in civil-military coalitions in six.

3. An example quoted by F. Khuri and G. Obermayer, (1974), 'The social bases for military intervention in the Middle East', in C. MacArdle Kelleher (ed.), *Political-military systems, comparative perspective*, Sage Publications, is from B. Aridi (1968), 'The role of the army in the process of development' (in Arabic), *al-Siyasa al-Dawliyya*, vol. 4, no. 13, 77–87. Aridi argues that 'the army is the most advanced institution in society and therefore capable of changing it'.

4. The thesis, apparent in most contributions of J. Johnson, (*The role of the military*) also appears in J.C. Hurewitz (1969) *Middle Eastern politics: the military dimension*, Praeger, New York, and in many others at the time.

5. The role of the army in the development of 'backward societies' and its class nature were discussed in the Soviet periodical *MEIMO 3* (1966) pp. 57–70, quoted by H. Carrere d'Encausse (1975), *La politique sovietique au Moyen-Orient*, Fondation Nationale des Sciences Politiques, Paris, p. 163.

6. A brilliant example of such treatment of Arab politics was given in I. Rabinovich's well-informed book, *Syria under the Baath, 1963–6: the*

144

army-party symbiosis, Shiloach Institute, Tel-Aviv (1982). Recent writers, such as N. Van Dam, 1979, do not escape the tendency.

7. The leading supporter of this thesis is A. Perlmutter in his polemical work (1974), *Egypt: the praetorian state*, Transaction Books, Brunswick, (New Jersey).

8. C. Wakebridge (1976), 'The Syrian side of the hill', *Military Review*, vol. 56, no. 2, pp. 20–30. An American officer, Wakebridge visited the Syrian Southern Front and Q.G. in Qatana with United Nations Forces (UNDOF). For an Arab denunciation of the 1967 defeat and responsibility of the military regime, see M. Khalil (1969), *Suqut il-Jawlan* (The fall of the Golan), Dar al-Yaqin, Amman.

9. In July 1982, following the loss of Khoramshar, Saddam Hussein eliminated eight members of the RCC. At the time, reports spoke of unhappiness in senior Iraqi ranks and of a reshuffle in the military command because of 'negligence and incompetence'. Another reshuffle took place after Fajr 5 (*Washington Post*, 30 July 1984).

10. In a recent article, L. Ware stresses the 'highly professional qualities of the Tunisian army' which never 'mounted a coup nor fomented a revolution' and is mainly 'dedicated to defence'. He also interestingly predicts that 'when Bourguiba leaves office or dies . . . Destourianism cannot help but undergo a final and irrecuperable dilution (so that) the military can be expected to intervene on a regular basis . . . (But) as it lacks elite experience, the Tunisian military is unlikely to adapt a formal political and ideological structure of its new position of power'. It is, thus, bound to follow the authoritarian military regime pattern of failure. L.B. Ware (1985), 'The role of the Tunisian military in the post-Bourguiba era', *Middle East Journal* vol. 39, no. 1, pp. 40–2.

On the other hand, the trial in September 1983 of 19 military men for their membership in the Islamic Liberation Party, a fundamentalist movement founded in Jordan, raises questions about concern over fundamentalist penetration in the Tunisian army.

11. Such information can be obtained through the London biweekly *Arab Report and Record* until 1981, then in daily newspapers such as *al-Ray-al-Amm* (Kuwait) and *al-Sharq al-Awsat* (London).

12. Just as domestic political measures are bound to reinforce foreign and Arab legitimacy, so foreign policy is used as a means of strengthening internal legitimacy. See Chapter 11 in this volume.

13. They reached the peak of their power at the time of Assad's illness, June 1984. See A. Drysdale (1985), 'The succession question in Syria', *Middle East Journal*, vol. 39, no. 2, p. 248.

14. 'I did not choose the army career by vocation. I would have become an engineer, but my family's income did not allow me to enter university,' said Colonel Abdel Karim Jundi to E. Rouleau. Quoted in 'La Syrie Baathiste ou la fuite à gauche', *Le Monde*, 13 October 1966.

15. During this period, Egyptian Muslim Brothers were infiltrating the Egyptian Army. Mitchell, R. (1969) *The society of the Muslim Brothers*, Oxford University Press, London, pp. 148–60.

16. Recent cinematographic works such as *al-Hudud* (To the frontiers) and M. Melhem's beautiful *Ahlam al-Madina* (Dreams of the city), or novels like N. Sulayman, *al-Misalla* (The obelisk), Dar al-Haqa'iq, Beirut,

ARAB MILITARY IN POLITICS

display the overwhelming presence of the military in Syrian daily life. In *al-Misalla* (1980), the group of young heroes who belong to various political parties such as the CP, Nasserist groups, the Palestinian Resistance, and even official Baath, is constantly under the intelligence network's control and influence.

17. *Bad al-Muntalaqat al-Nazariyya* (Theoretical perspectives) is the document adopted in October 1963 at the Sixth National Baath Congress at a time when Baathists were in power in Damascus as well as in Baghdad. It is still a fundamental charter for both Baathist branches.

18. In the party dailies such as *al-Baath*, *al-Thawra* and *Tishrin* and even more frequently in the union's weekly, *Kifah al Umma al-Ishtiraki*.

19. According to Y. Sadowski, 70 per cent of Syrian annual imports, (1 to 1.5 billion dollars worth of goods), are smuggled from Lebanon: Y. Sadowski (July-August 1985) 'Cadres, guns and money — eighth regional congress of the Syrian Baath', *Merip Report*, p. 6.

20. General Nabawi Ismail, who had already fled to the United States with his family.

6

Role of Religious Institutions in Support of the State

Sadok Belaid

GENERAL CONTEXT

Religion and political power have had strained relations throughout history. In various ways, they have always sought to dominate each other. Religion would consider political — 'temporal' — power as a necessary means to attain its spiritual goals, and conversely, political power would attempt to mobilise the ideological — 'spiritual' — power of religion in order to achieve its material goals. The relationship between religion and the state in the Western world exemplifies this dilemma: after a long period of domination over political power and then of resistance to change which lasted until the end of the nineteenth century, the Catholic Church finally lost its 'temporal' power and adamantly accommodated itself to the principle of separation between religion and state. The doctrine of 'secularism' and the 'privatisation' of religion are common expressions of the present balance of power between state and religion, which is clearly advantageous to the former.

At first sight, the position of Islam in the Arab world is dissimilar to the situation of the church in Western countries. The socio-cultural environment is different and is marked by the importance of religious movements. The problem of the relationship between Islam and the state itself is posed in terms which are basically different to those used in the Western world. According to the predominant view, in Islam there is no such thing as separation between the secular and religious domains, as the Islamic religion embraces inescapably both temporal and spiritual aspects of the Islamic community's life. There existed originally an understanding between the two parties — the state and the religious establishment — whereby, on one hand, the *'ulema* contributed to the legitimisation of the state and brought its support to state policy and, on the other, political power undertook to comply with orthodox doctrine

147

as defined by the 'ulema and to accept the supervision and the censure of the *fuqaha*.

This balanced relationship between political power and religious institutions was bound not to last and has proved to be an unequal alliance, as history abundantly has demonstrated. The political power has gradually integrated the religious establishment in its own structure.

More devastating, in certain cases, has been the impact of the colonial system on the personal position and the influence of the 'ulema. The reason lies in the fact that the colonial regime was based on a foreign system of religious and political values. Traditional Muslim institutions and establishments were progressively dominated by colonial authorities and lost power, prestige and credibility among the masses.

These fundamental contradictions persist in the contemporary Arab world and have taken on more dramatic form because of the contradictory changes in Arab politics. On the one hand, we witness a general renewal of the Islamic sentiment within Arab society as a whole, and the resurgence of militant Islamic movements advocating a return to original Islamic rule. However, the politically important feature of this renewal is that it is based on the conjunction of 'ulema power (or a section of the 'ulema) and the people's aspirations. As a result, 'Islam seems to have become the centre of political opposition and its adherents, somewhat unexpectedly, real contenders for power' (Piscatori, 1983, p. 1).

These two factors — widespread renewal of Islamic faith and the politicisation of Islam — are becoming an important political force states have to reckon with. The contemporary Arab political regimes — however progressive or conservative — cannot remain indifferent to this change and to the impact it may have on the political life of their societies. The actual or potential force that renewed Islam represents, and its manipulation by opposition parties on the political field, imposes on the state a policy of vigorous response, in order to neutralise the dangers generated by this threat.

Two different, and somewhat polar, responses have been adopted: either the 'secularist' attitude claiming a more or less strict separation of religion and state, as has been the case in Tunisia, at least in the early period of independence, and in Egypt under Nasser; or — because the secularist doctrine proved not to be politically rewarding — the old temptation for political power to exert its domination over the religious establishment. This has been the case of, amongst others, the Egypt of Sadat.

While not lacking in complexity it appears that a certain number of constants relating to the relationship between Islam and its institutions and political power can be drawn from the observation of both history and contemporary politics in the Arab world. Thus, Islam appears as a 'two-sided' phenomenon: it can be perceived as a religion, i.e. as an ideological force, or as an institution, i.e. as a sociological structure composed of a set of institutions and of a more or less coherent establishment. The observation of current Arab politics enables us to draw up a tentative systematisation of the various experiences in terms of relations between religion and the state. Three classes of cases can be distinguished. In the first, there exists a certain degree of harmony between Islam and the state, ideologically as well as institutionally. Being placed on an equal footing with political power, the religious institutions tend to willingly cooperate with the state, contributing to its legitimacy and supporting its policy. In the other two cases, the relationship between state and religion is characterised by the presence of conflict and opposition, which appear either on the ideological or on the institutional level. In one case, the state claims a major role as the guardian of Islam, until then monopolised by religious institutions. It then attempts to marginalise and weaken the traditional establishment: Algeria and Tunisia are examples of this. Finally, the conflictual relationship appears mainly on the institutional level. The state has no ideological differences with its opponents, but faces a powerful and challenging religious force, which mobilises its institutions and structures to gain political control: Egypt and Sudan illustrate this.

PARTNERSHIP; THE ARABIAN PENINSULA — SAUDI ARABIA

There is little doubt that the Arabian Peninsula political regimes are predominantly based on traditional values and Islamic principles and symbols. Islam is the cornerstone of construction of the whole society and of the state as well. More than in any other Arab country, the principle that 'Islam is a religion and a state' prevails. Islam is firmly proclaimed in the constitution as the state religion. Law and religion are strongly inter-connected and 'rest upon the infallible revelation of the Quran and its presumably infallible verification in detail by tradition' (Gallagher, 1968, p. 207).

The most serious challenge for this political religious partnership undoubtedly comes from its inescapable confrontation with modernisation or, more precisely, from the intrusion of Western modernist values on Islamic ideals, as defined and preserved by the traditional religious institutions. The more tightly a regime is linked to the traditional religious institutions, the more it will be vulnerable to the tensions and contradictions between modernisation and orthodoxy.

The Saudi Arabian regime represents a significant example of these complexities. Unlike the smaller Gulf sheikhdoms, the Saudi regime owes its existence to the alliance between political power and religion (Peretz, 1983, pp. 463–70). Unlike the surrounding states where Islam, despite its official status, is 'somewhat less salient as a political ideology' (Hudson, 1977, p. 167), the Saudi regime appears as a basically theocratic regime. As such, Islam is a constituent part of the state and the religious establishment is a major partner of the regime, a built-in piece, as it were, of the whole structure of the state.

Yet, the Saudis have proven to be much more resilient and adaptable to modernisation than political theorists expected, while at the same time, they have continued to adhere to Islamic orthodoxy. 'The Saudi solution to the legitimacy problems posed by modernity', as Hudson (1977, p. 180) has noted, 'has on the whole proved more successful than expected. Islamic and customary values have been harmonised with modern nationalism and secular values of progress and development.' These accomplishments are partly due to the skills and political shrewdness of outstanding rulers such as King Abd el-Aziz (Hudson, 1977, p. 172) and King Feisal, but this is not only a matter of personal capacities. Rather, these accomplishments were, to a large extent, generated by a successful mobilisation of Islam as an ideology in order to build not only a strong nation-state from disunited and continuously warring tribes, but also a modernising nation from a medieval, nomadic and backward society. This would not have been possible, if ideological mobilisation had not been successfully combined with the mobilisation of Islam as an institution.

As a spiritual partner, the religious establishment in Saudi Arabia enjoys more than in any other country in the Arab world, incontestable control over the ideology of state and governmental institutions. This effective control was made possible by the fact that, from the beginning of the century Muhammad Ibn Abd el-Wahhab 'bore the title of sheikh, the expounder of religious doctrine' and played the role of 'ideologist' in the nascent Saudi polity. After the institutionalisation of the Saudi regime, the 'ulema

150

was integrated into the royal family and into state structures, so that 'only in Saudi Arabia has neo-orthodoxy succeeded politically and maintained itself in full force until the present' (Pipes, 1980, p. 11).

On a larger scale, the 'ulema are strongly involved in control of the state's general policy and compliance with Islamic doctrine. They control the legitimacy of the ruling clan and as such, control succession to power and settle disputes related to this matter. In 1964, they played a key role in disputes between Saud Ibn Abd el-Aziz and his brother Feisal, and their *fatwa* (religious ruling) led to the replacement of Saud by Feisal (Piscatori, 1983, p. 61). In day-to-day matters, they exert direct control on the legislative and executive functions of the state. This control has proved effective in many crucial circumstances, the most significant being the strong and successful opposition by the 'ulema to the project of 'codification of the shariah' conceived by King Abd el-Aziz in 1927 and feared by the religious establishment to be an attempt by the state to manipulate and adulterate the original doctrine.

The 'ulema control judicial institutions and tribunals and such important sectors as educational, social and religious institutions. Since 1929, they have monopolised control of social morality, which they exert through the 'committees for the exhortation of good and suppression of evil'. Despite attempts by King Feisal to reduce their power, these influential committees (Piscatori, 1983, p. 61) even extend their jurisdiction over Saudis abroad.

As a political partner of the Wahhabis, the Saudi monarchy has won strength and stability. In that spiritual-temporal alliance, one should not overlook the very important fact that, since the origins of the Saudi-Wahhabi venture, royal authority was buttressed by the title of *imam*, acquired through Muhammad Ibn Saud's conversion in 1742 to Wahhabism. Since then, the head of the House of Saud has automatically been chief of the Wahhabi religious movement (Peretz, 1983, p. 466). One could expect that, because of the fusion of temporal and spiritual authorities, the original alliance would be unbalanced and ultimately lead to the subjugation of the spiritual partner — and this has largely been the case. The Saudi monarchy has displayed a rare shrewdness in using Islamic power to attain its political goals and to cement the stability of the regime.

First, thanks to the religious support and to the prestige of the title of imam, the Saudi monarchy has successfully dominated the independent and volatile tribes scattered all over the country and unified the nation. Wahhabi orthodoxy and its endorsement by the founders of their dynasty enabled the Saudis to validate their right

ROLE OF RELIGIOUS INSTITUTIONS

to rule and to establish their legitimacy. From its inception until now, the Saudi monarchy's legitimacy has been basically a religious one. This is the reason why the successive kings have been eager to stress their function as religious leaders and their devoted compliance with Islamic prescriptions.

Secondly, the Saudi monarchy has found in Islamic orthodoxy indisputable authority for the absolutist form of its government. The Saudi regime is a theocratic monarchy as well as an accepted absolutist regime, in as much as it accepts only God's rules and the Prophet's tradition. This explains the absence of constitutional law and of democratic mechanisms generally accepted in secularised modern regimes. 'A constitution in Saudi Arabia? With the Quran, we have the best and the oldest constitution in the world!' King Feisal has said in reply to Western critics of the Saudi regime (Piscatori, in Esposito, 1980, p. 126).

Thirdly, Saudi reliance on Islamic orthodoxy has enabled its rulers to combat successfully such challenging ideologies and 'competing sources of legitimacy' as Marxism — which they easily condemn as an 'atheist doctrine', or Baathism — which they condemn as an Arab version of Marxism, and Nasserism — which they condemn as a secularist and subversive Arab ideology. Indeed, a survey of the various 'progressive' or opposition movements which sporadically appear in Saudi Arabia demonstrates that none of these political ideologies 'seems strong enough to undermine the Saudi regime' (Sankari, 1980, p. 178), or represents a serious alternative to its Islamic legitimacy.

The most important challenge to the Saudi monarchy as a theocratic and orthodox regime comes from modernisation and its values which conflict with orthodoxy and religiosity. In as much as modernisation implies 'Westernisation', it inevitably means, at least in the opinion of the conservative religious establishment, conflict with such a puristic doctrine as the Wahhabist ideology. The Saudi 'ulema of the nineteenth century and the beginning of this one reacted very negatively to the first attempts by the state to introduce certain Western values and technologies (Piscatori, 1983, p. 59).

Nevertheless and despite these ominous signs, the Saudi monarchy has succeeded to a large extent — particularly since the 1970s — in steadily promoting modernisation, social and economic development. Without denying its fidelity and its commitment to the orthodox doctrine of Wahhabism, it has shown that even with a theocratic regime, Islam is not incompatible with a modernising state. Various means have been combined in order to neutralise the

152

possible resistance of the religious establishment, and indeed to involve it in the state's modernising policy for the purpose of reconciling innovations with orthodoxy and tradition.

Like many other other Arab countries, therefore, the Saudi regime has institutionalised its religious authorities. Members of the 'ulema, being dependent on 'the government for their salaries and positions . . . have become agents of the state. And because their methods of selection and education have been regularised they have become bureaucratised' (Piscatori, 1983, p. 61). This is not to say that 'only the shell of Wahhabism' (Lackner, 1983, p. 70) remains, but we are a long way from the period when 'ulema were powerful enough to oppose successfully the decisions of the king. This was the case in 1927. In present times, it seems that the 'ulema, though influential, have 'little independent political power' (Sankari, 1980, p. 178). The 1979 takeover of the Great Mosque of Mecca by a group of Sunni extremists is significant in this regard. Before the assault on the rebels by the Saudi security forces, the Saudi authorities had been 'careful to secure a fatwa. . . to legitimate their actions' and to condemn the invaders as *mufsidun fil ardh* (those who are corrupt on earth). 'They could have acted without a fatwa, but asking for one cost them nothing' (Piscatori, 1982, p. 61), and more importantly, they gained the support and thanks of the whole 'ulema community, thus strengthening their Islamic legitimacy.

The Saudi rulers have also tried to gain the support of the Islamic 'ulema before introducing flexibility in official orthodox doctrine. Whereas the original Wahhabi doctrine was based on strict observance of the traditional sources of Islam and on the most rigid school of interpretation — the Hanbali school — Saudi rulers took advantage of the flexibility of other schools to ensure the adaptation of official orthodoxy to modern society. Moreover, they have, to a certain extent, encouraged the 'progressivist' interpretation of basic principles such as justice and solidarity among believers, in order to establish and legitimise a new system of social security for the benefit of workers and the poor. By the same token, Saudi rulers have tended to take advantage of the teaching of the Hanbali school itself in order to mollify its rigidity. According to this school, which strictly adheres to the Quran and the Hadiths (traditions of the Prophet), there should be room for personal independent reasoning (*ijtihad*), whenever the texts are silent or vague. This principle has been interpreted in a very broad sense, so as to indicate that what is not clearly prohibited by the traditional sources should be taken as permissible. On this basis, it is evident that the rulers would be able to innovate with the approval of the 'ulema.

This erosion in the power of the religious establishment is likely to accelerate with the general political evolution of the country. This evolution may move in one of two contradictory directions. In the first, a strong fundamentalist movement would emerge in Saudi Arabia which, like the Ikhwan rebellion (1927–30), would accuse the present regime and the religious establishment of deviationism and corruption, and demand a return to the purist doctrine of Wahhabism. The siege of the Mecca Mosque in 1979 showed that such a movement should be taken seriously by the Saudi ruling elite. The second direction, which is at the other end of the spectrum, is the direct outcome of the modernisation policy, which would produce a new generation of Western-educated elite, a technocratic middle class and a wealthy bourgeoisie, calling for the liberalisation and democratisation of the political and social life of Saudi society.

Neither of these extreme movements is likely to overpower the present regime, given the strong control it exerts over the whole of society and the ability shown by the Saudi rulers in their handling of earlier crises. Yet it seems clear that they have learned from these troubles. After the shock of November 1979, the siege of the Mecca Mosque, which revealed serious unease in the country, in 1980 King Fahd created a constitutional committee headed by the interior minister, which was entrusted with drafting a constitution.

SPLIT: THE MAGHREB STATES

Since the Islamic expansion in the Maghreb, Islam and politics have been intertwined and their dialectical relationship has played a major role in the political evolution of this region. As a result, the Maghreb has inherited an ambivalent tradition of politicised Islam, which contrasts with the purity or even the ascetism of popular Islam. In other words, political Islam is to be differentiated from cultural Islam in the Maghreb countries.

The most serious blow to Islam during its long and uneasy relations with politics, occurred during the colonial period as the result of the policy of 'de-Islamisation' and acculturation undertaken by the colonial authorities. Islam was split into two: ideological Islam, which has served as a nationalist ideology of resistance; and institutional Islam, represented by corrupt 'ulema and religious institutions quiescent to the colonial authorities. Significantly, an important part of the religious establishment was under attack by the nationalist movements and the people during the pre-independence period.

Under these circumstances, it is no surprise that once in power, the Maghreb nationalist leaders, with the exception of Morocco, adopted from the outset a clear-cut distinction between institutional Islam and ideological Islam. They sought to discredit and weaken the traditional institutions and establishment (Achour, 1979, p. 65), but being aware of the paramount importance of Islamic feelings within the masses and of the political force Islam represented, they claimed Islam as a support base for their modernising policy.

The weakening of institutional Islam happened after independence in both Tunisia and Algeria. In Tunisia, the religious establishment backed the rebellion against the Bourguiba regime in the name of pan-Arabism and Islam. They were against the innovations in religious matters introduced by the modernisation policy undertaken by the government — hence, the virulent attacks directed by President Bourguiba against the 'old turbans', whom he held responsible for the decay of the country and accused of being an obstacle to the development of the nation. Between 1957 and 1960, Bourguiba launched the so-called 'reformist policy', which was aimed at dismantling the power of the religious establishment: the judicial and educational systems, the administration of the mosques and the land ownership system. The religious tribunals were integrated into a unified and state-controlled judicial system. Traditional education (Quranic schools, *medersas* and the University of Zituna) was taken over by the new Ministry of National Education. The imams, preachers and mufti were bureaucratised and put under the control of an office of religious affairs attached to the prime ministry. The religious endowments (*habous*) were dismantled and integrated into the state domain. Religious movements were overlawed as reactionary and obscurantist. These decisions, undertaken in the style of Kemal Atatürk, helped the regime to eliminate serious rightist opposition and to consolidate the 'lay' character of Bourguibian legitimacy.

During the colonial period in Algeria, Islam played a contradictory role. The Islam of the decaying marabouts and *zawiyas* was manipulated by the colonial authorities in order to extend their control, while the Islam of the reformist 'ulema in the 1930s played a notable, though unsuccessful role in the formation of national consciousness and was severely persecuted by French authorities (Ben Salah, 1979, pp. 58–61). As a result, the Islamic establishment lost its power and prestige and was marginalised as a nationalist force during the Algerian war of independence (Entelis, 1980, pp. 7–8). Once in power, the nationalist leaders distinguished between the reformist movement, which they co-opted, and the corrupt establishment and institutions, which they denounced, repudiating as anti-Islamic religious practices encouraged by the marabouts and zawiyas. These institutions were subsequently outlawed. The new regime found further reason for its attacks when the traditionalist institutions opposed the regime's modernisation policy. The association, Al-Qiyam (the values), which under the cover of reformism campaigned for the return to 'authentic' Islam, for the observance of the shariah and against land reform, was dissolved in September 1966 and definitively outlawed in March 1970.

In their assault against traditional forces, the new regimes in Tunisia and Algeria were projecting themselves as the true and authentic guardians of Islam. Both regimes had their own style, language and political goals, but the strategy remained the same: to neutralise a possible opponent and, by means of pre-emptive action, to monopolise the tremendous political power of Islam for the benefit of the regime.

The source of inspiration was also the same: the works of the contemporary Islamic philosophers, who called for a renewal of Islam centred on the original orthodoxy, the *salafiyah*. Like other Arab regimes, the new Tunisian and Algerian leaders sought to turn the salafiyah 'into an instrument and a pillar for their power. Thus the ideology of the religious institution became the ideology of the rulers, even the revolutionary ones among them' (Shalq, 1976, p. 61).

Tunisia adopted the so-called reformist policy. it emphasised the status of Islam as the religion of state and, in so doing, pre-empted criticism from its Islamist opponents. At the same time, the Bourguiba regime asserted the urgency of breaking obscurantism: the gates of *ijtihad* — individual reasoning — had to be reopened. Ijtihad meant that the regime could turn Islam to serve its own purposes.

The modernist Bourguiba, unlike Kemal Atatürk, whom he admired the most, never dared adopt a strictly secularist position in Islamic matters for fear of reviving the hostility of his opponents. Rather, he spared no pains, in his solemn speeches in the Zituna and Kairawan mosques, in explaining the Islamic nature of his innovations. He looked carefully at the Quran and the prophetic tradition for precedents likely to support such innovative views as the abolition of polygamy, the non-observance of the Ramadan restrictions or the equality of men and women. As regards polygamy, he argued that an intelligent reading of the Quran would clearly show God's distaste for the practice. As for Ramadan, he equated the struggle for economic development (*jihad al-akbar*, the greater holy war) with the holy war undertaken by Muhammad and he deduced from that authority not to fast. As for women's rights, he advocated that the new personal code represented a 'return to the authentic spirit of Islam'.

The Tunisian regime relied on more than persuasiveness of discourse. It resorted to the practice used in other Arab countries: *étatisation* of religious personnel, promotion of quiescent 'ulema to high posts, allocation of state subsidies for the construction or the restoration of mosques, allocation of public funds for religious/ cultural institutions, etc. Such generosities expected a *quid pro quo*: the issuing of fatwa or religious edicts in support of official policy, which the regime obtained on numerous occasions. When the system sometimes did not work, the fatwa was ignored and the recalcitrant 'ulema discreetly dismissed (Ben Achour, 1979, p. 69 and note 18).

In contrast to Tunisia, the Algerian regime has been from its inception a revolutionary and socialist system, directly influenced by Marxist doctrine. At first sight, the task of reconciling this ideology with Islam seems highly hypothetical. Indeed, during the first constitutional debates, some 'leftist' representatives were vociferous about the impossibility of such a reconciliation and advocated the creation of a secular state and its separation from religion (Etienne, 1966, p. 62). Although the attempts were unsuccessful, the new regime, aware of the paramount importance of Islam, finally sacrificed the purity of ideology for the sake of political convenience and Islam was officially made the 'state religion'. Following a resolution that used the same ambiguous wording as in Tunisia, the Algerian regime undertook to implement an Islamic policy — basically analogous to the Tunisian one — which consisted of the 'mobilisation' of Islam and the subjugation of religious people and institutions to the regime. This was done primarily by projecting Algerian socialism and a doctrine combining elements of Marxist ideals and Islamic values.

The Algerian rulers, like their Tunisian counterparts, had to make concessions to popular religiosity and traditions in order to alleviate social resistance to their progressivist doctrine and the need for political legitimacy imposed alterations on their doctrinal views. Thus, the Algerian regime, 'the quintessence of revolutionary policy' (Etienne, 1966, p. 140), was compelled to abandon birth control, a typically revolutionary programme accepted in many other Islamic countries, because of popular resistance grounded in traditional practices. Likewise, the personal code, the drafting of which provoked long and heated discussions between liberals and traditionalists, was finally diluted by traditional views, particularly regarding women.

Because of latent resistance to its revolutionary policies, the Algerian regime made a series of decisions intended to neutralise traditionalist movements. From its inception, the Algerian state has not been tolerant towards the religious institutions, which it has denigrated as reactionary and obscurantist. By outlawing them, it consolidated the monopoly of political legitimacy in the hands of the FLN. Like Tunisia but more systematically, it placed the religious institutions under the control of a Ministry of Religious Affairs. The ministry, which was reorganised in 1980, is responsible for 'preparing the coming generations for a better understanding of Islam, both as a religion and as a civilisation, and as a fundamental component of the Algerian personality' (Article 1).

This ministry has created new religious institutes and organised Islamic seminars on modern Islam. It has put under state control the religious 'ulema and monopolised the formation of a new 'institutionalised clergy'. An Islamic superior council, presided over by one member of the government, issues fatwas supporting state policy and provides the *imams* (preachers) and other religious personnel with official guidelines about the correct interpretation of Islamic rules and principles.

This does not mean that, either in Algeria or in Tunisia, the conflict between religion and political power is definitely settled. Whether drastic or moderate, state control is bound to generate reaction from religious groups. This resistance is constant and vigorous in Tunisia as well as in Algeria. For instance, the Tunisian government recently backed off from proposed modernist measures in response to social resistance and the religious establishment's opposition. A fundamentalist movement which emerged in Tunisia over the last ten years has grown so rapidly that it has compelled vigorous government response. In Algeria, fundamentalism has been equally persistent. Fundamentalist demonstrations that took place in various cities in 1982 and 1983 provoked the government to react strongly. Several fundamentalist leaders have been sentenced to prison. One of them, Sheikh Abdel Latif Sultani, died while under house arrest (March 1984). Thus in both countries, the dialectical movement of action-reaction has been triggered.

158

CONFRONTATION: EGYPT AND SUDAN

In other Arab countries, conflict between religion and political power developed earlier, and is at present entering a critical phase of open hostility. The extreme violence of this conflict and its seemingly endless character may be explained by the fact that, unlike in Tunisia and Algeria, the ideological and institutional aspects of Islam rather than being split up, are on the contrary, unified. And unlike Saudi Arabia, this unification of ideological and institutional Islam did not occur under the control of the state, but has been monopolised by the opposition. Islam has become politicised to the point that it has become a political force in its own right. The conflict between the state and the Islamic movement has become a struggle for the conquest of political power. This is what is happening in Egypt and Sudan.

In Egypt, the state was aware of the importance of Islam as a means of political control and sought to use religious institutions to consolidate its legitimacy and channel its ideology and policies throughout the country. This was the case under Nasser. 'The Ministry of Waqfs was used to establish domination over the Muslim religious leaders. Their Friday speeches were prepared by the government and prayer leaders throughout the Nile Valley preached state-supplied sermons on health, education, foreign affairs, and matters about which the government desired to educate the peasantry' (Peretz, 1983, p. 256). This was also the case with the Sadat regime. Under Sadat, al-Azhar 'ulema continued the long tradition of submission to the ruler of the time and gave Anwar Sadat the religious support he wanted. This was illustrated by the fatwa issued in May 1979 in support of his highly controversial trip to Jerusalem in 1977.

The state overlooked the fact that support given by an *'alim* 'largely disconnected from the populace' is politically useless and that the real political power of Islam would inevitably be mobilised by opposition parties capable of establishing a bridge between people's aspirations and Islamic social philosophy. This important gap has been filled partly by the Muslim Brotherhood.

The strength of the Muslim Brotherhood lies in the fact that it has obtained credibility within intellectual circles and some social classes that cannot be matched by the official religious establishment. It has also produced an easily accessible ideology in sharp opposition to official policy. In other words, the Islamic movement has been successful in capturing a kind of Islamic legitimacy and has become a serious challenge to the regime.

From its inception, the Islamic movement has been perceived by these regimes as a serious contender for power and a dangerous destabilising force. King Farouk persecuted the Muslim radicals and his Iron Guard killed their leader, Hasan al-Banna, in 1949. The Nasser regime, after a short period of ambiguous alliance, attacked and disbanded them. But at the same time, it 'used Islam to enhance the prestige of its revolution' (Peretz, 1983, p. 156) and mobilised Islamic institutions such as al-Azhar to support its policy. The Sadat regime, while making concessions to the mounting Islamic sentiment, harshly attacked the fundamentalist movement in 1977 and in 1981 imprisoning and prosecuting hundreds of members. The Mubarak regime has taken a more moderate line but has adopted a tough stand towards religious movements. After an informal truce in 1983 and 1984 and the relatively clement verdict of the court in the al-Jihad organisation's trial, about 50 fundamentalists were arrested in Cairo, Alexandria and el-Fayoum in July 1985. The Ministry of Waqfs took over several mosques, after the leaders of these movements called for a 'green march' and a popular meeting in Cairo in support of the immediate application of the shariah (Peretz, 1983, p. 251).

These incidents demonstrate how dangerous conflict between religion and state can be. Both parties are pushed to adopt extremist positions leading to violence and counter-violence, equally destructive for religion and the state. In the Egyptian case, the Islamic movement is pushed towards terrorism and political assassination, while the state is pushed toward an unfruitful policy of repression. Escalation could result in the dislocation of the whole society and the undermining of the structure and authority of the state itself.

Sudan is an illustration of this. The country is the 'ship adrift on Islam'. The political turmoil since independence cannot be blamed on Islam alone. Religious, ethnic, and social divisions have certainly played an important role in the dislocation of the society and the chronic instability of the political system. Yet, the unresolved conflict between state and Islamic forces appears to remain the major cause of political crisis in as much as neither state nor the Islamic forces have succeeded in exerting coherent and stable political authority over the country. What differentiates Sudanese politics from those of other Arab countries, is the seemingly endless succession of *coups d'état* and regime crises, the unpredictable alliances between opposing parties, the frequent breakdown of national reconciliations, the ever-changing ideological positions of political leaders and groups, and the overwhelming importance of tactics and opportunism.

As in Saudi Arabia, Islam has played a major role in the construction of an independent and Islamic state in Sudan. Mahdism in Sudan, like Wahhabism in Saudi Arabia, was the militant ideological mobiliser of Islamic forces during the nineteenth century. However, whereas Saudi Arabia's monarchy incorporated the spiritual power of the state ideologically and institutionally, Sudan, despite its theocratic tradition, did not cement such a fusion. The Sufi leaders have been reluctant from the start to intervent directly in political life, preferring to 'offer or withdraw their religious sanction for the existing political regimes' (Cudsi in Piscatori, 1983, p. 37). On the other hand, whereas Algeria and Tunisia outlawed traditional religious institutions, in Sudan the government was unable to because they were solidly implanted in the social and political culture of the country.

Sudanese political life has been deeply disturbed by the ambiguous position of the religious forces. Rivalries among the major sects have made it difficult for any to exert leadership strong enough to ensure stability and coherent political action. On the other hand, the central government was never strong enough to impose its authority over the religious groups. The Abbud military regime (1958–64) failed to introduce significant socio-political changes or to solve the serious economic crisis. When the Abbud regime was overthrown by a civilian coup in October 1964, and after the failure of a leftist government dominated by the Sudanese communist party, political power was captured by Islamist groups. Sadiq al-Mahdi and the Umma Party he reformed sought to modernise the state but this ambitious reformist programme was perceived by the religious leaders of the Ansar as a direct threat to the traditional institutions. The difficulties Sadiq al-Mahdi met within his own party were worsened by the old rivalry between the Ansar (Umma) and the Khatmiyya and allied factions led by al-Azhari. Just as these difficulties seem to be settled by an agreement reached on 23 May 1969, the military coup by Colonel Numeiry put an end to civilian rule.

With the Numeiry military regime, Sudan briefly experienced a new communist-oriented administration. The conflict was solved by the ousting of the communist ministers and the interdiction of the Communist Party and organisations. But in succeeding against the communists, Numeiry cut himself off from any strong legitimating base. After an abortive coup by the communists, Numeiry turned for support to the Sufi orders. Aware of the weakness of his own party, which was created only in 1972, he incorporated the Sufi orders into the Sudanese Socialist Union in 1976, set up a Ministry of Religious Affairs, undertook to subsidise the religious institutions and promote the observance of religious prescriptions in day-to-day matters, and pledged himself to make Islam the cornerstone of political and social life.

This, however, was not enough to consolidate the regime's control of the country. In July 1976, the Umma party led a coup against Numeiry. Although it failed, the attempt showed that the religious opposition was still strong, and that the state had still to pay the price of a general reconciliation with the various religious factions. A new 'National Reconciliation' was officially approved in July 1977, which increased the influence of the religious sects over the state, this time to the advantage of the Muslim Brotherhood. This first agreement was supplemented by another reconciliation agreement with Shariff Husain al-Hindi in April 1978.

In November 1981, however, Numeiry changed course yet again, dismissed his entire cabinet and the leadership of the Sudanese Socialist Union and appointed progressive and even Communist leaders. Against, this was not destined to last. In 1983–4, he made a decisive shift towards Islam. In September 1983, the sharia was reintroduced, replacing the civil and criminal codes. In June 1984, a series of amendments to the constitution in order to make it conform with Islamic rules were submitted by Numeiry to the People's Assembly. These initiatives encountered a growing opposition amongst the people and from some of the political factions. For example, Sadiq al-Mahdi was arrested for his criticisms of the Islamisation policy. An escalation of demonstrations and riots, repression and massive executions led to a national crisis and finally to the coup which ousted Numeiry from power in April 1985.

Numeiry's 17-year rule ultimately led to a dangerous crisis in the political and socio-economic life of Sudan. Without doubt, his opportunistic policies were partly responsible. But more fundamentally, Sudan's ills were caused by the confrontation that existed between the political authorities and the religious organisations, which undermined political stability and prevented the establishment of a secure base for political institutions.

In general, therefore, notwithstanding the continuing efforts by Arab regimes to use the religious establishment for the purpose of acquiring legitimacy, religion and politics seem destined to have a strained relationship, which can only lead to the weakening of both.

162

Political-religious conflict in the West was solved thanks to the secularist doctrine which calls for strict separation between church and state. The overwhelming difficulty with Islam is that such a doctrine is so unacceptable that few statesmen dare advocate it. Are state and religion condemned to live together in conflict and mutual distrust? Not necessarily, if both establishments endeavour equally to adapt to a compromise with one another. An extraordinary challenge for both Islam and state and a long-term task lie ahead.

7

Social Structure and Political Stability: Comparative Evidence from the Algerian, Syrian and Iraqi Cases

Jean Leca

The classic question of political sociology is concerned with the relations between the evolution of the social structure (the guiding principles for the allocation of scarce and valued resources; the identity, permeability, strength and wealth of beneficiary and deprived groups) and the political formula (the process of coercion, compromise and legitimacy which functions in a global collectivity). It is generally assumed that a causal relationship, functional or systemic, exists between the social constellation of interests (who benefits and who loses?) and the authority's moral order (who has the right and the power to master the political process? Who has the duty or the obligation to obey? What are the contents of the rules and the outcome of policies?)

For the past fifteen years most of the political Arab regimes can be considered as stable. Can the evolution of the social structure, both forming and formed by the nature of the government, provide part of the explanation for this stability?

POLITICAL STABILITY AND SOCIAL STRUCTURE: A STATIC MODEL

The concept of social structure can be used in a very abstract fashion to identify patterns of inequality, whatever they are. However, it is misleading if it rests on three concepts derived from the sociology of bourgeois society: (i) *the autonomy of the economic sphere* unified by the market with access to economic resources conditioning other resources, (ii) the *horizontal stratification* constituted by unequal access to the private ownership of the means of production, (iii) the *superposition* of units of analysis of the economic *structure*

164

and of units of analysis of *action*; not only do socio-political actors behave in general in conformity with economic interests as they see them (which in itself is quite commonplace) but political groups are, to paraphrase Lenin, 'the nomenclature of the social classes'.

Whatever their value in bourgeois societies, none of these concepts hold good in Arab societies (Bill, 1972; Eisenstadt, 1964; Chatelus and Schemeil, 1984; Batatu, 1985). Although they may apply to some historic situations or to specific substructures, they cannot be drawn on as part of a general paradigm. To throw light on this enigma it is not necessary to look to culturalist explanations or to dependency theories even though both have their value. Suffice it here to mention the long history of weakness in autonomous economic institutions (cities, feudal principalities, etc.) during the period of modernisation (Issawi, 1982, p. 170) and, in recent history, the importance of the economic role of the state, holder of oil rent, purveyor of employment, initiator of industry, instrument of investment, consumption and distribution of revenue (Chatelus, 1983; Batatu, 1984 and Luciani and Beblawi, 1987, vol. II, in this series). Where the economy is one of circulation more than production, access to rent is a more important principle of social structuration than the ownership of the means of production (though this is not so for real estate and commercial capital).

Three phenomena follow: (i) the importance of the political process (and of the state) in the constitution of social classes (for Egypt, see Waterbury, 1983, pp. 323 ff) and not only in their representation; (ii) a social articulation, complex determination and rating of categories and social functions, not exclusively manifest in occupation (Van Nieuwenhuijze, 1965, p. 77); (iii) the existence of multi-level identifications and the difference between classes and groups (ethnic and religious factions or local groups and clientele groups), with the latter more pertinent than the former to an understanding of social interaction (Bill, 1972). Since access to distribution is one of the principles of social structuration, and in consequence one of the issues at stake in the social struggle, group action is more immediately seen as normal and instrumental than class action.

The notion of social structure does not then imply the concept of a civil (i.e. bourgeois) society directly applied to the Arab world (Leca and Schemeil, 1983). Nor is it necessary to reduce the society to its kinship or corporative structure or to an ensemble of compound and decomposed groups (sometimes known as 'non groups' in anthropological language) connected by clientele relationships or lopsided friendships and dominated or crowned by a palace of ethnic clans, army officers and bureaucrats. Social mobilisation modifies the mosaic of solidarities without superseding the class, ethnic or factional action as the transformationist model would have it (Hudson, 1977, pp. 7–16).

The ideal *static* model of the relationship between social structure and political stability can thus be outlined, at least in the socialist republics of our study. Peripheral middle classes (non-bourgeois, coming from small rural cities) take state power and install a politico-economic formula based on the redistribution of wealth and political control of the economy. Agrarian reform, planning and expansion in the public sector, industrialisation and social spending are its main ingredients. This combination is only a variant of the big trade-off in the democratic capitalist states between equality and efficiency, analysed by Arthur Okun (1975). The allocation of revenue resources is only a way of avoiding confrontation and reinforcing the social stratification of those governed. Economic efficiency is not officially rejected. It is seen only as the outcome of political efficiency. Thus the growth of a new salaried middle class and a commercial and industrial private sector linked to the state is favoured. The difference between these states and the traditional monarchies (Heller and Safran, 1984) is that the new educated middle class is considered supportive of the regime and a factor in maintaining stability so long as resources are sufficient and their distribution accepted as equitable (that is, responsive to the different expectations of classes and groups).[1]

The trade-off with the new middle class has been important in the socialist republics, although it has never been presented as such. Whereas in Tunisia the government of Hedi Nouira was explicit about its strategy, in Algeria, on the contrary, the 1976 National Charter attributed the leading role for the future to the working class. Nevertheless, if we take our examples from socialist countries, it is because, despite their differences, the three regimes are sufficiently similar to test dynamically the model outlined.

SOCIAL CHALLENGES TO POLITICAL STABILITY: THE SPLIT IN THE MIDDLE CLASS AND THE DILEMMAS OF REDISTRIBUTION

(1) The 'new middle class' (NMC) is a vague concept which has borne the wear and tear of time quite well (Halpern, 1963; Bill, 1972; Turner, 1979; Heller and Safran, 1984). It does have

problems: (a) it is a *vague* concept which postulates a unity of position and condition of socio-professional workers competent in modern techniques, in whatever sphere they find themselves (administration, the army, enterprise or commerce), and attributes to them a common will for political modernisation; (b) it is an *elastic* concept which can just as well apply to menial jobs as to the upper civil service, to small entrepreneurs as to intellectuals; (c) it is a *residual* concept which rests on negative characteristics (neither the traditional merchant middle class, nor the big landowners, neither landless peasants nor proletariat;[2] (d) finally, it creates confusion between that middle class which formed the original political base for the regime, the peripheral middle class of the small rural towns, and that produced by the expansion of salaried employment, of consumption and of education. But these weak points are only the reverse side of a very fertile concept for which a better substitute has yet to be found.

The problem is the question of the destiny of this class. Can it remain an element of stability, dependent on the state for its reproduction but able to avoid and temper the resentment of the lower urban and urbanised classes and the dwindling peasantry, considering especially its lack of consumer ostentation, its austere habits and the authenticity of its cultural behaviour? It is possible that this middle class, modest and prosperous, ambitious and puritan, is only a fantasy in the minds of a leadership dreaming of Max Weber or Werner Lombart, or of Gambetta's new strata. Yet it is not a total figment of the imagination. The problem is that it sometimes tends to pay more attention to the religious opposition than to the nation state. Or is it possible that this class might split into an upper level of public and private managers and businessmen and a lower level of badly paid and barely committed salaried public employees (Waterbury, 1983, pp. 360–2)?

A double influence operates then, on the dual base of the patrimony (through continual access to oil revenue, foreign aid and international trade circuits) and the private ownership of the means of production and exchange. Neither of these bases of structuration necessarily obeys the same fundamental logic. The first rests on a commonplace logic, endogenous to groups: the patrimony is a sure and certain way of maintaining the family groups' social level, without running the risk of intergenerational downward mobility if the professional opportunities of one generation are lost for the next through rivalry or loss of palace favour. The second can be the result of a state strategy attempting to transfer onto the private sector the

SOCIAL STRUCTURE AND POLITICAL STABILITY

responsibility for meeting demands, creating employment and mobilising potential savings when its financial difficulties (debts, a fall in the oil income) no longer allow it to do without a bourgeoisie. But it is a risky strategy.

(2) Redistribution means that the NMC has that much more of a chance of being a stabilising group both when it benefits extensively (if not equally) from the resources accruing from oil revenue or foreign aid and also when state revenue stretches to cover classes with rising expectations. In a paper devoted to a comparison between Iranian and Nigerian social movements, Burke and Lubeck (1987) have convincingly argued that a regime's capacity to convert its oil wealth into collective goods and to co-opt the potential opposition determines its power to resist the challenge posed by popular Islam and cultural nationalism. In fact, the contrary would be surprising: whatever the source of wealth (annuities, industrial production or circulation), there is no reason why Muslim Arab societies should be spared the Tocquevillian tendency towards equality (i.e. refusal of excessive social rifts formerly considered natural); indeed, the opposite is more likely. Every spring must trickle through and water the entire social fabric. Not that great wealth is illegitimate (even Boumedienne's Algeria treated itself to a Messaoud Zghar). But if it becomes the negative symbol of the frustration of the excluded, that is if the social structure presents itself as a form of opposition between a predatory and corrupt group and all the rest (lower middle class, peasant smallholders, artisans, underemployed urban dwellers), popular protest could unite all those not belonging to the NMC and even its own frustrated members (those excluded both from the constitution of the patrimony and the private ownership of the means of production).

States redistributing wealth to the NMC can then find themselves facing a double challenge:

(a) The challenge of contradictory tendencies in redistribution. This is jointly rooted in rising expectations and the demand for equality, but the groups expressing such goals do not have the same objective. The upper middle class, who have received the first benefits, will be anxious to improve the standard and quality of their consumption while at the same time assuring their own reproduction by passing on material (notably real estate) and intellectual capital to their offspring (education for professional opportunities). The rest of the population wants the same things but on a lesser scale, which modifies the nature of the demand. A job, preferably salaried to give a minimal base income, and eventually a start in small scale

168

business, is the basic demand of those whose inadequate education (second rate diplomas and wasteage in the school system) bars them from the positions and returns that meet their minimal expectations. This is followed by a demand for the mass consumption of basic produce subsidised by the state. In the first instance, then, the state must enlarge and diversify the patrimonial and consumption market, in the second it must do the same thing in the labour market. It is not clear whether both can be done at the same time, since the jobs created to satisfy the latter do not necessarily produce the benefits which would satisfy the former, nor do they do so for the same people.

(b) The tendency toward opening the economy to the private sector appears to be an attempt to respond to this bottleneck. Could not the private owners of enterprises, commerce and services at one and the same time mobilise potential savings, create employment, develop disposable income and respond to the demand for consumption? Private entrepreneurs supported and protected by the state (but paying taxes to it), benefiting from a protected domestic market, in part through the state monopoly on foreign trading (although this is also an inhibition for entrepreneurs), are perhaps the dream solution of the socialist regimes. This only partially corresponds to the dependent development formula applied to Brazil by P. Evans: a non-agrarian class alliance among the industrial technocrats, the capitalists from protected industry, the state bureaucrats and nearly all urban consumers (Evans, 1979). As we shall see later, the regimes in our study can integrate farmers or at least rural dwellers.[3] In any case, in so far as the regime does not need to resort to exporting manufactured goods (because it can make do with exporting its hydrocarbons) and in this way can avoid the destabilisation of its political base by side-stepping direct confrontation with the international market, the creation of a bourgeoisie directly dependent on the state and oriented towards the domestic market can be a stabilising factor. But even if this bourgeoisie is a real entrepreneurial bourgeoisie there is a political price to pay. It is the manifestation of the social structure and inequalities by drawing attention to privileges (instead of concealing them within the state apparatus), especially if foreign debts and foreign bank pressures result in cost-cutting in the public sector, preventing it from playing out the residual redistribution role which it played with the creation of a public employment that was unproductive of anything but minimal social satisfaction.

169

SOCIAL STRUCTURE AND POLITICAL STABILITY

ALGERIA 1962–1985

The social base of the politico-economic formula: class links and class constraints

The Algerian politico-economic formula may be summarised by two characteristics: (a) *the combination of rationalities:* an economic rationality which demands the constitution of a self-supporting economy that must therefore be integrated and surplus-producing; and a political rationality which looks to the state to maintain a high level of allocation (in employment, consumer goods, social services) in order to transform political sovereignty into a means of satisfying social expectations; (b) *the constitution of an autonomous national society* which can superpose the political community and the economic community, in other words, lay the basis for a social structure on activities of production and exchange situated on the national territory. Hence there is an absolute priority accorded to state-sponsored industrialisation, the development of an administrative apparatus and the public services (see Benhouria, 1980; Benachenhou, 1982; Benissad, 1982; Lawless, 1985; Bennoune, 1985; and on agriculture, Mutin, 1980; Bedrani, 1982; Chaulet, 1984 and Pfeifer, 1985).

These two characteristics may perhaps be explained by the class nature of the Algerian state. By this term we do not mean the existence of a class link between a group clearly situated in the production process, and sectional or state elites, the latter recruiting from among the former. The hypothesis of a class link is simply not applicable to Algeria if one takes as a criterion of class the private ownership of the means of production and exchange. The urban and rural Muslim middle class studied by Ageron (1980) which was made up of middle-scale landowners, tradesmen, small industrialists and salaried executives and which constituted about 4 per cent of the population in 1954, participated in the FLN's decision-making process but did not itself hold a dominant position (see Quandt, 1969; Michel, 1972; Zartman, 1974 and 1984; Harbi, 1975; and Entelis, 1982).

Hardly anybody still maintains that the petty bourgeoisie has taken power. On the other hand a class link is plausible in two other senses of the term. It can refer to a political class whose members, regardless of their place in the economic division of labour and quite often without any fixed place therein, have a common investment in the political struggle because it is this that determines the ensuing

170

socio-political structures. But it must be recognised in that case that the class link becomes tautological, since the state does not recruit from any distinct group but, rather, is that group, and constitutes it,[4] or on the contrary, since it is the political resources of the state which alone can permit the creation of a socio-economic group.[5]

Class link can also refer to a group which is characterised first of all by its place in the cultural division of labour: in this sense Colonna (1983) could speak of the emergence between 1954 and 1962 of a literate petty bourgeoisie possessing as its principal capital a scriptural competence (in Arabic or in French, both lay and religious) and establishing itself at the centre of the political process. The objectives of the nationalist struggle were identified from then on with the particular interests of this group and the forms of struggle with the least costly means to achieve its objectives. The same is probably not altogether applicable to the whole political class (cf Harbi, 1975 and 1980), to whose diversity of origins and social trajectories Colonna herself draws attention, but it could well be interesting to extend the hypothesis of new cultural mediators to the decisions of economic policy. A highly-planned public sector economy makes the owners of technical knowledge and other organisers (the mameluks of modernity, to paraphrase Gellner, 1974) more functionally indispensable than the owners of the means of production. However, the class link cannot be here a principle of intentional action since in 1962 these mameluks who had graduated from institutions of higher education were still few in number in Algeria.

In fact, the principle which determines the relations between Algerian leadership and the social structure is not a common position in the production process but, rather, for the most part, a common distancing from the central economic positions of bourgeois society such as large landowners, industrial and commercial bourgeoisie, and salaried industrial workers. And with reason: these classes were weak, foreign or defeated as political classes. Industrialisation was set in motion by actors who saw in it above all a political goal and a political means to legitimise their power (particularistic interest) but also to fulfil their mission (ideological interest) in response to the class constraints weighing upon them.

In effect, class nature can also refer to the existence of class *constraints* which limit and induce various choices. With the exception of external constraints, the only (though heavy) constraints weighing upon Algerian decision-makers came from those whose access to the state as distributor of resources represented the

SOCIAL STRUCTURE AND POLITICAL STABILITY

expected and indispensable outcome of the liberation struggle. This access was the goal which limited the composite social base of the FLN, including small peasants and agrarian bourgeois or merchants; these two groups were, however, too lacking in cultural capital (in the case of the former) and in political and material strength (in the case of the latter: Algeria has no equivalent of the Tunisian Tahar Ben Ammar in its nationalist history) to obtain access to the state on its own terms.

In one sense, the decision-makers were under no internal constraint because no group was capable of opposing a legitimate project for a modern economy to the 1962 programme of Tripoli, but for the same reason the state could do nothing but redistribute foreign property, educate, allocate and, if possible, produce because it was there for that. After it produced independence, the production of a modern society was a necessary corollary, not only in the minds of the technocrats (who were in any case few in number) and of the politicians, but also for their clients, consumers of abandoned estates, of self-managed allotments and of public employment. What was thus one of the state's resources also acted as a constraint upon it: in order for Albert Hirschman's tunnel-effect to have full play, it was necessary that a large number of passengers got on the economic and public administration train (Hirschman, 1973). The result was an impetus towards exuberance (still using the terminology of Hirschman, 1968) of state-sponsored industrialisation. In this sense class constraint(s) pushed the state to regard industry more as a political instrument (of sovereignty and distribution) than as an economic instrument (of production and accumulation).

Algerian agriculture was not the subject of active policies until

Table 7.1: Algeria: share of agriculture and industry in labour force, Gross Domestic Product, planned public investment (in %)

	Labour force		GDP		Public investment		
	1	2	3	4	5	6	7
	1965	1983	1965	1984	1970	1977	1980–84
Agriculture	67	26.9	15	8	10	5.9	11.8
Industry (and hydrocarbons)	12	30.4	34	42	53	56	48.3

Source: 1 and 2: *World Tables: Social Data*, vol. II, World Bank, 1983; 3: *World Development Report*, World Bank, 1983; 4: *General Report on the Five-Year Plan 1980–84*, MPAT, 1985; 5 and 6: National Statistics Office, Algiers; 7: *Presentation of the Five-Year Plan 1980–84*, MPAT, 1980.

1980, because the rural world, source of legitimacy, was not the source of power (Colonna, 1980; Leca, 1980). The countryside was more the missionary field of agricultural production. Rural dwellers, who made up a significant section of the government, were not or were no longer farmers. Such sons of impoverished farmers as Ben Bella or Houari Boumedienne saw the countryside through their fathers' eyes: a distressed place offering neither new jobs nor surplus, and what is more, the site of respectable but archaic behaviour.[6] As for the rich countryside of colonial Algeria, which should have formed the capital for self-managed farming, the social movement to reclaim colonial land was quickly transformed into a policy objective led by political activists whom the peasants supported without committing themselves to production, which was made more and more difficult by the bureaucratisation of management (Blair, 1970).[7]

The Algerian social compromise

The Algerian social compromise may be summed up thus: oil revenues and access to foreign loans have permitted the generalisation of salaried employment, the creation of jobs without any corresponding extension of production and the reinforcement of managerial or bureaucratic activities. For instance, from 1967 to 1978 Sonatrach's employment tripled, while its output remained constant: in the fast-growing construction and public work sector, the value added by each worker had decreased by half from 1967 to 1982.

There has been a significant drop in unemployment in all sectors of activity. In 1966, 35 per cent of the active male population was unemployed, 23 per cent in 1977 and 11 per cent in 1984, showing

Table 7.2: Working male population of Algeria according to professional status (%)

	1966	1977
Employers	0.58	0.50
Independent	24.22	21.59
Co-operative workers	—	3.49
Seasonal workers	32.26	10.54
Full-time employees	35.15	60.00
Domestic workers	6.62	2.81
Non-declared	1.17	0.33

Source: *Statistical Annual of Algeria*, 1979.

SOCIAL STRUCTURE AND POLITICAL STABILITY

Table 7.3: Growth in employment in selected sectors (per thousand jobs)

	1967	1982
Industry	123	468
Construction and public works	71	552
Transportation	53	148
Trade and service	321	542
Government services	306	752
Agriculture	874	960

Note: Figures given here are different from the figures supplied by the 1980–84 Plan usually quoted by the international organisations.
Source: *General Directory of Statistics*, Statistical Series for 1967–1982, October 1984.

a sustained growth rate in employment of about 4.5 per cent per annum from 1967 to 1982. But the anticipated doubling of the active population between 1983 and 1999 as a result of demographic growth and of the entry of women into the labour market will necessitate an annual growth rate in employment of 5.5 per cent, a difficult objective.

Disposable incomes (salaries and profits) grew faster than productive capacity and the growth of imports and led to strong inflationist tendencies and a growing balance of payments deficit. Between 1967 and 1982, gross household incomes increased in real terms by 4.3 per cent annually while domestic consumption increased by 5.7 per cent annually. It was at this price that the economic system was able to function without coming under pressure from workers; but the incomes which they receive come not so much from values which they have created but rather from a part of the oil revenue.

Even though the purchasing power and standards of living of industrial workers have deteriorated (Thiery, 1982; Bernard, 1982), the organisation of the socialist management enterprises (Gestion socialiste des entreprises), the enactment of the general statute of the worker (Statut général du travailleur), the relative security of employment and the absence of pressure from state management to increase profitability, have up till now prevented the formation of broad social protest movements. Social tensions have taken the form of strategies of withdrawal from the workplace (see for example, Safir, 1985), of fairly tough local strikes, but not of an autonomous political class movement (Sraieb, 1985). The workers' movement may thus be represented as forming part of the state, legal society

174

SOCIAL STRUCTURE AND POLITICAL STABILITY

or '*hadara*', thus reinforcing the position of the left bureaucracy (Benkheira, 1985). In any case, there has been no development of a 'class-for-itself' movement with ideological and organisational autonomy. None of the massive social protest movements that Algeria has known (for example the Kabyle movement in 1980 or the demonstrations of marginalised youth in Oranie in 1982 or Constantinois in 1986) has presented such a character, even when these have resulted from a process of social differentiation.[8] Nor has Algeria experienced the degree of urban eruptions suffered by Tunisia, Morocco or Egypt as a result of massive rises in the prices of foodstuffs or (in the case of Morocco) the abrupt closing-down of educational establishments.

The system of distribution has not however prevented the crystallisation of social inequalities. One could even maintain that it has encouraged them, whatever the original intentions or the particular strategies of the social actors involved. The growth of nominal incomes has increased consumer demand, but the low productivity of the national productive system has not been able to provide the goods to meet this demand. In this vacuum, the most profitable branches of industry (construction, light industry, commerce) have grown stronger, in the sectors where public investment (of which 80 per cent is earmarked for hydrocarbons and heavy industry) has been lowest (see Benachenhou, 1983). Such a process has not led to the creation of a cosmopolitan sector connecting foreign and Algerian enterpreneurs, which is forbidden by the official ideology and by the state monopoly on foreign trade, but to the growth of a national sector constituted by the mobilisation of family savings through informal banks which lend at very high interest rates (between 25 per cent and 40 per cent) (Liabes, 1985, p. 136). Between 1967 and 1980 the purchasing power of manual workers stagnated or rose only slightly while that of private entrepreneurs increased by 56 per cent (Thiery, 1982, pp. 190–1). This indication of the vigour of the private sector became a major subject of debate at the sixth session of the Central Committee in December 1981: 'the state sector supports and reproduces private capital at all levels of the economy: in the distribution of wages, by protecting the market, by subsidising commodities, the state contributes to the structuration of an internal market and encourages the creation of a clientele . . . the restructuration of public enterprises and the role and function of private capital in economic development are dialectically connected' (Liabes, 1984). Algeria thus seems to have entered a new phase.

175

The private sector and the social structure since 1980

A study of Algerian private industry in 1972 concluded with the following observation:

> the private bourgeoisie of provincial and rural origin can rely only upon limited resources. It therefore orientates itself towards the nationalised sector and administration. It seeks to develop relations with senior state officials who can protect the interests of the private sector. (Peneff, 1981, p. 162)

This bourgeoisie, politically and culturally dominated and enjoying few marriage links with senior state officials, yet fulfilling economic functions for a small but demanding clientele and even recuperating exiles from the political class, has seen its social status evolve: the private sector is now the symbol of upward social mobility for workers who wish to become self-employed and for families planning their matrimonial strategy. A sociologist specialising in the El Hadjar steel plant writes:

> A private sector employer has today become someone who is looked up to, a 'maqla' with a high social visibility, who lives in a rich villa in the old colonial quarter, who marries off his children in sumptuous ceremonies and contributes to the building of a mosque. He has nothing in common with even a senior executive of El Hadjar, exhaused by the management of a complex organisation, living in a low rent building. In the early years of the El Hadjar site an employee of the National Steel Corporation would have been considered a good match by parents in search of a son-in-law. Nowadays matrimonial alliances have changed their objective, and nothing can match a good private capitalist. (El Kenz, 1983, p. 252)

Furthermore, the growth of the private sector has been encouraged by numerous regulations since Boumedienne's death.[9]

But it is nevertheless the case that the private sector creates few jobs in comparison with the public sector. From 1967 to 1982 public employment (including the administration) rose from 46 to 61 per cent of total employment, including a rise from 28 to 31 per cent of agriculture, 42 to 74 per cent of industry, 41 to 67 per cent of building and construction, 20 to 75 per cent of commerce, but from 71 to 51 per cent of transport. From 1979 to 1982 non-agricultural

Table 7.4: Growth in total non-agricultural employment, 1980–1982 and 1982–1984 (per thousand jobs)

	1980	1982	1984	Growth 1980–2	Growth 1982–4	% 1980–2	% 1982–4
Public sector (excluding administration)	889	1,033	1,217	144	184	16.1	17.8
Administration	660	752	842	92	90	13.9	11.9
Total public sector	1,549	1,785	2,059	236	274	15.2	15.3
Private sector	635	676	737	41	61	6.4	8
TOTAL	2,184	2,461	2,796	277	335	12.2	13.6

Source: *Maghreb-Machrek*, 1986b (from Bouzidi, 1984 and *The Second Five-Year Plan, 1985–1989*, Alger, MPAT).

SOCIAL STRUCTURE AND POLITICAL STABILITY

private employment (employers, employees and self-employed) rose by 9 per cent, employment in the public sector (excluding administration) by almost 20 per cent and employment in administration by more than 15 per cent (Bouzidi, 1984). In 1983 the non-agricultural public sector employed 1,920,000 people, or 73 per cent of the total non-agricultural workforce (compared with 70 per cent in 1979) and had created some 489,000 jobs between 1980 and 1983 (compared with 82,100 for the non-agricultural private sector), in other words, nearly 86 per cent of new non-agricultural employment.

Table 7.5: Non-agricultural private employment as of 31 December 1984 (per thousand jobs)

	Total	Self-employed	Salaried workers
Industry	127	41	86
Construction and public works	206	31	175
Commerce, transport and services	404	275	129
TOTAL	737	347	390

Source: *Maghreb-Machrek*, 1986b (figures from *The Second Five-Year Plan 1985–1989*, Alger-MPAT).

One can see from these figures (which are probably not completely reliable) that the private sector is very diverse and includes a large number of self-employed (some of whom are probably undeclared employers). According to the manpower statistics, the percentage of salaried workers is on the decrease. The private industrial sector is made up of businesses with a small workforce (except, relatively speaking, in the mechanical and textile industries). Only one private industrial enterprise employed more than 500 workers in 1982, while 4,700 out of a total of 5,700 companies employed between 1 and 20 workers (Hadjseyd, 1985); investment tends to be on a small scale and material is often obsolete, especially in the textile and food-processing industries. The National Statistics Office in its 1982 manpower survey registered for the private sector (both urban and rural) for 1983, 36,168 employers (of whom 9,860 were rural), 331,160 full-time workers, 106,170 seasonal workers and 756,900 self-employed. The structure of the sector is not very conducive to a class struggle between employers and workers.

178

SOCIAL STRUCTURE AND POLITICAL STABILITY

On the other hand, although the private sector receives only a tiny part of industrial investment (2.3 per cent in 1981) it employs 25 per cent of the population and realises 34 per cent of the added value (in the agro-alimentary branch these figures are 4 per cent, 34 per cent and 57 per cent respectively and in textiles 6 per cent, 45 per cent and 51 per cent (Amirouche, 1985). Monopoly profits on the market, the possibility of reducing the costs of production thanks to the low price of raw materials and intermediate products acquired from the public sector (Benachenhou, 1982; Semmoud, 1982), the virtual absence of social expenditures and the choice of payment systems (generally by the hour rather than by the month) create favourable conditions for the realisation of profits and the artificial inflation of added value.

In the course of the first Five-Year Plan, workers' incomes rose slightly (by about 3 per cent annually) while the incomes of the

Table 7.6: The development of incomes between 1979 and 1984 (in billions of dinars)

	1 1979 (in DA 1979)	2 Forecast 1984 (in DA 1979)	3 Actual 1984 (in DA 1984)	4 Actual 1984 (in DA 1979)
Wages and				
salaries	40.5	65.0	76.6	51.4
Agriculture	2.5	3.0	7.0	4.7
Non-agricul.	25.0	42.0	43.5	29.1
Administration	13.0	20.0	26.1	17.5
Non-salaried				
revenues	18.0	25.4	45.0	30.2
Agriculture	5.5	7.0	11.0	7.3
Non-agricul.	12.5	18.4	34.0	22.8
Transfers	8.8	15.5	19.7	13.2
Gross				
household				
incomes	67.3	105.9	141.3	94.8
Disposable				
incomes	—	—	131.4	88.1
Consumption	56.0	84.6	121.7	81.6

Sources: columns 1 and 2: *Presentation of the First Five-Year Plan 1980–1984*, MPAT, 1980; column 3: report on the results of the first plan in *Presentation of the Second Five-Year Plan 1985–1989)*, MPAT, 1985; column 4: *idem*, using the indicator for the increase in consumer prices established by the International Financial Statistics of the IMF and reproduced by the *Quarterly Economic Review, Algeria* 1985 annual supplement, p. 15. It is this only a rough calculation which must be subject to prudent interpretation.

179

SOCIAL STRUCTURE AND POLITICAL STABILITY

self-employed rose much faster (14 per cent annually). The presentation document of the second Five-Year Plan was probably not mistaken in its conclusion that 'in the course of previous plans the incomes of private entrepreneurs rose faster than had been forecast, thus contributing to inflationist tendencies and social inequalities'. These latter will no doubt be all the more manifest since non-agricultural salaried incomes have risen less rapidly than expected.

On the other hand, global consumption has increased less rapidly than forecast; and significant reduction in hydrocarbon resources which has led to a fall in investments and a serious disequilibrium in the balance of payments (*Maghreb-Machrek*, 1986a), has obliged the government to reduce domestic demand by about 5 per cent in an attempt to contain the external deficit. Such a contradiction, following a period of increased consumption, could make disparities of income a more sensitive issue. In fact, the statistics for consumer spending reflect both a general rise in the standard of living of the urban population (there have been increases for example in leisure and especially transport expenditures) and a widening of the gap in the quality of consumption. Habitations with up to seven people per room and consumption of subsidised commodities on the one hand, contrast with individual houses built 'at the initiative of the citizen', i.e. constructed on public land sold off cheaply by the state, on the other. Private habitations have multiplied in five years with the construction of over 100,000 units, while public housing fell 40 per cent behind target between 1980 and 1984, as 250,000 instead of 400,000 planned units were built.

The private sector is therefore developing, although it is still subject to control. The party, or a section of its leadership, is not prepared to allow the economic rationale of profitabiity (some would call it speculation) to gain precedence over the political rationale which governs distribution and social power. This is why there is a tendency to contrast the 'bad' private sector which is mercantile, speculative and remote from political power, although still the object of state subsidies, with the 'good' private sector, which mobilises savings, contributes to the growth of the standard of living, and combines the puritan and austere features of the nineteenth century Western bourgeoisie with the will to serve the national interest (Belaid, 1985). Echoing this attitude, certain employers (e.g. 'Parole du Privé', *Actualité-Economie*, June 1984) in the 'good' private sector emphasise their participation in the national effort, their complementarity with the public sector, and their acceptance of the state's monopoly of foreign trade, provided that a certain

180

SOCIAL STRUCTURE AND POLITICAL STABILITY

flexibility, and state aid for exportation in the form of subsidies, may be forthcoming. But above all, they insist on the need for autonomous organisation of their sector, presented as a means of eliminating its 'bad' side and establishing a decision-making partnership with the state. Still more interesting is the presentation of such re-structuration as the most appropriate organisation for *both* sectors, public and private. Here perhaps is manifested one of the guiding ideas of a section of the political elite: to make of the good private sector the instrument for rationalising the public sector so that it becomes more efficient, while however leaving the state in charge of access to profit and redistribution.

The rural classes and social stability

For its part, agricultural production has registered a decline in the socialist sector (self-managed lands and lands of the agrarian revolution) (Cote, 1985). As a result of the liberalisation of land transactions following the 1983 law, 500,000 hectares were shifted from the socialist to the private sector.

While large in comparison with its two North African neighbours, Algerian socialist agriculture has nevertheless declined, to the profit of a private middle peasantry which has a preponderant role in the production of meat and vegetables. Some of the agrarian revolution's co-operative structures have moreover been partially or wholly eliminated. One must nevertheless be wary of attaching too great an importance to legal distinctions between private and public sectors (the same applies for agricultural employment vs industrial and service sector employment) as a mechanical principle for the constitution and location of classes. In an important thesis which throws some light on the social basis of Algerian political stability, Claudine Chaulet emphasises the role of the family in explaining why the Algerian peasantry were quite willing to accept industrialisation while rejecting its apparent corollary, the industrialisation and intensification of agricultural production. As a result, the latter has stagnated in terms of absolute value. Indeed, many rural families, especially in the socialist sector, include sons working in industry, and fathers close to retirement as agricultural producers (not to mention sons who, as teachers and office workers, come to get produce from the farm) (Chaulet, 1984).

It is no longer a case of the extended autonomous family on its own lands, but rather the maintenance of cohesion among brothers,

181

and between conjugal units formed by brothers who are equal before the law. Wherever this cohesion has endured, it has given rise to two kinds of adaptation. Less frequently there have been associations of capitalist families covering several sectors, without however engaging in intensive agricultural production; more usually subsistence-oriented agricultural labour is combined with the salaried workforce and more of a non-agricultural nature. The rural family thus modifies the effects of urbanisation and industrialisation by contributing to the subsistence of a labour force mobilised by industry while at the same time benefiting from the support of non-agricultural employment.

The land is thus the repository of the family which looks to external sources of revenue to improve its standard of living. In this way oil revenues have been transformed into purchasing power produced by workers but not into new means of agricultural production. The social hierarchy that has been created is not founded upon the capacity to extract an agricultural surplus, that is to say upon the ownership (whether private or state-owned) of the means of production, but upon the relationship to apparatuses (both public and private) which distribute goods and services and determine the capacity to consume and accumulate. The relationship between the privileged clients and those excluded from redistribution may be more important that the relationship between owners and workers or small peasants (Chaulet, 1984, pp. 1048–55).

The combined impact of the extended family strategy and of differentiated access to the state's politico-economic circuits leads, according to Chaulet, to a triple rural class structure: (a) a rural bourgeoisie based on agricultural and more especially non-agricultural businesses, stronger in commerce than in agricultural production; (b) permanent workers on self-managed estates, unskilled full-time workers in the non-agricultural sector living in the countryside, co-operative workers and the small peasantry, constitute a rural proletariat who, because of familial cohesion and their relative security of employment, do not feel subject to the same exploitation as the isolated urban workers (but are more sensitive to inequalities of distribution), and are not antagonistic to either the state or the rural bourgeoisie; (c) a sub-proletariat with neither family support nor any secure source of income and belonging to no collectivity of kinship or of production, who may even be formal owners of a small plot of land, but are excluded (in particular by educational selection) from access to stable employment and services.

182

The development of the first two classes, in the context of a decline in agricultural production and expanding in industrial and commercial activities, tends to be a factor of support for the state (this is an optimistic interpretation which is not shared by Von Sivers, 1984). In any case, the stagnation foreseen in overall employment and the crisis of agricultural production are pushing the state to put forward (in a rather contradictory fashion) two recovery strategies: (1) incentives for autonomy in the utilisation of resources (and possibly even in the banking sector), which would tend to encourage the privatisation of agriculture, is a strategy imputed to the private bourgeoisie which has begun to be put into practice. It includes indemnities for landowners whose property was nationalised in the agrarian revolution, land transfers and broader provision of productive goods and credit to the private sector; (2) the inculcation of new techniques, the rationalisation of financial management, and the constitution of specialised workers' collectives, constitutes a strategy pioneered by state technocrats. It leads to an industrialisation of agriculture through a network of state farms controlled by engineers and technicians. The restructuring of the socialist sector is tending in this direction. The paradox is that if one accepts the analysis of Chaulet, there is no reason why the first strategy should particularly suit the rural bourgeoisie, which is obliged to confront the market, unless it receives exorbitant guarantees (complete liberty of wages and prices, and very broad tax exemptions as in Morocco), and still fewer reasons why the second strategy should suit the rural proletariat. If one is to go beyond a socially satisfying *status quo* (whose only fault is to be insufficiently productive), the first strategy remains the less improbable.

THE 'CORRECTIVE' MOVEMENT IN SYRIA: 1970–1985

In many respects the politico-economic formula in Syria is embedded in an external regional context and an internal social context[10] that is very different from that of Algeria. Baathist ideology makes Syria a province of the Arab nation, which conforms with the history of this province under the Ottoman Empire and as part of the United Arab Republic from 1958 to 1961. This might be of symbolic importance if it were not that the Palestinian and Lebanese situation induces the regime to devote nearly half its budget to military expenditure, a situation that in 1985 allowed a contraband traffic into Syria amounting to about 10 per cent of all

SOCIAL STRUCTURE AND POLITICAL STABILITY

its imports, to the profit of the army stationed in Lebanon. Unlike Algeria and Iraq, Syria does not have major oil resources[11] but it does have access to its own resources (i.e. not extracted from the society) from the Gulf and most likely also from Libya and Iran by virtue of its position as a frontline state in confrontation with Israel. Such resources covered more than 50 per cent of the budget in the late 1970s and only slightly less than 50 per cent in the mid-1980s, in loans and grants for both military and economic expedition (Longuenesse, 1985, p. 9; Chatelus, 1982, p. 254). Because of this, Syria evidently lives beyond its strictly national (or 'local' in Baathist language) means.

Table 7.7: Spending-production balance (in billions of Syrian pounds at 1980 constant prices)

	1980	1981	1982	1983
Total consumption	45.5	55.8	53.6	56.6
of which private	33.6	43.4	40.0	42.7
Administration	11.9	15.5	13.2	13.9
Total investment	14.1	14.4	14.8	16.3
of which public	9.0	8.9	9.2	10.9
private	5.0	5.5	5.6	5.4
Total spending	59.6	69.0	68.4	72.9
GDP	51.8	57.1	58.9	60.8
External net contribution	7.8	11.9	9.4	12.2

Sources: Compiled and simplified from the Central Bureau of Statistics, *Statistical Abstracts;* Economic Intelligence Unit, *EIU Regional Review, The Middle East and North Africa 1986.*

Syria is therefore in some ways an oil state by transference. But unlike countries with stable transfer economies, dependent only on market fluctuations, like Algeria or Iraq until the outbreak of war in 1980, Syria is influenced by fluctuations in the international political market, which in some way explains the strange variation of investment levels in the development plans, from over 40 per cent after 1973 to about 25 per cent in the 1980s, of which 18 per cent goes to public investment. The result is an almost total inability to develop a coherent industrial policy, a question we shall return to later.

The internal context can also be characterised in three respects. The most obvious is the salient and socially legitimate, although officially ignored presence of religious, sectarian and factional

184

SOCIAL STRUCTURE AND POLITICAL STABILITY

identities such as the Alawis who, with about 10 per cent of the population, were formerly a sect class (according to Batatu, 1981) and today are the central faction of Hafez al-Assad's rule. This does not mean that the ruling group either acts first and always in Alawi terms or that it does not find support and make alliances outside of this group. But the sect class faction occupies a disproportionate place for its numbers, and its group feeling allows it to respond impressively on behalf of the regime. There is also along tradition of town/country opposition that cannot be identified, as in Algeria, with colonialism vs nationalism. There, the decline of traditional cities, e.g. (Constantine, Tlemcen, Nedroma) has, in Algeria, made conquest of the city the symbol of national rule rather than a form of revenge against the very feeble traditional urban bourgeoisie. In Syria, this bourgeoisie and the landowning class were the social base of the parliamentary and dictatorial regimes prior to the union with Egypt of 1958 and the Baath seizure of power of 1963 (Picard, 1980; Batatu, 1981). This in large measure was a victory for the 'peasant hordes' and for the ruralisation of towns over the landowning oligarchy and old town-based bourgeoisie (Van Dam, 1979, p. 99). Meanwhile, among the political elites these long established classes were supplanted by sons of the peasantry and the middle class of the small towns (Maaoz, 1973; Van Dusen, 1975; Drysdale, 1981).

The differences between the Syrian and Algerian process stems neither from the nature of the social base nor the nature of the new regime's elite, but rather from the type of political culture, perhaps more 'Khaldunian' in Syria where the notion of holding state power and wielding it in the interests of one formerly excluded group has remained stronger. The divergence is especially due to the balance of power the struggles provoked. The power of urban elements and the strength of the industrial middle class, antagonised by the radical measures of the Baathist regime in 1966, precipitated the corrective movement in 1970, which continued to promote the countryside but did so with the aid of, and under the control of, the state (Metral, 1980, pp. 314f) which instituted for the first time an open policy from which the urban and Damascene private sectors benefited (Batatu, 1981, pp. 339–40).

The importance of the rural economy can be seen in its share of the GDP and the labour force. As elsewhere, agriculture in Syria is in decline but even so in 1983 it accounted for 19 per cent of the GDP (as against 29 per cent in 1965). The agrarian labour force represented 33 per cent of the total in 1980 (as against 52 per cent in 1965) (World Bank, 1983, 1985). The rural world is made up of

185

SOCIAL STRUCTURE AND POLITICAL STABILITY

Table 7.8: Landownership and distribution (as % of surface)

	10 ha	10 to 100 ha	100 ha	State lands
1913	25	15	60	—
1945	15	33	29	23

Source: Hannoyer, 1980, p. 288.

medium-sized holdings which had increased in number in the first half of the century.

The agricultural economic growth of the 1950s which marked the rapid development of capitalism in agriculture (Metral, 1980, p. 298) paved the way for the entry of the peasantry into the political arena and also for the first agrarian reforms in 1958, 1963 and 1966 under the Baathists (Garzouzi, 1963; Keilany, 1973; Metral, 1980; Springborg, 1981). But even as these reforms weakened the landowning class and increased the role of the state in agricultural policy and the control of inputs and markets, they did not noticeably develop the agrarian public sector (agrarian reform co-operatives and state farms) which held only 23 per cent of all cultivated land. The small and middle peasantry, beneficiaries of agrarian reform, retained their autonomy through the interplay of control and assistance which links them to the state: 'the development of market crops raised the monetary income of the peasantry and was accompanied by a rise in the standard of living . . . and by a new dependence' (Metral, 1980, pp. 316–17).The second aspect of the class structure worthy of mention is the numerical importance of the traditional urban petty bourgeoisie.[12] Independent workers and traders increased in number between 1960 and 1970 while medium-sized businesses decreased and the industrialised public sector became greater and more concentrated. (Longuenesse, 1979, explains it by reference to the material advantages offered by these occupations and the mechanisation of medium-sized enterprises which reduced their labour needs).

These characteristics of Syria in the 1970s explain the greater commitment of the state to agriculture where there was politically productive capital to be made,[13] and perhaps also the resistance of towns heavily populated by the petty bourgeoisie. They do not, however, contradict the schema outlined at the beginning of this chapter: the heavy engagement of the state in political industry, a large and meagerly productive administration and public sector that none the less provides jobs (more than two-thirds of the non-agricultural jobs,

186

SOCIAL STRUCTURE AND POLITICAL STABILITY

Table 7.9: Class structure of Syrian society in 1960 and 1970 (active population)

	1960	%	1970	%
Industrial and commercial bourgeoisie	19,750	2.2	10,890	0.7
Rural bourgeoisie	39,640	4.5	8,360	0.6
Working class	159,720	17.9	257,380	17.6
Agricultural proletariat	183,720	20.5	130,400	8.9
Traditional petty bourgeoisie				
— productive	51,300	5.8	103,350	7.0
— non-productive	59,600	6.7	112,740	7.7
Salaried intermediate (or middle) strata	132,530	15.0	234,930	16.0
Small peasantry	243,460	27.4	608.540	41.5
TOTAL	888,720	100.0	1,466,590	100.0

Source: Longuenesse, 1979.

exclusive of internal commerce), a growing if dominated private sector, a rural class interplay whereby the mechanism of access to the state is as strategic a factor as the ownership of soil and the control of the means of production.

The political industry, the bureaucracy and the public sector

The political rationale or the politico-military industry has been much more strongly emphasised in Syria than in Algeria (Chatelus, 1980; Seurat, 1982; Rivier, 1982; Sadowski, 1984).

The regime's politico-military functions in the region permit it 'to mobilise resources extending far beyond meagre profits of an industrial sector renowned for its lack of productivity' (Rivier, 1982, p. 119), but as we have seen, there is another side to the coin. Such external dependence can oblige the regime to cut its investments since it cannot contain either its military spending or its consumer subsidies, again only underlining the political rationale. This all works towards one end result: the economist cannot notice any strictly economic logic (for example, a heavy industry or an import substitution policy, Chatelus, 1980, p. 230) but he cannot miss the decrease in added value per job and in capital productivity (Longuenesse, 1985, p. 12). Costs become excessive, there is an underemployment of production capacity due to maintenance

SOCIAL STRUCTURE AND POLITICAL STABILITY

deficiencies and the dire lack of skilled workers, production units are implanted without any overall plan (Hannoyer, 1980; Seurat, 1980).

But here the sociologist may discern a social reproduction rationale. 'The primary justification for a factory is not the goal of showing a profit but the releasing of funds which in reality are themselves a source of power', thus symbolising the real presence of the state and providing employment, notably bureaucratic, in disproportionate measure (Seurat, 1982; Longuenesse, 1985 speaks more positively of the effects of this industrial policy). The evolution of the redistributive nature of the Syrian economy may be inferred from the gross domestic production structure.

Table 7.10: Evolution of the gross domestic production structure (as %)

	1970	1977	1983
Agriculture	19	16	18
Mining and manufacturing	25	22	17
Building and construction	4	7	7
Wholesale and retail trade	23	25	26
Transport and communication	8	7	7
Finance and insurance	7	6	5
Social and personal services	2	2	2
Government services	12	15	18

Source: Compiled by the author, see Table 7.7.

The relative decline in the value of industry and the growth of commerce and administrative services allow us to legitimately suppose that this distribution of revenue develops more rapidly than does production itself.

The politically induced and economically irrational creation and distribution of credit-jobs (Batatu, 1984, p. 13) has a dual effect: in the lower echelons, it increases the number of those who owe their jobs to somebody and thus are placed under a personal obligation; and in general it holds all those dependent on the state for their livelihood and opportunity for social advancement. Batatu (1984) points out that from 1960 to 1979 the number of state employees, including manual workers, leaped from 34,000 to 331,000, and argues that almost a quarter of the total population are in this situation and so eventually are members of the trade union organisations

188

linked to the ruling power (Longuenesse, 1985, p. 12). In the upper echelons, the interplay of factional and clientele interests transforms the public sector into a prebendal system (Sadowski, 1984; Longuenesse, 1985). The lower echelons and the upper echelons enjoy a virtually dialectical relationship; bound together ideologically and materially in defence of the public sector,[14] and all the more so since the lower echelons express themselves through trade union representatives, themselves partially dependent on the ruling power. They oppose one another in the recurring quarrel (in 1980 and 1985) over corruption and the bourgeois state, a quarrel periodically reactivated or simply tolerated by the leadership.

It is difficult clearly to analyse this type of crisis. When it becomes the object of toleration or official discussion, then its significance shifts from the original context to its presentation, organisation, and rival interpretations by rival groups. Not only does one man's efficient manager become another man's parasite but we can also discern a double entanglement, of politics and the economy on the one hand, of class, community, regional and factional interests on the other. The entire process conceals a multitude of strategies, of which some of the participants themselves are perhaps unconscious.

In 1985, the critique of the public sector and its functioning was undertaken by the trade unions and it is unthinkable that their discourse was not at least tacitly permitted by the president. It recalled certain themes of Algerian trade unionism in 1976 (Leca and Vatin, 1979, pp. 74ff) as well as the first critiques made in the post-Boumedienne era: the public sector, in particular, made massive use of imported goods with their consequent wastage and sold themselves to imperialism rather than developing the national potential. But Syrian trade unionisn went further, accusing public sector managers of seeking personal gain, a practice encouraged by the regime itself. Did this indicate a turning point towards the privatisation of the economy? The overall context would suggest a contrary interpretation: in criticising managers for their corrupt, anti-national practices, trade unionists had no intention of holding private bosses up as an example. Instead, when faced by a crisis, those in power stage-managed a scenario, about class struggle between workers and managers; the latter then became scapegoats from whom the leaders disassociated themselves and to whom they issued a warning by way of the union mouthpiece. This is state of affairs familiar to Algerians which confirms the earlier observation that the workers' movement is part and parcel of the state. This lower-upper opposition allows both symbolic and real causes to be found for the economic irrationality of public sector management when it becomes impossible to handle the crisis by increasing salaries because of the lack of finances (Longuenesse, 1985, p. 19). Upper managers are kept in a state of insecurity, thus perpetuating the clientele relationship.

The private sector

Since 1970 the private sector and its bourgeoisie have retained an important, although overshadowed, role which is why the political problems they pose in Algeria have never reached the same dimensions in Syria (a thorough study is still in progress: see Longuenesse, 1979; Amin, 1982). Class constraints weighing on the corrective movement were relatively simple: restore the confidence of domestic capital and of the bourgeoisie and petty bourgeois Sunnite merchants without losing the support of the peasantry and the wage and salary earners. A mixed political economy demands that socialist redistribution be upheld and maintained while at the same time a capitalist opening of the economy should be effected. Even though private investment (which remains stationary) equals about half the public investment allocated to the planning programmes, the private sector is in a minority in industry, both in terms of the value produced and size of labour force, and is only preponderant in real estate and domestic commerce, where speculation and the circulation of capital are necessary. Sunni traders benefit from this limited opening, which explains for some why, since 1978, the Muslim opposition has been unable to mobilise sufficient support (Ahsan, 1984). From this point of view the difference between the public and private sectors is not fundamental but only a means by which the regime can harness potential social and religious opposition.[14] But the high inflation rate (officially estimated at 20 per cent per annum), which does not bother the commercial and speculative sector, deeply affects urban workers in administration and industry.

The state which numbers these groups among its political base, or at any rate among its class allies, is doomed therefore to look for resources to transfer in order to maintain price and salary levels. In a sense, there is certainly a class struggle in the pure Marxist tradition over the question of salaries but it does not set the bourgeoisie against the proletariat for the control and exploitation of productive labour. Rather, it is the battlefield at the grassroots level and at top levels for the allocation and distribution of state resources.

Agriculture and the rural classes

As with Algeria, agricultural policies and problems are less important for present purposes than are certain aspects of the class structure after ten years of reforms. In Syria too, the reforms are marked by a combination of more flexible market mechanisms and intense state planning, since the state controls both water and credit, and the private sector holds almost 80 per cent of the cultivated land.

Françoise Metral posed the classic question in the conclusion to her 1979 article: 'kulak' (predominance of concentrated private farming) or 'collectivisation'? Posing the choices between support for high performance private ownership in the name of production, or for the co-operatives in the name of equal redistribution (Metral, 1980, pp. 321–2) or for the sake of political allegiances and control (Hannoyer, 1985, p. 28).

It is virtually impossible to answer this question fully given the wide diversity between regions in Syria (Metral, 1985). Two important examples come from the Euphrates and the Ghab (Hannoyer, 1985; Metral, 1985) where transferred oil rent gave impetus to ambitious projects. In the first, a fundamental difference seems to emerge between the rural bourgeoisie, who mastered their irrigation needs to become the main source of agro-industry production, and the lesser peasantry, bereft of capital and machinery and dependent on co-operatives in which they invest little economical labour but a good deal of political work (the playing out of factional and tribal conflicts destined to reap clientelist gains, especially jobs outside the village). Moreover, both strategies — class interest and political allegiance — can combine when the independent farmer shares in the running of a co-operative. What is more, neither group is stable.

Some members of the rural bourgeoisie may be downgraded whereas a lightweight peasant weaving his way through the local power network could turn any economic advantage to his political gain. The administration too has a dual rationale: centralised and rationalised management of economic resources where engineers are often much in evidence, and political, clientelist management of finance conceded to clans (and called misappropriation by the press). The agricultural enterprise becomes a means of forming a clientelist political base, thereby contradicting its own objective of intensifying production (Hannoyer, 1985). The end result is mystifying to the observer: has the state prepared the way for a class of private farmers to entrench themselves? Is this a state-assisted campaign which turns peasants into semi-urban workers? Is it a rationalisation of production by engineers? Still, these are not the most important questions.

More interesting is the fact that in a climate of relative economic efficiency (but starting at a fairly high level of productivity), the interplay between peasant family strategies and clientelist tribal distribution networks has opened new avenues for mobility and promotion to a great number of rural dwellers (Hannoyer, 1985, p. 29). So long as transferred resources allow the socio-political logic (allegiance and access to state resources) to win over the economic logic (production and bourgeois class interest), then the Syrian countryside remains a stable, if not legitimate, base and so it will remain as long as the number of those excluded from communal property and distribution networks does not increase excessively.

A study of Ghab shows similar mechanisms at work. Access to the state and army gives room for manoeuvre. Crops not provided for in the plan can be grown; allotments can be extended; external funds can be acquired (loans and paid jobs). As is true in Algeria, family brotherhood is again the key factor in all of these strategies with a double objective: diversify one's source of income and enlarge one's circle of contacts sufficiently to penetrate the state apparatus. In both examples, the mechanism for the transfer of state resources to private operators (Metral, 1985, p. 58), and the mixed social structure with its three components (independent farmers, salaried peasants or members of co-operatives and the state apparatus) are sources of support for the state in so far as class inequality is not sensitive enough an issue to cancel out the tunnel-effect mentioned above, and as long as demographic growth can be absorbed elsewhere than in agriculture (by emigration, trade, bureaucracy, the army or militia). As is often the case, the country-side is a support base for the state as long as it finds extra resources to supplement its means of production, and as long as its human surplus is transferred elsewhere. The problem evidently is to know if such a situation is durable. From this point of view, Iraq is in a better situation since it is the only one of three examples to import hired labour (estimated at one million) outright; but since 1981 Iraq, to all intents and purposes, has been living in a war economy.

IRAQ 1963–1985

The structural likeness between Iraq and Syria is evident in any comparison of the division of labour between agriculture and

SOCIAL STRUCTURE AND POLITICAL STABILITY

Table 7.11: The labour force in agriculture and industry, 1960–1980 (as %)[1]

	1960		1970		1980	
	Syria	Iraq	Syria	Iraq	Syria	Iraq
Labour force (%) in agriculture	54%	53%	51%	47%	33%	42%
Labour force in industry	19%	18%	21%	22%	31%	26%

Note: 1. The Iraqi figures offered by Sader (1982, p. 270) show quite a different picture. The agricultural labour force would have dropped from 52 per cent (in 1973) to 30 per cent (in 1977), the industrial one would here leap from 8.7 per cent to 20.1 per cent during the same period. Obviously, the bases of calculation are not the same. In any case, the similarity between Syria and Iraq is well established.
Source: *World Tables: Social Data*, vol. II, World Bank, 1983.

industry (with a deviation in the figures for 1980).

To be more precise, as the ever indispensable Batatu notes, the ethnic and religious structure is the same only reversed. Among the Muslim population in Iraq, 52 per cent are Shi'i, 20 per cent Sunni and 18 per cent Kurds, while in Syria 63 per cent are Sunni and 12 per cent Alawi.

Thus the core of the ruling element of Iraq also consists of a kinship group (closely related members of the Begat section of the Abu Nasir tribe), rests essentially on members of a minority sect (Sunni Arabs) and on country rather than city people (on middle and lower middle class families from the country towns of the Arab north-western parts of Iraq) and reflects the balance of forces in the army rather than in the country at large (the relative strength of the bloc of military officers originating from the country town of Takrit). (Batatu, 1981a, p. 344; for details see Batatu, 1978 and 1985)

As in Syria, the centre of power tends to fix itself around a tightly welded minority benefiting from the divisions among the Shi'i majority. Its ambition is not primarily Sunni but Arab, and Saddam Hussein has tried to widen his partisan base to Shi'is (Batatu, 1981b). None the less, he still depends on his particular identity for survival. He does not pursue a national class interest but, as a member of the peripheral middle class, he perceives problems in the same light as other sections of that class. Batatu (1985, p. 389f; see

193

SOCIAL STRUCTURE AND POLITICAL STABILITY

also Hudson, 1977, pp. 276f) detected here a factional-clientele logic consistent with the development logic of the entire middle class benefiting from the state, at the heart of which a higher class of state bourgeoisie is distinguishable (members of the commercial socialist sector whose members increased tenfold from 1970 to 1981).

The public sector and the private sector

When compared to Syria, Iraq shows a greater state hold on the economy, notably in agriculture and commerce, with the private sector being dominant only in the transport and communication, and construction sectors. These sectors have, since 1981, shown less growth in the GDP, but the fall in oil revenue caused by the war and the unreliability of Iraqi data make comparisons difficult.

Table 7.12: Public sector and private sector in certain economic sectors of the GDP (%)

	1980		1981		1982	
	Public	Private	Public	Private	Public	Private
Agriculture	46.9	53.1	53.1	48.7	52.7	47.2
Manufacturing	62.9	37.1	54.6	45.4	59.2	40.8
Construction	12.2	87.8	6.4	93.6	6.2	93.8
Transportation and communication	28.8	71.2	27.5	72.5	24	76
Trade	59.3	40.7	55.4	44.6	56.2	43.8
Subtotal	52.7	47.3	53.3	47.7	50.0	50.0
Mining and quarrying	99.7	0.3	98.6	1.4	98.7	1.3
Total	81.4	18.6	67.4	32.6	61.2	38.8

Source: Springborg, 1986.

In his essay, Springborg (1986) suggests a rapid growth in the private sector although, again, the figures must be corrected to allow for the decline in the oil sector.

These observations, confirmed by the respective share of each sector in gross domestic fixed capital (about 80 per cent for the public sector and 20 per cent for the private sector; as against 91 per cent and 8 per cent in 1979, because of the fall in oil investments), demonstrate a moderate growth in the private sector. The private sector is made up of small and medium sized enterprises, the vast majority of which employ less than 10 workers. As in Algeria, their share in added value (31 per cent for the entire industrial sector in

194

1977) and employment (30 per cent in 1978) (Sader, 1982, pp. 273–9) is more important than their share in investment. The large enterprises are to be found in the public sector although there is an appreciable number of private firms employing over 250 persons — more so than in Algeria — (20 as compared to 80 public sector companies), with the private firms going from an average of 500 to 700 employees between 1981 and 1982 compared to about 1,500 for those in the public sector (Springborg, 1986).

Infitah in agriculture

After the classic agrarian reform period in the 1970s, which placed about half of all cultivated land in collective farms and co-operatives by 1975 (Nyrop, 1979; Springborg, 1981), the Saddam Hussein government gradually changed direction. The number of collective farms diminished, many co-operatives were abolished, ownership ceilings were relaxed, usufruct rights were transformed from the state to private leasees, controls over recipients of agrarian reform land were progressively reduced and rents at low rates were granted by the government to Iraqis and other Arab nationals after the passage of law 35 in 1983. Credit has been more generously extended to private farmers, which enables them to purchase machinery; producers were given direct access to public wholesale markets or licensed private shops, and a joint venture was established to deal with the marketing of fruit, vegetables, and later on of field crops (see Springborg, 1986 for numerous details, except the statistics on agricultural land ownership, not released since 1979). The result has been growth in the private and traditional sector and stagnation in the public sector, which produces fixed crops at controlled prices.

This situation can be explained by two types of class constaints. One is upper middle class demand for more produce, even at higher prices and thus their reliance on the private sector, while the public sector continues to supply subsidised basic produce to the lower class. The other constraint is the need to satisfy the desire for social promotion felt by agents of the commercial socialist sector whose access to credit and inputs permits them to develop enterprises either parallel to, or together with, urbanite entrepreneurs. Hence, 'the symbiotic relationship between public and private sectors in which the latter exists by servicing the former, frequently provides the network in which the crucial contacts are made. Occasionally, these personal networks extend upwards into the political elite' (Springborg, 1986). Other groups may be observed in the rainfed regions: contractors, suppliers of machinery and equipment who receive about half the harvest, have fewer links with the national elite and are as yet only an amorphous group of supporters of the regime, more tied to the president himself than to the party. This verifies Hopkins's (1984, p. 7) hypothesis of a third wave of agrarian transformation. From the initial modernisation of large landholdings, followed by collectivisation or redistribution of land, to the constitution, with the blessing of the state, of a new private sector whose agents benefit economically and derive a political power base from their enhanced role.

CONCLUSION: CLASS SOCIETY, CLASS POLITICS AND SOCIAL UPHEAVALS

The foregoing account tends to bring Algeria and Iraq into line with each other, although the former is still well behind. There is the same overwhelming presence of an industrial public sector, the same political grip on the economy intent on redistribution and control, the same trend towards private sector development although only to quite a moderate extent (even though the private sector role in Iraqi agriculture seems more pronounced and so far at least there is no Algerian equivalent to the Buniyah family). Morever, the Algerian private sector exports very little and therefore the correlation between its growth and fluctuations in foreign trading as observed by Springborg in Iraq does not exist in Algeria. Springborg's hypotheses can then, with certain qualifications, be accepted.

(1) The single party power base is compromised by an extension of the private sector despite the attempt, more successful in Iraq than Algeria, to create joint ventures between the public and private sector. One-party systems are both ideologically and materially too fused to the public sector to find common ground with the employer interests of the private sector. Nor is it certain that the private sector is the consolidating base of Chadli Bendjedid's personal power (as Springborg maintains is the case with Saddam Hussein) and even if this were the case, any leader, no matter how authoritarian or sultanic, would find it difficult to overcome party resistance once he had lost his charismatic base or religious legitimacy).

(2) It is possible that the Arab political economies are evolving towards a centrist position. Those with a dominant public sector

196

whose state infrastructure is well-established tend to grant greater freedom of action to the private sector (Zartman, 1982, p. 31). The Gulf states, which from the start lacked autonomy *vis-à-vis* the traditional structure, are building state apparatuses that go beyond tribal and family relationships (in order to satisfy New Middle Class demands). This implies a rapid expansion of the public sector.

Secular patrimonial authoritarianism is more easily supported by a mixed structure which combines public and private sectors than it would be by a purely state economy (whose inefficiency would dissatisfy the emerging classes) or by a strictly private economy (which, by rendering visible the social structure of the groups, would exacerbate social conflicts and make them less easy to handle). The state can create classes but it is not necessarily able to give them political strength.

(3) One final hypothesis of Springborg's seems debatable however: 'an infitah class would itself constrain the ruler's options . . . A complete infitah leading to enhanced class solidarities and conflict would provide politically precisely what he does not want.' Hence the need for a mixed economy: 'Such an economy blunts class distinctions, thereby inhibiting the formation of firmly based political movements and thus perpetuating the very authoritarian rule that has presided over its development.' This logic is implicitly bound to the fact that the creation of classes leads to class action, action by groups identifiying themselves politically in terms of class and demanding political autonomy *vis-à-vis* the state. Corresponding to the economic market opened by the establishment of a private sector there should exist a political market opened by the establishment of class groups or factions. There is no empirical proof of this. The private sector growing up in the shadow of the state (and thanks to the public sector) certainly has an interest in gaining freedom of economic action, more access to credit and fiscal facilities, the freedom of cross-border traffic, but why should it have to undertake open political action when it can try to obtain all this at less cost to itself by remaining entrenched in bureaucratic or palace politics where the informal network of family, regional, and factional solidarity is at the heart of the game? It can, it is true, by virtue of its very existence, provoke class conflict and drive the workers and the excluded to demand freedom of political action which the bourgeoisie itself may not need. But as we have seen, the structural conditions for such class mobilisation do not exist either in the agrarian or the industrial sectors (given the rural class composition and the size of private enterprises in industrial life). What is more,

SOCIAL STRUCTURE AND POLITICAL STABILITY

the workers too, like the bourgeoisie have their demands (jobs, housing, subventioned low-price consumer goods, free medicine, educational opportunities) and these are also gained by way of bureaucratic and palace politics, or sometimes with local strikes or riots in the towns (although this is scarcely ever seen in Algeria) and not through any autonomous politicisation. The notion that a class structure, by simple virtue of its existence in the body politic, might destabilise populist-authoritarian regimes is related to the paradigm (erroneous in my view) of bourgeois society where economic and social relationships are meditated by citizenship and represented by political relationships in the public arena.

A society in which the social and economic relations are determined by the political ones and where the citizen does not enjoy autonomous political rights, but only the possibility of putting pressure on the bureaucracy through membership in a community or power group, might never experience the effect of the class structure binding the regime's roots so long as they are free from strong international constaints.

(4) The combination of bureaucratic authoritarian coercion and redistribution of wealth is not, for all that, a stable formula. Political action carried out by private factional, ethnic or religious groups is not always manageable. Moreover, the structure just described can also encourage another form of mobilisation. The most usual interpretation of Islamic or Islamist protest movements is as follows: secular nationalism supported by the new strata (New Middle Class intellectuals and the working class) is no longer a dominant force; Islamic ideology offers serious competition in that it both recuperates and dialectically surpasses nationalism. This Islam-based politics expresses at the same time (a) the desire for autonomy from foreign imperialism which is felt as a yoke of cultural aggression and material exploitation; (b) a revolt against the state which is seen as manipulative, corrupt and corrupting; and (c) the affirmation of a personal and collective identity, a bringing together again of spheres which bourgeois society separates (public/private, religious/political, economic/moral). This ideology finds its social base in the small towns and among those of a rural background, among young people who are relatively well-educated and politically informed, living in areas of rapid urbanisation (Etienne and Tozy, 1979; Ibrahim, 1980; Kepel, 1984 and 1985; Hermassi, 1984). Other commentators note that this social base is made up of certain segments of the lower middle-class whose leadership is a social mix including, among others, members of the rural elite (Ansari, 1984

198

and Chapter 9 this volume). In Algeria it is the rural middle class, and most especially its urbanised offspring, who are seen as the potential bearers of an Islamic ideology that can connect socialism and the sceptical and ecumenical Islamism of the state, and that in the rural world can supplant the tradition of self-reliance and abstentionism *vis-à-vis* the state (Von Sivers, 1984).

This contemporary Islamism, whatever its social content (e.g. whether or not it is favourable or hostile to the private ownership of the means of production) presents certain characteristic traits: an all-embracing ideology, egalitarian in the abstract and anti-individualist in practice, whose religious code is its root and source and not simply an instrument used for political ends. Such a common experience of resentment and frustration (in the economic, intellectual and symbolic spheres, giving three homothetic social categories) could be considered as progressive (Davis, 1984) or, on the other hand, a branch of the fascist family tree (Arjomand, 1984) (which is by no means a contradiction in terms). It does however form a relatively identifiable social unit through its symbolic content and by way of its organisation. It rejects partisan or institutional intermediaries and favours recruitment via family bonds or personal contacts in loosely organised and often very fragmented groupings. This does not prevent the unleashing of vast social movements for urgent material demands (often enough protest demonstrations against rises in food prices) and directed against the figureheads of corruption ('Western' shops and bourgeois districts, in the name of a religious code of justice which calls for an Islamic 'moral economy' (Burke, 1986)).

These movements are sometimes described as the revolt of the petty bourgeoisie (Fischer, 1982). This is most likely true in certain specified cases. But the essential seems to lie elsewhere; the redistributing state with its ever-increasing social weight has created a structure conducive to a total calling into question of its power (and that of the elites, groups and classes who seem to benefit the most). When there are no longer sufficient resources to provide for and satisfy those expecting minimal gratification (the impoverished peasantry, the urban sub-proletariat, unemployed skilled workers, those with decreasing spending power) the state becomes the target of manifold discontent which no class ideology can really express: the excluded (from many classes) in their turn reject the system that no longer has the means to integrate them into the allocation process.

From this point of view, the emergence of the private sector has a triple social significance, over and above the necessity for increased

SOCIAL STRUCTURE AND POLITICAL STABILITY

production (always a reason to justify a productive, non-parasitic, private sector). It is firstly the strategy for advancement of an upper middle class associated with the state. It is also, perhaps, an expression of the state's wish to indemnify itself, i.e. by offering up intermediate targets to social protest movements. But it renders the social structure and the social inequalities more visible.[15] The stratification of society and the privatisation of the state (Camau, 1984) are criticised together. The private sector, instead of coming to the aid of the authoritarian state, can in this way make it more fragile.

NOTES

1. The lack of resources can be smoothed over by the migration process. This aspect will not be dealt with in this paper, in spite of its utmost importance (cf. on Maghrebian migrations to France, Garson, 1981; Moulier-Boutang *et al.*, 1986 among many others; on inter-Arab migrations, Birks and Sinclair, 1980; Ibrahim, 1982; Serageldin *et al.*, 1983; Centre d'Etudes et de Recherches sur le Moyen Orient Contemporain, 1985). It is difficult to assess its relevance to our problem. It is likely that migration mitigates social tensions in the countries of emigration, and increases the supply of money and consumer goods available in the domestic markets, thus favouring the circulation process. Some studies show evidence of their positive impact on upward social mobility (Sabagh, 1982). More important, it is likely that they enhance cultural and confessional identities instead of class identities (Longuenesse, 1986).

2. For example Batatu, 1985, p. 386: 'By "middle class" I mean that composite part of the society which is plural in its functions but has in common an intermediate status or occupies a middle position between the propertyless and the proprietors and which includes, among other elements, army officers, civil servants, members of professions, merchants, tradesmen and landowners.'

3. On the seemingly opposite side, Morocco fully integrates the landowning bourgeoisie within the political formula (Leveau, 1984 and 1985). Benefiting from a favourable tax system, the landowners play an important role in supporting the regime. Morocco has no oil to export and has to rely on exports of citrus fruit to make up for the imports of wheat and oil.

4. In this particular case, it may be worth noting that the classical dispute in Western sociology, opposing instrumentalist to autonomist theories of the state, evolves in a peculiar way. Here the state is both totally autonomous (as an apparatus) since it is not manned nor manipulated by members of a specific economic class; and totally instrumental (as a process), being utilised by the political class (though not for its sole benefit) and being barred to anyone else.

5. Such a hypothesis is not groundless. But if the class link in reverse reminds us that the state can create classes, such a metaphor alone cannot

explain why the political class has made specific economic choices, leading to the creation of bourgeois classes. Mohamed Harbi is one of the few to have addressed the issue: emphasising the consensus among the rulers (populist culture and ideology, bureaucratic organisation and behaviour) in spite of their diverse class origins, he bases his explanation of their economic choices on 'the internal necessity . . . driving them to concentrate more and more power and to mold the national society to their own profit' (Harbi, 1980, p. 379).

6. The 1973 census of agriculture determined that 75 per cent of the farmers needed an additional source of income to make a living. In 1972 the Charter of the agrarian revolution pointed out that 425,000 farmers and their families (making up 72 per cent of the agricultural labour force) were below the subsistence level should they rely only on their holdings, 64 per cent of the farms occupied 29 per cent of the arable land, 13,000 farmers possessed more than 50 hectares (1.5 per cent of the farmers for 22 per cent of the arable land). Half of the private farmers did not use a metal plow, 10 per cent used fertilisers and 26 per cent used mechanical means (Mutin, 1980). In 1978, six years after the beginning of the agrarian revolution, the private farmers cultivated 60 per cent of the arable land and utilised only 23 per cent of the agricultural machinery. All those phenomena form a system. Private investment has none the less increased, in particular in aboriculture. That is probably due to the migrants' money (Karsenty, 1975, p. 141).

7. See also the policy of importing cereals which enabled the government to keep the producer prices artificially low while satisfying demand. By combining low retail food prices with low producer prices, the state was able to subsidise food consumption without excessively burdening the budget. Such political rationality did not extend, however, to other products (meat and vegetables) the prices of which skyrocketed. (See a more detailed account in Bedrani, 1982, pp. 111–64 and in Cleaver, 1982).

8. Can we interpret those movements in terms of class basis and class action in the classical sense? To some extent, Roberts explains the Kabyle movement by the dissatisfaction of the Kabyle bourgeoisie (Roberts, 1983) and Von Sivers attributes the religious resistance to the private peasantry (Von Sivers, 1984). It may also be so, but here the class is masked to such a point that it is almost impossible to pinpoint a political class consciousness of any sort.

9. For example the Act of 1985 regularising the illegal occupations of building sites, regulations encouraging private investments (Acts of August and December 1982 and decisions of December 1983 on private investment in petrochemical and heavy industries), fostering access to credit, providing facilities for importation, and granting fiscal advantages to the productive private sector (all the budgetary acts since 1983).

10. The terminology is not fully adequate: (1) the demarcation of domestic, regional and international contexts is particularly fuzzy; (2) the very notion of society is debatable in so far as it carries along several prejudices springing from the sociology of Western societies (cultural unification, class or group identities exclusive of cultural and communal identities, economic and social integration through the national market system). Cf. on the Syrian societies under the French mandate, Weulersse,

SOCIAL STRUCTURE AND POLITICAL STABILITY

1946, and on the contemporary period, Seurat, 1980, pp. 89, 119, and Michaud, 1981.

11. Syria's oil exports have made up 60 per cent of export revenues since 1974. Syria is also an oil importer since it cannot refine its own oil.

12. E. Longuenesse uses 'traditional' to point at the petty bourgeoisie (for example, the tradesmen and shopkeepers, in the usual Marxist terminology) and to differentiate it from the clerks and non-manual wage earners, part of the intermediate middle class. By 'traditional' she does not mean the traditional corporations in decline. This explains why, in her figures, the 'traditional petty bourgeoisie' (14 per cent of the labour force in 1960) is larger than the craftsmen (4 per cent, Halbaoui, 1965).

13. That does not preclude the impoverishment of a part of the peasantry. The rural world is in decline but, as Batatu has appositely pointed out,

if, therefore, in the long drawn out conflict between city and country, the city has been more and more overshadowing the countryside and growing in size, power and significance, the original city people themselves have been falling under. Even so, the city is having the final say, in as much as in the country people who are on the top of the heap now, are themselves being urbanised and transformed into citizens. (Batatu, 1981a, p. 338)

14. The opposition between public and private sector is accurately depicted as the complementarity of two forms of economic domination, rather than as a contrast between public and private interests (Hannoyer and Seurat, 1979, p. 38; Longuenesse, 1985, p. 27).

15. There are few quantitative analyses of social inequality. Samir Amin states that inequality is growing without always differentiating the absolute decline in the living standards of the poor masses from the relative gap between upper and lower strata (Amin, 1982, pp. 30–3 on land ownership and 120–32 on the overall issue. Most of the figures cited do not go beyond 1975).

8

Social Transformation and Political Power in the Radical Arab States

Rashid Khalidi

We intend to make you people into carbon copies of ourselves. . . . We have so many secret weapons you see. We will pacify you with Pepsi, sweeten you with deodorant and emasculate you with mouthwash . . . You're free now because you're poor; but we'll make you eager accomplices in your own enslavement. (Sheehan, 1964, p. 165)[1]

After an absence of over a decade, a visitor to the former twin capitals of radical Arab socialism, Cairo and Damascus, is struck by the great change in their outward appearance. The seas of shining cars and the roads and over-passes to go with them, the gleaming hotels, banks and boutiques, the expanses of flashing neons and garish billboards, all are new. They are the most obvious symbols of societies which seem closely in tune with the values of Western consumerism.

There is much that is still unique, distinct and Arab about both of these great cities, in spite of the changes they have undergone. But both have lost the bareness, the austerity, the look of strained poverty which characterised them in the 1960s, and which was consonant with the politics then espoused by their rulers. Appropriately, the new face of these two cities seems in keeping with the very different Arab politics of the mid-1980s.

It is impossible to pass judgement on a state's political system on the basis of such superficial impressions. Notwithstanding the glittering appearance of their capital cities, Egypt and Syria, like Algeria, Iraq and most other Arab states with large populations, still suffer from the ills of underdevelopment. Thus in 1977 the level of literacy in Syria, Egypt, Algeria and Iraq was only 53 per cent, 44 per cent, 35 per cent and 26 per cent respectively, and their

203

respective GNP *per capita* $910, $320, $1,110 and $1,550 (Ibrahim, 1982, pp. 59–61).

However, appearances are not entirely deceptive, and in spite of these grim facts, something has changed in these states. Similar mutations have remade the face of most Arab capitals over the past few years. They are part of a larger process which transcends the boundaries of individual Arab states and runs deep within their societies. This has been what we may loosely label *infitah*: a liberalisation of aspects of the economy and political system already under way in the early 1970s, and then greatly accelerated not so much as a result of government policies as by the wealth generated by the oil price boom of that era.

It is important to note that this wealth and the changes it brought affected not only the sparsely populated conservative oil-producing states of the Gulf, but also what used to be called the radical Arab states: Egypt, Syria, Iraq, Algeria, Sudan, Libya, and North and South Yemen. Of these eight states Egypt, Syria and (to a lesser extent) Iraq and Algeria,[2] will be the focus of this chapter.

The changes — indeed the reversals — in the internal and foreign policies of most of these states since the 1960s were rooted in this process of infitah. These shifts were not arbitrary and at times were not even the result of explicit policies. In a profound sense, they were a function of the socio-economic transformation engendered by a combination of indigenous processes of change and powerful exogenous forces. Notable among the latter were direct and indirect oil incomes.

Oil and gas revenues have been the motivating force of change in Iraq, Algeria and Libya — and to a far lesser extent in Egypt, which currently receives over 2 billion dollars annually from this source, and in Syria. Remittances from migrant workers in oil-producing states and direct subsidies from these states play a similar if less dramatic role in labour-exporting countries like Egypt, Syria, Sudan and the two Yemens (not to speak of Lebanon, Jordan and Tunisia, which fall outside the scope of chapter).

If there were any doubts about how much of a change has taken place in the four ex-radical states under discussion, it is necessary only to look at the individuals who run their political systems, societies and economies. The men at the top of the government bureaucracy, the officer corps, the security services, and the state and private sectors are quite different from the leaders of the 1950s and 1960s. This remains true, even when, as is often the case, they are the same individuals.

204

SOCIAL TRANSFORMATION AND POLITICAL POWER

They and their families own costly German cars, French clothes, Japanese consumer electronics and American home appliances. They live in expensive homes in heavily-guarded and exclusive neighbourhoods. They travel frequently, holiday and shop abroad, and when possible purchase property there. Their children learn English and/or French in school, and their ideal is to send them off to university in the United States or Europe.

Whatever they or their predecessors may have been in the decades of Arab radicalism, there is no way such men can any longer seriously be called revolutionaries. Indeed their current political conservatism would seem directly related to the fact that they are now beneficiaries of an established order which they have every interest in preserving.

Extrapolating from the current social conditions of members of this elite to the policies of the regimes they control, many recent events in the Arab world confirm the profound political importance of these transformations. Just as the restless young officers, teachers and students who dominated the Arab political scene of the 1950s and 1960s have evolved into balding, staid bureaucrats, so has the tone and tempo of Arab politics slowed down, even ossified, at least on the official level.

The contrast with the 1950s and 1960s could not be greater. Then adventurousness, passion and a spirit of self-sacrifice reigned in Arab political life. This sometimes reached the point of recklessness: the hasty Syrian-Egyptian union of 1958 and the vulnerable yet provocative postures of Syria and Egypt on the eve of the 1967 war come immediately to mind. Today, Arab politics are notable for the extreme caution and exaggerated concern for self-preservation with which most Arab regimes act, if they act at all.

Examples include the Arab world's timid response to the seven year-long Gulf war: even worse has been its impotence in the face of Israel's three month assault on Lebanon and the Palestinians in the summer of 1982 and the three-year occupation which followed. None of this led to disruption, or even to minor disturbances, in the course of normal life in most Arab countries (the largest demonstrations against the war and the massacres which followed took place in Israel). Nor has it led to serious efforts for common self defence or to concerted action either to put pressure on external powers, or to threaten their local interests.

The change from days gone by has not gone unnoticed. Twenty years ago, the Arabs were far poorer and weaker than today, and yet their leaders were actively wooed by both Washington and Moscow.

205

SOCIAL TRANSFORMATION AND POLITICAL POWER

Today, in spite of their new wealth, huge defence budgets[3] (which in most cases have bought them negligible defence capabilities) and massive holdings of US Treasury bonds, the Arab states show little ability to affect the policies of either superpower.[4]

External feebleness has been matched by a curious internal fragility, masked by the absence of political change. Major socio-economic transformations have not been accompanied by the political upheavals which once made the Arab world a byword for instability. On the contrary, a little-noticed phenomenon has been the virtual absence of fundamental changes of regime since 1970. Several leaders have died during this period, some violently, and others have been removed. However, with the possible current exception of the Sudan, in no case has this led to a fundamental change of regime, either in the conservative or the radical states. All have been superficially unchanging, if not necessarily stable, for at least 15 years, and in many cases much longer.

A look at the four ex-radical states under consideration reveals that all are ruled by essentially the same regimes as in 1970. Their leaders have sometimes been prominent for even longer. Hafez al Assad first filled a senior post in 1963: Hosni Mubarak in 1969; Saddam Hussein in 1968; Chadli Benjedid in 1963.[5] A similar phenomenon obtains in the other four: the recently overthrown Gaafar Numeiry as well as Muammar Qadhafi both seized power in 1969; by this date the military-tribal and party-based regimes which rule North and South Yemen, respectively, were firmly in place.

The key to how Egypt, Syria, Iraq and Algeria (and to a lesser extent the other four states) — dominated for so long by the same regimes and often the same individuals — went from being socialist-orientated, anti-American and apparently pro-Soviet, to what they are today lies in changes in the social bases of political power in the Arab world over the past few decades. We will now examine these further.

CHANGING RULING ELITES

The three coups of 1949 in Damascus marked the start of a two-decade process whereby the existing regimes of these eight states were successively overturned. The dramatic upheavals which marked this period were not always significant. Often, the most profound changes took place on another level and under a facade of temporary stability, but these coups and counter-coups served to

206

SOCIAL TRANSFORMATION AND POLITICAL POWER

show that the social order which had dominated Arab politics for many years was being replaced.

It is a commonplace that constitutional or monarchical regimes were thereby replaced by ones of a bureaucratic-authoritarian nature (Waterbury, 1983, pp. 6–12), dominated by military officers. It is also well known that these officers were generally lower-middle class and often of rural origins (Batatu, 1984, pp. 6ff), espousing a populist nationalistic ideology and often allied to or themselves members of clandestine radical political parties.

Although such changes in these four countries have been studied in depth (Batatu, 1978; Waterbury, 1983; Van Dam, 1979; Quandt, 1969), less attention has been paid to the fact that across much of the Arab world an era was passing. This was the age of the 'politics of the notables', to cite Albert Hourani's now classic term. Originally used to describe Arab urban politics under Ottoman rule, the term has been shown by Phillip Khoury[6] and others to describe aptly the functioning of politics during the mandate period and later. Important modifications in this traditional scheme took place before and after World War One,[7] but the essentials stayed the same and a socially homogeneous group continued to dominate politics.

This land-owning, office-holding and mercantile urban elite was different from country to country. It nevertheless had enough common characteristics for us to speak of its eclipse as being part of a pattern in the Arab core countries of Egypt, Syria and Iraq (related elites dominated Lebanon, Jordan and pre-1948 Palestinian Arab society). When this elite lost power, the traditional nationalist ideology and personality-based political parties it was associated with disappeared, as did the relatively free press and the forms of parliamentary democracy it had introduced or taken over from the colonial power.

An identical pattern did not obtain in the other states affected by the upheavals of the 1960s. Partly because of the way they were colonised and partly because of their distinct social structures, Algeria, Libya and Sudan underwent different transitions. So did the two Yemens: while the *ancien régime* in each had drawn much of its support from the tribes, the new regimes were in large part urban-based, although this distinction was never hard and fast either before or after their respective revolutions.

At the same time, there were important similarities between all eight countries. Hanna Batatu has suggested (1984, p. 7) that many key revolutionary leaders in both Algeria and Libya shared a pre-dominantly rural background with their Egyptian, Syrian and Iraqi

SOCIAL TRANSFORMATION AND POLITICAL POWER

counterparts. In most cases, the new rulers were considerably younger than those who had held power when the wave of revolutions began and represented an entirely new generation (one South Yemeni politician argued before independence that he had to be appointed president, since he was the only member of the new leadership over forty!)[8]

Unquestionably, however, the most striking similarity was the prominence of the military in the original takeovers and in the regimes they established. For a time, it looked as if these new regimes would retain a predominantly military character, whence books like Perlmutter's *Egypt: the praetorian state* (1974), Abdel Malek's *Egypt: military society* (1968), and other studies of the late 1960s and early 1970s. In fact, they did not remain praetorian states or military societies, if ever they were any such thing.

Beginning in Egypt,[9] which in this as in so many other respects has been the pioneer in the Arab world, a process of partial 'civilianisation' of these regimes began to take place. On the one hand, civilian technocrats were integrated into the governing apparatus and on the other — and more significantly — the top military members of this apparatus shed their uniforms, soon becoming nearly indistinguishable from their non-military colleagues.

Simultaneously with this process, which stretched over a decade from the mid-1960s, the military sector took over a growing share of both GNP and budget. The ostensible reason for this in most cases was external conflict (Egypt, Syria and Iraq with Israel; Iraq with Iran plus the Kurdish rebellion; Algeria with Morocco, etc.) Even in states where no such pretext existed, this growth continued. In the mid-1970s, Egypt reversed this process, a striking trend followed by the others, generally with a time lag of a few years.[10]

This phenomenon is exceedingly important, particularly in conjunction with the civilianisation of the government apparatus during the same period. It means that the military is not only getting a smaller share of the overall wealth of society, but is also forming a smaller proportion of that sector of society directly dependent on the state. Far from becoming 'military societies', those countries where the military took power are now moving in the other direction. This is happening is spite of regional conflicts which might have been expected to lead to higher defence outlays.

While the military is getting a smaller share of the pie, the officer corps in most states has been removed from direct involvement in the political process. Dissatisfaction has been prevented by higher pay, privileges and social status, glamorous new weapons systems

SOCIAL TRANSFORMATION AND POLITICAL POWER

and an increase in spending on defence in absolute terms over the period 1975–82 in all of these countries.

In the case of all except Egypt and the Sudan, a military supply relationship has been maintained with the USSR, even where the state's overall orientation is towards the West. This has been done partly to take advantage of low Soviet arms prices and thus get 'more bang for the buck', thereby keeping the military happy (although there are invariably other reasons for these states' link with the USSR and Western weapons are often attractive to them).

The result has been the depoliticisation of the armed forces in comparison with earlier periods. The current regimes have meanwhile taken the precaution of keeping a close watch over the military, use tight political and party control, secret police surveillance and periodic purges. In some cases paramilitary or parallel military forces have been created, often drawn from a particular sect, tribe or region, to serve as a counterweight to the regular armed forces.[11]

The net effect has been dramatic. In a region once notorious for military *coups d'états*, the armed forces have been largely absent from the ranks of the challengers to the holders of state power since 1970 (though the Sudan may prove to be the harbinger of a new trend). Indeed, the military has become a pillar of regime stability, proving vital for the repression of dissent, whether in Hama in 1982, or in Cairo in 1977 and 1986.

NEW AND PROSPEROUS CLASS

Over two decades, therefore, eight Arab regimes came to power by force and were then civilianised. Their armies were expanded but over time obtained a smaller share of both the GNP and the budget. The military was removed from politics, while serving to uphold those in power. How did the policies and social bases of these regimes change over this period?

Taking first Egypt, which here again preceded the rest, the high point of radical, *étatist* and socialist measures was the early 1960s. These followed a decade of reforms, partial nationalisations and half steps, and led to a major transformation of the Egyptian economy. A similar radical wave subsequently broke over the other seven states, though each took its own precise course.

By about 1970, these regimes had nationalised all heavy industry and most light industry; had taken over the private sector in banking,

209

insurance, export-import and often the wholesale trade and other sectors; had instituted rigid exchange controls and severely curtailed consumer imports and foreign travel. Most imposed extensive land reform. All had at least the rudiments of a planned economy and all developed close economic relations with the Soviet bloc, although many maintained economic links to the West even at the height of their socialist phase.

The state sector grew enormously as a result of these policies. According to Batatu (1984, p. 13), the number of state employees (counting the public sector but not the armed forces) grew as follows: in Egypt from 325,000 to 2.9 million from 1952 to 1976; in Syria from 34,000 to 331,000 from 1960 to 1979; and in Iraq from 85,000 to 662,000 from 1958 to 1978. This roughly eightfold increase over about two decades far outstripped the growth in population.

The price paid for these measures, taken in the name of 'unity, freedom and socialism' (in Baathist Syria and Iraq; in Egypt the same words were used but in a different order), was heavy. It included the disappearance of a free press, civil liberties and an open political system (where these had existed before the revolutionary wave struck), and a high level of repression.

Repression had been a feature of the mandatory and colonial era and indeed in one way or another had never been absent from the post-independence regimes. But the apparatus of control instituted by the military to suppress their rivals in the early years was new and sophisticated. It was retained and refined as these regimes matured, until they possessed a formidable mechanism for dominating society which was not dismantled in spite of the liberalising rhetoric which accompanied infitah.

The actual class composition of these regimes as they matured is hard to summarise beyond some of the observations made earlier. We have pointed out the lower-middle class and/or rural origins of many of those in key positions. This does not mean that the regimes they dominated did not include other elements. Urban upper-middle class technocrats were increasingly brought into important positions as time went on, in Egypt at an early stage, in Syria somewhat later and last in Iraq and Algeria. Some of these came from the old upper classes, whose members had either lain low or moved abroad and which made something of a comeback in the late 1970s.

In fact, what was taking place was the establishment of a hybrid new elite. This included ex-military officers of varying backgrounds, frequently but not always rural, and sometimes poor

(Waterbury, 1983, pp. 272–7); professionals and senior managers of the state sector and the government apparatus; well-to-do medium landowners; and a new group of businessmen, contractors, speculators and middle-men, some from the old upper classes, some with close links with those running the state sector, but all entrepreneurs of a kind which had seemingly disappeared in the 1960s.

Before this new formation could reach its current developed stage, a major shift had to take place in each of the states we are discussing. This was the ebbing of the 'radical' wave of the 1960s, which generally took place in the succeeding decade. The landmarks in this process are well-known: Sadat's complete reversal of Egypt's external alliances was only the most obvious external manifestation of what was happening. Domestically, the evisceration of the Arab Socialist Union after the Ali Sabri affair in 1971 and measures like the return of some nationalised and sequestered property showed that a major transformation was beginning. We are beholden to Sadat for the most fitting name for this new phase: infitah.

There were important shifts of policy in other states during the course of the 1970s, although they were rarely as dramatic as Sadat's moves. Among them was the limited economic liberalisation in Syria following the November 1970 coup, after which many propertied Syrians who had been in exile began to return. The Syrian private sector has benefited greatly, particularly from the liberalisation of imports and from the Damascus property and building boom of the 1970s and 1980s.

Another example of such shifts was the Iraqi regime's decisive abandonment of its alliance with the Communists in 1978–9. At the same time, many non-party technocrats, some of them links with the *ancien régime*, were brought into positions of responsibility in the economy and government. This coincided with an expansion of economic ties with the Western countries and a decline in trade and development links with the socialist states. Algeria's external economic relations followed a similar pattern in the late 1970s.

There was an anomaly in all this. On the surface, these regimes still appeared committed to the radical policies of the 1960s: the original slogans were still heard, identical words appeared on the mastheads of the same newspapers, the old faces still spoke the old words and the façade of good relations with the USSR and the hostility to the US and Israel was maintained. But underneath, something entirely new was stirring. Beginning visibly in Egypt in 1974 and spreading to the others with a time lag of a few years, infitah was growing into a powerful social and economic current.

211

SOCIAL TRANSFORMATION AND POLITICAL POWER

This does not mean that it won over the 'commanding heights' of the economy. As was pointed out by Waterbury (1983, p. 431) in the conclusion to his study of the Egyptian political economy over the past three decades, 'The state bourgeoisie has been weakened, but it is still the dominant force in the economy.' The state sector thus remains a powerful element, even if it is no longer particularly dynamic. This is all the more true in states like Syria, Iraq and Algeria, where the process of dismantling it has just begun, and where infitah is at an earlier stage than in Egypt.[12]

What infitah succeeded in doing was to win the hearts and minds of a broad stratum of society in all these countries. It did so in part by tapping the enormous pent up demands for consumer goods, imports, luxuries, foreign travel, investment opportunities, and at least the trappings of free expression. This had been dammed up over years of socialist austerity, war, and economic difficulties. Failing some outlet like infitah, this situation was probably bound to lead to open discontent sooner or later.

Avoiding such an explosion was undoubtedly a factor in the decisions of many regimes to go down this path. Another was the fact that so many of their key personnel had been won over to the new order and the symbols of consumption with which it was identified. They became allies within the 'new elite' of both the new entrepreneurs and members of the old commercial and landowning families making a comeback after the difficulties of the 1950s and 1960s. The result of this alliance was a boom in fields like property, construction, services, tourism, import of consumer goods — all sectors neglected during the socialist period.

This process may have done little for production in those basic sectors of these countries' economies, agriculture and industry[13] (Bourgey et al., 1982; Amin, 1982; Kubursi, 1983) and may well have benefited materially only a limited number of people. But it produced a 'trickle down effect' in one important sphere: that of the outlook, aspirations and ideals of a segment of society much broader than those who actually obtained something from infitah. The media played a key role in establishing the dominance of the freshly-acquired consumer values of the new elite. So did the experience of the many migrant workers from Egypt, Syria, Sudan and the two Yemens toiling in the oil-producing countries (Kerr and Yassin, 1982, p. 7; Ibrahim and Sabagh, 1982, pp. 48–53).

These new ideals had an impact, even when the rhetoric of the regimes still spoke of sacrifice, socialism and building a more equitable society. It was all the more potent where, as in Egypt, the

212

regime itself touted these values. And to the carrot of the wonderful things that could now be bought in the age of infitah was added the stick of inflation. As a result, the urban population began to be pushed out from under the umbrella of state subsidies and fixed prices where they had sheltered during the radical years.

It is only against the background of these rapid but profound changes and their creation of new social bases for the power of the regimes, that we can understand the shift in their foreign policies. In the case of Egypt it has been generally realised that a transformation inside that country has led to a reorientation of external policy, a realisation largely due to Sadat's public relations flair and his penchant for pushing things to, and often well beyond, their logical conclusions. However, in other Arab states the preoccupation of observers with their outworn rhetoric has often led to an insufficient appreciation of the extent to which they have changed both internally and in their external alignments.

Syria's acceptance of Security Council Resolution 338 (and thereby of SC 242), and then of Kissinger's mediation in 1973–74; its negotiation with the US (and indirectly with Israel) over its 1976 intervention in Lebanon; its acceptance of US Presidential Envoy Philip Habib's mediation in 1981 and then again in 1982; and its more recent willingness to receive repeated visits of US Assistant Secretary of State Richard Murphy in a similar capacity all bespeak an important evolution in the outlook of the Syrian leadership. This has continued in spite of the US-Syrian confrontation in Lebanon after the 1982 war and the accompanying harsh rhetoric.

The gradual Iraqi-American *rapprochement* which culminated in the re-establishment of diplomatic relations in 1984, and the change in the Iraqi position towards Israel, as symbolised by the 1978 Baghdad and 1982 Fez Arab summit resolutions (which for the first time committed it to accepting the existence of the Jewish state), are equally significant. Similar changes could be cited for Algeria, such as its negotiations with Iran on behalf of the US for the release of the Teheran embassy hostages, the exchanges of high level visits, or the growing extent to which its economy, like that of Iraq, is tied to the West.

In consequence, virtually the entire Arab governing class (including the rulers of these four ex-radical states) now in practice considers the US not as an enemy, but as an honest broker, if not a potential patron. Similarly, in spite of strong popular hostility towards Israel, in practice the Jewish state is no longer treated by the Arab regimes as an implacable enemy and an eternal regional

SOCIAL TRANSFORMATION AND POLITICAL POWER

pariah, but rather as a disputatious neighbour to be dealt with when possible via the always-available services of the US diplomacy.

These constitute momentous shifts from the attitudes of the 1950s and 1960s. They indicate the depth of change among the rulers of an Arab world which formally and superficially wears the same aspect as in 1970, with most of the same men, regimes, parties and structures still in place. As we have argued, what has changed has been these men themselves, the class they represent, and thus their aspirations and values.

The pre-eminent example is again provided by Anwar Sadat. By the time of his death, the ascetic revolutionary plotter of the 1940s was Sadat the star of American TV, the complete country gentleman with his briar pipe, his dogs and his English tweeds. Similarly, the same Saddam Hussein who was wounded while trying to assassinate Abd al-Karim Qasim, more recently was always impeccably dressed in pinstripe suits (at least until war with Iran led him to don a field marshal's uniform).

Equally important, the bureaucrats, army officers and secret policemen who support these rulers have also changed. Where once they carefully cultivated an image of dedication and selfless idealism, they now appear in a manifestly different light. The phenomenon extends well down the pyramid of power: it is not a case of absolute power corrupting the men only at the very top. It is easy to compare the early writings of Sadat or speeches of Assad with their later positions to show how they have changed. Underneath them, thousands of men who once wore khaki or shirt-sleeves now wear dark suits and Pierre Cardin ties, and more significantly, now think in a profoundly conservative way. A new elite has been established and is now maturing as it grows more prosperous.

DISTANCE BETWEEN RULER AND RULED

What of those not in the elite, those whose aspirations may have changed, and those whose expectations rose, but who have not yet had anything? What will happen if they cannot realise these aspirations or meet their expectations?

It can be argued that since oil wealth in large part fuelled infitah, and since it is unlikely to dry up immediately, any speculation about a crisis of unfulfilled expectations is at least premature. The current economic troubles of the oil-producing states and their potentially

214

grave consequences for the labour-exporting countries which are now economically dependent on them, cast some doubt on this argument.

The question may transcend oil together. The radical regimes of the 1950s and 1960s did not come to power solely as a result of a crisis of unfulfilled economic expectations. The traditional nationalist politicians like Shukri al-Quwwatli, Nuri al-Said and Mustafa Nahhas Pasha had aroused political expectations — for independence, freedom and dignity — and were judged by their peoples to have failed to fulfill them.

The 1980s are not the 1950s and history does not repeat itself, mechanically at least. In addition, it would be foolish in the extreme to underestimate the ruthlessness of those in power, the ferocity of their secret police or the firepower of their armed forces. They have developed a successful formula of graduated repression combined with controlled rewards and when it broke down in the past they showed little hesitation in unleashing these fearsome agencies on their citizens. If necessary, they could do so in future with equally few regrets.

However, these societies are still plagued by illiteracy and poverty, and are growing less self-sufficient in food production.[14] Given these facts, they cannot be called truly stable, especially when the bitter realities facing the mass of the people are contrasted with the wealth of the new elite.

This elite, however, is sizeable and its (largely Western) values permeate a large part of society. Such a diversified and powerful dominant group may be able to weather the discontent of the less-privileged, as those of previous eras could not. Manifestations of Islamic radicalism in most Arab countries indicate this may not be the case. A return to the purity of Islam does not necessarily mean a clash with Western values (depending on a given believer's understanding of Islam). But for many Muslims, there is a clash. It is hard to escape the impression that for them 'return to Islam' is a means of escape from and sometimes protest against values and developments in society which they do not approve of.

These are not original observations. But they sum up why Islam has become a main vehicle for dissidence in many Arab states. Another reason is that there is currently no viable secular alternative to Islam for expressing opposition to the *status quo* in the ex-radical states. This is partly because their regimes have rhetorically pre-empted the ground on which a radical secular alternative might stand. Indeed, they have made the ideas and policies of the radical

215

SOCIAL TRANSFORMATION AND POLITICAL POWER

left suspect in the eyes of the population. This is not surprising in view of the fact that they have changed course as much as 180 degrees, while their rulers' political discourse often still features the slogans of the long-gone radical days (Khoury, 1983b, pp. 228–9).

Political dissatisfaction, unfulfilled material expectations, and popular alienation from the new elite are not the only perils facing the once-radical regimes. There is also the strain resulting from defeats inflicted by external forces. Notable examples, such as the siege of Beirut, occupation of South Lebanon and the Iran-Iraq war, have already been cited. To these and other challenges — some going back 18 years, like the occupation of the Golan Heights, West Bank and Gaza Strip by Israel — there has been no meaningful Arab response.

These constant reminders that the rulers have failed to protect national dignity are important in view of the fact that the 1948 defeat and Arab impotence over the Palestine question and in the face of the West, sparked off the radical wave of the 1950s and 1960s. Unlike the rulers of today, the victims of these upheavals — the conservative old nationalist leaders, many of whom were as radical in their youth as their successors — never promised the Arabs unity, freedom and socialism. They had less to answer for than do their modern counterparts.

At the moment, none of the current rulers is being called to account, except by Islamic radicals. And those in power are supported by a far more extensive social base than their predecessors: the new elite which has matured under infitah. However, they can no longer manipulate the masses with the old populist Arab nationalism which served both the old politicians and many of the radical leaders so well in an earlier era: revived and remodelled by the latter, it is now thoroughly discredited.

Today the wild crowds which used to listen to such rhetoric are gone. There now exists a forbidding distance between rulers and ruled, a distance which is measurable in many ways. One is the massive walls and vehicle obstacles around government buildings and the homes of officials in Damascus and Baghdad to guard against car bombs. Another is the large numbers of armed troops, police and secret police guarding the streets of Cairo, Damascus and Baghdad. A third is the absence in recent years of once-familiar scenes of mob adulation of their leaders by the people of these and other capitals: now most Arab rulers are semi-recluses, moving in heavily guarded convoys from palace to palace.

Where once al-Nahhas, al-Quwwatli, Ben Bella, Nasser and

216

other leaders of both generations of 20th century nationalists aroused popular passions, the present incumbents are generally regarded with indifference. An example of this new attitude was the unconcerned reaction of Egyptians to Sadat's death. This was not solely because of his unpopularity. It is doubtful whether the current rulers of most Arab countries would be deeply mourned by their people.

This vast chasm between rulers and ruled reflects the gap between the elite, which supports the former, and the rest of the population. It is the best evidence that there has indeed been a transformation of the social bases of power in the once radical Arab states over the past few decades.

Whether the end of a cycle like that which ended with the upheavals of the 1950s and 1960s is at hand, or whether the current one has not yet been completed is unclear. What is certain is that in less than two decades the social formation now in authority in the ex-radical states has reached a stage of domination over state and society which the generation of Nuri Said, Shukri al-Quwwatli and Mustafa al-Nahhas took half a century to reach. In this relatively short time, however, a distance which is apparently unbridgeable has grown up between ruler and ruled.

NOTES

1. A character based on Kermit Roosevelt of the CIA is here addressing one modelled on Nasser.

2. Although trends affecting the entire group first arose in Egypt, Syria and Iraq, numerous specific observations about them do not apply to the other five states. The most similar to these three is Algeria and the greatest anomaly is South Yemen (which in many ways is an exception).

3. The combined defence budgets of all 18 Arab states came to well over 50 billion dollars in 1983–4, equal to the combined defence spending of the UK and France. The combined GNP or GDP of all 18 in 1982–3 was over 430 billion dollars.

4. An excellent example of how little Arab views count in Washington was the February 1985 visit of Saudi King Fahd, which, according to the condescending article by Bernard Gwertzman ('Rolling out the Reagan red carpet', *The New York Times*, 18 February 1985, p. A12) 'produced no significant agreements and no changes in either Saudi or American views', and of which an Arab specialist at the State Department said: 'Sooner or later it is going to dawn on Fahd that American policy has not changed. It is still pro-Israeli . . .'

5. Assad became commander of the air force in 1963; Benjedid one of five commanders of a military district in 1963 and a member of the 26-man

SOCIAL TRANSFORMATION AND POLITICAL POWER

Council of the Revolution the next year; Saddam became vice-chairman of the Revolutionary Command Council and assistant secretary general of the party in 1968; and Mubarak chief of staff of the air force in 1969.

6. In his Harvard PhD dissertation *The politics of nationalism: Syria and the French mandate, 1920–36*, to be published by Princeton University Press, and an introductory section of which has appeared as Khoury 1983a.

7. For some of these changes and some qualifications on Khoury's argument see Khalidi (1984) 'Social factors in the rise of the Arab movement in Syria', in S. Arjomand (ed.) *From nationalism to revolutionary Islam*, Suny Press, Albany.

8. The speaker is Qahtan al-Shabi, cited in Halliday (1974) *Arabia without sultans*, Penguin Books, Harmondsworth, p. 259.

9. In the late nineteenth century, Egypt led the Arab world intellectually; before World War One it was the first Arab country where basic elements of modern politics like the press, nationalist ideology, political parties and elections functioned; later, it led the radical transformation of the 1950s with authoritarian, Arab nationalist and socialist theory and practice; and for the past 15 years it has led the way in the other direction.

10. According to figures in the International Institute for Strategic Studies' annual *The military balance*, Egyptian defence spending, both as a percentage of GNP and in absolute terms, grew until 1974–5, then dropped precipitously. In Syria the upward trend was less rapid and started later, but was similar to that of Egypt, as was the subsequent downward trend, in spite of greatly increased expenditure in the 1981–2 due to the conflict in Lebanon. In the other six states (except Iraq, after the outbreak of the Iran war), trends followed those in Syria: defence spending rose in absolute terms, but at the end of the 1970s the rate of increase slowed, and spending began to decline as a percentage of both GNP and the state budget.

11. A striking example is the *saraya al-difa* in Syria, now much diminished in importance, but many others exist. Batatu, (1984), *The Egyptian, Syrian and Iraqi revolutions: some observations on their underlying causes and social character*, Georgetown University Center for Contemporary Studies, Washington DC, touches on the cases of Syria, Libya and Iraq.

12. Amin, (1982), *Irak et Syrie 1960–80: du projet national à la transnationalisation*, Editions du Minuit, Paris, pp. 144–8, concludes that the 'evolution of the Nasserist experience' illustrates the inevitability of Syria and Iraq following the Egyptian model, notwithstanding the residual importance of the state sector in both. The same idea is implicit in the analysis of Seurat, (1982) 'Etat et industrialisation dans l'Orient arabe (les fondements socio-historiques)' in Bourgey *et al.* (eds.) *Industrialisation et changements sociaux dans l'Orient arabe*, Editions du CERMOC, Beirut, pp. 54ff.

13. The feeble growth of industry manufacturing contributed only 10.5, 12, 13 and 13.6 per cent to the GNP's of Syria, Iraq, Algeria and Egypt from 1976 to 1980.

14. See Kubursi (1983), 'Arab agricultural productivity: a new perspective' in I. Ibrahim (ed.) *Arab resources, the transformation of a society*, Georgetown University Centre for Contemporary Arab Studies, Washington

218

DC, Table 2 which shows declining ratios of self-sufficiency for almost every food commodity produced in countries in the ECWA area from 1970 to 1977.

9

Limits of Ruling Elites: Autonomy in Comparative Perspective

Hamid Ansari

Ruling elite models have informed a generation of scholars concerned with Middle East studies. But nowhere have they been so extensively applied as in the study of Egypt. A great deal of reformulation and adaption has been made in the various approaches to unravel the secrets of a society whose history and politics continue to fascinate scholars and layman alike. For the purpose of analysis, however, these approached may be divided in to two major models: the elite-mass and the second stratum.

Each model emphasises an important aspect of social and political reality and ignores the other. The elite-mass model stresses ruling elites' autonomy, while the second stratum model put emphasis on the social base of support for the ruling elites. This essay will argue that greater insights into the problem of state stability can be gained by observing the interaction between ruling elites' autonomy and the limits imposed on them by the second stratum model. It will also show the limitations of these approaches and suggest possible ways for overcoming them in the light of recent developments in the Middle East.

The elite-mass model has dominated the field without any rival. As a consequence, the literature is replete with such concepts as the 'unincorporated society' (Moore, 1974, pp. 193–218), the 'Praetorian state' (Perlmutter, 1974); and 'patrimonial' (Springborg, 1979, pp. 49–69; and 1982) and 'neo-patrimonial' (Akavi, 1975, pp. 69–113) rule and elite will (Waterbury, 1983, pp. 32–40) — all conveying a near consensus on the autonomous character of the state and the absence of social restraints on the exercise of power by the ruling elites. By contrast, the second stratum approach presents a minority view on the links between the social and political orders and posits important questions concerning sources of political

220

stability for which the dichotomous approach has no adequate answer.

The dichotomous elite-mass approach does not deviate significantly from the classic ruling elite model which divides societies into rulers and ruled. The rulers constitute a small minority that dominates an undifferentiated mass. The instrument of rule in the hands of the dominant ruling elites is the military and government bureaucracy. Groups and classes, both of which are fundamental in the liberal and Marxist theories of development, respectively, are not counted for much, given their immature stages of development. In the majority of cases, they are excluded from consideration because of the underlying assumption that they do not constitute a threat to the ruling elites or exercise control over policy-making in any effective way. Thus the dichotomous elite-mass approach in its extreme form reduces the study of politics to the uncomplicated form of a small majority controlling and directing an undifferentiated mass.

Military intervention in Middle Eastern societies has generally reinforced the view of the autonomy of the ruling elites on the basis of assumptions largely drawn from the Latin American literature. For example, it has been observed that army officers intervene in politics autonomously and in accordance with their corporate interests. The impression gained is that Middle Eastern rulers, particularly the rulers drawn from the military ranks, are above society, unconstrained by its structure and untouched by the consequences of their decisions. It is further assumed that the authoritarian tendencies of the ruling elites are reinforced by a cultural disposition which teaches blind obedience to authority (Waterbury, 1983, p. 15).

In contrast, the second stratum approach assumes that power in its most rudimentary form originates in dependence on traditional support. Thus a fundamental point of departure for this approach is the assumption that the state and civil society are not separated by a gap as the conventional wisdom of the dichotomous approach dictates. Rather, it is assumed that the state and society are linked together by a social stratum whose intellectual origins can be traced back to the Italian thinker Gaetano Mosca. In the words of Binder (1978, p. 12):

> For Mosca, the second stratum is the necessary mediating instrument without which the ruling class or the ruling oligarchy cannot rule. The political function of the second stratum extends from

representation through expressive identification to the exercise of authority.

In a slightly modified version of Mosca's thesis, Binder points out that the 'second stratum', it must be remembered, is not the ruling class. The second stratum does not rule but is the stratum without which rulers cannot rule (Binder, 1978, p 26).

In order to understand fully the concept of the second stratum and its operational principles, it is important to bear in mind that its political necessity does not stem from its functional role. Necessity here must not be confused with functional indispensability. Rather, it is its particular characteristics and its specific situation in the society which together enable the second stratum to act as the mediating instrument. Egypt shares with a number of Middle Eastern countries the fact that diffusion of modernisation has left behind an uneven pattern of the regional development. The major differences lie between urban and rural areas and these differences continue to exist despite recent demographic changes as evident in the high rates of urbanisation and rural migration into the cities.[1]

The cultural-geographical bisector has been bridged traditionally by the intermediary role of locally influential individuals who are the heads of villages, the landlords or tribal chieftains. In Algeria and Tunisia, this role has traditionally been fulfilled by the *qaid*, while in Egypt it has been carried out by the *umdas* or the rural notables, the *yan*. In Iraq and Morocco, it was the tribal chieftains who acted as mediators and initiators of the process of national integration by representation at the centre. In Syria, the *zuama* and *mukhtars* mediated their local influence with the central authority. What unites these individuals is their traditional role as instruments of national integration. They are generally resident cultivators and, since they are more closely tied to the soil than the urban *dhawat* and *effendi* classes, they tend to regard themselves as the carriers of national culture and its most authentic representatives. Despite their localism, they have succeeded in forging kinship links with urban areas as more and more of their members attain higher education and come to occupy high positions in the military and government bureaucracy. Furthermore, although they are conscious of their economic interests, these elements do not constitute a cohesive class in the classical Marxist definition of the concept.

A variety of conditions could be explained in the light of the ruling elite model. Perhaps most salient is the persistence of the political order in many countries of the Middle East, despite the

LIMITS OF RULING ELITES

failure of reforms and the shifting orientations of the ruling elites. A quick scan of the Middle Eastern political scene shows clearly that in the majority of cases, the political orders, give or take a few changes in the political institutions, have proved to be extraordinarily resilient. What makes this resilience all the more extraordinary is that it has happened despite the recurrence of socio-economic crises brought about by the failures of 'socialist' and 'liberal' economic reform experiments.

Do the ruling elite models explain the persistence of the political order despite the failure of reforms? The most deficient model in explaining the persistence of the political order is the elite-mass approach for predicating ruling elite autonomy and for ignoring the social base of support to the authority at the centre and the limits such support may impose of the ruling elites. It is inevitable that under this approach the bureaucracy or the party, devoid of their extra-societal character, become instruments of control. The argument is strengthened further by the prevalence of a cultural disposition which inculcates blind obedience to the authority. In contrast, the second stratum approach emphasises the social base of support to the ruling elites.

In Binder's (1978, pp. 26, 36) interpretive scheme in the light of the second stratum approach, the political formula devised by the military officers who seized power in Egypt in 1952, reflected an alliance with rural middle class (RMC). In his view, the RMC is a class of locally influential landowners of moderate means (owners of 10 to 50 feddans) who constitute the backbone of the second stratum. Through the medium of the single party, the military oligarchy mobilised the RMC while it excluded from participation the outlawed and urban-based pre-revolutionary parties and political movements. Similarly, one may argue that the stability of the Syrian and Iraqi regimes stems from the efforts to mobilise the support of the small and middle peasantry through the Baath party. In Libya, it was the turn of the People's Bureau to mobilise the supportive elements and exclude from participation the disloyal individuals or the persons whole loyalties were held in doubt.

Parallel to the mobilisational efforts through the single party ran the agrarian reforms, since their purposes were almost identical. The reforms were meant to strip the traditionally dominant classes of their economic privileges and to isolate them politically. In Egypt, the agrarian reforms were implemented gradually and each time the ceiling was lowered, until it reached 50 feddans per individual or 100 feddans per family. This is in addition to the famous socialist

223

decrees which deprived the wealthy classes of their huge urban-based resources.

The Baath regime in Syria implemented a much more radical agrarian reform that the one adopted by the Egyptians at the time when Syria and Egypt were united in the United Arab Republic. As pointed out by Ziad Keilany (1980, p. 221), the Baath party made strenuous efforts to extend its authority into villages after removing the rural power of the landlords through the agrarian reforms. In fact, the land reform programme itself was used as a vehicle to establish political linkage extending between the revolutionary elite and the masses in the villages and neighbourhoods. The regime of Colonel Qadhafi went to the extreme of refusing to recognise private property. although his extremist outlook was more influenced by the need to deprive the traditionally dominant class and men of the Sanusi order of their economic resources and, consequently, their political power than by an egalitarian impulse.

The reforms, however, failed to satisfy the expectations of the peasant masses. On the contrary, the experience of both Syria and Egypt shows that there has been a rise in the influence of the rich and middle peasants. Egypt is a prime example of a country whose agrarian reforms failed to stem the rise of rich and middle peasants to positions of influence. As an indication of the extent of their influence, it has been pointed out that they 'control about 62 per cent of the farming area and high as 80 per cent to 90 per cent of the agricultural machinery. Their position has been further enhanced by *infitah*, or the "open door" policy.' (Batatu, 1983, pp. 70–1). Keilany, among others, has also shown that the traditional power of landlords in Syria has persisted, creating a rival power to the peasant unions which the Baath Party had attempted to organise.

How do we explain the failure of reforms? From the perspective of the elite-mass approach, the reforms failed because of the personal predilections of the rulers themselves, their political orientations, fears and hesitations which may be summed up as the 'elite will'. In the words of Waterbury (1983, pp. 37–8), the failure of reforms in Egypt was related to Nasser's own fears and hesitations:

> Nasser refused to use the iron fist, not because of signals from the countries of the core (they abounded) nor because of his class predilections, if he had any. Rather his course was set by his very real unwillingness to sacrifice, as he put it, the peasant generation for those of the future and to unleash potentially uncontrollable elements of class conflict.

Waterbury, however. leaves unexplained the reason why the rulers would feel motivated to wear the egalitarian mask in the first place. If they were autonomous, why would they feel compelled to enact reforms or respond favourable to egalitarian demands? Paradoxically, if there were no limits on the autonomy of ruling elites, why would they retreat from implementing more radical reforms once they initiated them? Finally, what is the basis for assuming that the abandonment of reforms would prevent class alienation and the exacerbation of class conflicts? Is it not more reasonable to assume the exact opposite, that is, the failure of reforms would increase class alienation and conflicts?

Binder's explanation (1978, p. 7) of the reasons behind the failure of reforms is congruent with his explanation of the attempts exerted by the ruling oligarchy to mobilise the RMC support and exclude from participation the pre-revolutionary elites. According to him, the RMC was like 'lucky Pierre, always seems to turn up as a beneficiary of the system'. He further points out that as consequence of the agrarian reforms:

> The great absentee landowners who were connected with the palace or with the Wafd were deprived of part of their wealth and most of their political influence, leaving the more traditional rural segment of the second stratum in virtually undisputed dominance. (Binder, 1978, p. 26)

It is not surprising, according to Binder, that the agrarian reforms did not go below the 50-feddan limit — the threshold beyond which the interests of the RMC would have been directly affected.

Although there is strong empirical evidence to support the second stratum approach, the problem is the lack of rigorous definition of the relations between the ruling oligarchy and the second stratum and of the second stratum itself. A rigorous definition of the second stratum is difficult to achieve because it does not constitute a cohesive class.[2] Although members of the second stratum give the appearance of a homogeneous class by virtue of their traditional outlook and their pervasive local and national influence, they are divided by wide gaps of wealth and prestige. It must be noted that neither the agrarian reforms nor the party bureaucratic-penetration of the countryside eliminated the traditionally influential elites who constituted the wealthiest rural strata. In Egypt, the new leadership promoted by the central authorities in the rural areas and the traditional leadership overlap. In Syria, they coexist as rival centres of power. Party leaders are sometimes forced by the exigencies of circumstances to seek compromise with the traditional elites.

Binder's assumptions regarding the intermediary role of the RMC were based on an uncertain graduation of landownership arbitrarily drawn by the Bureau of Statistics.[3] Empirical evidence tends to show that the traditionally influential elites are highly stratified in terms of property ownership and the amount of influence exerted both at the national and subnational levels. In so far as Egypt is concerned, the most influential nationally and subnationally are the wealthiest. But this does not mean that the small peasant with the proper kinship connections is without influence in his locality. In other words, it seems that the role of the second stratum extends above and below the RMC, i.e. the large landowners who were not influential in the pre-revolutionary era and the small farmers.

This emphasis on the stratified and incohesive character of the second stratum as an instrument of mediation is directly related to the shifting ideological and policy orientations of the ruling elites, a subject to which we turn later in this chapter. Suffice it now to say that an historical review would reveal that it was the upper stratum or *kibar al-ayan* who continued to exercise their intermediary role, except for brief periods when the ruling elites put on the radical mask.[4] Iliya Harik's study of power relations within a village community under the impact of the centre's party-bureaucratic penetration, revealed the dynamic nature of the social base of power at the local community level under Nasser.[5] His research led to the conclusion that in the period which preceded the radicalist trends in the mid-1960s, the rich farmers, who may be regarded as equivalent to Binder's RMC, displaced the traditionally dominant elites who were most closely identified with the *ancien régime* in the local party and bureaucratic organs.

In the radical period which coincided with the Kamshish Affair of 1966 and the formation of the Higher Committee for the Liquidation of Feudalism (HCLF) and lasted until the outbreak of the June 1967 war — the so-called mobilisation period — the rich farmers suffered a setback, while the small farmers rose to positions of influence thanks to the leadership groups organised by the central authorities and to the various party organs whose main aim was the mobilisation of the small farmers. This took place at the time when the urban areas were seething with discontent and when, under the hegemonic control of the authorities, the left emerged on the political scene as a counterforce to the underground movements representing the Wafd and the Muslim Brotherhood. The Kamshish

Affair and the investigations launched by the HCLF reflected the last stage in the radical attitude of the central authorities toward the dominant rural elites. This was followed by a reversal in policy orientation which led to the re-emergence of the upper stratum and middle farmers, although they were weakened by the turmoils in the mid-1960s.

The re-emergence of the rich and middle farmers at the local community level coincided with the emphasis on order and stability by a regime whose confidence was shaken by the June 1967 defeat. One may appreciate the second stratum as a source of political stability by studying a situation where it does not exist. It has been observed that a rural middle class in Iran was conspicuous by its absence. Furthermore, Iran is the only country in the Middle East whose agrarian reforms were almost revolutionary in their consequences. A scholar has pointed out that:

> The two Pahlavi monarchs in Iran gradually broke the power of the tribal chiefs, local notables, the trade and merchant guilds and eventually of the nationalist politicians who had acted as a bridge between the old politics and the new. This facilitated appeals to an undifferentiated mass, without traditional intermediaries. (Bakhash, 1983, p. 61)

As a consequence of the agrarian policy adopted by the Shah, the removal of the traditional landlord class brought the Shah face to face with the recalcitrant peasants. This in turn increased his reliance on the bureaucracy as an instrument of control. By contrast, the agrarian reforms in Egypt had the opposite effect. They reversed the phenomenon of landlord absenteeism, while consolidating the rural notables who had traditionally acted as the mediating instrument between the regime and the peasant mass. Thus while it may be said that the agrarian reforms in Iran revolutionised the countryside and even set the stage for the revolutionary upheaval which engulfed the country shortly before the fall of the Shah, the reformist policies of Nasser produced the opposite effects of stabilising the countryside and strengthening the power of the state. The only exception to this general trend was the mobilisation period, when the ruling elites appeared to be determined to take strong measures to bring about social change in the countryside.

The question now is what motives the ruling oligarchy to put on the egalitarian mask? An important element missing in the elite-mass approach is the socio-political implications of the social origins of

LIMITS OF RULING ELITES

the ruling oligarchy. Egypt shares with Syria, Iraq and Libya the fact that the ruling elites are drawn from the lower middle classes and have generally shown the tendency of appealing to the sentiments and values of their class origins. In fact, the leaders of Syria and Libya come from the most downtrodden classes. In the words of Batatu (1983, pp. 67–8), the Alawites from which the ruling military officers are drawn:

> Constituted the most numerous and poorest peasants to the west, south and east of the Alawi Mountains. Under the Ottomans, they were abused, reviled and ground down by exactions, and, on occasions, their women and children were led into captivity and disposed of by sale. Their conditions worsened with the deepening commercialisation of agriculture and after World War One became so deplorable that they developed the practice of selling or hiring their daughters to affluent townspeople. It is such conditions that drove them to enroll in great numbers in the state armed forces, a fact which eventually was instrumental in their rise to the political dominance which they now enjoy.

In Libya, quoting Colonel Muammar Qadhafi, Anderson writes (1983, p. 139):

> The officers have the conscience to recognise the people's claims better than others. This depends on our origin which is characterised by humbleness. We are not rich people: the parents of the majority of us are living in huts. My parents are still living in a tent near Sirte. The interests we represent are genuinely those of the Libyan people.

Iraq is also no exception to what appears to be a general pattern. Again, according to substantial documentary evidence presented by Batatu (1978, pp. 1004–7), the ruling officers reflected the rise of inferior tribal and small elements to positions of power, Zartman (1980, p. 4) further points out that in Algeria:

> A new elite from small towns and villages eliminated the colonial rulers in 1962 . . . In Tunisia, the Neo-Destour party which came to power in 1956, was centred above all in the rural villages of the Sahel, although the Sahelis came into a majority in the political elite only in 1970.

228

The Egyptian officers who captured power in 1952, by contrast, did not come from a homogeneous socio-economic background. Among them were officers who were the sons of the rich umda class as, for example, Marshal Abdel Hakim Amer. Others were connected with the landed aristocracy and had close associations with the palace, such as Ali Sabri. Nevertheless, Nasser and Sadat, the two Egyptian leaders who controlled their country's destiny successively in the last three decades came from the class of small landowners. It has been pointed out that Nasser's father owned less than five feddans while Sadat's father owned two and a half feddans. It is not surprising, therefore, that Nasser turned out to be the nemesis of the landed elites and champion of the downtrodden *fellahin*, or the small and landless peasants.

Social origins may sensitise the ruling elites to the egalitarian demands and to the problems of equity in general. Nonetheless, as the behaviour of Sadat well testifies, no determinate relationship can be discerned between social origins and political behaviour. In contrast to Nasser, Sadat showed a preference for Parisian clothes and the easy, luxurious life; he had 35 houses spread all over the country. In his late years, Sadat's opulence contrasted sharply with his social origins, as Heikal has so starkly revealed in the *Autumn of fury*. The question is how do we explain the contradictory behaviour of Nasser and Sadat in the light of the ruling elite models? How do we explain the shifting socio-political orientations of the ruling elites which at times sharply contradict what influence social origins may have had on their perception of political reality?

A significant element missing in both the elite-mass and the second stratum approaches is the pressure exerted by the lowest rural strata and the very small farmers. It has generally been assumed that Middle Eastern peasants are politically quiescent. It has been assumed that the agrarian reforms were implemented from above and that the peasants played no part in them. Waterbury (1983, p. 325), for example, conveys the impression that the agrarian reforms had a 'tunnel effect' on the peasants, meaning the accommodation of one stratum of peasants, while the rest of the rural population awaited their turn patiently. Waterbury goes further by asserting that there has been no sign of peasant involvement in Egyptian political life since 1952. On the other hand, Binder maintains the view that the ruling elites were more keen on keeping the lid on social changes than hotly pursuing egalitarian principles. Egalitarianism was sacrificed in the interest of maintaining the alliance with the RMC.

History, however, conveys a different impression. The Egyptian peasants have been able to bring pressure upon ruling elites from time to time, although they have failed to change the social order. Peasant rebellions coincided with major historical events such as the French invasion in 1798, the Urabi revolt that led to British occupation in 1882, the 1919 revolt for national independence and, finally, the rebellious spirit of the peasants manifested itself in isolated incidents of violence in some villages before and after the army seized power in 1952. It has even been suggested that the limited agrarian reforms were carried out in 1952 to prevent further polarisation in the countryside and to stem the revolutionary tide among the peasants (Abdel Malek, 1968, pp. 68–70). Accumulated evidence thus tends to reveal that the submissiveness of the peasant is only skin deep, and, given the emergence of circumstances such as a major reshuffle of power at the centre, the propensity to rebel may manifest itself (Baer, 1969, p. 108).

Perhaps nowhere in the Middle East has the revolutionary consciousness of the peasant been more revealed than in the Algerian war of independence. It would have hardly been possible for the leaders of the Algerian revolution to persist in a long and protracted struggle against the French colonialists without the Algerian peasantry (Hermassi, 1972, pp. 128–130). But both the Algerian revolution and the 1919 nationalist revolt in Egypt were turned on and off by the elites. In both instances, the elites turned out to be more conservative than the peasants, despite the former's rhetoric about the revolutionary change and the egalitarian outlook. Nonetheless, Nasser and the leaders of the Algerian revolution learned how difficult it was to contain the revolutionary impulse of the peasants once they were stirred by the hope of reforms.

By examining the contradictions resulting from the pressure of reforms and considerations of rule, we are in a better position to explain the conflicting policy orientations of the ruling elites. In Kalecki's view, a crisis situation emerges when the ruling elites are forced to surrender their egalitarian outlook in the interest of preserving the stability of the political order through their alliance with the lower middle classes in urban areas and with the rich farmers (Radwan, 1979, p. 200). The basis of Kalecki's critique of the Nasserist leftist experiment can also be used to explain the failure of the liberal order instituted by Sadat. The emergence of competitive urban interests can be no less threatening to the alliance than Nasser's policy which was based on limited participation and mobilisation of supportive elements.

The discussion thus far has concentrated on the ruling elite's ideological and policy shifts. What is left to be analysed is how these shifts affect classes divided by wide socio-economic gaps. This is a hard empirical question whose relevance to countries undergoing a similar experience ranging from China to Mexico can be inferred from the historical development in Egypt.

The foundation stone for traditional influence was laid down before the middle of the nineteenth century, which witnessed the formation of privately owned large estates. The interpenetration between landed interests, on the one hand, and commerce and industry, on the other, throughout the past century did not eliminate one of the distinguishing features of the former, that is, their intermediary role between the centre and the periphery. The main reason behind their persisting political role is the fact that their dominant status came as a result of social differentiation at the local community level rather than being externally imposed. Local status such as village or tribal leadership went hand in hand with the formation of large estates. As the century progressed, these indigenous elements were catapulted to national prominence. More so, when the central authorities took recourse to parliamentary representation and to the recruitment of indigenous elements in growing government and military bureaucracy. They gradually displaced the Turco-Circassians in the upper hierarchies of the provincial and central governments.

The third quarter of the nineteenth century saw the conversion of Egyptian agriculture into a gigantic cotton plantation as a consequence of the famine resulting from the American Civil War. The level of prosperity for the landed elites increased and with that, the temptation to seek the comforts of city life in preference to the drab and dreary rural existence. Absenteeism, however, was checked by the powerful influence of kinship. With the advantage of hindsight, it can be well asserted that the intermediary role of the traditional elites would have been lost had the temptation of city life proved to be too strong to resist.

The British rule between the occupation of Egypt in 1882 and the establishment of the constitutional monarchy in 1923 led to the strengthening of the power and influence of the landed grandees of *kibar al ayan*. In this period, the lopsided development in land distribution became the endemic feature of the agrarian structure down the century. Statistics taken towards the end of the last century revealed that the holders of large estates of over 50 feddans were fewer than 12,000 (1.3 per cent) and their cultivated area amounted to 2.2 million feddans (44.0 per cent). By contrast, the small owners of 5 feddans or less were 760,000 (83.3 per cent) and their share of the cultivated land was 1.1 million feddans (21.7 per cent). Between these two strata were the middling owners (five to 50 feddans) who amounted to 140,000 (15.4 per cent) cultivating an area of 1.8 million feddans (34.3 per cent).

The British colonial power instituted reforms to curb the worst abuses of local power, while aspiring to win the loyalty of all rural classes. Nonetheless, as the events during the massive nationalist uprising in 1919 had demonstrated, the only elements which called into question the nationalist agitation against the British rule were the rural upper stratum, kibar al-ayan. They were driven to support the colonial power not out of loyalty to the central authority or foreign power, but due to the fear caused by peasant unrest and its repercussions on local privileges. It is not surprising to note that in both instances — the Urabi revolt which led to the British occupation in 1882 and the nationalist uprising in 1919 — peasant agitations tempered the revolutionary behaviour of some kibar al-ayan, who threw all caution to the wind by joining the nationalists.

Independence and the establishment of a constitutional monarchy did not bring any noticeable change in the social hierarchy established during the colonial period. On the contrary, the political institutions came to reflect the dominant agrarian interests. Competitive urban interests representing the king and the palace-created parties, on the one hand, and the British consul, on the other, led to the strengthening of local interests. Thus it may be argued that the politics of Egypt in the period between the establishment of the monarchy and its overthrow by the army officers in 1952 bore a strong family resemblence to Iraqi politics during the seesaw struggle between the king and the British mandatory power which enhanced the local power of the tribal chieftains and the large landowners (Batatu, 1978, pp. 86–134). Furthermore, as shown by Frey (1975) in his study of Turkey, localism tends to become an important political factor under such conditions as the emergence of competitive party interests.

A system dominated by large agrarian interests produces its own nemesis either in the form of rural unrest or massive rural migration to the cities that would most likely provide added fuel to political extremism on the left or right of the political spectrum. At the time when the army officers seized power in July 1952, Cairo was in the grip of social violence perpetrated by the Muslim Brotherhood and Misr al-Fatat. Even the Wafd found an opportunity in extremism to enhance its dwindling popularity. Urban violence, however, concealed a much more troublesome social unrest in the rural areas. Land prices and rental rates skyrocketed to the extent that many thoughtful Egyptians became convinced that the only way out of the chaotic situation was to invest power in the hands of a strongman. Nasser appeared to be a fulfillment of that desire.

In her survey of developments in Mexico from 1911 to the present, Sanderson (1984, pp. 102–4) revealed the close connection between political stability and agrarian policy. She observes that agrarian reforms were launched whenever a crisis appeared to threaten the stability of political order. Peasant unrest and pressures for land redistribution were much more obvious in Mexico than in Egypt. Nonetheless, the discovery of agrarian reforms as a means to consolidate rule and even to win a measure of popularity was made shortly after the army officers seized power in Egypt. A parallel development with Mexico was the discovery of the single-party as a means of mobilising the supportive elements and eliminating from the political process the elements hostile to the revolution. In Egypt, the political formula devised by the army officers was the mobilisation of rural support and the exclusion from participation of outlawed political parties and movements that belonged to the *ancien régime*. The implementation of these policies surprisingly left traditional influence, including kibar al-ayan, in a dominant position. The political elites who were hurt most by these policies were the absentee owners and the urban-based politicians.

In a country with limited resources and paucity of land for redistribution, revolutionary rhetoric is bound to clash with objective reality. The agrarian reforms in the early stage of the army seizure of power benefited a very small margin of the peasantry, while it left the majority dissatisfied. The limited nature of the reforms is clear even if we take in to consideration all the successive stages of reforms whose cumulative effects benefited twelve per cent of the peasantry. If we take into consideration the fact that the agrarian reforms of the Shah of Iran affected roughly 90 per cent of the peasantry, then there is ground for the claim that the White Revolution was indeed revolutionary in its consequences in comparison to the Egyptian reforms. It is ironical, however, that it was Nasser rather than the Shah of Iran who appeared to be radically bent upon revolutionary change.

Behind the revolutionary rhetoric, Nasser continued to sustain the illusion that he could turn the single-party and the bureaucracy into revolutionary instruments until the outbreak of the Kamshish Affair

LIMITS OF RULING ELITES

in 1966. The latter acted as the catalyst which brought the dissatisfied peasants and the urban leftist intellectuals together in a rare moment — and only for a short interval. Leftist radicalism in the 1960s was a worldwide phenomenon. Kamshish was Egypt's cultural revolution during which the single-party and the bureaucracy were questioned as legitimate means of bringing about revolutionary change. The main target of leftist criticism was the fact that, despite the successive agrarian reforms, there was no perceptible change in the relations of production in the countryside. On the contrary, the dominant agrarian interests continued to exercise their influence either directly or through kinship connections over the very means used by the central government to divest them of their local privileges. Kamshish provided the opportunity for the dissatisfied peasants to put pressure on the central authorities to take measures which would have been detrimental to the stability of the regime.

The Higher Committee for the Liquidation of Feudalism (HCLF) was formed in the wake of the Kamshish Affair with the objective of ending exploitation in the countryside. The formation of the HCLF lends the impression that Nasser anticipated a socialist revolution led by the left and decided to preempt it by leading the revolution himself in a bureaucratic fashion. The HCLF was headed by Marshal Abdel Hakim Amer, the vice-president and Commander General of the Armed Forces. Most of its members belonged to the top echelons of the single-party, the government bureaucracy and the military establishment. Throughout the 16 agricultural provinces, the HCLF brought charges against the so-called feudalists that led in many cases to banishment from villages, land expropriation and sequestration and dismissal from government services.

The critical aspect of the activities which accompanied the Kamshish was that the authorities appeared to be striking at the foundations upon which the state was erected. In reality, however, they were feeble attempts to let the wind out of leftist sails. What bears witness to the latter is the quick suppression of the Kamshish Affair, the dissolution of the HCLF and the cessation of all activities against the so-called feudalists. The significance of this episode is that it marked the end of an era in which equity and economic growth appeared to be a realistic solution to the twin problems of underdevelopment and maldistribution. The first symptom of the impending socialist crisis was the failure to meet the objective of the first five-year plan (1960–5) due to lack of capital. The deepening

234

of the socialist crisis was reflected in the events which followed the June War defeat in 1967. Apart from the dissolution of the HCLF, the so-called feudalists were allowed to return to their villages and the ousted officials and local government employees were reinstated.

China provides ample examples for countries with a radical past searching for an explanation for the surrender of egalitarianism. Such pragmatic considerations as offering incentives to increase production is perhaps the primary legitimising principle. Nonetheless, short of a spectacular economic growth — which is doubtful in the case of Egypt — and because of diminishing returns, it is inevitable that the socio-economic gap would widen, to the cost of the majority of the population. In Sadat's Egypt, the situation proved to be much more intractable for those who stood to lose their socialist inheritance under the gospel of infitah. The undoing of Nasserism by Sadat was nothing more than negating step by step the socialist gains behind the guise of supremacy of laws, economic and political liberalisation. Religion was brought into the picture as a political expedient to sanctify property and to eliminate from the political scene leftist elements. Political participation and economic rationalisation were endorsed to negate the ill-effects of political repression and the curtailment of freedom to pursue economic gains. All these objectives were subsumed under the slogan of 'faith and science'.

Nonetheless, all the strategies of power consolidation were tainted by their worst consequences. Let us take each strategy and unravel the contradictions it created. Sadat's manipulation of religion to augment his position led to severe repercussions among members of the Christian Coptic minority. The appeals made in the name of religion had the unintended effect of arousing Islamic militancy among the same socio-economic groups to whom Nasser appealed in the name of socialism. The important difference is that Islamic militancy under Sadat lacked institutional mediation, while its autonomous existence proved to be a significant destabilising element.

Economic liberalisation meant in effect removing the restrictions on free trade and the restoration of property which had been placed under sequestration during the socialist era. The unintended consequences were reflected in the reverse process of the agrarian reforms and property sequestration. As Nasser realised that it was impossible to limit the hopes of the peasants once they were stimulated by a redistributive policy, Sadat came to the realisation that there were no limits to the satisfaction of the dispossessed classes once the legitimacy of taking from the rich in order to give to the poor was called into question.

Political liberalisation meant the destruction of the single-party organisation and the recognition of plurality of interests as sanctified by the multi-party system. But once the principle of freedom of association had been recognised, all the barriers which had so far prevented the old order from reasserting itself were removed. Sadat had no legitimate excuse for not bending to the logic of his own strategic thinking and recognising the formation of the New Wafd, the symbol of the old order.

All these unintended consequences came to a head in 1977, the year in which Sadat launched yet another of his surprises by visiting Israel to break through the psychology of hostility which marked the relations of the two countries. This was also the year when opposition to the policy of infitah began to gather momentum amid news of the kidnapping and execution of the Minister of Religious Endowment by an Islamic militant group. However, two major events preceded the peace initiative. One event captured newspaper headlines all over the world and the other was noticed only by those to whom it was directed. The first event was the food riots, which were symptomatic of the limits of deradicalisation. The second one was the resurrection of the Kamshish Affair in the form of a trial in which those who had been prosecuted during the socialist era became the prosecutors. The trial of the 'torturers of Kamshish' among former army officers and retired state officials coincided with the hearings of the Complaints and Grievances Committee of the People's Assembly against those who participated in the activities of the HCLF. It was like putting the state on trial for its own misdeeds against the traditionally influential elites during the socialist era.

Sadat could now bask in the assurance of traditional support. Just before the curtain was drawn on the Sadat regime, the Wafd party was in a state of dissolution. Its close urban ally, the Bar Association, was in shambles and the Islamic militants were either in prison or in hiding. Sadat exceeded Nasser in his widespread repression and succeeded in conveying the impression that Egypt was in the grip of political instability. The impression was strengthened with the news of his assassination at the hands of the Islamic militant group. On the other hand, the smooth transition of rule to his vice-president Hosni Mubarak, the revitalisation of 'democratic rule' as evidenced by the restoration of the repressed political parties and the electoral results of the People's Assembly, all convey the opposite impression of a stable political order.

In conclusion, there is no doubt that the application of the concept of the second stratum has advanced our knowledge about one aspect of political reality in the Middle East which is missing in the dichotomous elite-mass approach. Nonetheless, a better and more realistic understanding of Middle East politics is possible through analysis of the interactions between the autonomy of the ruling elites, as reflected by the shifts in ideological and policy orientations, and the second stratum. Such an approach will explain several problem areas which so far Middle Eastern studies have failed to resolve. The main problem is the relation between the ruling elites and their instrument of rule. What has been generally missing is an understanding of the pressures from below and their impact on the political orientations and the socio-economic policies of the ruling elites. By understanding the nature of these pressures, we will be able to put together a more realistic picture of the conflicting forces which produce crises of development in the Middle East.

It may be true that the growing sophistication of the instruments of social control explain the continuity and persistence of the political order. Yet, it must be made clear that there are also counter-destabilising tendencies which are apparent in the attitude of the peasants or ruler migrants among the urban lower middle classes. However the absence of social and economic reforms seems to be fundamentally related to the complacency of the ruling elites about the stability of their political order. From time to time they are forced to act when pressures erupt into sporadic street violence, but once the pressures recede, the ruling elites retreat behind the trenches of the second stratum.

NOTES

1. The distinctions are more visible in Morocco and Algeria than in Egypt, which formed the basis of the policies formulated by the French colonialists and the nationalist leaders. See Hermassi Elbaki (1972), *Leadership and national development in North Africa: a comparative study*, University of California Press, Berkeley.

2. Binder argues that the rural middle class (RMC) is a compliant instrument in the hands of the ruling elites since it was neither conscious of its class interests nor did it act as a collectivity. His use of the concept of class is therefore, as he puts it, a bit of ordinary language. L. Binder (1978), *In*

LIMITS OF RULING ELITES

a moment of enthusiasm: political power and the second stratum, University of Chicago Press, Chicago, p. 31.

3. The official statistics do not reflect the actual size of landholdings under cultivation which often includes leased-in land and freeholds held together. Nor do these statistics reflect the extent of property concentration resulting from cultivation of lands nominally divided among family members or illegally held properties. See Abdel-Fadil, M. (1975), *Development, income distribution and social change in rural Egypt: 1952–70*, Cambridge University Press, Cambridge.

4. Waterbury rejects Binder's thesis that the RMC, in an moment of enthusiasm, embraced the Egyptian revolution, became its embodiment, and served as a 'referent or source of values for the Nasserist elite'. According to Waterbury, the RMC was merely tolerated and not infrequently harassed. See Waterbury, J. (1983), *The Egypt of Nasser and Sadat: the political economy of two regimes*, Princeton University Press, Princeton (New Jersey), pp. 274 and 303.

5. In his critique of the dichotomous ruling elite model, Iliya Harik observes that 'less significance has been attributed to leaders' relations to one another or to their power base, strategies, and interrelations at various levels in society. When the concept of power is conceived as a dynamic relationship whereby one actor induces or forces compliance from another, the power network of which their relationship is a part is overlooked . . . a power distribution pattern is a gradation network. National leaders, regardless of how overbearing their power is, have to relate to other dealers in power at every level of society.' See Harik, I. (1974), *The political mobilization of peasants: a study of an Egyptian community*, Indiana University Press, Bloomington, p. 26.

6. See Samir Radwan's argument on the application of the concept of the 'intermediate state' as developed by Michel Kalecki in Dharm Ghai (ed.) *Economy of income distribution in Egypt*, Holmes and Meier, New York, pp. 512–13.

10

Class and the State in Rural Arab Communities

Nicholas Hopkins

While the ploughman thought of how well the new blade penetrated the soil, the worms underneath may be pardoned for taking a different view. (M.N. Srinivas, 1976, p. 257)

As the rural communities of the Arab world undergo an agrarian transformation by moving towards a capitalist economy, there are changes both in their internal structure and organisation and in their relationship to the wider national society of which they are a part. In particular, there are changes in the class structure of these communities reflecting both changes in the internal political economy and also growing and evolving role of the state. This chapter analyses the political economy first of two Arab villages, one Tunisian and one Egyptian, and then of the Bedouin population of Saudi Arabia, and stresses the problem of the integration of rural communities into the state. It seeks to use this material to explain state stability through an understanding of its relations to local society. These communities are chosen because of the availability of appropriate data: there is no suggestion that they are typical, though the underlying processes are. The methodology is a comparative one, in which not only the similarities but also the contrasts illuminate the general pattern.

Rural communities are linked into the national society through the interlocking class structures, but cultural and symbolic factors also play a role. The Saudi case illustrates the most far-reaching effort to create a national culture, in the form of Wahhabi Islam (Grand-guillaume, 1982). Saudi Arabia is both by far the 'newest' of the three nations and, as the only one not to be colonised, the oldest state in its present form. In Tunisia the national culture is linked to the epic struggle against colonialism, won in 1956, and the role of Habib

CLASS AND STATE IN RURAL ARAB COMMUNITIES

Bourguiba; the colonial period and its aftermath are a deep rupture in Tunisian history. Egyptian history is marked by the penetration of the economy by capitalism and colonialism and by the accomplishments of the 1952 revolution, but also by considerable continuity of rural institutions and even of particular families.

A metaphor may express my basic attitude: even though the sailor may control the boat, he does not control the ocean; just because the boat continues to float does not mean that it controls the water. The boat is of course the state. As the metaphor suggests, there are a lot of activities that reflect individual interests and their pursuit; there are local political, social, and power structures in which the state intervenes tardily and inefficiently or unknowingly, if at all. From the state's viewpoint, it is dealing with a 'citizen-client', not with an autonomous actor. But autonomous actors ('worms' in Srinivas's metaphor) exist.

Production is a relatively autonomous sector. So we can start with some analytical sense of the mode of production as the base for (local) politics, values and the formation of the wider system. Although much more complex definitions of the mode of production are useful for some purposes, here it means essentially a particular combination of the forces of production and productive relations and this chapter is more concerned with the latter than the former. Thus we can start with the labour process — the social organisation of production, the social relations between individuals which derive from the work experience — at the local level.

From the labour process emerges the class system, 'Class' refers to two or more groups of people related by an opposite position with regards to the means of production, for instance, landowners and hired workers. Classes ultimately imply a national framework, and therefore a national division of labour, and hence some kind of absorption of the local community into the body politic regulated by the state. Class analysis is possible at the local level, so long as one recognises the limitation that some classes, while absent, influence the local scene. There is a useful sense in which a national (or pan-Arab) system of class can only be the sum of many local systems, if we accept that class relations and class consciousness emerge first of all from the everyday interpersonal relations people have.

The model posits that rural society comes to occupy a different position in society as a whole, moving from relative autarky to a well-integrated position in a larger whole, articulated by the state, as a function of the role of socio-economic class formation. Another part of the process is the integration of the national society into the

240

world economic system, typically in a 'dependent' position.

The role of the state is primordial, yet limited. Its existence initially reflects the urban and international political arenas. The pre-colonial, colonial, and post-colonial states have all intervened in such matters as agricultural policy, land tenure and land reform, infrastructure projects, education and the provision of public services. It is appropriate to speak of the penetration of rural communities by the state, of their 'capture' by the state. Yet these phrases simply imply that the rural communities were there in the beginning and are still there. They can only be penetrated if they have an independent existence. Although the state usually argues that its activities are justified by its concern for the general welfare, there is nonetheless usually a hidden agenda, which is the support that such activities give to enhancing the state's own continuing role within its society.

The discourse of the state often assumes that nothing goes on in society except by the initiative of the state. Nothing, of course, could be further from the truth. There are many dynamic forces present in rural communities. They are full of individuals seeking to advance their own interest by political, economic or even religious action. Such individuals are alert to take advantage of any changes in their environment, including most notably those created by state interventions of various kinds. This tendency means that sometimes the outcome of state policies is unpredictable. The actual shape of events in the evolution of rural communities is thus a combination of the policies of the state and the goal-seeking behaviour of individuals.

TESTOUR (TUNISIA)

Political economy

Testour has a population of around 7,500 and lies in an interior prolongation of the Mediterranean coastal plain. Founded by Andalusian Muslims expelled from Spain shortly after 1609 (Hopkins, 1977a), it began under government auspices and has always been depended on a centralised state. Despite its relatively small size, Testour always appeared as an urban centre for its immediate hinterland. The colonial period after 1881 did not affect the traditional situation until land around Testour was alienated to French farmers who developed a mechanised, speculative, market-orientated agriculture after 1925. This coincided with the reduction in the scope of local self-government in the face of a centralised colonial administrative system. These two simultaneous pressures seem to have inspired Testour's early participation in the nationalist movement (Hopkins, 1980). Independence in 1956 resulted in the departure of the European farmers in the area. While many local farmers, large and small, profited from this, the bulk of the colonists' land was acquired by the government which then tried a series of experiments with cooperatives and state farms. Testour regained a form of self-government through the workings of the party and the other institutions of independent Tunisia. During the 1960s the national government bypassed the town of Testour in an effort to build socialism directly on agriculture. Since the 1970s there has been a return to private agriculture, except on state land, and the farmers of Testour have come into their own again.

The two main kinds of farming are extensive 'dry-farming' on the hill and plains and intensive irrigation in the bottom lands along the river. Agriculture is based on private ownership of land and the extensive use of hired labour (Hopkins, 1977b). Private ownership of land allows some to control more of an economic resource than they can themselves utilise and this sets up the conditions for the appearance of some kind of class relations between those who own land and those who work it. At present, farm workers are mobilised by owners who exploit their land directly, using machines and hiring workers by the day as they need them. The power of decision rests in the owner's hands. Meanwhile, the area that can be irrigated from the Mejerda river or from wells has been expanded considerably. These areas are generally devoted to market crops such as fruit, peppers or potatoes, that are labour intensive. The labour is hired. Increasingly, the social landscape is dominated by the presence of a class of large farmers and a class of workers.

The economy of Testour is closely linked to the agricultural patterns of its hinterland and the emergence of a dominant pattern of market-orientated agriculture has had important implications for the urban structure of the market town and service centre. Over the last century, the town has changed from a self-sufficient community to a link in the centralised organisation of Tunisian agricultural and other productive activity. One revealing change is the growth of employment outside agriculture, particularly in government service and in small-scale industry. The townspeople now face a rural economy including peasant farmers operating according to the domestic mode of production as well as larger farmers and cooperatives subject to the logic of the capitalist mode of production.

242

The point of articulation of these different modes of production and styles of life is the market of Testour. On market day (Friday), people from Testour's hinterland come into town to buy consumer goods, sell produce, deal in animals, transact business at the government offices, visit the bath, or attend the Friday prayer in the mosque. To some extent, the town serves as a centre for crops moving towards the Tunis wholesale market, only an hour and a half away by truck. Increasingly, while Testour's fruits and vegetables are sold in Tunis, the local greengrocers supply themselves in Tunis with similar crops from other towns for sale in Testour. Thus from a local economy with a fair degree of self-sufficiency, Testour has become an integral cog in a national system.

Household, women and social order

The household continues to be an important element in the town's social organisation. Traditionally (and to some extent at present) the household is the focus for the sexual division of labour. By and large, in Testour this means that the men work at production and the women at transformation. Thus the men raise the sheep and shear the wool and the women prepare the wool into cloth by cleaning, carding, spinning and weaving. The men farm and the women transform the wheat in to couscous, the quinces into jam, dry the peppers, and so on. The principal workplace of the women is in the house, particularly in the courtyard of the house, while the men work outside the house, either in the shops in the village or in the fields and gardens.

Norms concerning the movement and behaviour of women are very much on people's minds in Testour. In principle, the women are discouraged from leaving the house too much. Even for these outside visits, women are supposed to cover themselves with a white cloth known as the *safsari* and avoid the long market street. Men's movements are also restricted. They rarely visit each other's houses, but instead socialise in public areas such as cafés or shops in the market. The strict controls on women's behaviour (and in a different way on men's behaviour) are only applicable in Testour itself, so that when women visit Tunis of another town they feel less inclined to wear the *safsari*, and freely enter the market. Since Tunis is only 80 km away, this is an important safety valve. Nevertheless, the emphasis given to such controls suggests that there is a need to maintain strict discipline in the household. By protecting the formal separation of the sexes, the sexual division of labour is enhanced, and the maintenance of this division of labour is necessary for the reproduction of the society.

What is true for local society may also be of some interest to the state, for the reproduction of national society supposes many local processes. The relationship between the symbolic and the economic role of women illustrates this linkage between local and national reproduction. The social control of women symbolises and creates their 'inferior' status and this status in turn determines the fact that women are generally paid lower wages for comparable work in agriculture, Thus, the discrimination against women, by creating a cheap source of alternative labour, acts to limit men's wages as well and hence to reinforce national as well as local class distinctions. (Mernissi, 1982)

Islam provides the symbols of the unity and integration of the town. The chief architectural symbol of the town is the main mosque, built in the seventeenth century in an 'Andalusian ' style (Marçais, 1942), and considered one of the architectural treasures of Tunisia. A pattern of smaller mosques linked to the principal families in the town has largely disappeared, leaving only the ruins. From the point of view of popular belief, the main shrine of Sidi Ali el-Arian is important. This saint is considered the 'ancestor' and protector of the town, particularly against state predation (Hopkins, 1977a). The annual festival in his honour each spring is a major event. There are many other saints' shrines in his honour and in the popular mind Testour is protected by its ramparts of saints. Some of these saints are considered to be the ancestors, real or spiritual, of the large families in the town, while others are simply people noted for their sanctity during their lifetime.

Politics and class

The two principal classes in Testour are the result of the agrarian structure: the class of the relatively large landowners and the class of the agricultural workers. Many in this latter category are not considered to be authentic Testouris and live in shantytown-like peripheral quarters. They are mostly people whose fathers or grand-fathers immigrated to this area during the colonial period to work on the colonial farms, since local people preferred not to do this. Two other important classes are the petty bourgeois shopkeepers, together with some farmers who largely meet their labour needs from within their households and so are neither hirers nor hired; and lastly the new intellectuals, schoolteachers and civil servants. The 'new intellectuals' both represent the state in the town and also occupy their own class position *vis-à-vis* the other groups. While the party branch is able to control the political process in the town, there is some evidence of conflict outside the party framework that has a definite class configuration.

Testour is not a microcosm of the class structure of Tunisia. In particular, the upper reaches of the bourgeoisie and the administrative elite are not represented within the town itself and yet they are clearly significant in terms of the town's development since they determine policy decisions at the national level.

During the colonial period, most of the large landowners were imitating the French capitalist farmers and moving towards a pattern of mechanisation, market orientation and hired labour. Perhaps for this reason, they were not in the forefront of the nationalist movement. It is possible to trace the existence of two factions in the town, a relatively pro-French faction of the establishment and a relatively anti-French faction in opposition to it from as early as 1910 and through until Tunisian independence in 1956 (Hopkins, 1983a, pp. 125–40). The nationalist movement, thus to some extent corresponded to an existing cleavage in the town and this had a class dimension. Although the first leader of the nationalist movement in Testour was a large landowner, most of the rank and file were shopkeepers, who were largely involved in the final phases of the nationalist movement, just before and after independence; most of the 'militants' credited with having 'sacrificed' during this period were from this category.

By the mid-1970s the educational qualifications of the new intellectuals were beginning to give them a role in the politics of the town, They began to move into the posts on the party cell and the town council. However, they are also essentially allied to the large landowners and generally follow policies in the interest of these people. Thus the political cleavage is generally between the class of those who work as hired labour in agriculture and construction and all the others. The new intellectuals and the large landowners control access to the party cell board. No worker has ever been a candidate for this board and workers generally vote only on instructions from a 'patron'. Interestingly, no large landowners are themselves on this board, nor do they participate in elections. However, several are members of the town council — perhaps because the town council deals with issues like zoning that are of immediate material impact.

The early phases of the transformation of Tunisian rural society took place during the colonial period and were influenced by the presence of colonial farmers. Since the breakdown of the colonial system. some large Tunisian farmers have emerged as a powerful group, but they are in competition for political power both with those whose legitimacy is based on political militancy in the past and with those whose claim is based on education in the present. There is substantial hired labour in agriculture and construction and a continuing migration to the city and away from agriculture. Class distinction appears in a relatively sharp form. Some political conflict between classes has begun to appear and there is a complicated pattern of class alliances. some of the recent clashes in Tunisia, involving the trade union, the party and the 'street', clearly manifest this sharpening class distinction, some of whose roots are in agrarian change.

MUSHA (EGYPT)

Setting and history

Musha village lies about 400km south of Cairo, in Upper Egypt, Among the largest Egyptian villages, its population is around 18,000 people and the village land area is around 5,000 feddans (2,000 hectares). The land in Musha yields two crops a year, with a sharp distinction being made between summer crops such as cotton, maize and sorghum, and winter crops such as wheat, beans, lentils, chickpeas and bersim. Livestock is also important, mostly for dairy produce and for fattening out (Hopkins *et al.*, 1980). Rainfall is negligible and all water is supplied through irrigation.

Local politics are influenced by patterns of social organisation in the economic domain. Musha is characterised by a relatively large gap between the wealthy and the poor, and the introduction of mechanisation in agriculture has accentuated that difference. At the same time, the fractionisation of the labour process in agriculture has had an impact on the class stratification pattern.

The role of the state

The state in Egypt has intervened extensively in the reconstruction of the landscape and the accumulation of capital. During the nineteenth century, the state fostered the three parallel processes of creation of private landholding, drawing rural Egypt into the international market through cotton marketing and improvement of the irrigation system to provide perennial irrigation. These three processes, which have continued until the present, have integrated rural Egypt into the national and international system.

The Musha landscape was initially less affected than the delta or Middle Egypt by the changes in irrigation. In the nineteenth century, dikes were strengthened and sluices built. The most significant change was introduced by the large landowners and labour contractors who brought in pumps to raise ground water for irrigation during the off-season. This process began with steam pumps in the early twentieth century and was consolidated after the introduction of diesel pumps in the 1930s. It was the introduction of pumping that allowed for a double crop rotation including cotton. The completion of the Aswan High Dam in 1964 (Fahim, 1981) had a major impact on the environment of the Musha area. The annual flood stopped altogether and instead water was supplied to the farmers by a network of canals (Abul-Ata Azim, 1977). The existing diesel pumps were modified to lift water from these canals. This consolidated double-cropping. The first tractors made their appearance in Musha around 1950 (Saab, 1960) and the present level of tractorisation goes back to around 1970, following the big push towards this goal under Abd al-Nasser in the 1960s (Bremer, 1982).

State intervention in land tenure laws has also had an impact on social stratification in the village. The creation of private landholding led to the creation of a landed class and the institution of agrarian reform was an effort to limit the influence of that class (Saab, 1967; Warriner, 1969). The first law in 1952 had the effect of eliminating the very largest estates and setting up agrarian reform cooperatives in their place. The 1961 law reduced the ceiling on landholdings even further, created a system of mandatory cooperatives corresponding to each village and guaranteed tenants the right of access to their land. The first law had only a marginal effect on Musha, and the second law led to the expropriation of three per cent of the total land area, not enough to alter the land distribution pattern significantly, The 1961 law also led to the formation of a cooperative which exemplified the ambitions of the state to control agriculture in detail (El-Shagi, 1969). The cooperative was responsible for monitoring agriculture in general, and in particular the crop rotation cycle and the planting of required crops such as cotton, wheat, beans and lentils.

Social relations of production

The social relations of production in agriculture have important implications for the emergence of social class. These social relations are a function of the level of technology and of the patterns of control of technology.

Wealth in land and machines is highly concentrated. There are about 1,500 landholders in Musha and around 1,200 actual farm enterprises, while approximately 45 per cent of the households in the village are landless (Hopkins, 1983b). About 13 per cent of the landholders hold more than five feddans, about twice the national average size of this group. The average holding is more than three feddans, compared with a national average of two, and the largest farms are over 100 feddans, The seven largest farms in the village occupy about 20 per cent of the land, they own 27 per cent of the 48 tractors and have a share in 46 per cent of the 70 pumps.

The contrast between mechanised and non-mechanised operations is significant. In Musha, all water lifting, ploughing, threshing and most hauling are done mechanically. Tasks done by hand include sowing, application of chemicals, irrigating, weeding, pest control (apart from aerial spraying), harvesting, sacking, loading, winnowing and some transport involving the use of camels and donkeys. Generally, the mechanised tasks are those formerly performed by animal traction. This pattern is fairly typical of Egyptian villages (Hopkins, Mehanna and Abdelmaksoud, 1982).

The social organisation of water lifting in Musha can serve as an example (Mehanna *et al.*, 1983). The vertical distance that water is lifted from the government canal is usually less than one metre. The water then flows in to an irrigation ditch, which delivers the water to the fields where the farmer takes charge of it. In addition to the farmer, the other roles include the watchman, also responsible for allocating water from a pump to its client farmers, the mechanic responsible for keeping the pumping engine running and the owner (or owners) of the pump. The farmer must pay a fee to the owners for each watering and an annual fee to the watchman for each feddan. Some degree of cooperation is thus required, but the cooperation is organised in a way compatible with the general hierarchical nature of the social organisation. The fundamental relationship is the one of clientship between the farmer and the pump owners and their employees.

The unequal relationship between the machine owner and his client is as important for tractors as for pumps. The 34 owners of

Musha's 48 tractors perform all the ploughing and threshing for the entire village and all other farmers must come to them for these services. Even though farmers retain, in principle, the freedom of choice between tractor owners (as they do not for the pumps), this freedom is, in practice, limited by indebtedness, a preference for neighbours, or the greater facility of having all farmers in one zone use the same tractor.

The organisation of work tends to create a stratification system in the village based on unequal exchanges between households. Those households that control the mechanised means of production and more land, are in a favourable position. The pattern of labour transfer between households can be on an exchange or a reciprocal basis, but is most often between households that control the means of production and the others, and takes the form of hired labour.

The household plays a key managerial role. The household derives its role from the place it held in the days of subsistence agriculture when the household corresponded to the technology — animal traction and manual labour — and there were many fewer non-agricultural occupations. Now that the labour process involves a complex blending of credit and inputs from cooperatives, hired labour, hiring of machines and supply of water, it has become divided and is only reunified by the skill of the individual farmer.

Households do not provide much of their own labour, but they do decentralise the control of hired labour and thus they minimise the need for hierarchical control of labour. They can fulfil this function because the small size and shifting composition of work groups favour the ability of the household head to make micro-adjustments and decisions. Only the household head follows the crops throughout the cycle even though others do the work. Furthermore, the small farmer household is a relatively more efficient organiser of labour than the capitalist farmers would be if they used their control of machinery to take on the task of mobilising and controlling labour.

It is, however, extremely important to point out that somewhere between a third and a half of the village's households do not directly rely on agriculture for a living, but on salaried jobs, trades and crafts. Many of the landless work outside agriculture and a few merchants and government workers do very well. Many of these are not directly affected by the relations of production in agriculture, though they are part of the general system to which these relations of production give rise.

Politics and class

The political history of Musha over the last century has been marked by the wealthiest families in the village (as in Sirs al-Layyan, cf. Berque, 1957). These families are often large, extended families, veritable lineages, whose size reflects their wealth. Particularly in the 1930s, some new families were able to join ranks of the wealthiest class, but without modifying the nature of the system itself. Leading members of these families represented the major national political parties, and some were elected to parliament on the Wafd ticket. The Wafd Party at this point represented the Egyptian national movement in the same way that the Neo-Destour Party did in Tunisia, only here it was the traditional leaders rather than the rebels who struck up an association with it. Members of these families still occupy major political roles in the village.

The religious institutions reinforce the verticality of social links. There are about 20 mosques in Musha; with one exception, they are clearly associated with families or with neighbourhoods organised around families. Thus, in this way, the mosques reflect and reinforce the strength and importance of the families, while the one exceptional mosque symbolises the unity of the community as a whole. The most obvious form of organised religion in Musha, after the mosques themselves, are the sufi brotherhoods. The local sections of these brotherhoods are organised according to a tight hierarchy, usually centred around a leader whose position is hereditary. This hierarchy reflects the ranking of individuals in the community at large. Thus the brotherhoods are organised by the dominant class, draw most of their members from the working class and serve to extend patterns of economic domination into the religious and ideological realm.

There is objective social differentiation in Musha. One could talk about a class of large landowners (let us say those farming 25 feddans or more) and a class of more or less landless agricultural workers, with others, particularly government workers and shopkeepers and grain merchants, scattered in between. However, the work situation does not always rely on sharp class distinctions as in Testour because of the small work groups, the use of children and outsiders, and the patron-client nature of the linkages between the large farmers and their regular workers. Non-agricultural wealth does not seem to have the same effect as far as class is concerned. Thus, the two main groups are less well defined as categories than in Testour, although their individual members are very visible. As in Testour, the national bourgeoisie and the administrative elite are absent from the village.

The complexity of the case makes it hard to argue that the stratification in Musha is leading to classes aware of their collective interests. The nature of machine hiring and wage labour, as in a real sense a relationship between households, tends to reinforce the patron-client or vertical ties between people. This is also buttressed by traditional religion, even if education and modern religion (here including so-called religious fundamentalism) push in the opposite direction. Many of the off-farm jobs are part of a national division of labour rather than a village or household division. The growth of this sector should gradually integrate the village into a national class organisation with feedback to the agrarian structure.

The process is certainly complex in Egypt, where depeasantisation began in some senses 150 years ago and the dependency of all peasants on the market was complete by the end of the nineteenth century, Moreover, social hierarchies at the village level have millenia of existence in Egypt. Broadly speaking what we can observe here is a situation where: (i) the role of the state has been overwhelming in creating a new landscape through modification of the irrigation system and imposition of constraints on the accumulation of large estates; (ii) nevertheless, many capitalist farmers emerged in the last half century; (iii) a substantial part of the population consists of free, waged labour; (iv) the continued importance of the household as an organiser of labour for many people represents an 'obstacle' to the agrarian transition; (v) in any case, education and migration are allowing many to escape the system altogether by situating their work and hence their primary source of income outside agriculture; and (vi) there has been a substantial continuity of religious and political structures, reflecting the continuity of the class hierarchy.

AL-MURRAH BEDOUIN (SAUDI ARABIA)

Context

The Kingdom of Saudi Arabia is a much more newer polity than either Tunisia or Egypt. It was constituted in its present form in 1932, after a series of conquests by Ibn Saud in which he extended the range of his power from Najd, in the centre of the peninsula, to the east (Hasa oasis and the Gulf coast, where the oil is located), the

CLASS AND STATE IN RURAL ARAB COMMUNITIES

west (the Hijaz, including the holy cities), the south (the Asir province; the movement stopped short of taking over the Yemen where another dynasty and centralised government already existed), and the north (the area of the Shammar and the Rwala). In his rise to power, Ibn Saud relied initially on forces raised from Bedouin elements of the peninsula, sometimes operating as tribal groups and sometimes incorporated into the religious forces known as the *Ikhwan*, though eventually the sedentary oasis dwellers and slaves took over the leading role.

Though the role of religion (Wahhabism) was an important element in the rise of Ibn Saud, it is entirely possible that without two external factors, this rise would have been simply one more episode in the long cycle of rise and fall of dynasties in the Arabian peninsula (Montagne, 1947, pp. 137–89). These two external factors were, on the one hand, the international political conjuncture of World War One and its aftermath, in which the House of Al-Saud became at least sporadically British clients, relying on Britain for arms in particular; and on the other hand, the discovery of oil in the Eastern Province, which led to American involvement with the kingdom and royal house. Thus the political centralisation stabilised as a result of forces in the international arena. Within the kingdom, this meant that the relationship of local communities, whether settled or bedouin, to the emerging state was coloured both by relative newness and by the element of conquest or forced absorption (Abdulfettah, 1981, for local variability; and Grandguillaume, 1982, for the process of cultural homogenisation).

The Al-Murrah

One of the groups incorporated into the Saudi state were the Al-Murrah Bedouin, living in the southern part of the Eastern Province (Cole, 1975). This group of around 15,000 people in 1970 were traditionally camel herders ranging from the area around the oasis of al-Hasa in the north to the Empty Quarter in the south; they also had traditional attachments to the Najran area on the Yemeni border, Their ecological adaptation was to the difficult conditions of the true desert; yet their need for urban and agricultural specialities brought them into symbiosis with the settled populations.

The Al-Murrah had the flexible segmentary social arrangements typical of a pastoral group in difficult terrain. During the summer, when water was scarce, groups based on a lineage or a clan clustered

252

around oases and wells, dividing themselves into individual household groups of perhaps 25 individuals. In the winter, the individual household was more independent, and migrated in search of pasture. This geographically imposed pattern also allowed for the constitution of larger and smaller groups for purposes of warfare and raiding.

Under the traditional tribal system of the Arabian Peninsula, the integration of a group like the Al-Murrah into larger political formations was an extension of the segmentary lineage structure of the bedouin. It operated through political and marital alliances, joint raids, rivalry and treachery. It was important for the Al-Murrah, for instance, that a woman from their leading family had married from a powerful Jiluwi clan that controlled the Eastern Province within the Saudi system (Cole, 1975, p. 100). However, to say that integration is an extension of segmentation does not mean that the system worked the same way all the way to the top. The Al-Murrah, like other bedouin groups, have a leader, the *amir*. The amir generally emerges from the same leading family from one generation to the next, but continuity in one family requires political success: 'The position of amir is an achieved status which can be maintained only through the continued success of the leader and his close relatives' (Cole, 1975, p. 98; also Lancaster, 1981, p. 95). 'The amir has no right to negotiate on behalf of the tribe but, being the most influential man in a position to negotiate, he has an obligation to do so'. The amirs remain settled near the town of Abqaiq in order to be accessible to the Al-Murrah and also near the urban bases of Saudi power. Their political role requires them to intervene in all cases involving individual members of the Al-Murrah; in the past it often involved speaking for the interests of the whole tribe.

To some extent, this pattern was modernised through the National Guard. The amir of the Al-Murrah commanded a unit in the National Guard that was largely made up of Al-Murrah. The reserve National Guard both to some extent replicates the tribal structure, and is a major way to channel income to the bedouin. Ibrahim and Cole (1978, p. 29) report that in a group of 35 Al-Murrah families, 34 had at least one member in the reserve National Guard; in 1977 this produced a monthly cash income of about SR 2,000.

In recent years the Al-Murrah have known many changes. The availability of trucks has allowed them to exploit pastures beyond the traditional range; the trucks can be used either to haul animals to pasture or to haul water to the animals and thus allow grazing in areas away from water points, as well as rapid mobility to utilise the pasturing opportunities created by erratic rainfall. The state has also drilled new wells and thus created new water points and modified the environment. The Al-Murrah are increasingly willing to sell their camels, but do not depend on the herds for a regular cash income (Ibrahim and Cole, 1978), in part because so many of them work for the government or in the oil fields. There have been pressures on the Al-Murrah to settle, and to place their children in schools: the Al-Murrah seem divided on how to respond to these pressures.

Both the state and the bedouin, including the Al-Murrah have been trying to take immediate and short-term advantage of changes in the physical and social environment. The outcome of over-exploitation has sometimes been degradation of the environment:

> What appears to have happened is that unplanned, spontaneous and partial efforts at modernisation by both the government and the bedouin are leading to the potential destruction of rangelands as a result of overgrazing and vehicular traffic, without the nation having benefited from a short-term increase in its domestic meat supply. (Cole, 1981, p. 142)

Yet with all this, the Al-Murrah have been marginalised with the Saudi state. The development of the country has been based on the exploitation of oil and the centre of this development has been the cities. The contrast between the urban and the nomadic or bedouin populations has been increased, with most of the benefits going to the former group. Although distinctions within the wider society have grown, the bedouin themselves remain a fairly homogenous group, lacking internal class distinctions. The reorganisation of the national economic system has left a different place for animal husbandry (there has been little effective effort to utilise the animal resources of the country to supply the local market with meat; instead there has been an effort to make the country self-sufficient in wheat), and this has new implications for local communities. In the late 1970s, the Saudi Ministry of Planning estimated that 35 per cent of all the male labour force (excluding nomads) were engaged in the low growth, low productivity and low wage sectors of agriculture and personal and community services (Cole, 1981, p. 134).

Cole's study of the Al-Murrah has recently been confirmed by an analysis of the Rwala Bedouin, some of whom live in the northern provinces of Saudi Arabia, around al-Jouf and in the Wadi Sirhan

254

(Lancaster, 1981). The proximity of the Rwala to the borders of Jordan, Iraq and Syria allows greater flexibility and the top political leadership resides outside Saudi Arabia. But the ecological pressures are comparable and the adaptations to modern life (including the role of the National Guard and the availability of jobs in the oil sector) are similar. Like the Al-Murrah, the Rwala are susceptible to the blandishments of the state, but strive to retain a degree of personal independence: 'The Rwala have adapted the new economy to fit their own requirements' (Lancaster, 1981, p. 146). Their traditional link to the wider society has been through the amir, but the growing integration of individuals into the Saudi state system undermines this. Lancaster (1981, pp. 79–80) maintains that 'the relationship between the Rwala and the bureaucracy is not a happy one', especially now that the bureaucracy tends to invade the desert rather than remain in the towns and that the 'problem is magnified because the Rwala have little concept of the state'. The Rwala and the Al-Murrah make a distinction between *al-dawlah* (the state or bureaucracy) and *al-hukuma* (the Saudi royal family or governors); they are loyal to the latter and fearful of the former, but fear that the state is taking over the government.

Class, politics and the Saudi state

The class nature of the Saudi state is rapidly developing in ways that leave an increasingly inglorious place for the nomadic populations. In the major cities a bureaucratic and commercial bourgeoisie has appeared, deriving the major part of its income from importing consumer goods on the one hand, and extracting a 'rent' from foreign firms and individuals anxious to do business (and to construct) in Saudi Arabia on the other hand. This bourgeoisie is intermingled with the ruling clans to form a hegemonic alliance. Both the workers in the oil industry and local populations throughout the country have been restless and have occasionally had to be suppressed (Islami and Kavoussi, 1984; Halliday, 1975, pp. 65–9).

The most striking aspect of the developing class structure of Saudi Arabia is the role played by foreign workers. A large proportion of the productive work in the country is done by foreign workers brought in to the country under contract (at least 43 per cent of the civilian employment was non-Saudi in 1980, Islam and Kavoussi, 1984, p. 38). The cities and towns nowadays are cosmopolitan in that one sees clusters of Asians, Arabs of different

255

origins and Westerners. One sees shop signs, for instance, not only in Arabic and English, but also in various Indian languages, Turkish etc, and each group has its own network of restaurants, barbers, tailors and other services. There is a tendency towards using ethnic or national origin as the basis for organising the workforce, resulting in an ethnic division of labour. Yet this emphasis on nationality and on legal distinctions among people only partially masks the growth of an exploitative class structure made possible by the flows of money generated by oil. Control over this foreign labour force is decentralised to the level of individual employer or labour contractor and is backed up by a legal system of visas and residence permits (Ibrahim, 1982).

The bedouin largely stand outside this system; in fact in 1977 they seemed relatively worse off than ten years earlier (Ibrahim and Cole, 1978, p. 110). Some individuals may penetrate the system by becoming labour contractors and thus entering it at the bourgeois level. But the majority have developed a life style that leaves them free to realise their values in other ways, for instance by allowing them to retain patterns of physical mobility, sociability and inter-personal relations based on the presumption of equality. Their relation to the central authority is still in principle mediated through the traditional political system, however modified in practice this may be by the demands of bureaucratisation.

In analysing the Saudi state, it is important to consider the role of the bedouin and the other marginalised rural and traditional urban populations within the same framework as the immigrant workers. In effect, these two categories are both examples of subordinated groups. But whereas the immigrant workers are controlled by making them individually dependent on individual Saudi entre-preneurs, with the support of the state through the requirement of work permits and visas, the bedouin and the other traditional popula-tions are controlled through a policy of subsidies that both guide their economic and social choices and bind them to the state as the source of the subsidies. Thus in recent years, there have been considerable subsidies available to those who build a house (Lancaster, 1981, p. 109 mentions the figures of SR 300,00) or start a farm, whereas the subsidies available for animal husbandry are lower. The bedouin have adapted to this new ecology by spreading their bets in characteristic fashion. Thus, some members of an extended family retain an interest in pastoralism (sheep for income, camels for security), while others accept jobs in government or the private sector, or experiment with agriculture. While some live in new houses in the towns, their relatives remain in tents and individuals can move back and forth.

CONCLUSION

Each of the three cases shows a distinct pattern of the integration of a rural community into the state, yet the overall outcome is similar, The state may gradually be growing stronger, but the local communities and people retain considerable vitality and initiative. The mariner is not yet master of the sea. In each case, the result is as much the matter of individual actions taken by people at the local level as it is of deliberate state policy, yet in each case, these people must include the opportunities opened up by state policy as part of the ecology within which they operate.

In Tunisia and in Egypt, integration of the local community into the national structure goes apace with the growth of a capitalist agriculture. At the local level, this capitalist agriculture reflects the skills of farmers able to take advantage of new opportunities in marketing, new crops and an changing technology. It also leads to the growth of class structures within such local communities as Testour and Musha. In Saudi Arabia, both the starting point and the ending point are different. Though the bedouin tribes have a highly differentiated internal structure, they have been incorporated *en masse* into the emerging class system of the national polity. While on the one hand, their traditional leaders, the amirs, retain the right of direct access to the rulers, thus giving them a sense of continuity with a more illustrious past, on the other, they are being bypassed by the growth of a class system based, in the cities, on an alliance of Saudi bourgeoisie, multinational corporations and foreign labour. Thus here the dynamics are largely those of the wider society, whereas in Tunisia and Egypt, the endogenous evolution of the rural communities is a notable factor.

From a point of view of rural people in all three countries, the state represents primarily a pool of resources that they can exploit. Thus the involvement of the state in the ecological changes in Egyptian agriculture, or the efforts of the Tunisian state to co-operativise agriculture, or the willingness of the Saudi state to subsidise agriculture in order to achieve a goal of self-sufficiency in wheat production, all modify the nature of resources available to local people and guide their choices accordingly. These choices reflect not just the options offered by the state, however, but also the values and goals of rural people.

As the basis of production in local communities is modified, new social roles and groups are born and the local manifestations of a class system begin to appear. Weber points out that 'classes are formed in accordance with relations of production and the acquisition of wealth', and that 'all technological and economic convulsions and upheavals . . . thrust the class situation into the foreground' (Weber, 1978, p. 54). He further stresses that ' class situations arise only in the context of a community', adding that, 'The collective action which leads to the emergence of a class situation, however, is not in its essence an action undertaken by members of the same class but one involving relations between members of different classes' (Weber, 1978, p. 47). In other words, the interesting dimension is not the existence of something static called a class, but the presence of a class structure in which differences of wealth and power over economic resources, expressed in the relations of production, influence the behaviour of individuals. If individuals orient their social action in this situation, and give it meaning, then it is class action.

The material presented in this paper shows that a class situation is most nearly present in Testour, where the relations of production involve a good deal of wage labour, which political action takes into account. The Egyptian case appears intermediate, in that, although wage labour is present, it is not the relations of production but status distinctions that are the basis for political action. The Saudi bedouin case represents the opposite extreme. There is no evidence for emergence of a class situation within the bedouin community, which in fact is marked by a rather militant egalitarianism, but class and status distinctions within the wider community are perhaps the sharpest of all, precisely because status distinctions (e.g. nationality) are increasingly coming to define economic class. Whether the bedouin will have a collective place in this new social order or will fragment and take their places as individuals remains to be seen. In the Tunisian and Egyptian cases, the class situation within the local communities reflects, at least partially, that of the national community and serves to integrate them into the national community in the form of the state.

The developments within local communities in the Arab world have significance for the strength of the state. People appear bound to the state by self interest, by a desire to share in the resources that the state can make available. They do not let the state define all their actions, and a variable but considerable range of behaviour remains outside the influence or even knowledge of the state. Economic and political behaviour is more likely to reflect local concerns of prestige and status and the emerging local class situation than national policies. Yet the willingness of people in rural communities to support the state is crucial to the survival of the state. If the state is an expression of the society and the society is becoming integrated in a horizontal way through class formation, then the involvement of rural communities in this process fosters their integration into the national society and the state. This process seems more advanced in Tunisia and in Egypt than in Saudi Arabia, but everywhere it owes relatively little to the intended outcome of state policies.

At the same time, the social bases of Arab unity are enhanced to the extent that the life experiences and the class situations in the different countries provide more of a basis for common viewpoints. If the process of integration through class formation occurs within each state, could it one day apply to the Arab world as a whole?

ACKNOWLEDGEMENTS

Research in Testour was carried out principally in 1972–3 with financial support from the Smithsonian Foreign Currency Program and the Social Science Research Council. The research was part of a joint programme conducted with Dr Abdelkader Zghal of the University of Tunis. Research in Musha was carried out in 1980–1 with financial support from the American Research Center in Egypt and the Population Council Middle East Awards Program. It was locally sponsored by the University of Asyut. Part of the analysis of the Musha data was done while I was on sabbatical leave from the American University in Cairo at the Center for Middle Eastern Studies, Harvard University, in 1982–3. I wish to thank all these institutions and their representatives for their support. The section on Saudi Arabia is based on reading, but I have benefited enormously from conversations with Professor Donald Cole of the American University in Cairo. Thanks to the FAO, I made a brief trip to Saudi Arabia (Sakaka and Wadi Sirhan) in 1984.

11

Arab Regimes: Legitimacy and Foreign Policy

Adeed Dawisha

When a regime embarks on foreign activity, the analyst can usually uncover a variety of motivating factors. In this, the analysis of Arab politics is no different from the analysis of politics in any other international regime. One can list a number of political, ideological, economic and geo-strategic reasons for Syria's decision to intervene in Lebanon and for its consciously anti-American policies, for Iraq's invasion of Iran in September 1980, for the support accorded to revolutionary groups such as the Palestinians and Eritreans by the conservative regime of Saudi Arabia, for Morocco's active pursuit of its claims on the Western Sahara, and for Libya's interventionist activities in Africa and the Middle East.However, one factor which has always been, and continues to be a potent motivating force of foreign policy in Arab politics is the effort by Arab regimes to legitimise their rule by undertaking foreign ventures. It is no exaggeration to argue that in all the above examples, the efforts by regimes at domestic legitimisation constituted a primary, if not the only, motivating factor.

This is not to suggest that the search for legitimacy necessarily motivates Arab leaders to embark on foreign ventures. However, given the environment in which Arab politics operate, it is easy to see why there is such a strong correlation between foreign policy and domestic legitimacy. Conflict in the area is endemic: there is the perennial Arab-Israel struggle; there is the constant conflict over territorial issues born out of the colonial legacy and in some cases still not satisfactorily resolved; there are the immense number of sectarian and ethnic divisions that cut across state boundaries, causing not only intra-state, but also inter-state, conflict; and finally there is the identification by the citizens of the various Arab states with the universalist values of Arabism and Islam. Not only do these

260

two ideological forces tend to weaken people's identification with their own states, Arabism and Islam also are regularly used by Arab leaders to appeal to the loyalty of the citizens of other Arab states, thus undermining the legitimacy and stability of their regimes.

Aware of the potential for conflict in their area, Arab states have tried to limit the opportunities and regulate their relations through regional institutions and practices such as the League of Arab States and the summits of the Arab Heads of State. The Arab political environment, whether conflictual or cooperative (or both), is characterised by an intense level of inter-state activity. It is this kind of environment that makes foreign policy such a convenient vehicle for regime stability and legitimacy.

The concept of legitimacy has been explored by many different theorists, and whereas the thrust of their analyses may differ, they all tend to agree that, in the final analysis, only uncoerced acceptance by the citizens of the state makes a government legitimate. According to David Easton 'what differentiates political interactions from all other kinds of social interactions is that they are predominantly oriented toward the authoritative allocation of values for society. . . . An allocation is authoritative when the persons oriented to it consider that they are bound by it' (Easton, 1965, p. 50). Similarly, Max Weber, identifies three types of legitimacy: the traditional, the charismatic and the legal-rational. In the first and second types, obligations and loyalty are to a person, the traditional chieftan or the heroic or messianic leader; in the third type, obligation is to the legally established impersonal network of institutions (Weber, 1957, pp. 325–8). In all three types, however, legitimacy is defined in the context of people's acceptance of their governments and of their leaders. Thus, in discussing the second type of legitimacy, that of a charismatic leader, Weber posits this as a relationship in which the people perceive qualities in an individual which impel them to follow him, and as such, 'it is the duty of those to whom he addresses his mission to realise him as their legitimate and charismatically qualified leader' (Gerth and Wright Mills, 1970, p. 247). Again, the definition refers to a relationship between governors and governed, in which the latter enter uncoerced into the relationship. Herbert C. Kelman puts it succinctly. He defines a government as legitimate:

When it is perceived as having the right to exercise authority in a given domain and within specified limits. Thus, when the administration of a legitimate political system makes certain demands, citizens accept them, whether or not they like them. An individual citizen may or may not be convinced of the value of the action he is asked to take; he may or may not be enthusiastic about carrying it out; and he may, in fact, be very unhappy about it. If it is within the limits of legitimacy, however, he willingly meets the demand without feeling coerced, and considers it his duty to do so (Kelman, 1969, p. 279).

This relationship is institutionalised in Western political thought and practice through the creation of political institutions. By facilitating the participation of the citizen in the body politic, these institutions become the symbols of system legitimacy, and the means by which citizens show their acceptance of the political system. The seventeenth century English philosopher John Locke argued (Locke, 1960) for a legislative power to run alongside, and independently of, executive power. Moreover, he contended that the legislative power should be superior to the executive, and that legislative institutions would be the means by which people participated actively, through representation, in the affairs of the state. As an example, he said that people's properties should not be taxed or taken from them except by their own consent or that of their representatives.

It is this tradition of representative democracy which underpins the whole notion of legitimacy in Western societies. Legitimacy in this sense is invested not in the ruler but in the political system as a whole. In North America, Europe and Japan, it is the parliamentary system of government that is legitimate, and government officials, elected through the institutions of this system of government, acquire their own legitimacy from the legitimacy of the system.

Lacking legitimacy based on mass participation through political representation, and realising how crucial legitimacy is for the stability of the political order, political leaders in the Arab world constantly endeavour to win the acceptance of their population, or at least their acquiescence in their leadership. This is usually done through the leader's efforts to create in the minds of his people an image of himself as a meritorious and successful leader. This is a difficult and uncertain process; indeed, it is like a journey on a Cairo bus: not only will one get a bumpy ride, but one may never arrive at the final destination. However, when an Arab leader embarks on the hazardous mission of acquiring legitimacy through success and achievements, he starts with some favourable omens that relate to the apparent susceptibility of Arab populations to the notion of centralised and authoritarian regimes.

262

Prior to the birth of the modern Arab state, the core societal units in the Arab world were (many would argue continue to be) the tribe, the village and the extended family. For centuries, the pattern of political loyalty in the tribal and village communities was hierarchical, with authority focused on the Sheikh or Rais. Although he was bound by tribal and village laws and customs, the Sheikh or the Rais, assisted by elders and religious personages, acted as the central authority, the final arbiter of power and the ultimate dispenser of justice. Similarly, the extended family has traditionally been hierarchically structured with authority resting in the hands of the oldest member. Deference to, and respect for, family elders creates a far greater conformity within an Arab family than is usually the case in a Western family, where intra-family relationships are less hierarchical. Transferred to the national milieu, therefore, the respectful and ready acceptance, in a tribal, village or family context, of a hierarchical social structure with a clearly identifiable authoritative personage at the top tends obviously to lessen rebellious tendencies among the populations against authoritarian regimes.

Even more crucial in this context is the role of Islam. As the religion of the overwhelming majority of the Arab people, Islam tends to pervade social custom and to dominate cultural and political attitudes. To this day, many of the values, norms of behaviour and attitudes of the Arab populations emanate from the inspiration and moral teachings of Islam. Accepting no separation between state and religion, Islam represents for the Muslim Arab much more than a system of spiritual guidance; it is accepted as a comprehensive social, political, legal and cultural system, and as such, even after years of 'modernisation' and 'secularisation', Islam remains a powerful and pervasive force in the Arab world.

Islam tends to bestow legitimacy on the centralised structure of political authority in the Arab world. The first major decision that the first Muslim community had to make was the election of the first Khalifa (successor) on the death of the prophet Mohammad. The Khalifa was given religious and political authority, a decision based on the Sunna (the traditions of the prophet) that religious and temporal power are inseparable. Moreover, the centralisation of authority is embodied in Islamic political heritage through the pronouncements of renowned Muslim jurists, theologians and philosophers in the centuries following the death of the prophet. Thus, according to the fourteenth century philosopher of history Ibn Khaldun, 'It is in the nature of states that authority becomes concentrated in one person' (Issawi, 1950, p. 114).

These same jurists prescribed almost total obedience to the ruler by fostering the belief that 'rebellion was the most heinous of crimes'; a doctrine which was consecrated in the juristic maxim, 'sixty years of tyranny are better than one hour of civil strife' (Gibb, 1955, p. 15). The famous eleventh century theologian al-Ghazali teaches that, 'An unjust ruler should not be deposed if strife would follow' (Hourani, 1962, p. 14). It is true that theologians, such as al-Mawardi (d. 1058), had argued that if the ruler did not fulfill his function, he should be removed from power, but none could indicate how this could be done legally or constitutionally. On the other hand, jurists such as al-Ash'ari (d. 935), 'Not only denied any right of popular revolution, but also emphasised the Caliph's full claim to obedience even if he had disregarded or violated his duties' (Khadduri, 1955, p. 12). This school of thought was extended some centuries later by the constitutional theorist Ibn Jama'a (d. 1333), who argued that, 'Self-investiture by armed force is lawful, and obedience is due to such a ruler' (Rosenthal, 1958, p. 45). The fact that Ibn Jama'a wrote under the militaristic rule of the Mamluks may explain his point of view. Nevertheless, his views, and the views of the other theologians, constitute prescriptive knowledge embodied in the culture and heritage of the Arab/Muslim people, and as such must have an impact on the way contemporary Arab populations have reacted to authority.

This may explain in part the endurance of authoritarian rule in the Arab world. In every Arab state (apart from Lebanon), the centralisation of power in the hands of one man has been the dominant feature of Arab politics over the last four decades. Opposition parties and groups hardly exist except in clandestine forms, and with the notable exception Kuwait, where opposition officially exists, they are blatantly manipulated by the regime. Institutions, such as parliaments and assemblies are sometimes created by the regimes to act as rubber stamps for government policies. And when assemblies, parties and mass organisations outgrow their original purpose or begin to act independently, they are ruthlessly cast aside by the ruling group. President Gamal Abd al-Nasser created three successive mass parties between 1953 and 1962. Nor did he feel himself to be necessarily bound by the decisions of his cabinet. Professor Boutros Boutros-Ghali, in analysing the working of Egyptian foreign policy under Nasser, states that 'The formulation of foreign policy . . . is strictly the prerogative and sole responsibility of the chief executive. The extent to which the executive is guided by the counsel of his principal associates, including the minister of foreign affairs, is a matter of personal choice' (Boutros-Ghali, 1963, p. 320). Professor Ghali, who later became Minister of State for Foreign Affairs under Nasser's successor, Anwar Sadat, must have congratulated himself many times on how true his analysis was. Similarly, the dazzling array of Libyan institutions of supposedly mass participation, from the Arab Socialist Union to the various popular committees, are the product not so much of Libya's democratic traditions, which itself is a contradiction in terms, but of the restless soul of Libya's sole ruler, Muammar Qadhafi.

Naturally, some Arab countries can point to political institutions that participate fully in the decision-making process. The Neo-Destour party in Tunisia, the FLN in Algeria, the NLF in South Yemen and the Baath in Syria and Iraq are all long-standing organisations that are capable of setting limitations on the chief executive's freedom. Even in these cases, however, power, in the final analysis, resides with the chief executive, for to set limitations is not for formulate or reverse policies, and to argue a point is not to make the argument stick. To generalise from the Syrian case, the late Ahmad Iskander, Syria's Minister of Information until his death in 1983, confirmed in an interview that in meetings with the top membership of the Baath Party, the President was the dominant personality, and the final decision on any policy was always the President's responsibility (Dawisha, 1980, pp. 102–3). Whatever the regime, therefore, the power to make decisions and enact policies in the Arab world continues to reside with the man at the top, and it is he who dominates the decision-making process and who determines the country's policy orientations. Unlike the pluralistic models of political behaviour, therefore, in which the chief executive derives his authority (defined as the legitimate exercise of power) from the legitimacy of the political system, political theory and practice in the Arab world have tended to elevate the ruler to a position of dominance over the legal-institutional structure, thus making the legitimacy of the political system dependent on the authority of the ruler.

Authoritarian leaders, however, cannot trust the survival of their political orders to the force of history alone. Conspirators as the majority of them are, they need more than the assurances of the past to make them sleep comfortably at night. They know that the attitudes of nations are shaped not only by the memories of the past, but also by the experiences of the present. The past influences people's perceptions of the present; but the present provides an ever-changing environment that constantly expands the limits of human

ARAB REGIMES

and intellectual horizons. This in turn modifies the people's memory of their past.

The curse of the present for the Arab authoritarian rulers is the impact of the process of modernisation on their traditional societies. With increasing urbanisation, accelerated education and creeping Westernisation, traditional values and attitudes, which could be relied upon to underpin the stability of the Arab regimes, were bound to be questioned. Tribal values were being gradually eroded by urban living, the expansion of economic life began to dissipate the physical unity and inner coherence of the family, and Islam was confronted by Western secularism. In short, the Arabs of the second half of the twentieth century were demanding more of their rulers than their forefathers ever did. The traditional values of their political culture still held sway over the minds of the Arabs, but increasingly, as their eyes opened to new social and political realities in the world around them, they began to demand changes to their own political situation.

Just as the process of modernisation proved to be curse for the rulers, it ended as a curse for the ruled as well. For with modernisation came technological advancement, and that placed in the hands of the rulers methods of social and coercive suppression that made earlier means of population control pale into insignificance. However, the rulers knew only too well that more was needed to ensure the stability of their regimes, so a two-pronged maxim was followed: put fear in people's hearts, but also try to win their support, no matter how grudgingly given. On the other side of the fence, the ruled realised very quickly through bitter experience the futility of demanding genuine and full political participation; at least, however, they could demand intelligent and worthy leaders. Once the needs of the rulers and the demands of the ruled converged, achievements in foreign policy, magnified and exaggerated by the states' propaganda machines into great heroic acts, became, from the 1950s onwards, a central legitimising agent for Arab leadership.

The process began with Gamal Abd al-Nasser in the mid-1950s. His defiance of the West in a number of dramatic political acts ranging from his attacks on the Baghdad Pact, through the purchase of Soviet weapons, to the momentous decision to nationalise the Suez Canal company in 1956 won much support among the Egyptian population, humiliated as it was by almost a century of British presence on its soil. And when the Suez expedition, mounted by Britain and France in alliance with Israel, failed to wrest the Suez Canal from Egyptian control, the process of the

266

domestic legitimisation of Nasser's regime was complete. According to a commentator, who hardly counts as an admirer of Nasser, Suez gave the Egyptian president 'almost unlimited credit in his own country and throughout the Arab world' (Laqueuer, 1968, p. 36). Through skillful and effective use of his propaganda machine, Nasser created in the minds of his people an image of himself as the first genuinely local hero who not only had dared to defy the might of the West, but had actually won. From then on, Nasser's legitimacy as Egypt's president, and the legitimacy of the political order which he had created were not to be questioned, until the 1967 war with Israel, which, as an episode of Nasser's controversial history, was the complete antithesis of Suez. We shall come back to the 1967 war below.

The man to succeed Nasser as president of Egypt in 1970 was Anwar Sadat, a man who had spent all his political life under the towering shadow of his predecessor. Indeed, Nasser himself used to refer to Sadat as *Bikbashi Aywa* — Colonel Yes-man. When, by virtue of his being Vice-President (a largely ceremonial and inconsequential role) at the time of Nasser's death, Sadat ascended to the presidency, his credibility, to say nothing of his legitimacy, was very low indeed. Yet the new, and allegedly makeshift president had learned well from his predecessor, and a series of bold foreign policy measures that surpassed even the exploits of Nasser, had, within a few years of his ascension to power, established him as the undisputed leader of his country.

The process began in 1972 when, in a bold move, he expelled over 21,000 Soviet personnel from Egypt. Given that most observers had by that time concluded that Egypt had become a political and military satellite of the Soviet Union, Sadat's dramatic act increased his prestige immeasurably both inside Egypt and in the Arab world. This was followed by the greatest 'achievement' of his eleven years as president — the launching of the October 1973 war against Israel and the successful military crossing of the Suez Canal. Until it happened, no one had thought it possible, not even the renowned experts of Western intelligence. And when it happened, and when everyone knew that it was Sadat who made it happen, the man finally emerged from the shadow of Nasser. In the words of Fouad Ajami, 'The war provided Sadat with his great act. The crossing of the Suez Canal became the mandate to create his kind of Egypt' (Ajami, 1981, pp. 95–6). The propagandists lost no time in making the October war not only the foundation upon which the legitimacy of Sadat's Egypt rested, but also a sort of moral dividing line between an old defeated and oppressive Egypt under Nasser and a new, heroic and invigorated Egypt of Sadat. The term *al-'Ubur* (the crossing) became the symbol of the new legitimacy; it became 'the crossing from defeat to victory, division to unity, shame to dignity, oppression to justice, terror to security' (Ajami, 1981, p. 96). Sadat had arrived; at last, he was his own man, needing no patron, memories of the past. He had became *al-Rais* in his own right. A major foreign policy 'success' had established Sadat as the unchallenged leader of his country.

For a while, he tried to sustain his authority with domestic achievements. The crossing of the Canal was supposed to be followed by the 'economic crossing' and the 'political crossing' in Egypt. Liberalisation of the socialist economic order and democratisation of the authoritarian political system were to follow now that Egypt had overcome the 'cycle of shame' and Sadat had established his legitimacy. Sadat, who three to four years earlier had been the brunt of the Egyptians' famed sardonic humour, was single-handedly transforming Egypt: from a socialist to a capitalist economy, from a pro-Soviet to a pro-American country, and from an authoritarian to a democratic state.

All this, however, met with little internal applause. Economic liberalisation (*infitah*) did no more than stir the lethargic Egyptian economy, creating hardly the promised land that Sadat and his propagandists confidently predicted. But it did create a rich class of people, seemingly dedicated to conspicuous consumption, whose antics and excesses fuelled the resentments of those, the majority of Egyptians, whose own economic situation not only did not improve, but in relative terms actually worsened. And while the shift from pro-Soviet to a pro-American orientation was met at first by almost universal approval, America's image was gradually eroded by the regime's conscious effort to equate Egypt's promised economic revival with America's help and encouragement. So, as the infitah began to falter, the blame was being increasingly directed not only at the regime, but also at the outside power which encouraged and, in the eyes of many Egyptians, actually planned the economic strategy.

Most disappointing was the failure of the political liberalisation of Egypt. Sadat would talk incessantly about democracy in Egypt; his propagandists would paint a glowing picture of genuine political representation, and of a free and dynamic electorate filled with the kind of affection and admiration for their president that persuaded no less than 98 per cent of them consistently to vote for him and for all his policies. Of course, as usually happens in the Arab world, the reality did not correspond to the regime's claims. The people, whose perception and intelligence more often than not have been grossly underestimated by Arab regimes, could see Sadat's democracy for the sham that it actually was. Sadat was allowed, in the wake of October 1973, to experience the seductions of absolute power, and like all addicts, it was too much to ask the man to share his 'high' with someone else. For all the protestations of the president and his men, and for all the cosmetic changes that they tried to affect in the political institutions of the country, Egypt remained an authoritarian political system, dependent for its *raison d'être* on the legitimacy of 'the man at the top'.

It was no coincidence, therefore, that Sadat's 'historic' trip to Jerusalem came when it came. By 1977, the glow of al-'Ubur was beginning to markedly recede; nothing much had come out of the other crossing — Egypt's political and economic liberalisation; and generally the universal optimism of the immediate post-1973 era was giving way to mounting scepticism and cynicism directed towards the regime, its policies, its rhetoric and its promises. It was therefore time for yet another 'heroic' foreign policy act — the dramatic trip to Jerusalem at the end of 1977. Of course, the Jerusalem trip was dictated by a number of factors, many of which were of an ideological and strategic nature. But there can be little doubt that the initiative, in its announcement and its execution, in the publicity that surrounded it, and in the manner by which the Egyptian propaganda machine used it to resurrect the tarnished image of the president, was also meant to achieve what the October war and the expulsion of the Russians had once achieved for the domestic legitimacy and stability of the Sadat regime.

The evidence is still not conclusive, but it looks as though this last of Sadat's heroic acts was not the domestic success that he had anticipated. The Egyptians did not want war with Israel but neither, it seems, were they ready for fully-fledged peace, and as such the Jerusalem trip and the subsequent Camp David accords, which made Sadat an American superstar, did little to allay the alienation of the mass of Egyptians from the unpopular domestic policies of his regime. Sadat's assassination, and the sheer nonchalance with which the ordinary Egyptian reacted to his death was testimony to that.

In contrast, Syria's risky foreign policy activities in the wake of Israel's invasion of Lebanon in 1982 seemed to go a long way towards cementing the authority and stability of President Assad. This was especially crucial to the Syrian president, as he and a number of key members of Syria's leadership belong to the minority Alawi community. The Sunni Muslims, who constitute the vast majority of the Syrian population, have had a long-standing antipathy towards the Alawis. The orthodox Sunnis have long considered the Alawi sect, which is an esoteric offshoot of Ismaili Shi'ism that seems to have absorbed animistic and Christian beliefs, as bordering on the heretical. Moreover, the contrast between the Alawis' recent political ascendency and their traditional inferior social and material status was bound to fuel the resentment of the Sunni Syrian population.

Sensitive to this underlying tension, President Assad endeavoured throughout the 1970s, to make the Baath Party the main ideological base and political arm of his regime. This tended to blur the regime's dependence on the Alawi community for its security. The situation changed dramatically with the onset of the 1980s. The growing opposition of the well-organised and highly fanatical Muslim Brotherhood to the Assad political order led to a number of bloody encounters, culminating in the uprising in the predominantly Sunni city of Hama in February 1982. During three weeks of seemingly limitless brutality, thousands of Muslim Brothers and innocent civilians were killed and almost half the city was razed to the ground primarily by the units of Siraya al-Difa, a crack, impeccably-trained military force made up entirely of Alawis and commanded by the President's brother, Rifat al-Assad. During this period, in terms of legitimacy, the Assad regime went through probably its weakest period. It was perceived by the Sunni majority population as a blatantly sectarian regime, wholly dependent on coercion that was ruthlessly perpetrated by members of its minority sect.

Paradoxically, it was Israel's invasion of Lebanon in June 1982 that restored to the Assad regime the credibility which it had almost completely lost after the Hama incident. By projecting Syria as the only Arab country that dared to confront Israel militarily, the Damascus government put itself forward as the champion of the 'Arab nation' (Khaddam al-Halim, 1983, p. 15). What is more, the Syrian leadership's obstinate stand, in the face of seemingly overwhelming odds, against the Israeli-Lebanese 17 May agreement, and later against the might of America's military power, brought Hafez al-Assad and his colleagues immense credit in Syria and in the Arab world. When the Americans ignominiously withdrew and the Israeli-Lebanese agreement was abrogated, Assad's prestige soared.

This series of foreign policy 'achievements', regained for President Assad the legitimacy he had lost after Hama in early 1982. The

Syrian president had no doubt hoped that his vigorous portrayal of Syria's 'steadfastness' as a heroic defender of Arab rights would create in the country an image of the Assad regime that was more 'Arab' and less 'Alawi'. Whatever the sectarian characteristics of his regime, therefore, President Assad would be embraced by the virulently Arabist Syrian population as a true and committed Arab leader, for he knew that to project himself as fighting on behalf of the 'Arab nations' was probably the best way to erase from the people's perceptions the regime's Alawi affiliations.

Assad's endeavours were risky, for a possible defeat at the hands of the Americans or the Israelis could have had the opposite effect on the Syrian population; he would not have been the successful and courageous defender of Arab rights, but the reckless adventurer who brought shame and despair on his country. I return here to a point I made earlier: the path towards legitimacy through foreign policy acts has been a risky, even hazardous, practice for Arab leaders. In the case of President Assad, he had emerged 'victorious' by the spring of 1984, and as a result, his legitimacy was seemingly restored and his position consolidated. But there have also been failures — cases when leaders went too far, miscalculated and lost.

The most obvious example was the June war of 1967. The prestige of President Nasser in the mid-sixties had been undermined by an almost continuous economic crisis, which itself was exacerbated by Egypt's morale-sapping and financially-ruinous military intervention in Yemen. Moreover, the acclaimed leader of Arab nationalism's cautious policy towards Israel, which was in stark contrast to his fiery rhetoric, put his credibility in question among many Egyptians as well as Arabs. When in the spring of 1967, therefore, tension on the Syrian-Israeli borders abruptly increased with Israeli leaders making veiled threats about the Syrian regime and with rumours circulating about Israeli massing of troops on the Syrian border, the chance for Nasser to seize the moment to re-establish his prestige was too good to be missed. In May 1967, he decided to ask the United Nations to pull its peace-keeping forces out of Sinai, to assert Egyptian sovereignty over the port of Sharm al-Sheikh and to close the straits of Tiran to Israeli shipping. Once the implementation of these decisions achieved his political objectives of restoring his regime's credibility Nasser, who did not particularly want to fight Israel, began to wind down the crisis through superpower diplomacy. He obviously hoped that the superpowers, fearful of being drawn into the conflict, would compel Israel to accept the newly created situation, leaving him with a great political victory

ARAB REGIMES

that would silence his critics and erase from their minds Egypt's economic ills and its disastrous intervention in the Yemen. It almost worked, except that nobody had calculated for the presence in Israel of leaders who were just as adept at the game of risk-taking.

Nasser was to rule Egypt until his death in 1970, but the end of his charisma, and of his almost mystical hold on the masses were signalled by the June 1967 defeat. 'He would stay in power' Ajami writes, 'not as a confident, vibrant hero, but as a tragic figure, a symbol of better days, an indication of the will to resist' (Ajami, 1981, p. 85). The people stayed with Nasser; but they were no longer bound to him.

A more recent example of an Arab leader who used foreign policy to broaden his mass support, until he over-reached himself, is President Saddam Hussein of Iraq. In Hussein's case, however, the initial efforts at legitimisation were carried through by domestic reforms. Using Iraq's immense oil wealth, Hussein embarked in the mid and late 1970s on massive development and social welfare programmes which were aimed at broadening his support in the country. With an eye towards bridging the gap between rich and poor, he vigorously pursued policies that included rapid improvements in housing, education and medical services, and enacted legislation on social security, minimum wages and pension rights.

By 1979, foreign policy was beginning to supplant domestic reform as the main vehicle for Hussein's legitimisation. Seizing the opportunity left by Egypt's withdrawal from Arab politics because of Camp David, the Iraqi President embarked on diplomatic activity during 1979 and 1980 aimed at establishing Baghdad as the core of Arab political action and himself as the central figure among Arab leaders. In a speech in April 1980, Hussein declared that Iraq had 'always had a unique historical position within the Arab nation' and that 'the Iraqi army will remain strong to defend the honour of all Arabs fighting foreign forces' (Al-Thawra, 17 April 1980). Two months earlier, the President in a much trumpeted proclamation had enunciated his Arab National Charter which set out and communicated to other leaders in the area Hussein's ideas on future Arab political action.

Beyond the Arab world, President Hussein lobbyed hard to bring the conference of the leaders of the non-aligned world to Baghdad in September 1982, a move that would have given Hussein the opportunity to assume the mantle of leadership of the non-aligned world. In order to pave the way, throughout 1980 the Iraqi received

272

more than 30 Third World heads of state and prime ministers. All this activity certainly had the desired effect. By the end of 1980, Hussein had successfully changed his image from that of a ruthless but anonymous party-man in the early 1970s to one of a meritorious and substantial popular leader. With his domestic legitimacy seemingly guaranteed, President Hussein set out to make the 1980s the decade in which he would fill the void of Arab charismatic leadership vacated by Nasser after the 1967 defeat. And the young, ambitious Iraqi president might have succeeded had it not been for the intervention of the old and frail, but ruthlessly committed, Ayatollah Khomeini.

The entry of Iraq's armed forces into Iran in September 1980 was motivated by a number of reasons, not least by Khomeini's obstinate insistence on imposing his brand of revolutionary Islam on Iraq. It is true that the Iraqi leaders were concerned about the new Muslim Iranian regime 'trying to instigate fanaticism, resentment and division among the peoples of the area', (*Al-Thawra*, 18 September 1980) and it is also true that the new Tehran leaders resolutely dismissed all Iraq's overtures for neighbourly relations, preferring instead to mount increasingly hostile verbal onslaughts against Hussein and the Baath Party. Nevertheless, there seems to have been more that mere defensiveness in the Iraqi decision to invade Iran in 1980.

The reports coming from Iran had painted a picture of the political order as one of utter chaos, with a number of competing centres of power that were more interested in fighting each other than building a viable political structure. The news about the economy was hardly any better. Oil production had fallen sharply; there was a foreign currency reserve crisis, and food and consumer shortages were rampant. Most crucially, after the collapse of the Shah's army, Iran's fighting capability was thought to be almost negligible; most of Iran's officer corps had fled, been executed or put in prison, and the equipment, lacking spare parts, was becoming nearly unusable. What is more, the Iranian clergy had succeeded in alienating almost the entire international community. In short, the aggressively expansionist revolutionary Iran of September 1980 was, by all accounts, an easy target for a bold military operation by the Iraqi leader, frustrated as he was by Iran's seemingly limitless hostility towards him and his regime.

Once he had convinced himself that a military operation against Iran would not be costly and would be successful, Hussein could immediately see the benefits that would accrue to him in Iraq and the Arab world generally, once this 'bold' feat was achieved. He would go to the Arab summit conference scheduled in Amman two months later as the first Arab leader since independence who had been able to defeat a foreign enemy. And if he could do it in less than the six days it took Israel to defeat Nasser, then all the better. He would immediately and without question be raised to a level above that of his Arab competitors like Syria's Assad, King Hussein of Jordan and King Khalid of Saudi Arabia. How could anyone ever again challenge the status of the dynamic young leader who had transformed his country economically and socially, had become a major figure internationally, and had inflicted a humiliating defeat on a major power that could have become a main threat to the stability of many Arab regimes? In the exuberant days of 1980, when everything seemed to go well for Iraq, Saddam Hussein probably could almost hear the late President Nasser declaring the young leader of Iraq the natural heir to the mantle of Arab leadership. With all this, his legitimacy inside Iraq, as the leader who had achieved the ultimate in success, would probably be guaranteed for life.

It is said that dreamers eventually come down to earth with a painful thud; and Hussein's dreams were to shatter against the rock of religious commitment and revolutionary enthusiasm. The hopes for swift and famous victory never materialised; the conflict became a war of attrition that cost Iraq dearly. Economic development was arrested and reversed, social cohesion began to show signs of strain, and as more and more of Iraq's youth sacrificed their lives in this senseless war, the people's morale sank deeper into despair. In this mood of hopelessness, they could hardly be expected to applaud the leader who plunged them into this seemingly unending abyss. It was not that Hussein had completely lost his support, since he still had much good will from earlier days, and in any case, Iraqis resented Tehran's insistence on the removal of Hussein as a condition for the cessation of fighting, for people do not, as a rule, take kindly to foreign powers interfering in their domestic affairs. But the halo of merit and success, which had underpinned Hussein's legitimacy, had deserted him, and he was left to pick up the pieces and somehow try to start the whole process of establishing legitimacy all over again.

Whether the leader is successful or not, the way in which he acquires legitimacy in the Arab world must make his tenure, by the very nature of the process, a transient phenomenon. Success in a particular foreign policy venture will fuel people's enthusiasm — but only for a while. Sooner of later, the enthusiasm will wane, and the leader will have to provide the population with yet another dose of visible and applaudable achievements. The Arab leader has to have a career portfolio of successive 'success stories' in order to maintain his credibility, his legitimacy and ultimately the stability of his political order. It is only through genuine participation in the political process by the people that the unshakable and permanent legitimacy of the political order is guaranteed. There is, however, no sign that the Arab leaders are ready for such a fundamental departure from the present order of things, and as such, foreign policy seems destined to continue to play a central role in the legitimisation of Arab leaders and their political orders.

12

Conclusion: Reasons for Resilience

Adeed Dawisha

How stable are contemporary Arab states really? That was the question posed in the introductory chapter. On the face of it, Arab states seem to be extraordinarily resilient: since the onset of the 1970s state structures, on the whole, have remained intact; there have been no Iranian-type societal convulsions, and when rebellions have occurred (such as the Islamic uprising in the Syrian city of Hama and the takeover of the Grand Mosque in Mecca), they have been quickly and effectively suppressed by state power. Indeed, the faces of most of the Arab political leaders who were in power in 1970-1 have continued in the late 1980s to look down on their public from high billboards in public squares.

These are powerful arguments that auger well for the future survival of the Arab state. Yet doubts remain. Has the state survived so far because it has been able to legitimise its political and social order, or has survival been simply a function of overwhelming state power and control? Many analysts in the past have pointed to power as the major reason for state survival. Increasingly, in the late 1970s and 1980s analysts endeavoured to look beyond the state power into the varied and complex institutions that constituted the link between the general public and the political elites. These institutions, whether organisational (bureaucracies, military, parties) or cultural (religion, social units), seemed to represent a more sophisticated explanatory device for the understanding of state resilience and survival.

But, as Zartman cautions in the introduction it is simply not realistic to underestimate the effectiveness of internal security apparatuses in the Arab state, both as an instrument to control potential opposition, and as a means of combatting such opposition in the event control fails. And indeed, as has been pointed out earlier, technological advancement, coupled with a steep rise in the purchasing power of the Arab states in the wake of the 1974 rise in oil prices, meant that state authorities would acquire new methods of coercion and suppression that made earlier means of population control pale into insignificance. In many Arab states these days it is only the recklessly courageous and zealously committed who would dare oppose government policies and actions.

Beyond the brute force of state violence, state authorities control other aspects of individuals' lives which tend to undermine peoples' ability or willingness to mount a vigorous challenge to the regime. For example, in almost all Arab countries, the media, and therefore the dissemination of information, is an easy and frequent target of state manipulation. Even in the least illiberal of Arab states, the press operates within strictly circumscribed parameters that it transgresses at its peril. No Arab country can boast a radio or television station that is not government-owned or operated. Such persuasive dominance over information and ideas allows the state to interfere vigorously with what people know and to shape political and social aspirations.

Real as state power and control undoubtedly are, it is simplistic to see them as the sole reason for the apparent resilience of the Arab state. The chapters in this book have explored facets of the contemporary Arab state that might explain its stability. The state appears to have used a number of non-coercive methods to bestow legitimacy on the political order and safeguard its structures. Arab regimes have followed a two-pronged maxim: put fear in peoples' hearts but try to win their support, no matter how grudgingly given.

One means of acquiring support has been the effort by Arab regimes to co-opt influential, and potentially or actually destabilising groups into the body politic. In a world where Islam permeates peoples' lives, it is evident that the state would endeavour to use religious institutions as a support-base for state authority. Belaid points to two methods. From the very beginning of the Saudi state, Wahhabi orthodoxy and its endorsement of the Saudi dynasty, enabled the House of Saud to legitimise its rule and the absolutist form of its government. It also allowed the ruling family to combat other competing (and, given the nature of Saudi rule, clearly subversive) sources of ideology such as Marxism and Arab nationalism.

The Tunisian and Algerian regimes used religious institutions in a different way, by labelling the institutions of traditional Islam corrupt, obstructionist and deviationist. By means of preemptive action, they assumed the role of authentic guardians and true

CONCLUSION

interpreters of Islam. Not only did they undermine opposition to their rule but they acquired an important source of legitimacy.

More generally, Arab regimes have endeavoured to cement state stability by extending socio-economic benefits to hitherto excluded groups, or by incorporating into the political/administrative process emerging social classes with rising political expectations. The efforts of the Baath regime of Saddam Hussein to bridge the socio-economic gap between rich and poor in Iraq was an important reason (but still one amongst many) for Iran's failure to incite the Iraqi Shi'ites to rebel against the Baghdad government. Since the bulk of Iraq's poor were Shi'ites, Baghdad's socio-economic measures, such as compulsory minimum wages, a social security scheme and free health and education programmes went a long way towards diluting the religious bonds between Iran's ayatollahs and their co-religionists in Iraq.

In other Arab countries, the problem was different. For example, because of its small population, Saudi Arabia satisfied the economic demand of its society easily and rapidly. But the economic bonanza was bound to lead to a process of modernisation which inflated the ranks of the technocratic middle class. Until the early 1970s, the political/administrative structure was dominated by the royal family and its close clan and tribal allies. The steep rise in the number of highly qualified middle class technocrats could have been a destabilising factor if not absorbed into the system. In the mid-1970s, the bureaucratic structure of Saudi Arabia was substantially expanded in order to absorb this emergent class. More significantly for the stability of the House of Saud, a number of cabinet portfolios were given to non-royal technocrats for the first time in 1975, thus giving this class access to the highest level of decision-making.

The problem is that whereas in the early years of political/ bureaucratic expansion, the system could absorb an influx of people, by the early 1980s, the cost-effectiveness of this expansion was diminishing. At present, as Ayubi points out, the creation of jobs in Saudi Arabia has become almost an objective in its own right, with little regard for what these recruits are supposed to do. The problem is not unique to Saudi Arabia or the oil-rich Gulf states. In many Arab countries today, there are more qualified people than the industrial and manufacturing base needs. The surplus goes into the bureaucracy, where they do little but absorb a significant proportion of public expenditure. All this has led inevitably to inefficiency, absenteeism and corruption.

It is difficult to see how Arab regimes could change a practice that

278

serves them well politically, for the sake of cost-effectiveness. As Ayubi explains, bureaucracies are becoming invaluable to political leaders because they are well equipped to cope with hostile political environments. A clear hierarchical structure and a strict chain of command make for quick and effective response to political threats.

In the Arab one-party systems, new blood is also recruited via the channels of the ruling party. Hinnebusch makes the case for Syria, but his argument is equally true for Iraq, South Yemen and even Tunisia. He contends that the party has been a major channel of elite recruitment and patronage. It has also been the means through which the interests of thousands of participants are articulated and, to an extent, incorporated into policy. By incorporating an active constituency with a stake in the regime, Hinnebusch argues, the party has been able to give the regime a sturdiness and modicum of legitimacy that contrasts sharply with the ephemeral, narrowly-based regimes of the past.

The most significant aspect of the resilience of the Arab state is the change in the role and self image of the military. In the 1950s and 1960s, the most destabilising sector of society was, without doubt, the army. The dominance of the military over the political process was such that political structures almost became hostage to the whims of ambitious army officers. The contemporary period, however, has witnessed the gradual civilianisation of Arab republics, to the extent that the old dominance of the military over the political process seems to have been arrested or even reversed. Khalidi argues that, rather than constituting challenges to the holders of power, the military has become a pillar of the regime's stability.

The evidence for what two decades ago might have been an outlandish statement is not difficult to find. It was customary in the 1950s and 1960s to expect the armed forces to wrest power from the incumbent leaders in the wake of serious challenges to the existing regimes. From the mid-1970s onwards, the picture changed. A short-lived, but bloody, Shi'ite rebellion in the south of Iraq in 1977 might have developed into a serious threat to the Baathist regime had it not been for the Iraqi armed forces. It is a testimony to the seriousness of the rebellion that President Hussein and the Baath Party decided immediately afterwards to woo the Shi'ite population with socio-economic concessions. Similarly, it was the Syrian armed forces which suppressed the 1982 rebellion in the city of Hama by the fanatically anti-Assad Muslim Brothers. President Sadat of Egypt, too, turned to the army in 1977 when faced with massive anti-government riots in Cairo and other Egyptian towns, nor would

CONCLUSION

his successor, President Mubarak, have been able to crush the uprising by Egypt's central security forces in 1986 had it not been for the country's military machine.

The harnessing of these diverse groups into the political and social order may, according to some analysts, have deeper, more ideological roots. With the exception of Marxist South Yemen, the economic philosophies of the contemporary Arab states bear little resemblance to the strident socialist ideals of the 1960s.

Even the socialists of today — Assad of Syria and Hussein of Iraq — are socialist more in name than in deed. Increasing economic liberalisation has been enthusiastically supported by a population frustrated by years of socialist austerity. Policies such as the encouragement of the private sector have won the support of the powerful urban middle and upper-middle classes in particular. And it is from these classes that the military officers, aspiring politicians, bureaucrats, professionals and businessmen emerge.

The problem for the Arab states is how to reconcile economic liberalisation and a centralised political order. Strict authoritarianism encompassing a dominant central figure is still the major characteristic of contemporary Arab political systems. Thus, for example, while Hinnebusch cautions against taking the Baath Party in Syria lightly, he points out that its role is circumscribed by the presidential regime into which it has been incorporated. The same applies to Iraq, North Yemen, Tunisia, Algeria and other Arab countries. And as for the much heralded political committees and congresses of Libya's 'grass-roots democracy', Hinnebusch asserts that democracy from below is channelled and controlled from above, and that Qadhafi and his colleagues remain the top political elite, ruling on the basis of charismatic legitimacy and coercive power.

The same characteristics are repeated in the bureaucracies. Ayubi contends that what we have in the Arab world is a system of administrative authority in which all power emanates from a single political leader, and where the influence of others derives in rough proportion to their perceived access to him or their share in his largesse. This shapes not only the political but the professional attitudes of Arab bureaucrats who are singularly unwilling to take responsibility. The natural inclination is to refer everything to the next step up.

The pace of social and economic development during the 1950s and 1960s made the centralisation of power a coherent political system. The revolutionary nationalist/socialist republics argued for an authoritarian political system in order to modernise. People

280

agreed that the daunting effort of catching up with the West left neither the time nor the need for the endless political debates so characteristic of multi-party systems and pluralist societies. The socialist model, drawing its inspiration from the Socialist Bloc and depending almost exclusively on the public sector, necessitated the active participation of the state, which was naturally compatible with authoritarianism. On their part, the Arab monarchies, basing their legitimacy on traditional tribal and religious symbols, with populations relatively unaffected by Western secularist notions, naturally clung to patriarchical authoritarian rule.

Times, however, have changed. The process of modernisation has had an impact on every aspect of life in the Arab world. It has thus been a major cause of political and bureaucratic policies of the 1970s and 1980s. Primarily Western-oriented as it has been, modernisation of the Arab states must also take responsibility, if not wholly then at least in part, for the rejection of the socialist economic order and the increasing tendency toward *infitah* and the encouragement of the private sector. The new elites drawn primarily from the urban middle and upper-middle classes seem more interested in economic advancement and political participation than in 'revolutionary' ideas and activities.

All this may suggest that unlike the 1950s and 1960s, authoritarian and personalised rule may no longer be compatible with the economic and intellectual/psychological environment of the 1980s. This may be the reason why this decade has witnessed efforts by a number of Arab regimes to liberalise their political orders.

Parliamentary elections surprisingly free of state interference have been held in a number of Arab states in the 1980s. Morocco, which has the longest tradition of party politics in the Arab world, held its 'most genuine of elections' in 1984 in which a large number of parties and independents took part. Kuwait, another country with a relatively long electoral past which had suspended the constitution and dissolved the national assembly in 1976, reactivated the democratic experiment in 1981. A second election was held in 1985, and in both cases vociferous critics of the ruling Sabah family were elected, a clear sign of the lack of interference by the state. The electoral experiences in Jordan and Egypt in 1984 have been similar and the people went to the polls relatively unimpeded by the state security organs.

The problem is that the parameters of political participation in all these cases were set by the rulers. There can be little doubt that representative democracy continues to be hostage to the will of Arab

CONCLUSION

authoritarian leaders. In all these cases, an important motivation for liberalising the political system has been the leadership's conviction that such a move would be useful to the functioning of the system. As Zartman observes in the Moroccan case, even the Frontists, the most implacable, and sometimes violent, enemies of the Moroccan monarchy, were useful to the system, since the regime could point to them as examples of the limits of participation and of the fate of total opposition. And once it had made its point, it could, in a show of royal magnanimity, both pardon them and exhibit its control.

The times ahead for democratic participation in the Arab world, even in this circumspect form, will not be easy. The democratic experience will be harassed and constrained every inch of the way by leaders who, accustomed to absolute power, have tended to characterise opposition as subversive, even traitorous. Having tasted absolute power, Arab leaders, like all addicts, are reluctant to share their 'high' with anybody else; and since almost no Arab leader is willing to put his trust in the people voluntarily to usher him and his associates back into power, they are reluctant to help the democratic experiment further, lest it get out of hand.

And in any case the Arab leaders may decide that in times ahead (and here we are not talking about the immediate future), strict control, rather than more political liberalisation, will be the surest way to ensure survival. With the sharp fall in the oil prices that occurred in the mid and late 1980s the ability of Arab governments to win support through socio-economic reforms will become more limited in the 1990s. With decreasing revenues, Arab leaders will find it that much more difficult to sustain subsidies, extend basic services and satisfy rising expectations. This in turn may lead to increased societal discontent that will necessitate a radical response from Arab governments. Rather than a broadening of the democratic experiment, the future may witness mounting state control, centralisation and oppression in the Arab world.

But this is not an immediate problem. For some time to come, the stability of the Arab state will continue to rest on the ability of political leaderships to exercise effective control through coercion to co-opt individuals and groups into the administrative and political structure; to extend economic and social benefits to hitherto excluded sectors of society; and to satisfy the hunger of the urban middle and upper-middle classes for an increasing role in the political process by allowing them limited political participation and representation. As long as these functions are performed, the

282

Arab state will continue to be resilient. But it is not the durable resilience of the system whose legitimacy is based on the full participation of the people in the body politic.

Bibliography

Abd al-Fattah Munji, M. (1975) (ed.) *Bahth hasr wa taqdir al-ihtiyajat min al-'amala bi al-qita' al-am* (employment in the public sector . . .), Institute of National Planning, Cairo

Abd Allah, U.F. (1983) *The Islamic Struggle in Syria*, Mizan Press, Berkeley, (California)

Abd al-Rahman, U. (1982) *Al-Biruqratiyya al-naftiyya wa mu'adilat al-tanmiya* (petroleum bureaucracy and the dilemma of development), National Council for Culture and Arts, Kuwait

Abdel Malek, A. (1962) *Egypte: Société Militaire*, Le Seuil, Paris

———— (1968) *Egypt: military society: the army, the left and social change under Nasser*, Vintage Books, New York

Abdel Moneim, A.F. (1984) *Professional associations in the Egyptian political system*, a doctorate dissertation presented to the Faculty of Economics and Political Science, Cairo University, Giza

Abdulfettah, K. (1981) *Mountain farmer and fellah in Asir, southwest Saudi Arabia: the conditions of agriculture in a traditional society*, Erlanger Geographische Arbeiten, Sonderband 12

Abu Uras, M. (1969) 'The military and the revolution' (in Arabic), *Dirasat Arabiyya*, 5, no. 11, pp. 7–84

Abul-Ata Azim, A. (1977) 'The conversion of basin irrigation to perennial systems in Egypt' in E. Worthington Barton (ed.), *Arid land irrigation in developing countries*, Pergamon, Oxford

Adam, H. (1985) 'South Africa: the search for legitimacy', *Telos*, 59

Ageron, C.R. (1980) 'Les classes moyennes dans l'Algérie coloniale: origine, formation et évaluation quantitative', in CRESM, 51980° pp. 52–74

Ahsan, S.A. (1984) 'Economic policy and class structure in Syria: 1958–80', *International Journal of Middle East Studies*, 16, pp. 301–23

Ajami, F. (1981) *The Arab predicament: Arab political thought and practice since 1967*, Cambridge University Press, Cambridge

Akavi, S. (1975) 'Egypt: neo-patrimonial elite', in Frank Tachau (ed.), *Political elites and political development in the Middle Ease*, Halsted Press, New York, pp. 69–113

Allush, N. (1968) 'The people's war is the only way to victory' (in Arabic) *Dirasat Arabiyya, vol. 4, no. 7*, pp. 45–56

Almond, G. and Coleman, J. (eds) (1960) *The politics of developing areas*, Princeton University Press, Princeton, (New Jersey)

Almond, G. and Powell, B.G. (1966) *Comparative politics: a developmental approach*, Little, Brown, Boston, (Massachusetts)

Amin, S. (1982) *Irak et Syrie 1960–80: du projet national à la trans-nationalisation*, Editions du Minuit, Paris

Amirouche, A. (1985) 'Présentation empirique du stock d'équipement en matériel des enterprises industrielles privées en Algérie', *Revue du CENEAP*, (Centre national d'études et d'analyses pour la planification), 2, Algiers, pp. 63–78

BIBLIOGRAPHY

Anderson, L. (1983) 'Qadhafi's Islam', in Esposito, J.L. (ed.), *Voices of resurgent Islam*, Oxford University Press, Oxford

Ansari, H.N. (1984) 'The Islamic militants in Egyptian politics', *International Journal of Middle East Studies*, 16, pp. 123–44

Arab Institute of Planning in Kuwait (AIPK) and Centre for Arab Unity Studies (1983) *Al-'amala al-ajnabiyya fi aqtar al-khalij al-'arabi*, (foreign employment in countries of the Arabian Gulf), CAUS, Beirut

Arab Lawyers Union (ALU) General Secretariat (1956) *Book of the Second Arab Lawyers Conference*, Cairo

—— (1957) *Book of the Third Arab Lawyers Conference*, Cairo

—— (1958) *Book of the Fourth Arab Lawyers Conference*, Cairo

—— (1959) *Book of the Fifth Arab Lawyers Conference*, Cairo

—— (1960) *Book of the Sixth Arab Lawyers Conference*, Cairo

—— (1964) *Book of the Seventh Arab Lawyers Conference*, Cairo

—— (1965) *Book of the Eighth Arab Lawyers Conference*, Cairo

—— (1967) *Book of the Ninth Arab Lawyers Conference*, Cairo

—— (1968) *Book of the Tenth Arab Lawyers Conference*, Cairo

—— (1970) *Book of the Eleventh Arab Lawyers Conference*, Cairo

—— (1974) *Book of the Twelfth Arab Lawyers Conference*, Cairo

—— (1979) *Documents of the Thirteenth Arab Lawyers Conference*, Tunis

—— (1980) *Documents of the Fourteenth Arab Lawyers Conference*, Rabat

—— (1984a) *Documents of the Fifteenth Arab Lawyers Conference*, Sousa

—— (1984b) 'Forty years on the path of right and Arabism' in *Report of the Secretary General, fifteenth conference*, Tunis

—— (1985) *International Bulletin*, Cairo

—— (1983–5) *Al Haq* (ALU journal), Cairo; (1984–5) *International Bulletin*, Cairo

Arabian Government and Public Services (1983) *Directory*, Beacon, London

Arjomand, S.A. (1984) 'Introduction: social movements in the contemporary Near and Middle East' in Arjomand, S.A. (ed.), *From nationalism to revolutionary Islam*, Macmillan, London, pp. 1–27

Arrow, K. (1951) *Social choice and individual values*, Wiley, New York

Ashford, D. (1961) *Political change in Morocco*, Princeton University Press, Princeton, (New Jersey)

—— (1967) *National development and local reform*, Princeton University Press, Princeton, (New Jersey)

Ashqar, R. (1981) 'The armies of the Mashreq and Israeli military challenges in the eighties' (in Arabic) *Shuon Arabiyya*, 2, pp. 175–91

Al-Awaji, I.M. (1971) *Bureaucracy and society in Saudi Arabia*, unpublished PhD thesis, University of Virginia

Ayubi, N. (1980) *Bureaucracy and politics in contemporary Egypt*, Ithaca, London

—— (1982a) 'Bureaucratic inflation and administrative inefficiency: the deadlock in Egyptian administration', *Middle Eastern Studies*, 28, no. 3

—— (1982b) 'Organisation for development: the politico-administrative framework of economic activity in Egypt under Sadat', *Public*

BIBLIOGRAPHY

Administration and Development, 2, no. 4

────── (1982–3) 'The politics of militant Islamic movements in the Middle East', *Journal of International Affairs*, 36, no. 2, autumn/winter

────── (1983) 'The Egyptian brain drain', *Journal of Middle East Studies*, 15

────── (1984) 'Local government and rural development in Egypt in the 1970s', *Cahiers africains d'Administration Publique*, 23

Aziz, M. *(1979) Anmat al-infaq w'al-istithmar fi aqtar al-khalij al-arabi* (expenditure and investment patterns in countries of the Arabian Gulf), Institute of Arab Research Studies, Cairo

Badie, B. and Birnbaum, P. (1983) *The sociology of the state*, Chicago University Press, Chicago

Baer, G. (1969) *Studies in the social history of modern Egypt*, Chicago University Press, Chicago

Bakhash, S. (1983) 'Revolutions in the Middle East and North Africa in comparative perspectives', in W.G. Miller and P.H. Stoddard (eds), *Perspectives on the Middle East: proceedings of a conference*, Middle East Institute, Washington DC

Baram, A. (1981) 'The June 1980 elections to the National Assembly in Iraq: an experiment in controlled democracy', *Orient*, 22, no. 3, pp. 391–412

Barrada, H. (1980) 'La monarchie, la gauche et l'alternance', *Jeune Afrique*, *1043*, pp. 194–9

Batatu, H. (1978) *The old social classes and the revolutionary movements of Iraq*, Princeton University Press, Princeton, (New Jersey)

────── (1981a) 'Some observations on the social roots of Syria's ruling military group and the cause for its dominance', *Middle East Journal*, 35, pp. 331–44

────── (1981b) 'Iraq's underground Shia movements: characteristics, causes and prospects', *Middle East Journal*, pp. 578–94

────── (1982) 'Syria's Muslim brethren', *MERIP Reports*, *110*, pp. 12–20

────── (1983) 'The Egyptian, Iraqi, Syrian revolutions: comparisons', in Miller, W.G. and Stoddard, P.H. (eds), *Perspectives on the Middle East 1983: proceedings of a conference*, Middle East Institute, Washington DC

────── (1984) *The Egyptian, Syrian and Iraqi revolutions: some observations on their underlying causes and social character*, Georgetown University Centre for Contemporary Arab Studies, Washington DC

────── (1985) 'Class analysis and Iraqi society', in Ibrahim and Hopkins, pp. 379–84 (reprinted from *Peuples méditerranéens*, 1979)

Beblawi, H. and Luciani, G. (1987) 'The Arab rentier state', in *Nation, state and integration in the Arab world* (vol. 2, Croom Helm, London)

Bedrani, S. (1982) *L'agriculture algérienne depuis 1966*, Economica, Paris

Belaid, A. (1985) 'La necessaire clarification', *La Révolution Africaine*, 12, pp. 25f (September)

Ben Achour, Y. (1979) 'Islam perdu, Islam retrouvé', *Annuaire de l'Afrique du Nord*, pp. 65–74

Benachenhou, A. (1973) 'Forces sociales et accumulation du capital au Maghreb', *Annuaire de l'Afrique du Nord*, pp. 315–42

────── (1982) *L'expérience algérienne de planification et de développement*, Office des publications universitaires, Algeria

Ben Dor, G. (1982) 'Egypt', in R.E. Harkavy and E.A. Kolodziej (eds)

286

Security policies of developing countries, Lexington Books, Lexington (Kentucky)

Benhouria, T. (1980) *L'économie de l'Algérie*, Maspero, Paris

Benissad, M.E. (1982) *L'économie du développement de l'Algérie: sous-développement et socialisme*, Economica, Paris

Benkheira, M.H. (1985) 'Etat et mouvement ouvrier dans l'Algérie indépendante', in Sraieb, N. *et al. Le mouvement ouvrier maghrébin*, CNRS, Paris, pp. 197–208

Bennoune, M. (1985) 'The industrialization of Algeria: an overview', in Barakat, H. (ed.), *Contemporary North Africa: issues of development and integration*, Centre for Contemporary Arab Studies, Washington DC, pp. 178–213

Ben Salah, T. (1975) 'Systéme politique et systéme religieux en Tunisie', *Revue tunisienne de droit*, 6, p. 249

——— (1979) *La république algérienne*, Librairie général de droit et de jurisprudence, Paris

Bendix, R. (1964) *Nation-building and citizenship*, John Wiley and Sons, New York

Bernard, C. *et al.* (1982) *La politique de l'emploi-formation au Maghreb 1970–80*, CNRS, Paris

——— (1986) 'L'emploi en Algérie', unpublished

Berque, J. (1957) *Histoire sociale d'un village egyptien au XXe siècle*, Mouton, Paris

Bianchi, R. (1984) *Interest groups and political development in Turkey*, Princeton University Press, Princeton, (New Jersey)

Bill, J.A. (1972) 'Class analysis and the dialectics of modernisation in the Middle East', *International Journal of Middle East Studies*, 3, pp. 417–34

——— and Leiden, C. (1979) *Politics in the Middle East*, Little Brown, Boston, (Massachusetts)

Binder, L. *et al.* (ed.) (1971) *Crises and sequences in political development*, Princeton University Press, Princeton, (New Jersey)

——— (1978) *In a moment of enthusiasm: power and the second stratum*, University of Chicago Press, Chicago

Birks, J.S. and Sinclair, C.A. (1980) *International migrations and development in the Arab region*, International Labour Office, Geneva

Blair, T.L. (1970) *The land to those who work it: Algeria's experiment in worker's management*, Anchor Books, Garden City, (New York)

Blau, P.M. (1964) *Exchange and power in social life*, Wiley, New York

Bourgey *et al.* (1982) *Industrialisation et changements sociaux dans l'Orient arabe*, Editions du CERMOC, Beirut

Boutros-Ghali, B. (1963) 'The foreign policy of Egypt', in J.E. Black and K.W. Thompson (eds), *Foreign policy in a world of change*, Harper and Row, New York

Bouzidi, A.M. (1984) 'Emploi et chomage en Algérie (1967–83)', *Les Cahiers du CREA* (Centre de recherches en économie appliquée), 2, Algiers, pp. 57–76

Bremer, J. (1982) *Alternatives for mechanization: public cooperatives and the private sector in Egypt's agriculture*, PhD thesis, Kennedy School of Government, Harvard University

Brown, L.C. (ed.) (1966) *State and society in independent North Africa*,

BIBLIOGRAPHY

Middle East Institute, Washington DC

Budge, I. and Farlie, D.J. (1981) 'Predicting regime change: a cross-national investigation with aggregate data, 1950–80', *Quality and Quantity, 15*, pp. 335–64

Burke III, E. and Lubeck, P. (1985) *Explaining social movements in two OPEC countries: divergent outcomes in Nigeria and Iran*, (mimeo)

—— (1986) 'Understanding Arab social movements', *The Maghreb Review*

—— and Lubeck, P. (1987) *Comparative studies in society and history*, Rienner, Boulder, Colorado

Bu Roways, A.M. (1982) *Encyclopedia of the Arab lawyer*, first edition (4 volumes), Arab Organisation for Studies and Publication, Beirut

Callaghy, T. (1984) *The state-society struggle: Zaire in comparative perspective*, Columbia University Press, New York

Camau, J.S. and Sinclair, C.A. (1980) *International migrations and development in the Arab region*, International Labour Office, Geneva

Camau, M. (1978) *Pouvoir et institutions au Maghreb*, Cerés Productions, Tunis

—— (1984) 'L'etat tunisien: de la tutelle au désengagement', *Maghreb-Machrek, 103*, pp. 8–38

Centre d'etudes et de recherches sur le Moyen-Orient Contemporain (1985) *Mouvements communautaires et espaces urbains au Machreq*, Beirut

—— (1985) *Migrations et changements sociaux dans l'Orient arabe*, CERMOC, Beirut

Centre de Recherches et d'Etudes sur les Sociétés Méditerranéenes (CRESM) (1979) *Développements politiques au Maghreb*, CNRS, Paris

—— (1980) *Les classes moyennes au Maghreb*, CNRS, Paris

Chackerian, R. and Abcarian, G. (1983) *Bureaucratic power in society*, Nelson Hall, Chicago

—— and El-Fathaly, O. (1983) 'Administration and the forgotten issue in Arab development', in I. Ibrahim (ed.) *Arab resources: the transformation of a society*, Croom Helm, London

—— and Shadukhi, S.M. (1983) 'Public bureaucracy in Saudi Arabia: an empirical assessment of work behaviour', *International Review of Administrative Sciences, 69*, no. 3

Chatelus, M. (1980) 'La croissance économique, mutations des structures et dynamisme du déséquilibre', in Raymond, A. (ed.) *La Syrie aujourd'hui*, CNRS, Paris, pp. 225–72

—— (1982) 'Le monde arabe vingt ans après: de l'avant pétrole à l'après pétrole — les économies des pays arabes', *Maghreb-Machrek, 101*, pp. 5–45

—— and Schemeil, Y. (1984) 'Towards a new political economy of state industrialisation in the Arab Middle East', *International Journal of Middle East Studies, 16 (2)*, pp. 251–65

Chaulet, C. (1984) *La terre, les frères et l'argent*, Thèse lettres et sciences humaines, Université Paris V, roneo

Chazan, N. (1983) *The anatomy of Ghanaian politics*, Westview, Boulder, (Colorado)

Cohen, R. and Service, E. (1978) *The origins of the state*, ISHI, Philadelphia

Cole, D. (1975) *Nomadism and the nomads: the Al-Murrah bedouin of the empty quarter*, Aldine, Chicago

288

—— (1981) 'Bedouin and social change in Saudi Arabia' in *Journal of Asian and African Studies*, *16 (1–2)*, pp. 128–49

Colombe, M. (1951) *L'évolution de l'Egypte 1924–50*, Maisonneuve, Paris

Colonna, F. (1980) 'Paysans et encadreurs: à propos des transferts de savoirs et de modèles entre villes et campagnes en Algérie' in Rassam, A. and Zghal, A.K., *Système urbain et développement au Maghreb*, Cerès Productions, Tunis

—— (1983) 'Les spécialistes de la médiation: naissance d'une classe moyenne au Maghreb' in *Histoire sociale de l'Algérie*, *8*, Publications du centre de recherches et de documentation en sciences sociales et humaines, Oran

Cooper, M. (1982) 'The demilitarisation of the Egyptian cabinet', *International Journal of Middle East Studies*, *14*, no. 2, pp. 209–25

Coser, Lewis (1956) *The function of social conflict*, The Free Press, New York

Cote, M. (1985) 'Campagnes algériennes', *Méditerranée*, Revue géographique des pays méditerranéens, *55 (3)*, pp. 41–50

Criscuolo, J. (1975) *Armée et nation dans les discours du Colonel Boumedienne*, Université P. Valéry, Montpellier

Cudsi, A. (1983) 'Islam and politics in Sudan', in Piscatori, (ed.) *Islam in the political process*, Cambridge University Press, Cambridge

Dahl, R. (1966) (ed.) *Political oppositions in western democracy*, Yale University Press, New Haven, (Connecticut)

—— (1973) *Regimes and opposition*, Yale University Press, New Haven, (Connecticut)

Davis, E. (1984) 'Ideology, social class and Islamic radicalism in modern Egypt', in Arjomand, S.A. (ed.), pp. 134–57

Dawisha, A.I. (1978) 'Syria under Assad, 1970–8: the centres of power', *Government and Opposition*, *13*, no. 3

—— (1980) *Syria and the Lebanese crisis*, Macmillan, London

—— (1986) *The Arab radicals*, Council on Foreign Relations, New York

Day, A. (1986) *East Bank/West Bank*, Council on Foreign Relations, New York

Debbasch, C. *et al.* (1970) *Pouvoir et administration au Maghreb*, CNRS, Paris

Deeb, M. (1979) *Party politics in Egypt: the world and its rivals 1919–39*, Ithaca Press, London

Degenhardt, H.W. (1983) *Political dissent*, Gale Research, New York

Dessouki, A.E.H. (1978) 'The transformation of the party system: Egypt, 1952–77', in *Cairo Papers in Social Science, Democracy in Egypt*, *1*, *Monograph Two*, American University in Cairo, pp. 7–24

—— (1984) 'Intikhabat 1984', *Al-Ahram*, 15 June

—— and Labban, A. (1981) 'Arms race, defence expenditures and development: the Egyptian case 1952–73', *Journal of South Asia and the Middle East Studies*, *4*, no. 3, pp. 66–77

De Tocqueville, A. (1954) *Democracy in America*, Vintage Books, New York

Devlin, J. (1982) 'Syria' in R.E. Harkavy and E.A. Kolodziej (eds), *Security policies of developing countries*, Lexington Books, Lexington, (Kentucky)

Downs, A. (1957) *An economic theory of democracy*, Harper and Row, New York

Drysdale, A. (1981) 'The Syrian political elite, 1966–76: a spatial and

BIBLIOGRAPHY

social analysis', *Middle Eastern Studies*

—— (1982) 'The Syrian armed forces in national politics: the role of geographic and ethnic periphery', in Kolkowicz, R. and Korbonski, A. (eds), *Soldiers, peasants and bureaucrats*, George Allen and Unwin, London, pp. 52–76

Dubar, C. and Nasr, S. (1976) *Les classes sociales au Liban*, Fondation Nationale des Sciences Politiques, Paris

Durkheim, Emile (1964) *The division of labour in society*, The Free Press, New York

Duwaidar, Muhammad (1983) *Al-Ittija al-rai' bi al-iqtisad al-misri* (the rentier orientation of the Egyptian economy), Munsha'at al-Ma'arif, Alexandria

Easton, D. (1965a) *A framework for political analysis*, Prentice Hall, Englewood Cliffs, (New Jersey)

—— (1965) *A systems analysis of political life*, John Wiley, London

Egyptian Bar Association, *Al-Muhamat*, Cairo; several issues, particularly 1984–5

Eisenstadt, S. (1964) 'Convergence and divergence of modern and modernising societies: indications from the analysis of the structuring of social hierarchies in Middle Eastern Societies', *International Journal of Middle East Studies*, 8, pp. 1–27

—— (1966) *Modernisation: protest and change*, Prentice Hall, Englewood Cliffs, (New Jersey)

El Kenz, A. (1983) *Monographie d'une expérience industrielle en Algérie: le complexe sidérurgique d'El Hadjar (Annaba)*, thèse de doctorat détat en sciences humaines, Université de Paris VIII

Entelis, J.P. (1980) *Comparative politics of North Africa: Algeria, Morocco and Tunisia*, Syracuse University Press, Syracuse, (New York)

—— (1982) 'Algeria: technocratic rule, military power', in I.W. Zartman (ed.), *Political elites in Arab North Africa*, Longman, New York, pp. 92–143

—— (1985) *Algeria: the revolution institutionalised*, Westview, Boulder, (Colorado)

Eqbal, A. (1966) 'Trade Unionism' in L.C. Brown (ed.), *State and society in contemporary North Africa*, Middle East Institute, Washington DC

Esposito, (1980) 'Islam and development', Syrian University Press, Syracuse, (New York)

Etienne, B. (1966) in *Revue de l'Occident Musulman et de la Méditerranée*, first semester, p. 62ff

—— and Tozy, M. (1979) 'Le glissement des obligations islamiques vers le phénomène associatif à Casablanca', *Annuaire de l'Afrique du Nord*, pp. 235–59

Evans, P. (1979) *Dependent development*, Princeton University Press, Princeton, (New Jersey)

—— Rueschmayer, D. and Skocpol, T. (1985) (eds), *Bringing the state back in*, Cambridge University Press, Cambridge

Fahim, H. (1981) *Dams, people and development: the Aswan high dam case*, Pergamon Press, New York

Al-Farsi, F. (1982) *Saudi Arabia: a case study in development*, Kegan Paul International, London and Boston

Fathaly, O. and Palmer, M. (1980) *Political development and social change*

290

BIBLIOGRAPHY

in Libya, Lexington Books, Lexington, (Massachusetts)

Fischer, M. (1982) 'Islam and the revolt of the petit bourgeoisie', *Daedalus*, *111*, pp. 101-25

Finer, S.E. (1974) *The man on horseback*, Penguin, London

Forst, R. (1976) 'Origins and early development of the Union Marocaine du Travail', *International Journal of Middle East Studies*, *7 (2)*, pp. 271-87

Frey, F. (1975) 'Patterns of elite politics in Turkey', in Lenczowski, G. (ed.), *Political elites in the Middle East*, American Enterprise Institute, Washington DC

Gallagher, F. (1968) 'Islam', in Stills, D.L. (ed.), *International Encyclopedia of Social Sciences*, Macmillan, New York, *8*, p. 207

Garson, J. (1981) 'Les Algériens', 'Les Marocains' in Garson, J.P. and Tapinos, G. (eds), *L'argent des immigrés*, papers and documents of the INED, PUF, Paris, pp. 31-70 and 133-72

Garzouzi, E. (1963) 'Land reform in Syria', *Middle East Journal*, winter-spring

Gellner, E. and Micaud, C. (eds) (1972) *Arabs and Berbers*, Lexington Books, Lexington, (Massachusetts)

―――― (1974) 'The unknown Apollo of Biskra: the social base of Algerian puritanism', *Government and Opposition*, pp. 277-310

―――― (1981) *Muslim society*, Cambridge University Press, London

―――― (1983) 'The tribal society and its enemies', R. Tapper (ed.), *The conflict of tribe and state*, Croom Helm, London

Gerth, H.C. and Wright Mills, C. (1970) *From Max Weber*, Routledge and Kegan Paul, London

Gibb, H. (1955) 'Constitutional organisation: the Muslim community and the state', in Majid Khadduri and Hubert J. Liebesny (eds), *Law in the Middle East*, Middle East Institute, Washington DC

Gordon, D. (1986) *Decolonisation and the state in Kenya*, Westview, Boulder, (Colorado)

Grandguillaume, G. (1982) 'Valorisation et devalorisation liées aux contacts de cultures en Arabie Saoudite', in P. Bonnenfant (ed.), *La peninsule arabique d'aujourd'hui*, *2*, pp. 623-54

Gubser, P. (1983) *Jordan: crossroads of Middle Eastern events*, Westview, Boulder, (Colorado)

Gurr, T.R. (1974) 'Persistence and change in political systems 1800-1971', *American Political Science Review*, *68*, pp; 1482-1504

Haddad, G. (1971) *Revolutions and military rule in the Middle East*, *t. 2.*, *The Arab states, part 1: Iraq, Syria, Lebanon and Jordan*, R. Speller, New York

Hadjseyd, M. (1985) 'Quelques aspects de l'évolution du secteur privé industriel', *Revue du CENEAP*, *2*, Algiers, pp. 49-62

Halbaoui, Y. (1965) 'La population et la population active en Syrie', *Population*, pp. 697-714

Halliday, F. (1975) *Arabia without sultans*, Penguin Books, Harmondsworth

Halpern, M. (1962) 'The Middle Eastern armies and the new middle class' in J. Johnson (ed.), *The role of the military in underdeveloped countries*, Princeton University Press, Princeton, (New Jersey)

―――― (1963) *The politics of social change in the Middle East and North Africa*, Princeton University Press, Princeton, (New Jersey)

291

BIBLIOGRAPHY

Hannoyer, J. and Seurat, M. (1979) *Etat et secteur public industriel en Syrie*, Centre d'études et de recherches sur le Moyen-Orient contemporain, Beirut
——— (1980) 'Le monde rural avant les réformes', in Raymond, A. (ed.), *La Syrie d'aujourd'hui*, CNRS, Paris, pp. 273–96
——— (1985) 'Grands projets hydrauliques en Syrie: la tentation orientale', *Maghreb-Machrek*, pp. 24–42
Harbi, M. (1975) *Aux origines du FLN: le populisme révolutionnaire en Algérie*, Christian Bourgeois, Paris
——— (1980) *Le FLN, mirage et réalité: dex origines à la prise du pouvoir (1945–62)*, Jeune Afrique, Paris
Heikal, M (1983) *Autumn of fury: the assassination of Sadat*, Random House, New York
Heller, M. and Safran, N. (1984) Saudi Arabia and the new middle class, Harvard Middle East Papers
——— (1985) *The Middle East military balance*, Jaffe Centre for Strategic Studies, Tel Aviv
Helms, C. (1984) *Iraq: Eastern flank of the Arab world*, Brookings Institution, Washington DC
Hermassi, E. (1972) *Leadership and national development in North Africa: a comparative study*, University of California Press, Berkeley
——— (1984) 'La société tunisienne au miroir islamiste', *Maghreb-Machrek*, *103*, pp. 39–56
Hinnebusch, R. (1976) 'Syria under the Baath: state formation in a fragmented society', *Arab Studies Quarterly*, 4, no. 3, pp. 177–99
——— (1984a) 'Charisma, revolution and state formation: Qadhafi and Libya', *Third World Quarterly*, 6, no. 1
——— (1984b) 'Syria: the role of ideology and party organisation in local development', in Louis J. Cantori and Iliya Harik, *Local politics and development in the Middle East*, Westview Press, Boulder, (Colorado)
——— (1984c) 'The re-emergence of the Wafd party', *Sixteenth International Journal of Middle East Studies*, *1*, pp. 99–121
——— (1984d) 'The National Progressive Party', *III Arab Studies Quarterly*, 4, pp. 325–51
——— (1985) *Egyptian politics under Sadat: the post-populist development of an authoritarian-modernising state*, Cambridge University Press, Cambridge
Hirschman, A.O. (1968) 'The political economy of import-substituting industrialisation in Latin America', *The Quarterly Journal of Economics*, *82 (1)*
——— (1970) *Exit, voice and loyalty*, Harvard, Cambridge, (Massachusetts)
——— (1973) 'The changing tolerance for income inequality in the course of economic development', *The Quarterly Journal of Economics*, 87 (4)
Hodges, T. (1981) 'Political conflicts sharpen', *New African*, April
Hooglund, E. (1982) *Land and revolution in Iran: 1960–80*, University of Texas Press, Austin, (Texas)
Hopkins, N.S. (1977a) 'Notes sur l'histoire de Testour', in *Revue d'Histoire Maghrebine*, 9, pp. 294–313
——— (1977b) 'The emergence of class in a Tunisian town', in *International Journal of Middle East Studies*, 8, pp. 453–91
——— (1978) 'The articulation of the modes of production: tailoring in

292

Testour', in *American Ethnologist, 5,* pp. 468–91

—— (1980) 'Testour au dixneuvieme siecle', in *Revue d'Histoire Maghrebine, 17–18,* pp. 19–31

—— *et al.* (1980) *Animal husbandry and the household economy in two Egyptian villages,* report to the Catholic Relief Services and USAID, Cairo

—— Mehanna, S. and Abdelmaksoud, B. (1982) *The state of agricultural mechanisation in Egypt, results of a survey, 1982,* Ministry of Agriculture, Agricultural Mechanisation Project, Cairo

—— (1983a) 'The social impact of mechanisation', in Richards, A. and Martin, P. (eds), *Migration, mechanisation and agricultural labour markets in Egypt,* Westview Press, Boulder, (Colorado) and American University in Cairo, Cairo, pp. 181–97

—— (1983b) *Testour ou la transformation des campagnes maghrebines,* Cerés Productions, Tunis

—— (1984) 'Development and Centre Building in the Middle East', in Cantori, L.J. and Harik, I. (eds), *Local politics and development in the Middle East,* Westview Press, Boulder, (Colorado)

Hourani, A. (1962) *Arabic thought in the liberal age, 1798–1939,* Oxford University Press, London

Hudson, M. (1977) *Arab politics, the search for legitimacy,* Yale University Press, New Haven

—— (1983) 'The Islamic factor in Syrian and Iraqi politics', in Piscatori (ed.), *Islam in the political process,* Cambridge University Press, Cambridge, p. 73ff

Huntington, S. (1969) *Political order in changing societies,* Yale University Press, New Haven

—— and Dominguez, J. (1975) 'Political development', in Greenstein, F. and Polsby, N. (eds), *Handbook of political science,* Addison-Wesley, New York

Hurewitz, J.C. (1969) *Middle East politics: the military dimension,* Praeger, New York

Ibrahim, S.E. and Cole, D.P. (1978) 'Saudi Arabian bedouin, Cairo papers', *Social Science, 1,* no. 5

—— (1980) 'Anatomy of Egypt's militant Islamic groups', *International Journal of Middle East Studies, 12,* pp. 423–53

—— and Sabagh, G. (1982) 'Oil, migration and the new Arab social order', in Kerr, M.H. and Yassin, E. (eds), *Rich and poor states in the Middle East,* Westview Press, Boulder, (Colorado) and American University in Cairo, Cairo, pp. 17–70

—— and Hopkins, N. (eds) (1985) *Arab society: social science perspectives,* American University in Cairo, Cairo

Ionescu, G. and de Madariaga, I. (1968) *Opposition,* Watts, London

Islam, N. and Henault, G. (1979) 'From GNP to basic needs: a critical review of development administration', *International review of administrative sciences, 45,* no. 3

Islami, A.R.S. and Kavoussi, R.M. (1984) *The political economy of Saudi Arabia,* University of Washington, Seattle

Issawi, C. (1950) *An Arab philosopher of history,* John Murray, London

—— (1982) *An economic history of the Middle East and North Africa,* Columbia University Press, New York

BIBLIOGRAPHY

Janowitz, M. (1977) *Military institutions and coercion in the developing nations*, Chicago University Press, Chicago

Jarry, E. (1984) 'La première enterprise de Syrie, Milihouse, n'a de militaire que le nom', *Le Monde*, 6 May

Karsenty, J. (1975) 'Les investissements dans l'agriculture algérienne', *Annuaire de l'Afrique du Nord*, pp. 115–42

Kaufman, M. (1981) 'In India, there's a demonstration for any occasion', *New York Times*, 23 April

Keilany, Z. (1973) 'Socialism and economic change in Syria', *Middle Eastern Studies*

—— (1980) 'Land reforms in Syria', *Middle Eastern Studies*, 16, p. 221

Kelman, H.C. (1969) 'Patterns of personal involvement in the national system: a social-psychological analysis of political legitimacy', in J.N. Rosenau (ed.), *International politics and foreign policy: a reader in research and theory*, The Free Press, New York

Kepel, G. (1984) *Le prophéte et le pharaon*, La Découverte, Paris

—— (1985) 'Les oulémas, l'intelligentsia et les islamistes en Egypte: système social, ordre transcendental et ordre traduit', *Revue français de science politique*, 35 (3), pp. 424–45

Kerr, M. and Yassin, S. (eds) (1982) *Rich and poor states in the Middle East: Egypt and the new Arab order*, Westview Press, Boulder, (Colorado)

Khaddam al-Halim, A. (1983) Interview in *al-Mostaqbal*, 19 November, p. 15

Khadduri, M. (1955) *War and peace in the Law of Islam*, Johns Hopkins University Press, Baltimore, (Maryland)

—— (1978) *Socialist Iraq, a study in Iraqi politics since 1968*, Oxford University Press, Oxford

Khatibi, A. (1972) *Etudes sociologiques sur le Maroc*, Société d'études economiques, sociales et statistiques, Rabat

Khoury, P. (1983a) *Urban notables and Arab nationalism: the politics of Damascus 1860–1920*, Cambridge University Press, Cambridge

—— (1983b) 'Islamic revival and the crisis of the secular state in the Arab world: an historical appraisal', in I. Ibrahim (ed.), *Arab resources: the transformation of a society*, Croom Helm, London

Khuri, F. and Obermayer, G. (1974) 'The social bases for military intervention in the Middle East', in C. MacArdle Kelleher (ed.), *Political-military systems: comparative perspectives*, Sage Publications, London

Al-Kubaisi, A. (1982) *Al-Idara al-'amma w'al-tanmiya bi dawlat al-imarat al-muttahida* (public administration and development in the UAE), Dar al-Khalij, Al-Shariqa

Kubursi, A. (1983) 'Arab agricultural productivity: a new perspective', in I. Ibrahim (ed.), *Arab resources: the transformation of a society*, Croom Helm, London

Lackner, H. (1983) Manca il titolo, in Piscatori (ed.), *Islam in the political process*, Cambridge University Press, Cambridge, p. 70

Lancaster, W. (1981) *The Rwala bedouin today*, Cambridge University Press, Cambridge

Laqueuer, W. (1968) *The road to war*, Penguin Books, Harmondsworth

Laski, H.J. (1935) *The state in theory and practice*, W.H. Allen, London

Lasswell, H. and Kaplan, A. (1950) *Politics and society*, Yale University Press, New Haven, (Connecticut)

294

Lawless, R. (1985) 'Algeria: the contradictions of rapid industrialisation', in Lawless, R. and Findlay, A. (eds), *North Africa: contemporary politics and economic development*, Croom Helm, London, pp. 153–90

Leca, J. *et al.* (1979) *Developpements politiques au Maghreb*, CNRS, Paris

——— (1980) 'Ville et système politique: l'image de la ville dans le discours officiel algérien', in Rassam, A. and Zghal, A.K. (eds), *Système urbain et développement au Maghreb*, Cerès Productions, Tunis, pp. 290–317

——— and Schemeil, Y. (1983) 'Clientélisme et néo-patrimonialisme dans le monde arabe', *International Political Science Review, 4*

——— and Vatin, J.C. (1975) *L'Algérie politique: institutions et régime*, Fondation Nationale des Sciences Politiques, Paris

——— and Vatin, J.C. (1979) 'Le système politique algérien', in Centre de Recherches et d'Etudes sur les Sociétés Mediterranéenes, pp. 15–90

Lehmbruch, G. and Schmitter, P. (1982) *Patterns of corporatist policy-making*, Sage Publications, London

Leveau, R. (1976) *Le fellah marocain, défenseur du trône*, Colin, Paris

——— (1984) 'Aperçu de l'évolution du système politique marocain depuis vingt ans', *Maghreb-Machrek, 106*, pp. 7–36

——— (1985) *Le fellah marocain, défenseur du trône*, Presses de la Fondation Nationale des Sciences Politiques, second edition

Liabes, D. (1984) *Capital privé et patrons d'industrie en Algérie 1962–82*, Centre de Rechercheen Economie Appliquée, Algeria

——— (1985) 'Une approche strictement économique du secteur privé est-elle possible?', *Revue du CENEAP, 2*, pp. 118–37

Locke, J. (1960) *Two treatises of government*, Cambridge University Press, London

Long, D.E. (1976) 'Saudi Arabia', *The Washington Papers, 39*, Sage Publications, Beverly Hills, (California)

Longuenesse, E. (1979) 'The class nature of the state in Syria', *MERIP*

——— (1985) Syrie: secteur public industriel, les enjeux d'une crise', *Maghreb-Machrek, 109*, pp. 5–23

——— (1986) 'Migrations et sociétés dans les pays du Golfe', *Maghreb-Machrek, 112*, pp. 8–21

Lowi, T. (1969) *The end of liberalism*, W.W. Norton and Co, New York

MacIver, R.M. (1926) *The modern state*, Oxford University Press, London

Maghreb-Machrek (1986a) 'Dossiers et documents: l'Algérie face au contre-choc pétrolier', *Maghreb-Machrek, 112*, pp. 94–100

——— (1986b) 'dossiers et documents: le secteur privé en Algérie', *Maghreb-Machrek, 113*

El-Mallakh, R. (1982) *Saudi Arabia, rush to development*, Johns Hopkins University Press, Baltimore, (Maryland) and London

Maaoz, M. (1973) 'Society and state in modern Syria', in Milson, M. (ed.), *Society and political structure in the Arab world*, Humanities Press, New York

Al-Marayati, A.A. (1972) *The Middle East: its government and politics*, Duxbury, Belmont, (California)

Marçais, G. (1942) 'Testour et sa grande mosquée: contribution à l'étude des Andalous en Tunisie', in *Revue Tunisienne, 49–50–51*, pp. 147–69

Marouf, N. (1982) 'Administrative development in Kuwait, *Arab Journal of Administration*, April

Al-Mashat, A.M. (1984) *Professional associations in the Egyptian political system*, doctorate dissertation presented to the Faculty of Economics and Political Science, Cairo University, Giza

McLennan, B. (ed.) (1973) *Political opposition and dissent*, Dunellen, New York

Mehanna, S. *et al.* (1983) *Water allocation among Egyptian farmers: irrigation technology and social organisation*, American University in Cairo, Cairo

Mernissi, F. (1982) 'Les femmes dans une société rurale dependante: les femmes et le quotidien dans le Gharb', in *Maghreb-Machrek*, *98*, pp. 4–45

Metral, F. (1980) 'Le monde rural syrien à l'heure des réformes', in Raymond, A. (ed.), *La Syrie d'aujourd'hui*, CNRS, Paris, pp. 297–326

——— (1985) 'Etat et paysans dans le ghab en Syrie: approche locale d'un projet d'état', *Maghreb-Machrek*, *109*, pp 43–63; English version in Ibrahim, S.E. and Hopkins, N. (eds), *Arab society: social science perspectives*, American University in Cairo, Cairo, pp. 336–54

——— (1986) 'Transferts de technologie dans l'agriculture irriguée en Syrie: stratégies familiales et travail féminin', in Cannon, B. (ed.), *Terroirs et sociétés dans le monde arabe*, Etudes sur le monde arabe 2, Maison de l'Orient, Lyons

Michaud, G. and Carrè, O. (1983) *Les frères musulmans*, Gallimard, Paris

——— (1981) 'Castes, confessions et société en Syrie: Ibn Khaldoun au chevet du progressisme arabe', *Peuples méditérannéens*, *16*

Michel, H. (1972) 'Algérie', in Centre d'Etudes et de Recherches sur les Sociétés Mediterranéenes, *La formation des élites politique maghrébines*, Pichon et Durand-Auzias, Paris

Mintzberg, H. (1979) *The structuring of organisations*, Prentice Hall, Englewood Cliffs, (New Jersey)

Montagne, R. (1947) *La civilisation du désert*, Hachette, Paris

Moore, B. (1966) *Social origins of dictatorship and democracy*, Beacon, Boston, (Massachusetts)

Moore, C.H. (1974) 'Authoritarian politics in unincorporated society: the case of Nasser's Egypt', *Comparative Politics*, *6*, pp. 193–218

——— (1980) *Images of development*, MIT Press, Cambridge, (Massachusetts)

El-Mossadeq, R. (1981) *Les forces politiques face au problème de la democratisation du Maroc*, University of Paris, Paris

Moulier Boutang, Y., Garson, J.P. and Silberman, R. (1986) *Economie politique des migrations clandestines de main d'oeuvres*, Publi-sud, Paris

Al-Muhamoun, (journal) Syrian Bar Association

Mourad, K. (1972) *Le Maroc à la recherche d'une révolution*, Sindbad, Paris

Muna, Farid A. (1980) *The Arab executive*, Macmillan, London

Murad, Z. (1966) 'About the revolutionary probabilities for the military in the national revolution for liberation' (in Arabic), *al-Talia*, *2*, no. 11, pp. 40–8

Mutin, G. (1980) 'Agriculture et dépendence alimentaire en Algérie', *Maghreb-Machrek*, *90*, pp. 40–64

BIBLIOGRAPHY

Nasr, S. (1982) 'Les travailleurs de l'industrie manufacturière au Machrek: Irak, Jordanie, Palestine, Liban, Syrie', in Bourgey, *et al.*, *Industrialisation et changements sociaux dans l'Orient arabe*, Editions du CERMOC, Beirut, pp. 147–70

Nettl, J.P. (1968) 'The state as a conceptual variable', *World Politics*, 20, no. 4, pp. 559–92

Niblock, T. (1982) (ed.) *Iraq: the contemporary state*, Croom Helm, London

Nurallah, K. (1978) 'Administrative development and socio-economic development in the Arab world' (in Arabic), *Al-Mustaqbal al-arabi*, 1, no. 4

Nyrop, R.F. (1979) *Iraq: a country study*, Washington DC

Okun, A. (1975) *Equality and efficiency: the big trade-off*, Brookings Institution, Washington DC

Othman, O.A. (1979) 'Saudi Arabia: an unprecedented growth of wealth with an unparalleled growth of bureaucracy', *International Review of Administrative Sciences*, 45, no. 3

Ottoway, D. (1984) 'Malaise is apparent after Egyptian election', *Washington Post*, 3 June

Owen, R. (1983) 'The political environment for development', in I. Ibrahim (ed.), *Arab resources, the transformation of a society*, Croom Helm, London

Palmer, M., Alghofaily, I. and Alnimir, S. (1984) 'The behavioural correlates of rentier economics: a case study of Saudi Arabia', in Stookey, R. (ed.), *The Arabian Peninsula: zone of ferment*, Hoover Institution, Stanford, (California)

Peneff, J. (1981) *Industriels algériens*, CNRS, Paris

Peretz, D. (1983) *The Middle East today*, Praeger, New York, p. 57

Perlmutter, A. (1974) *Egypt: the praetorian state*, Transaction Books, Brunswick, (New Jersey)

Pfeifer, K. (1985) *Agrarian reform under state capitalism in Algeria*, Westview Press, Boulder, (Colorado)

Picard, E. (1978) 'Syria returns to democracy', in G. Hermet, R. Rose and A. Rouguiè (eds), *Elections without choice*, Macmillan, London, pp. 129–44

—— (1979a) 'Clans militaires et pouvoir ba'thiste en Syrie', *Orient*, Hamburg, pp. 49–62

—— (1979b) 'Ouverture économique et renforcement militaire en Syrie', *Oriente Moderno*, 59, no. 7–12, pp. 663–76

—— (1979c) 'Le rapprochement syro-iraquien', *Maghreb-Machrek*, 83, p. 9

—— (1980) 'La Syrie de 1946 à 1979', in Raymond, A. (ed,), *La Syrie aujourd'hui*, CNRS, Paris, pp. 143–84

Pipes, D. (1980) 'This world is political!!!', and 'The Islamic revival of the seventies', in *Orbis*, 24, 1, pp. 9–41

Piscatori, J.P. (1983) *Islam in the political process*, Cambridge University Press, Cambridge, p. 1

Al-Qabbaj, M. (1984) (ed.) *Democracy in Morocco* (in Arabic), Dar al Mustaqbal Al Arabi, Cairo

Quandt, W.B. (1969) *Revolution and political leadership: Algeria,*

1954–68, MIT Press, Cambridge, (Massachusetts)

—— (1983) *Saudi Arabia*, Brookings Institution, Washington DC

Rabinovich, I. (1982) 'Syria', in R.E. Harkavy and E.A. Kolodziej (eds), *Security policies of developing countries*, Lexington Books, Lexington, (Maryland)

Radwan, S. and Les, E. (1979) 'The state and agrarian change: a case study of Egypt 1952–77', in Ghai, D. and others (eds), *Agrarian system and rural development*, Holmes and Meier, New York

Rashid, A. (1975) 'Government and administration in the UAE', *Bulletin of Arab Research and Studies*, 6

Rassam, A. and Zghal, A.K. (eds), (1980) *Système urbain et développement au Maghreb*, Cerès Productions, Tunis

Raymond, A. (ed.) (1980) *La Syrie aujourd'hui*, CNRS, Paris

Reid, D. (1981) *Lawyers and politics in the Arab world*, Bibliotheca Islamica, Minneapolis, (Minnesota)

Riker, W. (1962) *The theory of political coalitions*, Yale University Press, New Haven, (Connecticut)

Rivier, F. (1982) 'Rente pétrolière et politiques industrielles des états non pétroliers: Egypte, Jordanie, Liban, Syrie', in Bourgey *et al.*, *Industrialisation et changements sociaux dans l'Orient arabe*, Editions du CERMOC, Beirut, pp. 169–47

Roberts, H.J.R. (1980) 'Towards an understanding of the Kabyle question in contemporary Algeria', *The Maghreb Review*, pp. 115–224

—— (1983) 'The economics of Berberism: the material base of the Kabyle question in contemporary Algeria', *Government and Oposition*, pp. 218–35

Rokkan, S. (1966) 'Mass suffrage, secret voting and political participation', in Caser, L. (ed.), *Political sociology*, Harper and Row, New York, pp. 101–31

Rosen, L. (1984) *Bargaining for reality*, University of Chicago, Chicago

Rosenthal, E.I.J. (1958) *Political thought in medieval Islam: an introductory outline*, Cambridge University Press, Cambridge

Saab, G. (1960) *Motorisation de l'agriculture et developpement au Proche-Orient*, SEDES, Paris

—— (1967) *The Egyptian agrarian reform: 1952–62*, Oxford University Press, New York

Sabagh, G. (1982) 'Migration and social mobility in Egypt', in Kerr and Yassin, *Rich and poor states in the Middle East: Egypt and the new Arab order*, Westview Press, Boulder, (Colorado), pp. 71–95

Sader, M. (1982) 'Le développement industriel de l'Irak', in Bourgey *et al.*, *Industrialisation et changements sociaux dans l'Orient arabe*, Editions du CERMOC, Beirut, pp. 235–81

Sadowski, Y. (1984) *Political power and economic organisation in Syria*, PhD dissertation, University of California, Los Angeles

Safir, N. (1985) 'A propos de la constitution du travailleur collectif dans l'industrie mécanique algérienne', and 'Quelques aspects sociaux du développement de l'industrie mécanique', in *Essais d'analyses sociologiques*, 2, OPU-ENA L, 2, Algeria, pp. 191–218 and 219–66

Safran, N. (1984) *Saudi Arabia*, Harvard University Press, Cambridge, (Massachusetts)

BIBLIOGRAPHY

Al-Salim, F. (1982) *Al-Khadamat al-hukumiyya fi dawlat al-kuwait* (Government services in the State of Kuwait), University of Kuwait, Kuwait

Sanderson, S.R. (1984) *Land reform in Mexico, 1910–80*, Academic Press, New York

Sankari, (1980) 'Islam and politics in Saudi Arabia', in Esposito (ed.), *Islam and development*, Syracuse University Press, Syracuse, (New York)

El-Sayed, M.K. (1983) *Society and politics in Egypt: interest groups in the Egyptian political system* (in Arabic), Dar al Mustaqbal Al Arabi, Cairo

Schattschneider, E.E. (1960) *The semi-sovereign people*, Holt, Rinehart and Winston, New York

Schatzberg, M. (1980) *Politics and the State in Zaire*, Westview, Boulder, (Colorado)

Schiff, Z. (1984) *Israel's Lebanon war*, Simon and Schuster, New York

Schmitter, P.C. (1971) *Interest conflict and political change in Brazil*, Stanford University Press, Stanford, (California)

Seale, P. (1965) *The struggle for Syria*, Oxford University Press, London and New York

Sehimi, M. (1979) *Juin 1977: étude des elections legislatives au Maroc*, SOMADED, Casablanca

——— (1985) 'Les elections legislatives au Maroc', *Maghreb-Machrek*, *107*, pp. 23–51

Semmoud, B. (1982) 'Croissance du secteur industriel privé en Algérie dans ses relations avec le secteur national', *Revue canadienne des études africaines, 2*

Serageldin, I. *et al.*, (1983) *Manpower and international labour migration in the Middle East and North Africa*, World Bank, Oxford University Press, Oxford

Seurat, M. (1980) 'Les populations, l'état et la société', in Raymond, *La Syrie aujourd'hui*, CNRS, Paris, pp. 87–141

——— (1982) 'Etat et industrialisation dans l'Orient arabe: les fondements socio-historiques' in Bourgey *et al.*, *Industrialisation et changements sociaux dans l'Orient arabe*, Editions du CERMOC, Beirut, pp. 27–67

El-Shadi, El-Shagi (1969) *Neuordnung der Bodennutzung in Aegypten*, Weltforum-Verlag, Munich, (IFO-Institut für Wirtschaftsforschung, Afrika-Studien 36)

Shalq, F. (1976) *The other Lebanon*, Beirut

Sharabi, H. (1966) *Nationalism and revolution in the Arab world*, Van Nostrand, New York

Sheehan, R. (1964) *Kingdom of illusion*, Morrow, New York

Simmel, G. (1955) *Conflict*, translated by Kurt H. Wolff; *The web of group affiliations*, translated by Reinhard Bendix, The Free Press, New York

Society of Arab Association of the Maghreb, eighteenth conference of Bar Associations of the Maghreb, *Reports and Resolutions*

Springborg, R. (1978) 'Professional syndicates in Egyptian politics, 1952–70', in *International Journal of Middle East Studies*, 9, pp. 275–95

——— (1979) 'Patrimonialism and policy-making in Egypt: and the tenure policy for reclaimed land', *Middle East Studies*, *15*, pp. 49–69

——— (1981) 'Baathism in practice: agriculture, politics and political culture in Syria and Iraq', *Middle Eastern Studies, 15*

BIBLIOGRAPHY

—— (1982) *Sayyid Mir'i: family power and politics in Egypt*, University of Pennsylvania Press, Philadelphia

—— (1986) 'Iraqi *infitah*: agrarian transformation and growth of the private sector', *Middle East Journal*, 40, no. 1, pp. 33–53

—— (1986a) *Infitah, agrarian transformation, and elite consolidation in comtemporary Iraq*, IPSA world conference, Paris (published in *The Middle East Journal*, winter)

Sraieb, N. *et al.* (1985) *Le mouvement ouvrier maghrébin*, CNRS, Paris

Srinivas, M. (1976) The remembered village, Oxford University Press, Delhi

Stork, J. (1979) 'Oil and capitalism in Iraq', *Peuples Méditerranéens — Mediterranean People*, 9, p. 145

Syria, Ministry of State for Cabinet Affairs (1984) *The importance of administrative development and the creation of a specialised agency thereof, memorandum* (in Arabic), Damascus

Syrian Bar Association, *Al-Muhamoun*, Damascus; several issues, particularly 1979–81

Thiery, S.P. (1982) 'Emploi, formation et productivité dans l'industrie algérienne', in Bernard, C. *et al.*, *La politique de l'emploi — formation au Maghreb 1970–80*, CNRS, Paris

Tilly, C. (ed.) (1975) *The formation of national states in western Europe*, Princeton University Press, Princeton, (New Jersey)

Turner, B.S. (1979) 'The middle classes and entrepreneurship in capitalist development', *Arab Studies*

Van Dam, N. (1979) *The struggle for power in Syria: sectarianism, regionalism and tribalism in politics, 1961–80*, Croom Helm, London

Van Dusen, M. (1971) *Intra and inter-generational conflict in the Syrian army*, unpublished PhD dissertation, Johns Hopkins University Press, Baltimore

—— (1975) 'Syria: downfall of a traditional elite', in Tachau, F. (ed.), *Political elites and political development in the Middle East*, Schenkman/Wiley, Cambridge

Van Nieuwenhuijze, C.A.O. (1965) *Social stratification and the Middle East*, Brill, Leiden

—— (1971) *Sociology of the Middle East*, Brill, Leiden

Vatikiotis, P. (1961) *The Egyptian army in politics*, Indiana University Press, Bloomingdale

Vatin, J.C. (1982) 'Religious resistance and state power in Algeria', in Cudsi, A. and Dessouki, A.E.H. (eds), *Islam and power in the contemporary Muslim world*, Croom Helm, London

Von Sivers, P. (1984) 'National integration and traditional rural organisation in Algeria 1970–80: background for Islamic traditionalism?', in Arjomand, S.A. (ed.), *From national to revolutionary Islam*, Macmillan, London, pp. 94–118

Wai, D. (1981) *The Afro-Arab conflict in the Sudan*, Africana, New York

Warriner, D. (1969) *Land reform in principle and practice*, Clarendon Press, Oxford

Waterbury, J. (1970) *The commander of the faithful*, Columbia University Press, New York

—— (1976) 'Corruption, political stability and development',

Government and Opposition, 11, pp. 426–45

——— (1983) *The Egypt of Nasser and Sadat: the political economy of two regimes*, Princeton University Press, Princeton, (New Jersey)

——— (1984) *The Egypt of Nasser and Sadat: the political economy of two regimes*, Princeton University Press, Princeton, (New Jersey)

Watkins, M. (1934) *The state as a concept of political science*, Harper and Brothers, New York

Weber, M. (1947) *The theory of social and economic organisation*, Oxford University Press, New York and London

——— (1978) Weber: selections in translation, W.G. Runciman (ed.), Cambridge University Press, Cambridge

Weinbaum, Marvin G. (1979) *Bureaucratic norms, structures and strategies in agricultural policies in the Middle East*, paper submitted at the Middle East Studies Association Annual Conference, Salt Lake City, (Utah)

Weinstein, John M. (1981) 'A structural analysis of the moderniser's dilemma', *Comparative Development, 16*, no. 3 and 4

Weulersse, J. (1946) *Paysans de Syrie et du Proche-Orient*, Paris

Wickwar, Hardy (1963) *The modernisation of administration in the Near East*, Khayat, Beirut

World Bank (1983) *World tables: social data*, vol. II, IBRD, Washington DC

——— (1985) *World development report*, IBRD, Washington DC

Wright, J. (1982) *Libya: a modern history*, Johns Hopkins University Press, Baltimore, (Maryland)

Zartman, I.W. (1964a) *Problems of new power*, Atherton, New York

——— (1964b) *Destiny of a dynasty*, University of South Carolina Press, Charleston

——— (1967) 'Political pluralism in Morocco', *Government and Opposition, 2 (4)*, pp. 568–83

——— (1970) 'The Algerian army in politics', in C. Welch (ed.), *Soldier and state in Africa*, Northwestern University Press, Evanston, (Illinois)

——— (1974) 'Algeria: a post-revolutionary elite', in Frank (ed.), *Political elites and political development in the Middle East*, Schenkman/Wiley, Cambridge

——— (1975) 'L'élite algérienne sous la présidence de Chadli Bendjedid', *Maghreb-Machrek, 106*

——— (ed.) (1980) *Elites in the Middle East*, Praeger, New York

——— (ed.) (1982) *Political elites in Arab North Africa*, Longman, New York

——— (ed.) (1986) *The political economy of Morocco*, Praeger, New York

Zghal, A. (1980) 'Classes moyennes et développement au Maghreb', in CRESM, pp. 1–39

Ziadeh, F.J. (1968) *Lawyers, the role of law and liberalism in modern Egypt*, Stanford University Press, Stanford, (California)

Index

Abbud 161
Abu Dhabi: bureaucratisation
18–19
Abu Ghazala, Abdel Halim 126
Abu Issa, Farouk 113
Abu Wafia, Mahmud 77
Achour, Habib 83
Aflaq, Michel 132
Ahrar Party (Egypt) 51, 55, 56,
76–7
Alawi 44, 122, 129, 135, 143,
185, 193, 228, 270–1
Algeria 86, 161, 184–5, 189–95,
265, 280
agriculture 172–3, 181–3
class structure 166, 170–83,
199, 222, 228, 230
ideological involution
203–17
lawyers' association 95
military expenditure 136–7
political stability 3, 6, 8, 13
public vs private sector
176–81
role of military 120–2,
124–7, 129–31, 133, 135,
138, 141–2, 144
state and religion 149, 155–8,
277
Amir, Abdel Hakin 229, 234
Arabism (Pan) or Arab
Nationalism 36, 43, 155,
260, 277
Arab Lawyers Union 106–7,
112–14
Arab Socialist Union (ASU)
in Egypt 50, 52, 54, 74, 97,
104, 125, 142, 211
in Libya 36–7
armed forces (military) 10, 35,
43, 116–44, 207–9, 279
al-Asali, Sabri 108
al-Ash'ari 264
al-Assad, Hafez 4, 44, 46–8,
102, 105–7, 111, 12–3,

128–9, 140–1, 185, 206,
214, 269–71, 274, 279–80
al-Assad, Rifat 129, 143, 270
Atatürk 136, 155–6
al-Azhar University (Egypt)
159–60
al-Azhari 161

Baath 122–3, 132, 134, 142,
152, 183, 210, 223–4, 265,
280
in Iraq 124, 129;
in Syria 43–50, 58, 101, 105,
117, 120, 127–8, 185,
270, 273, 278–9
Bahrein 95, 98
al-Banna, Hasan 160
al-Baradei, Mustapha 103
Bedoucracy 29
Ben Ammar, Tahar 172
Ben Amru, Ahmed 108
Ben Barka, Mahdi 76
Ben Bella 8, 173, 216
Benjedid, Chadli 3, 8, 9, 125–6,
133, 196, 206
Ben Salah, Ahmed 81–2
Black September (1970) 5
Bouabid, Abderrahim 64, 68
Bouabid, Maati 65, 108
Boumedienne, Houari 3, 4, 8, 9,
117, 120, 125–6, 133, 168,
173, 176, 189
Bourguiba, Habib 3–4, 81, 84,
155–6, 240
Bucetta, Muhammad 108

Camp David 272
Catholic Church 147
class 164–202, 220–37, 240
bourgeoisie
capitalist 10, 136
commercial 109
petty 170–1
state 44, 169
landowners 109

305

INDEX

middle class 10, 117, 166–8,
  185ff
peasants 10
proletariat (workers) 10, 166
second stratum 221ff
centralisation 26–7
Chad 9
China 231, 235
Communist Party 86
  in Iraq 134
  in Morocco 70
  in Sudan 161–2
  in Syria 134
  in Tunisia 82
Copt 97–8, 235

al Dawa 79
democracy 10, 42, 62, 65, 128,
  262, 268–9, 281–2
Druse 135

education 20, 25, 50
Egypt 8–9, 62, 175, 185, 224,
  281
  bureaucratisation 14–16, 23,
    25–6, 31
  class in rural community 239,
    246–51, 257–9
  foreign policy 266–9, 271–2
  ideological involution 203–17
  lawyers' association 44–8,
    79, 100–5, 108–12,
    114–15, 236
  military expenditure 136–7
  nature of the state 23–4,
    228–37
  parties in 35, 45, 50–8,
    73–81, 86
  political stability 4, 6
  professional associations 32,
    94
  role of military 117, 120–2,
    124–7, 129–32, 135, 138,
    141–2, 144, 279–80
  state and religion 148–9,
    159–60
employment 177–8
Eritrea 260

Fahmi, Marqus 97
Farouk (King of Egypt) 8, 160
al Fasi, Allal 65–7
food riots 3–4, 236, 279
food subsidies 53, 175
France 8, 99, 230, 266
Front (Party in Morocco) 76,
  282

General Union of Tunisian
  Workers (UGTT) 81, 83
al-Geyoushi, Mahmoud 106
al-Ghazali 264
al-Ghazzi, Sabri 108
Green Book 38, 40

Habib, Philip 213
al-Hafiz, Amin 123
Hama (Syria) 4, 129, 209, 270,
  276, 279
Hassan II (King of Morocco) 3,
  64–5, 109–10
al-Hindi, Sheriff Husein 162
Hussein (King of Jordan) 5, 274
Hussein, Saddam 5, 121–2, 124,
  132, 142, 193, 195–6, 206,
  214, 272–4, 278–90
Hydrar, Ali 129

Ibn Khaldum 263
Ibn Jama'a 264
Ibrahim, Abdullah 68
Idris al Sanusi (King of Libya) 8
Ijtihad 156
Ikhwan (Saudi Arabia) 23, 154,
  252
industrialisation 25, 50, 117
Infitah 13, 16, 55, 75, 143, 204,
  211–14, 216, 224, 235, 268,
  281
Iran 25, 168, 184, 213, 227,
  260, 278
Iran–Iraq war 5, 121, 124, 129,
  132–3, 136, 208, 216, 260,
  273–4
Iraq 86, 184, 232, 265
  agriculture 195–6
  class structure 192–6, 222–3,
    228

306

foreign policy 260, 272–4
ideological involution
   203–17, 280
lawyers' association 94–5,
   112
military expenditure 136–7
political stability 5–6, 279
public vs private sector 194–5
rentier state 141
role of military 116–17,
   121–4, 127, 129–35, 139,
   141, 144
Iskander, Ahmad 265
Islam 36, 38, 147–63, 168,
   198–9, 215, 235, 244, 260,
   263, 273, 277–8
Islamic Tendency Movement
   (MTI) (Tunisia) 82
Islmaili 135, 270
Israel 47, 55, 75, 82, 86,
   103–4, 116, 118, 131, 141,
   144, 184, 205, 208, 211,
   213, 216, 236, 260, 267,
   269–71, 274
Istiqlal Party (Morocco) 65–8,
   71, 109

Japan 20
Jerusalem trip to, 53, 159, 269
Jews 97
Jordan 142, 204, 207, 274, 281
bureaucratisation 14, 19, 31
lawyers' association 95, 112
military 121
political stability 5–6
remittances 24

Kairawan mosque (Tunisia) 156
Kamshish (Egypt) affair of 226,
   233–6
al-Kaylani, Rashid Ali 116
al-Kazar, Nadim 134
Khairallah, Adnan 142
Khalif 263
Khalil, Mustafa 53
Khatmiyya 161
al-Khawaga, Ahmed 104
Khomeini, Ruhollah 273
al-Khoury, Fayez 97

al-Khoury, Fares 97, 108
Kissinger, Henry 213
al-Kozbari, Maamoun 108
al-Kozbari, Mawaffaq 106
Kurds 193, 133, 208
Kuwait 164, 281
bureaucratisation 14, 17, 26
lawyers' association 95, 98
nature of state 21

land reform 43, 210, 223,
   233–4, 227, 230, 233, 235,
   247
Lawyers' Union 94–115
League of Arab States 261
Lebanon 9, 142, 204–5, 207,
   216, 264
lawyers' association 94–5,
   98, 112
political instability 5
legitimacy
and foreign policy 260–75
of the military 130
and parties 36
and stability 6
of the state 7–8
Libya 13, 86, 122, 184, 204,
   207, 228
foreign policy 260
lawyers' association 95, 112
party 35–43, 45, 58, 223,
   265, 280
political stability 4, 6

el Mahdi, Sadiq 161–2
Mahdism 161
Mahmud, Muhammad 112
Makhuf, Adnan 129
Marx, Karl 24
marxism 37, 152, 157, 190,
   222, 277, 280
Mauritania 9
lawyers' association 95
al-Mawardi 264
Mecca, siege of Great Mosque
   in 1979 153–4, 276
Mestiri, Ahmed 83
Mexico 231, 233
migration (foreign workers) 23

307

INDEX

migrants' remittances 204
Mohammad V (King of
  Morocco) 3, 4
Morocco 62, 120, 127, 130,
  133, 175, 183, 208
  class structure 222
  lawyers' association 94–7,
    99–101, 107–10, 112,
    114–15
  military 121
  political stability 3, 4, 6, 8
  political system and
    opposition 64–73, 78, 86,
    281–2
  state and religion 155
Mubarak, Hosni 8, 10, 52, 56,
  74–6, 79, 80, 110, 126, 160,
  206, 236, 280
Muhammad, Ali 20
Muhammad, the Prophet 157,
  263
Muhi al-Din, Fuad 53
al-Murrah (Tribe in Saudi
  Arabia) 252–5
Murphy, Richard 213
Muslim Brotherhood 43, 106,
  134, 159–60, 162, 226, 232,
  270, 279
Mzali, Mohammed 82–3

an Nahhas, Mustafa 215–17
Nasser, Gamal Abdel 8, 9, 24,
  31, 50–1, 54, 55, 58, 74,
  103, 111, 118, 122, 125–6,
  140, 158, 159, 216, 224,
  226, 229–30, 233, 235–6,
  247, 264, 266–8, 271–2,
  274
Nasserism 37–8, 43, 152
National Democratic Party
  (Egypt) 51, 52–4, 74–7, 104
National Liberation Front (FLN)
  (Algeria) 124–6, 142, 158,
  170, 172, 265
National Progressive Unionist
  Party (Egypt) 51, 55, 56, 74,
  77
Nigeria 168
non-aligned countries 272–3

Nouira, Heidi 81, 166
Numeiry, Gaafar 5, 110, 161–2,
  206

Obeid, Makram 108
oil revenue (rent) 173–4, 191,
  204, 215
Oman 95
Osman, O.A. 142

Pahlavi, Muhammad Reza 227,
  233
Palestine 95, 112, 132, 183,
  205, 216, 260
Party of Progress and Socialism
  (Morocco) 70
Popular Unity movement (MUP)
  (Tunisia) 82

Qadhafi, Muammar 4, 8, 36–43,
  206, 224, 228, 265, 280
Qasim, Abdel Karim 117, 214
al-Qasimi, Zakir 105
Qatar 95
al Quwwaitli, Shukri 215–17

Rentier State 21–3, 29, 165
al-Rokabi, Mesbah 112
Rwala (Tribe in Saudi Arabia)
  254–5

Sabri, Ali 211, 229
Sadat, Anwar 4, 8, 9, 10, 24,
  50–2, 55, 56, 74–6, 79, 80,
  103–4, 109–10, 111, 125–6,
  132–3, 142, 148, 159–60,
  211, 214, 217, 229–30,
  235–6, 265, 267–9, 279
Sahara (Western) 67–70, 260
as Said, Nuri 215
Salameh, Ibrahim 141
Sanusi 224
al Saud
  Abdel Aziz ibn Saud 150–1,
    251–2
  Fahd ibn Abdel Aziz ibn
    Saud 5, 154
  Faisal II ibn Abdel Aziz ibn
    Saud 5, 150–2

308

INDEX

Khalid ibn Abdel Aziz ibn
Saud 5, 274
Saud ibn Abdel Aziz ibn
Saud 151
Saudi Arabia 95, 118, 161, 274
bureaucratisation 14, 17, 23
foreign policy 260
marginalisation of bedouins
239, 251–7
military 121, 129
nature of state 21
political stability 5–6, 277–8
state and religion 149–54
Shariah 95, 100, 160, 162
Shi'a (Shi'i) 133, 193, 270,
278–9
Shishakli, Adib 105, 109
al-Shourbagui, Abdel 104
Sidki, Bakr 116
Sidqi, Ismail 111–12
Social Democratic Party
(Tunisia) 83
Social Destourian Party (Tunisia)
81–4, 228, 250, 265
Socialist Labour Party (Egypt)
52, 55, 56, 74–7
Soviet Union 8, 90, 205–6, 209,
267, 269
State, definition of 6–9
Sudan 204, 206–7, 209
lawyers' association 95, 110
political stability 5, 7, 122
state and religion 149, 160–2
Sudanese Socialist Union 149,
160–2
Suez canal 24, 116, 266–8
Sultani, Sheikh Abdel Latfi 158
Summits (Arab) 261
Amman (1980) 274
Baghdad (1978) 213
Fez (1982) 213
Sunni 12, 133–5, 153, 190, 193,
270
Syria 86, 193, 265, 274
agriculture 185–7, 191
bureaucratisation 14, 19
class structure 183–92,
222–5, 228
foreign policy 260, 269–71

ideological involution
203–17, 280
industrial sector 187–8
intervention in Lebanon 47,
124, 183–4, 213, 260,
269–70
lawyers' association 94–103,
105–9, 111–12, 114–15,
128
military expenditure 136–7,
183
political stability 4, 6
public vs private sector 189
remittances 24
role of the military 117–23,
127–32, 134–5, 138–44
role of the party 35, 43–50,
58, 279

al Takfir wal Hijra 23, 79, 132
Takrit (Iraq) 134, 193
al-Takriti, Hardan 134
taxation in Libya 40
in Syria 140–1
Tilimsani, Omar 79
Tlas, Mustafa 121
Trade unions and/or professional
associations 32, 70–1,
88–115
Tunisia 62, 121–2, 161, 175,
204, 250, 281
class structure 166, 222, 228,
239, 241–6, 257–9
lawyers' association 95
state and religion 148–9,
155–8, 277
political stability 3–4, 6
political system 81–4, 265,
279–80
Turkey 25, 136, 232

Uganda 40
Umma Party (Sudan 161–2
Union Nationale des Etudiants
Marocains (UNEM) 67, 70,
72–3
Union Nationale des Forces
Populaires (UNFP-Morocco)
65, 67, 69–71

309

INDEX

Union Socialiste des Forces
Populaires (USFP-Morocco)
67–9, 71–2, 78, 109
United Arab Emirates
bureaucratisation 14, 18–19
lawyers' association 95
nature of state
United Kingdom 266
United States 8, 51, 75, 82,
205–6, 213–14, 252, 260,
270–1
Urabi 230, 232

Wafd Party (Egypt) 51, 54, 55,
74–5, 77–8, 79, 80, 83, 103,
105, 108, 112, 225–6, 232,
236, 250
Wahabi(sm) 151–3, 161, 239,
252, 277

Wahhab, Muhammad ibn Abdel
150
War of June 1967 1, 116, 120,
125, 235, 267, 271–2
War of October 1973 132–3,
267, 269
Weber, Max 25–6, 64, 167, 261

Yemen Arab Republic (North) 9,
125, 271–2, 280
Yemen, People's Democratic
Republic (South) 95, 122,
204, 206–8, 265, 279–80

Zaim, Husni 120
Zituna University (Tunisia)
155–6
Zghar, Massaoud 168